COMPLYING WITH THE AMERICANS WITH DISABILITIES ACT OF 1990

Revised Edition

Edited by Kathryn Shane McCarty

National League of Cities

Revised Edition
Copyright © 1991 by the
National League of Cities
Washington, D.C. 20004
ISBN # 0-933729-70-7

Additional copies of this Local Officials Guide are available at
$60.00 per copy for officials of NLC direct member cities and state
municipal leagues. The price for all others is $75.00

To order, send a check or money order to:
National League of Cities
Publications Sales
1301 Pennsylvania Avenue NW
Washington, D.C. 20004
(202) 626-3150

TABLE OF CONTENTS

FOREWORD

As cities, towns, and counties across the United States take steps to comply with the Americans with Disabilities Act of 1990 (ADA), we are pleased that the National League of Cities (NLC) can assist in their efforts by providing technical guidance on this subject. NLC has taken a leadership role in advising cities on compliance with disability rights legislation over the years. This is our latest contribution to that effort.

This *Local Officials Guide* highlights all of the major issues that local officials will face as they move towards compliance with the ADA. The Act is a comprehensive and far-reaching piece of federal legislation that will have a tremendous impact on local government operations and facilities. Most aspects of local government programs, services and facilities will be affected by the ADA. Indeed, the employment practices and policies of local governments will have to be reviewed and, in some instances, amended in order to comply with the law and related regulations. Local officials even have an oversight role as places of public accommodation and commercial facilities come into compliance.

It is important to recognize that the goal of the Americans with Disabilities Act is a positive one. The results of nondiscrimination on the basis of disability will make our society more open — inviting participation by and ensuring equal rights to all individuals regardless of their abilities or disabilities.

This book and our related training efforts on ADA compliance reflect NLC's commitment to assist municipal officials in their efforts to comply. Because of this commitment, we invite comments and discussion about the ideas and strategies offered in this guidebook. We hope that you find it useful.

Donald J. Borut
Executive Director
National League of Cities

William E. Davis, III
Director, Center for Education
and Information Resources

PREFACE

Focusing on the issues of local government compliance with a civil rights statute affecting disabled Americans has been a case of *deja vu* for me. More than a decade ago, I was an assistant project director on NLC's Section 504 Demonstration Compliance Project. As I began to network and glean information on ADA, I was able to renew old friendships as well as my spirit.

Asking talented, knowledgeable authors, busy with other assignments, to produce detailed, legal copy within four short weeks was asking a great deal. I know, because I was faced with the same challenge. I would like to express my sincere thanks to the three other contributing authors — Katharine L. Herber, David Coburn and Florence Stewart — for their outstanding efforts.

A special thanks is offered to Leslie Shechter, Legal Consultant to the Tennessee Municipal Technical Advisory Service, and Marie Allen Murphy, Legal Services Coordinator, Tennessee County Technical Assistance Service, for contributing several key appendices. Because of their experience in preparing a similar guidebook for Tennessee cities and counties, they were very helpful and knowledgeable about what to include in ours. Another special acknowledgement is due for the outstanding self-evaluation checklists prepared by the Texas Governor's Committee for Disabled Persons. We greatly appreciate the willingness of Executive Director Virginia Roberts to share these fine tools with local government officials nationwide.

The reviewers of this compliance manual were equally wonderful. Mary McKnew, a former NLC staff member and now a member of Governor Booth Gardner's staff in Washington state, offered her knowledge, her insights, and a sensitivity to the topic that few could offer. Charles Goldman, a noted Washington, D.C. disability rights attorney, provided oversight from the concepts to the specifics. We could never have accomplished this manual without his assistance. Darla Fera, a professional editor and subject expert on ADA, performed miracles with the manuscript. Clint Page performed the finishing touches that turned this manuscript into a *Local Officials Guide*.

William E. Davis III, Director of the Center for Education and Information Resources, marshalled the resources and offered guidance to make this compliance manual possible. Virginia Mayer offered behind-the-scenes support that got us started and then kept us on schedule.

Many thanks to all who contributed their time, thoughts, and writing ability to make this compliance manual a reality.

Kathryn Shane McCarty
Director, Information Services
National League of Cities

ABOUT THE AUTHORS

David Coburn is a partner in the Washington, D.C. law firm of Steptoe and Johnson. He specializes in transportation law and regularly advises carriers of all types concerning their obligations under federal laws, including the Americans with Disabilities Act and other employment-related laws. Mr. Coburn is Chairman of the Transportation Committee of the Section of Administrative Law and Regulatory Practice of the American Bar Association and serves on the education committee of the Association of Transportation Practitioners. Before joining Steptoe and Johnson, he was a director in the law firm of Short, Klein and Karas, P.C. Mr. Coburn is a graduate of Brandeis University and Georgetown University Law Center.

Ronald S. Cooper is a partner in the Washington, D.C. law firm of Steptoe and Johnson, where he specializes in federal regulations of employment. He has litigated employment cases in the federal district courts and appeals courts and has participated in a number of U.S. Supreme Court cases. Before joining Steptoe and Johnson, he served as law clerk to Judge Walter P. Gewin of the U.S. Court of Appeals for the Fifth Circuit and in the Fair Labor Standards Division of the Solicitor's Office in the U.S. Department of Labor. Mr. Cooper has been a frequent speaker and author on employment law topics, including the Americans with Disabilities Act. He is the principal author of a book on the application of the Fair Labor Standards Act of state and local governments, published by the National League of Cities and ICMA. Mr. Cooper also serves on the Advisory Board for the "The Disability Law Reporter Service," published by Prentice Hall. He served for ten years as an adjunct professor on the graduate faculty at the Georgetown University Law School, where he taught a seminar on employment law.

Katharine L. Herber serves as the Legal Counsel to the Center for Policy and Federal Relations at the National League of Cities.

Ms. Herber previously served in a similar capacity at the National School Boards Association and in the U.S. Senate. She is a former assistant prosecutor and administrative law judge. She is a graduate of Gonzaga School of Law, the National Judicial College, and the Institute on International and Comparative Law in Guadalajara, Mexico.

Kathryn Shane McCarty is the Director of Information Services at the National League of Cities. She served as the editor of this *Local Officials Guide to ADA Compliance*. Ms. McCarty has an expertise in the field of disability rights. She was the Assistant Project Director of NLC's Section 504 Compliance Demonstration Project in 1979 - 1981. She has direct experience in Section 504 compliance since she assisted the city of New Orleans achieve its compliance objectives. She also served as the Section 504 Coordinator for a small community in the Pacific Northwest. Ms. McCarty is a graduate of Denison University and the School of Public Affairs at the University of Washington.

Florence Keys Stewart is a freelance writer, editor, and management consultant. She is presently employed at the National League of Cities' Municipal Reference Service. She has taught in the Business Division of Northern Virginia Community College. Ms. Stewart is a graduate of Howard University School of Business.

INTRODUCTION

By Kathryn Shane McCarty

"Every man, woman and child with a disability now can pass through once-closed doors into a bright new era of equality, independence, and freedom." President George Bush's speech on July 26, 1990

The Americans with Disabilities Act (ADA) — Public Law 101-336 — was enacted on July 26, 1990. The ADA is codified as 42 U.S.C. 12101 - 12213. This landmark legislation provides comprehensive civil rights protection to individuals with disabilities in the areas of employment, public accommodations, state and local government services and programs, and telecommunications. The ADA prohibits all state and local governments and some private businesses from discriminating on the basis of disability.

The legal citations provided in this book refer either to the Americans with Disabilities Act of 1990 as codified (42 U.S.C. 12101-12213) or the *Federal Register,* not the Code of the Federal Register. Since copies of the regulations implementing Titles I, II, and III of the ADA are included in the appendices,k the editor chose to make all legal citations to the sections and pages of the *Federal Register,* not the codified reference.

For future reference, it may be important to know where to find the ADA regulations as codified in the CFR. The citiations to this code are:

- 28 CFR Part 35 — Nondiscrimination on the Basis of Disability in State and Local Government Services;
- 29 CFR Part 1630 — Equal Employment Opportunity for Individuals with Disabilities;
- 29 CFR Parts 1602 and 1627 — Recordkeeping and Reporting Under Title VII of the Civil Rights Act of 1964 and the Americans with Disabilities Act;
- 49 CFR Parts 37 and 38 — Transportation for Individuals with Disabilities.

Ramifications of the Americans with Disabilities Act

This *Local Officials Guide to ADA Compliance* provides information and step-by-step instructions on how to comply with the ADA. This is a comprehensive, far-reaching law that has a direct impact on many aspects of municipal operations from employment to service delivery.

Most of the provisions of the ADA, however, build on an existing framework — that of Section 504 of the Rehabilitation Act of 1973, as amended, and the Civil Rights Act of 1964, as amended. Where jurisdictions have complied with the nondiscrimination and record keeping provisions of Section 504, they have a head start.

In addition, many state and local governments have enacted handicapped accessibility and nondiscrimination laws over the past fifteen years. If your community is in compliance with your state or local laws, you may be well on your way to complying with ADA. The critical step needed is to check.

Begin by reviewing what you already do, to determine what access and nondiscrimination laws are already being followed and how they compare with the ADA provisions. This should be your first step towards compliance. It may be time-consuming, but it may prove to be cost-effective in the long term.

In many instances, your state governor's committee for disabled individuals and your state's human rights commission may have already investigated the distinctions between existing state laws and the ADA requirements. Call your state offices to see if they can assist with your compliance review and your self-evaluation process.

What is in this Local Officials Guide

Chapter 1 provides an extensive summary of the law and the regulations issued by several federal agencies. This chapter sets the context for the compliance manual offering background on the legislation, the rulemaking process, and the effect on state and local laws.

The definition of who is covered and who is excluded under this statute is also summarized in this first chapter. You will, however, will find references to the definition as it applies to specific titles, as well.

It is important to note that additional regulations and technical guidance on ADA compliance may emerge from federal agencies after the publication date of this manual. Use the resource guide to contact agencies to receive copies of the latest materials.

Chapter 2 describes how the services, programs, and facilities of all local governments must be offered in a nondiscriminatory manner to any qualified disabled person. This chapter explains the critical concepts of program accessibility and undue hardship.

All local governments must ensure that their employment practices, policies and procedures do not discriminate against individuals with disabilities. The employment provisions are covered under both Titles I and II of the Act. To begin with, all local jurisdictions must comply with the Section 504 regulations issued by the U.S. Department of Justice, with an effective date of January 26, 1992. These regulations are codified in 28 CFR Part 41. The DOJ Section 504 regulations offer guidance on how small communities must amend their employment practices and policies to ensure nondiscrimination on the basis of handicap (substitute - disability).

Jurisdictions with fewer than fifteen employees are not exempt from compliance. The Department of Justice reversed its position on an exemption for smaller communities, stating in the final rule that "Congress intended to cover the employment practices of all public entities." The effective date for employment-related compliance is January 26, 1992, as it is for program accessibility under Title II.

Chapter 3 explains the employment provisions of the ADA as mandated by the EEOC regulations. It includes a summary of what jurisdictions must do to comply, based on the number of city employees. All local governments with fifteen or more employees are subject to Title I of the Act. The Equal Employment Opportunity

Commission (EEOC) has the lead responsibility for outlining the requirements and enforcing the nondiscrimination provisions related to employment.

Chapter 4 describes the impact that ADA will have on public accommodations. In many cases, the facilities classified as "public accommodations" are covered under federal handicapped access laws for the first time. However, where state and local building codes require handicapped access, the provisions of ADA may not be unfamiliar.

Title III of the ADA affects three types of construction and facility modification: (1) "readily achievable" removal of barriers; (2) new construction; and (3) alterations. In order for places of public accommodation to comply, the owners will have to follow the ADA Accessibility Guidelines (ADAAG) as issued by the Architectural and Transportation Barriers Compliance Board (ATBCB).

Chapter 5 focuses on the complex issues of how public transportation agencies are going to reach compliance with ADA. The rule is based on U.S. Department of Transportation's (DOT) Section 504 regulations, but has been rewritten and is now more pervasive. Anyone responsible for compliance with the DOT regulations should recognize that this is an overview only and that further research will be required to fully understand the compliance requirements.

Chapter 6 explains the two federal accessibility standards now available for local governments to use when complying with ADA. The access guidelines produced by ATBCB provide the new standard for places of public accommodation, public buildings, and commercial facilities. These are based in large part on the ANSI A117.1-1980 requirements, although deviations do exist and, in some instances, are new in their entirety. The 1984 Uniform Federal Accessibility Standards (UFAS) are an alternative to the ADAAG technical standards for any public buildings. An explanation of both standards is provided in this chapter.

Chapter 7 contains the material to help the reader understand the steps needed to achieve compliance with the ADA. The self-evaluation checklist is the first step in assessing one's facilities, programs, and routine practices.

If an organization or affected party determines that structural modifications are necessary to one's physical setting, the transition plan specifies the steps necessary to complete the changes and the timeframe for completion.

The grievance procedure is necessary to facilitate the prompt and equitable resolution of complaints alleging discrimination on the basis of disability. All three of these tools and requirements are explained in this chapter.

Chapter 8 outlines the enforcement provisions under ADA and explains the potential penalties, fines and payment of attorneys' fees.

The appendices are extensive and offer some outstanding resources, including sample checklists, policies, a glossary of terms, a resource list of disability organizations, and copies of the Americans with Disabilities Act of 1990 and two key regulations — U.S. Department of Justice regulations implementing Subtitle A of Title II and the EEOC regulations implementing Title I.

1
THE LAW AND
THE POLITICS

By Kathryn Shane McCarty

The U.S. Congress drew upon previous civil rights laws when drafting the Americans with Disabilities Act of 1990 (ADA) that prohibits discrimination on the basis of disability.

The purpose of the American with Disabilities Act of 1990 (ADA) is clearly stated in Section 2 (b) of the Act as follows:

■ to provide a clear and comprehensive national mandate for the elimination of discrimination against individuals with disabilities;
■ to provide clear, strong, consistent, enforceable standards addressing discrimination against individuals with disabilities;
■ to ensure that the Federal Government plays a central role in enforcing the standards established in this Act on behalf of individuals with disabilities; and
■ to invoke the sweep of congressional authority, including the power to enforce the fourteenth amendment and to regulate commerce, in order to address the major areas of discrimination faced day-to-day by people with disabilities.

The underpinnings of ADA are derived from Section 504 of the Rehabilitation Act of 1973, as amended (29 U.S.C. 701-796) and Title VII of the Civil Rights Act of 1964 (42 U.S.C. Secs. 2000a and 2000d). Section 504 prohibits discrimination on the basis of handicap in federally assisted programs and activities. Therefore, jurisdictions that receive federal funds have been legally mandated to comply with Section 504 for nearly twenty years. Officials of jurisdictions that have done so in the areas of physical and program access and employment practices, should review their practices to ensure compliance with ADA, since ADA does differ from Section 504.

The ADA extends disability discrimination prohibitions to all state and local governments, whether or not they receive federal funds. All local governments must comply with the Title II provisions of the ADA. Compliance is mandatory; it is not linked to federal funding as it was under Section 504.

Rulemaking History

The U.S. Department of Justice (DOJ) published a notice of proposed rulemaking implementing Titles II and III of the ADA in late February 1991. After reviewing nearly 3,000 comments, the U.S. Department of Justice issued its final regulations on Titles II and III on July 26, 1991, the first anniversary of the Act's passage. The Architectural and Transportation Barriers Compliance Board (ATBCB) issued its ADA accessibility guidelines (ADAAG) as an appendix to the DOJ regulations on July 26, 1991, as well. The Title II and III regulations issued by DOJ designate the ADAAG guidelines as meeting compliance under the ADA.

The effective dates for compliance vary depending on the section of the regulation; the effective compliance date for most local government activities and practices, however, is January 26, 1992.

On the same day (July 26), the Equal Employment Opportunity Commission (EEOC) issued final regulations implementing the nondiscrimination provisions regarding employment under Title I of the Act. All local governments, regardless of the number of employees or size of the budget, must begin by complying with the employment provisions mandated under Title II which are effective on January 26, 1992. As of July 26, 1992, a local government or public accommodation with twenty-five or more employees must meet the EEOC requirements. For employers with fifteen to twenty-four staff members, the compliance deadline is delayed until July 26, 1994. All local governments employing fewer than fifteen employees are required to comply with Title II as it relates to employment practices. The effective date for Title II compliance is January 26, 1992.

Justice Department officials advise that all local governments, regardless of the number of employees, comply with the EEOC regulations as they pertain to employment as soon as possible, preferably by January 26, 1992.

The Department of Transportation (DOT) issued final regulations implementing the transportation provisions of the Americans with Disabilities Act in the Federal Register on September 6, 1991. The rule contains provisions on acquisition of accessible vehicles by private and public entities, requirements for complementary paratransit service by public entities, and the provision of nondiscriminatory accessible transportation service. The Architectural and Transportation Barriers Compliance Board (ATBCB) published accessibility guidelines on the same day and the DOT regulations mandate the ADAAG guidelines as the official standard.

The effective dates for transit compliance vary depending on the section of the DOT rule. Those compliance dates will be explained in more detail in Chapter 5, which deals with public transit.

Defining "Disability"

Understanding the definition of who is covered under ADA is critical. There is a historical context for individuals covered by this Act, i.e., Section 504 of the Rehabilitation Act of 1973 and the Fair Housing Act. In order to prohibit discriminatory practices effectively, local government officials need to understand the categories included and excluded under the ADA definition of "disability".

The legislative record on ADA indicates that Congressional leaders wanted the legislation to reflect the current terminology most in line with the sensibilities of most Americans with disabilities.

"The use of the term 'disability' instead of 'handicap' represents an effort by Congress to make use of up-to-date, currently accepted terminology ... No change in definition or substance is intended nor should one be attributed to this change in phraseology" (56 Fed.Reg. 35698).

Therefore Section 3(2) of the Act defines disability in much the same way as it was previously defined in Section 504:

The term "disability" means, with respect to an individual,

- a physical or mental impairment that substantially limits one or more of the major life activities of such individual;
- a record of such an impairment; or
- being regarded as having such an impairment.

Thus the term "disability" is defined as meeting one of three conditions. If an individual falls into any one of the three categories (and their condition is not listed as one of the exemptions), then the individual cannot be discriminated against based on disability.

The terms "physical or mental impairment", "major life activities", "has a record of such impairment" and "regarded as having an impairment" are all critical to fully understanding the definition of who is covered under ADA. These terms are defined in the U.S. Department of Justice regulation (28 CFR Part 35), issued on July 26, 1991. These definitions are explained in Chapter 2 within the context of who is covered under Title II. They also can be found in Chapter 3 as defined in the EEOC regulations (29 CFR Part 1630).

It should be noted that individuals who are HIV positive or have contracted AIDS are covered under the definition of "disability" within the context of ADA. In order to be covered under the employment provisions of the ADA, however, individuals must not pose a direct threat to their own health or safety or the health or safety of other individuals in the work environment.

Qualified Individual with a Disability

Under Subtitle A of the Title II, the term, "qualified individual with a disability" means:

an individual with a disability who, with or without reasonable modifications to rules, policies or practices, the removal of architectural, communication or transportation barriers, or the provision of auxiliary aids and services, meets the essential eligibility requirements for the receipt of services or the participation in programs or activities provided by a public entity.

This definition attempts to ensure that those individuals who are qualified for services or program participation are entitled to receive such services or engage in such programs without regard to their disability. This definition directly applies to the services and programs of local governments.

There is also a slightly different definition of a "qualified individuals with a disability" as cited in the Title I regulations affecting the employment provisions of the ADA. The qualified individual with a disability must:

- satisfy the requisite skill, experience, education, and other job-related requirements of the position such individual holds or desires, and
- with or without reasonable accommodation, perform the essential functions of the position.

This definition is explained extensively in Chapter 3, which deals with employment.

Exclusions

Homosexuality and bisexuality are excluded as disabilities, because they are not physical or mental impairments; they are instead considered sexual orientations (Section 511, 42 U.S.C. Sec. 12211).

The Section 511 of the Act, as well as the U.S. Department of Justice and EEOC regulations, indicate that the following conditions are not included in the definition of "disability":

tranvestism, transsexualism, pedophilia, exhibitionism, voyeurism, gender identity disorders not resulting from physical impairments, or other sexual behavior disorders; compulsive gambling, kleptomania, or pyromania; or psychoactive substance use disorders resulting from current illegal use of drugs (56 Fed.Reg. 35698).

State and Local Laws

The Americans with Disabilities Act of 1990 does not preempt existing state and local laws dealing with accessibility and nondiscrimination on the basis of disability. Charles D. Goldman, Esq. notes in his *Disability Rights Guide, 2nd Edition*, that:

> State and local laws are critically important.... While [ADA] will be phasing into applicability through 1994, these [state and local] laws are in effect now.... Furthermore, every state has a law requiring accessibility for persons with disabilities in buildings.

> In approaching state laws affecting employment practices and handicapped persons, it is important to note that those laws are commonly found in state civil rights, human rights, or anti-discrimination statutes.[1]

Goldman's research and the inventory included in his book emphasize the critical importance of reviewing your state and local laws related to individuals with disabilities. Where state and local laws are more stringent than the federal requirements under ADA, the state and local laws will remain in force. For example, "the D.C. Human Rights Act of 1977 (D.C. Law 2-38) prohibits discrimination in employment, housing, commercial space, public accommodations and educational institutions on the basis of 'physical handicap'. This D.C. law applies to all employers and provides private rights of action and allows for the recovery of damages and attorney's fees for discrimination."[2]

---

1 Charles L. Goldman, "The Americans with Disabilities Act", *The Washington Attorney*, Vol. 5, No. 4, March/April, 1991, p.36.

2 Charles L. Goldman, *Disability Rights Guide, Practical Solutions to Problems Affecting People with Disabilities,* (Lincoln, NE: Media Publishing, 1991)

The provisions of the ADA do not preempt this local statute, since it provides greater protection to disabled individuals than the ADA.

If the state and local requirements do not meet the minimum standards of the ADA, city officials should amend their local codes to mandate compliance with the ADA requirements, including the accessibility standards.

It is important to remember that state and local building codes affect the construction and renovation of privately owned buildings considered places of public accommodation or commercial facilities, which fall under Title III of the Act. It is essential to review and amend state and local building codes to determine whether they meet or exceed ADA requirements for places of public accommodation and commercial facilities.

2 PUBLIC SERVICES

By Katharine L. Herber

Subject to the provisions of this title, no qualified individual with a disability shall, by reason of such disability, be excluded from participation in or be denied the benefits of the services, programs, or activities of a public entity, or be subjected to discrimination by any such entity (42 U.S.C. 12132).

Subtitle A of Title II of the Americans with Disabilities Act of 1990 protects individuals with disabilities against discrimination by public entities. The regulations implementing this subtitle of ADA (28 CFR Part 35) were published in the *Federal Register* by the Department of Justice (DOJ) on July 26, 1991. DOJ's Office on Americans with Disabilities Act has the lead responsibility for enforcing the public services provisions of the Act that directly affect the general operations of state and local governments. Subtitle B of Title II, which applies to public transportation provided by public agencies or local governments, is explained in Chapter 5.

This chapter outlines the responsibilities of local governments to comply with Subtitle A of Title II of the Act. The key terms "disability" and "qualified individual with a disability" are defined at the beginning of the chapter. After reviewing this chapter, you should also read Chapter 7, "Action Steps Towards Compliance" and the appendices to begin developing an action plan for achieving compliance.

Under Title II, all local governments regardless of the number of employees or whether or not they receive federal funds, must comply with the employment provisions of Section 504 of the Rehabilitation Act of 1973, as amended, as referenced in Subtitle A of Title II. The compliance deadlines vary for different local governments of various sizes and for different parts of the regulations, but there are some compliance dates and activities that all local governments must meet.

■ By July 25, 1992, all local governments, regardless of size, must comply with 28 Code Of Federal Regulations (CFR) Part 41 (refers to Section 504) as it pertains to employment.

- After July 26, 1992, local governments with twenty-five or more employees must comply with the Title I regulations issued by EEOC. Cities, towns, villages and counties with fewer than twenty-five employees must comply with 28 CFR Part 41, as it pertains to employment.
- After July 26, 1994, local jurisdictions with fifteen or more employees must comply with the Title I regulations. Municipalities, towns, and villages with fewer than fifteen employees must comply with 28 CFR Part 41, as it pertains to employment.

If you wish, you can simply comply with the EEOC regulations, thus knowing that your jurisdiction has met the requirements mandated by the ADA.

Who Is Covered?

Individual with a Disability (56 Fed. Reg. 35717, Sec. 35.104)

Under Title II, an individual with a disability is any person who:

- has a physical or mental impairment that substantially limits one or more of his or her major life activities; or
- has a record of such an impairment; or
- is regarded as having such an impairment.

Disability Based on Impairment (56 Fed. Reg. 35717, Sec. 35.104)

An individual is considered to have a disability based on a physical or mental impairment if he or she has:

- any physiological disorder or condition, cosmetic disfigurement, or anatomical loss affecting one or more of the following body systems: neurological, musculoskeletal, special sense organs, respiratory (including speech organs), cardiovascular, reproductive, digestive, genitourinary, hemic and lymphatic, skin and endocrine;
- any mental or psychological disorder such as mental retardation, organic brain syndrome, emotional or mental illness, and specific learning disabilities; and/or
- any contagious or noncontagious disease or condition, such as orthopedic, visual, speech, and hearing impairments, cerebral palsy, epilepsy, muscular dystrophy, multiple sclerosis, cancer, heart disease, diabetes, mental retardation, emotional illness,

specific learning disabilities, HIV disease (whether symptomatic or asymptomatic), tuberculosis, drug addiction, and alcoholism.

Major life activities are functions such as caring for one's self, performing manual tasks, walking, seeing, hearing, speaking, breathing, learning, and working.

Disability Based on an Individual Having a Record of a Physical or Mental Impairment

An individual is considered to have a record of a physical or mental impairment if he or she has a history of, or has been misclassified as having, a mental or physical impairment that substantially limits one or more major life activities.

Regarded as Having an Impairment

An individual will be regarded as having an impairment if he or she has:

■ a physical or mental impairment that does not substantially limit major life activities but that is treated by a public entity as constituting such a limitation;
■ a physical or mental impairment that substantially limits major life activities only as a result of the attitudes of others toward such impairment; or
■ no physical or mental impairments but is treated by a public entity as having an impairment.

Exceptions

There are several exceptions to the definition of physical or mental impairment.

Conditions that Do Not Qualify as Impairment (56 Fed. Reg. 35717, Sec. 35.104)

The following conditions do not qualify as a physical or mental impairment:

■ homosexuality or bisexuality;
■ physical characteristics (e.g., green eyes or red hair), age and common personality traits (i.e., poor judgment or a quick temper where these are not symptoms of a mental or psychological disorder); and
■ environmental, cultural, economic or other disadvantages (e.g., having a prison record or being poor).

Certain Disorders and Behaviors
(56 Fed. Reg. 35717, Sec. 35.104)

The term "disability" does not include:

- transvestism, transsexualism, pedophilia exhibitionism, voyeurism, gender identity disorders not resulting from physical impairments, or other sexual behavior disorders;
- compulsive gambling, kleptomania, or pyromania; or
- psychoactive substances use disorders resulting from current illegal use of drugs.

Unlawful Current Use of Drugs
(56 Fed. Reg. 35719, Sec. 35.131)

The Act does not prohibit discrimination against an individual (including an individual with a disability) based on that individual's current unlawful use of drugs. However, a local government may not discriminate on the basis of unlawful drug use against an individual who is not currently engaging in the unlawful use of drugs and who

- has successfully completed a supervised drug rehabilitation program or has otherwise been rehabilitated successfully;
- is participating in a supervised rehabilitation program; or
- is erroneously regarded as engaging in such use.

Qualified Individual with a Disability
(56 Fed. Reg. 35717, Sec. 35.104)

A qualified individual with a disability who, with or without reasonable modifications to municipal rules, policies or practices, the removal of architectural, communication, or transportation barriers or the provision of auxiliary aids and services, meets the essential eligibility requirements for the receipt of services or the participation in programs or activities provided by a local government.

Threats to Public Health and Safety

The preamble to the regulations explains how the "direct threat" or questions of safety apply to local government programs. The principles established in Section 36.208 of the Title III regulations, codified as 28 CFR Part 36, are applicable. A local government, therefore, is not required to permit any individual (including a qualified individual with a disability) who poses a direct threat to the health or safety of others to participate in or benefit from a public service, facility, program, privilege, or advantage.

A "direct threat" is defined as a significant risk to the health or safety of others that cannot be eliminated by a modification of policies, practices, or procedures, or the provision of auxiliary aids and services.

A determination whether an individual with a disability poses a direct threat to the health and safety of others is to be made under the three-part test established by the U.S. Supreme Court in *School Board of Nassau County v. Arline*. This case is referenced in the preamble of the DOJ regulations (56 *Fed. Reg.* 35701).

Using the Arline test, a local government must make an individualized assessment, based on reasonable judgment that relies on current medical evidence to determine:

- the nature, duration, and severity of the risk;
- the probability that the potential injury will actually occur; and
- whether reasonable modifications of policies, practices, or procedures will mitigate or eliminate the risk.

Overview of Title II Requirements

Subtitle A of Title II of the ADA extends the prohibition of discrimination established by the Rehabilitation Act of 1973 (Section 504) to all local government services, programs, or activities (including employment practices). In addition to an expanded definition of who is covered, the new rule requires all local governments to make sure that programs are accessible, sets specific standards for what constitutes discrimination on the basis of mental or physical disability, and institutes a complaint mechanism for resolving allegations of discrimination.

Effective Compliance Dates

Title II sets several deadlines for compliance with these new requirements.

Program Accessibility

By January 26, 1992 all local government programs are to be accessible to individuals with disabilities.

Self-Evaluations

Self-evaluations of services, programs, policies, and procedures are to be completed by January 26, 1993.

Existing Facilities and Buildings

Nonstructural changes are to be made as soon as practicable, but no later than January 26, 1992.

Structural changes are to be made as expeditiously as possible, but no later than January 26, 1995.

Employment

Local government employment policies must ensure accessibility to individuals with disabilities by January 26, 1992.

New Construction

Any new construction or alterations to buildings or facilities begun after January 26, 1992 must provide access for individuals with disabilities.

Municipal Information and Special Procedures Requirements

Notice Requirement
(56 Fed. Reg. 35718, Sec. 35.106)

No later than January 26, 1992, each local government must:

- make available to any interested individual information that describes application of the rules governing nondiscrimination on the basis of a disability in services, programs, or activities offered or provided by the municipality and
- apprise such individuals of the protections against discrimination assured them by the Act.

Self-Evaluation Requirement
(56 Fed.Reg. 35718, Sec. 35.105)

No later than January 26, 1993, each local government must:

- evaluate its current services, policies and practices (including employment policies and practices), and their effects, that do not (or may not) satisfy the requirements of the new regulations;
- make any modifications to such services, policies, and practices necessary to assure compliance with the new rules; and
- provide an opportunity for interested individuals and groups to submit comments as part of the self-evaluation process.

For at least three years following completion of the self-evaluation, a local government that employs fifty or more individuals must maintain on file and make available for public inspection:

- a list of the interested persons consulted;
- a description of areas examined and any problems identifies; and
- a description of any modifications made.

The self-evaluation requirement does not apply to policies and practices for which a local government has already met the self-evaluation requirement of a regulation implementing Section 504 of the Rehabilitation Act of 1973.

Special Rules for Local Governments that Employ Fifty or More Employees

Local governments with fifty or more employees are required to designate at least one employee to coordinate compliance efforts, adopt a grievance procedure, and develop a transition plan.

ADA Coordinator

Designation of Responsible Employee (56 Fed. Reg. 35718, Sec. 35.107)

A local government that employs fifty or more individuals must designate at least one employee to coordinate its efforts to comply with and carry out its responsibilities under rules governing nondiscrimination on the basis of disability in state and local government services (Subtitle A of Title II), including investigation of complaints arising out of allegations that the local government has failed to comply with the new law. The local government must make available to all interested individuals the name, office address, and telephone number of the designated employee or employees.

Although the designation of a ADA coordinator is required only in jurisdictions with fifty or more employees, it is recommended that all local governments designate a responsible employee for overseeing ADA compliance.

Grievance Procedure

Adoption of a Grievance Procedure (56 Fed. Reg. 35718, Sec. 35.107)

Only local governments that employ fifty or more individuals must adopt and publish grievance procedures. But it is advisable for all local jurisdictions to develop and publish grievance procedures, if only to avoid facing a grievance without one in place. These grievance procedures must provide for prompt and equitable resolution of complaints alleging any action prohibited under the rules governing nondiscrimination on the basis of disability in state and local government services (Subtitle A of Title II).

Transition Plan

Transition Plan (56 Fed. Reg. 35720, Sec. 35.150(d))

No later than July 26, 1992, a local government employing fifty or more individuals must develop a transition plan identifying all structural changes needed to a facility to achieve program accessibility. The transition plan must set forth the steps necessary to complete such changes and a timeframe for doing so.

At a minimum, the plan must:

- identify physical obstacles in publicly owned or leased facilities that limit the accessibility of its programs or activities to individuals with disabilities;
- describe (in detail) the methods that will be used to make the facilities accessible;
- specify the schedule for taking the steps necessary to achieve compliance with this section and, if the time period of the transition plan is longer than one year, identify steps that will be taken during each year of the transition period; and
- indicate the official responsible for implementation of the plan.

If the local government is responsible for maintaining or installing streets, walkways, sidewalks, or roads, the transition plan must include a schedule for providing curb ramps or other sloped areas where pedestrian walks cross curbs. Walkways serving public accommodations, commercial facilities, governmental entities and employers (the entities covered by the Act) should be dealt with first, followed by walkways serving other areas.

A local jurisdiction may want to create some mechanism for setting priorities when determining the location of retrofitted curb ramps. For example, a curb ramp committee comprised of disabled citizens and other community leaders could review and prioritize the Department of Public Works' capital improvement plan to determine where curb ramps will be installed. All citizen requests, along with anticipated new development, could be factored into the decision-making process.

Notice, Comment Period And Public Availability

The local government must give to all interested persons, including individuals with disabilities or organizations representing individuals with disabilities, the opportunity to submit comments on the transition plan. A copy of the transition plan must be made available for public inspection.

Exemption From Transition Plan Requirements

If a local government has already complied with the transition plan requirements of a Federal agency regulation implementing Section 504 of the Rehabilitation Act of 1973, then the transition plan requirement applies only to policies and practices that were not included in the previous transition plan.

Municipal Services, Activities, and Programs

Title II applies to all services, programs and activities (including employment practices) provided or made available by a local government or any of its instrumentalities, agencies, or contractors.

Prohibited Discrimination (56 Fed. Reg. 35718, Sec. 35.130(b))

In providing any aid, benefit, or service, a local government may not, directly or through contractual, licensing, or other arrangements, discriminate on the basis of disability:

- deny a qualified individual with a disability the opportunity to participate in or benefit from the aid, benefit, or service;
- afford a qualified individual with a disability an opportunity to participate in or benefit from the aid, benefit, or service that is not equal to that afforded others;
- provide a qualified individual with a disability with an aid, benefit, or service that is not as effective in affording equal opportunity to obtain the same result, to gain the same benefit, or to reach the same level of achievement as that provided to others;
- provide different or separate aids, benefits or services to individuals with disabilities or to any class of individuals with disabilities than is provided to others unless such action is necessary to provide qualified individuals with disabilities with aids, benefits, or services that are as effective as those provided to others;
- aid or perpetuate discrimination against a qualified individual with a disability by providing significant assistance to an agency, organization, or person that discriminates on the basis of disability in providing any aid, benefit, or service to beneficiaries of the public entity's program;
- deny a qualified individual with a disability the opportunity to participate as a member of planning or advisory boards; or
- otherwise limit a qualified individual with a disability in the enjoyment of any right, privilege, advantage, or opportunity enjoyed by others receiving the aid, benefit, or service.

The new rules do not prohibit a local government from offering otherwise permissibly separate or different services, programs, or activities to qualified individuals with a disability. However, local government officials may not deny a qualified individual with a disability the opportunity to participate in services, programs, or activities that are not separate or different, despite the existence of permissibly separate or different programs, services, or activities.

A local government may not impose a surcharge on a particular individual with a disability or group of individuals with a disability to pay the cost of measures (auxiliary aids or program accessibility) that the local government is required to provide to assure nondiscriminatory treatment under the Act (56 *Fed. Reg.* 35718, Sec. 35.130(f)).

Other Municipal Activities (56 Fed. Reg. 35718, Sec. 35.130 (3))

At a minimum, a local government must ensure that it does not:

■ use criteria to select procurement contractors that subjects qualified individuals with disabilities to discrimination on the basis of disability;

■ administer a licensing or certification program in a manner that subjects qualified individuals with disabilities to discrimination on the basis of disability, nor may it establish requirements for the programs or activities of licensees or certified entities that subject qualified individuals with disabilities to discrimination on the basis of disability (The programs or activities of entities that are licensed or certified by a public entity are not, themselves, covered by Title II);

■ impose or apply eligibility criteria that screen out or tend to screen out an individual with a disability or any class of individuals with disabilities from fully and equally enjoying any service, program, or activity, unless such criteria can be shown to be necessary for the provision of the service, program, or activity being offered;

■ exclude or otherwise deny equal services, programs, or activities to an individual or entity because of the known disability of an individual with whom the individual or entity is known to have a relationship or association.

Integrated Setting (56 Fed. Reg. 35719, Sec.35.130(d))

A local government must administer its services, programs, and activities in the most integrated setting appropriate to the needs of qualified individuals with disabilities. However, an individual with a disability is not required to accept an accommodation, aid, service, opportunity or benefit provided under the ADA that the individual chooses not to accept.

The DOJ regulations, however, do not authorize the personal representative or guardian of an individual with a disability to decline food, water, medical treatment, or medical services for that individual.

Health And Drug Rehabilitation Services (56 Fed. Reg. 35719, Sec. 35.131 (b))

A local government may not deny health services, or services provided in connection with drug rehabilitation, to an individual on the basis of that individual's current unlawful use of drugs, if the individual is otherwise entitled to such services. However, a drug treatment or rehabilitation program may deny participation to individuals who engage in unlawful use of drugs while they are in the program.

This provision does not prohibit a city, town, or county from adopting or administering reasonable policies or procedures, including but not limited to drug testing, designed to ensure that an individual who formerly engaged in the unlawful use of drugs is not now engaging in current unlawful use of drugs.

Drug Testing (56 Fed. Reg. 35719, Sec. 35.131 (c))

A local government agency or department may adopt or administer reasonable policies or procedures regarding drug testing. Drug testing may be used to determine if individuals (either employees or applicants) are now engaging in the illegal use of drugs.

Smoking (56 Fed. Reg. 35719, Sec. 35.132)

The Act does not preclude the prohibition of, or the imposition of restrictions on, smoking in a publicly-owned facility.

Discrimination In Public Sector Employment

The Title II regulations provide that no qualified individual with a disability may, on the basis of disability, be subjected to discrimination in employment under any service, program, or activity conducted by a local government (56 *Fed. Reg.* 35719, Sec.

35.140(a)).These regulations specifically provide that the prohibition against employment discrimination on the basis of disability applies to all local governments on January 26, 1992, notwithstanding the number of individuals the local government employs.

The preamble to the regulations suggests that DOJ and the Equal Employment Opportunity Commission (EEOC) would work together to issue regulations that specifically address municipal employment. However, because those regulations are not expected to be available until after January 1, 1992, local government officials should immediately begin to familiarize themselves with the Title I regulations, as well as those issued by the Section 504 regulations issued by DOJ (28 CFR Part 41).

If no joint DOJ-EEOC public sector employment regulations have been issued by January 26, 1992, local governments must meet the following regulatory requirements.

Program Accessibility

Prohibited Discrimination (56 Fed.
Reg. 35719, Sec. 35.149)

In general, no qualified individual with a disability shall, because a municipality's facilities are inaccessible to or unusable by individuals with disabilities, be excluded from participation in, or be

---

Employment Compliance Dates

■ January 26, 1991 - July 25, 1992: All local governments, regardless of size, must comply with 28 Code Of Federal Regulations (CFR) Part 41 (references to Section 504) as it pertains to employment.

■ After July 26, 1992: Local governments with 25 or more employees must comply with the Title I regulations issued by EEOC. Cities, towns, villages and counties with fewer than 25 employees must comply with 28 CFR Part 41, as it pertains to employment.

■ After July 26, 1994: Local jurisdictions with 15 or more employees must comply with the Title I regulations. Municipalities, towns, and villages with fewer than 15 employees must comply with 28 CFR Part 41, as it pertains to employment.

denied the benefits of the services, programs, or activities of a public entity, or be subjected to discrimination by any municipality.

Existing Facilities (56 Fed. Reg. 35719-20, Sec. 35.150)

A local government must operate each service, program, or activity so that the service, program, or activity, when viewed in its entirety, is readily accessible to and usable by individuals with disabilities.

The general rule should not be interpreted to mean that a local government is necessarily required to:

- make each of its existing facilities accessible to and usable by individuals with disabilities;
- take any action that would threaten or destroy the historic significance of an historic property; or
- take any action that it can demonstrate would result in a fundamental alteration in the nature of a service, program, or activity or in undue financial and administrative burdens.

Burden of Proof

When local government officials believe that a proposed compliance action would fundamentally alter the service, program, or activity or would result in undue financial and administrative burdens, they have the burden of proving that the compliance action would result in such alteration or burdens.

The head of the public agency or a designee must determine whether compliance would result in such alteration or burdens after considering all resources available for use in the funding and operation of the service, program, or activity. A written statement of the reasons for reaching that conclusion must accompany the determination.

If an action would result in such an alteration or such burdens, a municipality must take any other action that would not result in such an alteration or such burdens but would nevertheless ensure that individuals with disabilities receive the benefits or service provided by the municipality.

Compliance Activities

A local government may comply with the program accessibility requirements through a variety of means, including the redesign of equipment, reassignment of services to accessible buildings, assignment of aides to beneficiaries, home visits, delivery of services at alternate accessible sites, alteration of existing facilities and construction of new facilities, use of accessible rolling stock or other conveyances, or any other methods that result in making its services, programs, or activities readily accessible to and usable by individuals with disabilities.

Structural changes are not required in existing facilities where other methods will achieve compliance with this section. However, in making alterations to existing buildings, the local entity must meet the accessibility requirements for new construction and alterations (UFAS or ADAAG standards).

In choosing among available methods for meeting the program accessibility requirements, a local government must give priority to those methods that offer services, programs, and activities to qualified individuals with disabilities in the most integrated setting appropriate.

Historic Preservation Programs

Historic Preservation Programs
(56 Fed. Reg. 35720, Sec.
35.150(b)(2))

To meet the program accessibility requirements in historic preservation programs, a local government must give priority to methods that provide physical access to individuals with disabilities. Where a physical alteration to an historic property is not required because it would threaten or destroy the historic significance of the property or result in a fundamental alteration of the service, activity, or program, program accessibility may be achieved through alternate means, including:

■ using audiovisual materials and devices to depict those portions of an historic property that cannot otherwise be made accessible;

- providing guides to take individuals with disabilities into or through portions of historic properties that cannot otherwise be made accessible; or
- adopting other innovative methods.

Time Period For Compliance

Structural changes in facilities to satisfy the program accessibility requirements, must be made as expeditiously as possible, but in no event later than January 26, 1995.

New Construction and Alterations (56 Fed. Reg. 35720, Sec. 35.151)

Each facility or part of a facility constructed by, on behalf of, or for the use of a local government must be designed and constructed so that the facility or part of the facility is readily accessible to and usable by individuals with disabilities, if the construction began after January 26, 1992.

Each facility or part of a facility altered by, on behalf of, or for the use of a municipality in a manner that affects or could affect the usability of the facility or part of the facility must (to the maximum extent feasible) be altered in such manner that the altered portion of the facility is readily accessible to and usable by individuals with disabilities, if the alteration was commenced after January 26, 1992.

Accessibility Standards

Design, construction, or alteration of facilities in conformance with the Uniform Federal Accessibility Standards (UFAS) or Americans With Disabilities Act Accessibility Guidelines for Buildings and Facilities (ADAAG) will comply with the regulatory requirements for new construction and alterations. Departures from particular requirements of either standard by the use of other compliance methods is permitted when it is clearly evident that the other methods provide equivalent access to the facility or part of the facility.

Both standards are described in some detail in Chapter 6.

The elevator exemption provided for in the ADAAG does not apply to any publicly owned or leased facility or building.

Alterations To Historic Properties

Alterations to historic properties must comply (to the maximum extent feasible) with UFAS or ADAAG. However, if it is not feasible to provide physical access to an historic property in a manner that will not threaten or destroy the historic significance of the building or facility, alternative methods of access must be provided (i.e., audiovisual materials, guided tours, or other innovative methods).

Curb Ramps

Curb ramps are required as follows:

- Newly constructed or altered streets, roads, and highways must provide curb ramps or other sloped areas at any intersection where there are curbs or other barriers to entry from a street level pedestrian walkway.
- Newly constructed or altered street level pedestrian walkways must include curb ramps or other sloped areas at intersections to streets, roads, or highways.

Local Government Communications

Local Government
Communications (56 Fed. Reg.
35721, Subpart E)

Local government communications with applicants, participants, and members of the public with disabilities must be as effective as communications with others.

Auxiliary Aids and Services (56
Fed. Reg. 35721, Sec. 35.160(b))

A local government must furnish appropriate auxiliary aids and services where necessary to afford an individual with a disability an equal opportunity to participate in, and enjoy the benefits of, a service, program, or activity conducted by a public entity. In determining what type of auxiliary aid and service is necessary, a local government must give primary consideration to the requests of the individual with disabilities.

Appropriate auxiliary aids and services may include reading devices and readers when necessary to ensure equal participation and opportunity to benefit from any government service, program, or activity (such as reviewing public documents, examining demonstrative evidence, filling out a voter's registration form, or taking an examination). The preamble to the regulations points out that television and videotape programming produced by a local government are covered activities and that access to the audio portions of such programming may be provided by closed captioning.

Telecommunications Devices for the Deaf (56 Fed. Reg. 35721, Sec. 35.161)

This section requires that where a local government communicates by telephone with applicants and beneficiaries, telecommunication devices for the deaf (TDDs) or equally effective telecommunication systems must be used to communicate with individuals with impaired hearing or speech. Where provision of telephone service is a major function of the agency (for example at city hall or a public library), TDDs should be available.

Telephone Emergency Services (56 Fed. Reg. 35721, Sec. 35.162)

Telephone emergency services, including all 911 emergency services, must provide direct access to individuals who use TDDs and computer modems. This means that all emergency 911 services must be adapted to receive calls from TDDs and computer modems. It is not satisfactory to install a separate seven-digit telephone number to handle emergency calls from hearing or speech impaired individuals using telecommunications devices for the deaf.

Information and Signage (56 Fed. Reg. 35721, Sec. 35.163)

A local jurisdiction must ensure that interested persons, including persons with impaired vision or hearing, can obtain information about accessible services, activities, and facilities. There must be signs at all inaccessible entrances to each facility, directing users to an accessible entrance or to a location at which they can obtain information about accessible facilities. Each accessible entrance of a facility must be identified with the international symbol for accessibility. In airports, public auditoriums, and other public facilities, signs near telephone banks should direct individuals in need of a TDD to the nearest location.

Duties (56 Fed. Reg. 35721, Sec. 35.164)

A local government is not required to take any action under regulations governing communications that it can demonstrate would result in a fundamental alteration in the nature of a service, program, or activity or in undue financial and administrative burdens.

Where local government officials believe that the proposed action would fundamentally alter the service, program, or activity, or would result in undue financial and administrative burdens, the jurisdiction has the burden of proving that compliance would result in such alteration or burdens. A determination that compliance would result in such alteration or burdens must be made by the head of the public agency or his or her designee after considering all resources available for use in the funding and operation of the service, program, or activity and must be accompanied by a written statement of the reasons for reaching that conclusion.

If an action required to comply with regulations governing communications would result in such an alteration or such burdens, a local government must take any other action that would not result in such an alteration or such burdens but would nevertheless ensure that, to the maximum extent possible, individuals with disabilities receive the benefits or services provided by the public entity.

Preparing for Compliance with the Public Service Provisions of Title II

■ Designate an ADA compliance coordinator to oversee to the planning, training and implementation of compliance activities.

■ Provide public notice to all interested parties on who the ADA coordinator is and anticipated compliance steps.

■ Conduct a comprehensive self-evaluation, noting where compliance with Section 504 has occurred previously and where changes are needed to achieve either program accessibility or structural modifications.

■ Prepare a transition plan which describes all structural changes, how they will be corrected, the timeframe for completion, and the responsible official.

■ Develop a grievance procedure for handling complaints.

■ Conduct sensitivity training for city employees who have direct contact with the general public, so they can learn how to provide services in a nondiscriminatory manner.

■ Review the employment provisions of Title II to ensure compliance.

■ Take the steps necessary to ensure that disabled individuals can readily communicate with city programs and services. Determine how your 911 emergency dispatch service will become accessible to hearing and speech impaired citizens.

■ Be sure that all new facilities and major alterations meet with UFAS or ADA-AG standards for accessibility.

■ When reviewing your services to determine whether they met the "program accessibility" test, give special consideration to the objective of providing services in the "most integrated setting possible".

■ Use representatives from disability organizations wherever possible to advise your department on how to provide program access in the most integrated setting possible.

3
EMPLOYMENT
PROVISIONS

By Katharine L. Herber

No employer covered under the ADA shall discriminate against a qualified individual with a disability ... in regard to job application procedures, the hiring, advancement or discharge of employees, employee compensation, job training and other terms, conditions and privileges of employment. (42 U.S.C. 12112)

Under Title I of the ADA (29 CFR Part 1630), local governments must make "reasonable accommodations" to the known physical or mental impairments of otherwise qualified individuals unless the result would create an "undue hardship" on the employer (56 *Fed. Reg.* 35736). (Title I covers private as well as public entities with fifteen or more employees.) The Equal Employment Opportunity Commission (EEOC), the lead federal agency for enforcing the employment provisions of the ADA, published regulations implementing Title I in the *Federal Register* on July 26, 1991.

This chapter explains the conditions, prohibitions, responsibilities and steps that local governments must take as employers under Title I of the ADA. Although Title I specifically applies to public employers with fifteen or more employees, the requirement to ensure nondiscrimination in employment affects all local governments regardless of their number of employees or size of the budget. Section 35.140 of the Title II regulations clearly states that those local governments not covered under Title I must meet the requirements of Section 504 of the Rehabilitation Act of 1973, as established in 28 CFR Part 41, as those requirements pertain to employment.

However, the Section 504 regulations do not outline specific ways for smaller jurisdictions to comply with the employment provisions of the ADA. For this reason, it is advisable for officials of all local governments to review this chapter with the intent of complying with the EEOC regulations. Justice Department officials have indicated that compliance with the EEOC regulations would provide a "safe haven" for all local governments.

Who is Covered Under Title I?

Qualified Individual With a Disability (56 Fed. Reg., Sec. 1630.2(m))

A qualified individual with a disability means an individual with a disability who:

- satisfies the requisite skill, experience, education and other job-related requirements of the position such individual holds or desires, and
- with or without reasonable accommodation, can perform the essential functions of the position.

Determining if an individual is a "qualified individual with a disability" must be done at the time of the employment action in question. The determination may not be based on speculation that the individual will become unable to perform the job in the future or that the individual may cause the municipality's health insurance or workers' compensation costs to increase.

Relationship or Association with a Disabled Person (56 Fed. Reg. 35737, Sec. 1630.8)

Any qualified individual, with or without a disability, is protected from discrimination on the basis of an association or relationship with an individual who has a known disability. These protections, which apply to hiring, promotions, and transfers as well as to other benefits and privileges of employment, are not limited to those who have a family relationship with an individual with a disability. For example, an advocate, volunteer, or friend cannot be discriminated against because they are supporters of disabled individuals.

Assessing Qualifications

Determining whether an individual with a disability is qualified for the position involves two steps. The first step is to determine if the individual satisfies the prerequisites for the position (i.e., appropriate education, skills, licenses, etc.). The second step involves determining whether the individual can perform the essential functions of the position held or desired, with or without reasonable accommodation.

Determining if an individual is qualified must be made at the time of the employment decision. The decision should not be based on speculation that the employee may become unable to perform the job functions in the future or may cause increased health insurance premiums or workers' compensation costs.

Essential Functions (56 Fed. Reg., Sec. 1630.2(n))

Essential functions are ones that the individual who holds the position must be able to perform unaided or with the assistance of reasonable accommodation. To determine whether a function is essential, consider the following factors:

- whether the position exists to perform a particular function;
- the number of other employees available to perform that job function or among whom the performance of that job function can be distributed (this may be a factor either because the total number of available employees is low, or because of the fluctuating demands of the business operation); and
- the degree of expertise or skill required to perform the function.

All relevant evidence should be considered in making a determination that a function is an essential function. For example, written job descriptions prepared before advertising or interviewing applicants for the job; the employer's judgment as to what functions are essential; collective bargaining agreements; work experience of past employees in the job or of current employees in similar jobs; the time spent in performing the particular function; and the consequences of failing to require the employee to perform the function are facts relevant to the determination of whether a particular function is essential.

The inquiry into essential functions is not intended to second guess an employer's business judgment with regard to production standards, whether qualitative or quantitative, nor to require employers to lower such standards.

Exceptions

Unlawful Use of Drugs (56 Fed. Reg. 35736, Sec. 1630.3(a) - (c))

An individual currently engaging in the unlawful use of drugs is not an individual with a disability for the purpose of Title I where the employer acts on that basis. Unlawful use of drugs refers both to the use of unlawful drugs and to the unlawful use of prescription drugs.

Individuals who are (1) erroneously perceived as engaging in the unlawful use of drugs, but are not in fact unlawfully using drugs and/or (2) no longer unlawfully using drugs and who have either been rehabilitated successfully or are in the process of completing a rehabilitation program are not excluded from the definition of the terms "disability" and "qualified individual with a disability." However, these individuals must still establish that they meet the requirements of these definitions in order to be protected by the ADA.

A local government may ask individuals to make reasonable assurances that they are not currently engaged in the unlawful use of drugs and may ask for evidence that they are participating in drug treatment programs and/or evidence (such as drug test results) that they are not currently engaging in the unlawful use of drugs.

Sexual Disorders, Compulsive Behaviors and Psychoactive Substance Use Disorders (56 Fed. Reg. 35736, Sec. 1630(d))

The following disorders or behaviors are not included in the definition of "disability" under the Act:

- transvestism, transsexualism, pedophilia, exhibitionism, voyeurism, gender identity disorders not resulting from physical impairments or other sexual behavior disorders;
- compulsive gambling, kleptomania or pyromania; or
- psychoactive substance use disorders resulting from current illegal use of drugs.

Homosexuality and Bisexuality (56 Fed. Reg. 35736, Sec. 1630(e))

Homosexuality and bisexuality are not impairments and, therefore, are not defined as disabilities. They are considered sexual orientations.

Disability Determination (56 Fed. Reg. 35735, Sec. 1630.2(g) - (I))

Under the ADA, an individual is considered to have a disability if that individual (1) has a physical or mental impairment that substantially limits one or more of that person's major life activities, or (2) has a record of such an impairment, or (3) is regarded by the municipality as having such an impairment.

Physical or Mental Impairment (56 Fed. Reg., Sec. 1620.2(h))

A physical or mental impairment is any physiological disorder or condition, cosmetic disfigurement, or anatomical loss affecting one or more of several body systems or any mental or psychological disorder. Whether an individual has an impairment is to be determined without regard to mitigating measures (for example, medicines or assistive or prosthetic devices).

**Characteristics, Conditions and
Traits Not Considered Impairments**

Physical, psychological, environmental, cultural and economic characteristics that are not considered impairments include physical characteristics (e.g., eye color, hair color, left-handedness, or height, weight or muscle tone that are within "normal" range and are not the result of a physiological disorder); characteristic predisposition to illness or disease; conditions that are not the result of a physiological disorder (e.g., pregnancy); common personality traits (e.g., poor judgment or a quick temper) where these are not symptoms of a mental or psychological disorder; and environmental, cultural or economic disadvantages (e.g., poverty, prison record or lack of education). In addition, although advanced age is not an impairment, various medical conditions commonly associated with the aged may constitute impairments (e.g., arthritis or hearing loss).

**Major Life Activities (56 Fed. Reg.
35735, Sec. 1630.2(i))**

Major life activities are basic activities that the average person in the general population can perform with little or no difficulty. Major life activities include: caring for oneself, performing manual tasks, walking, seeing, hearing, speaking, sitting, standing, lifting, reaching, breathing, learning, and working.

**Determination Whether the
Disability Is Substantially Limiting
(56 Fed. Reg. 35735, Sec.
1630.2(j))**

Determining whether the disability is substantially limiting must be done on a case-by-case basis, without regard to such mitigating measures as medicines, or assistive or prosthetic devices. Under the regulations, an individual is not substantially limited in a major life activity if the limitation does not constitute a significant restriction when compared with the abilities of the average person when viewed in light of the following factors:

- the nature and severity of the impairment;
- the duration or expected duration of the impairment; and
- the permanent or long term impact or the expected long term or permanent impact of, or resulting from, the impairment.

If an individual is not substantially limited with respect to any other major life activity, the individual's ability to work must be considered (if an individual is substantially limited in any other major life activity, no determination should be made as to whether the individual's ability to work is also substantially limited).

To determine whether the limitation in the major life activity of working is substantial, look at the following factors:

- the geographical area to which the individual has reasonable access;
- the job from which the individual has been disqualified because of an impairment, and the number and types of jobs utilizing similar training, knowledge, skills or abilities, within that geographical area, from which the individual is also disqualified because of the impairment (class of jobs); and/or
- the job from which the individual has been disqualified because of an impairment, and the number and types of other jobs not utilizing similar training, knowledge, skills or abilities, within that geographical area, from which the individual is also disqualified because of the impairment (broad range of jobs in various classes).

Disability Based on a Record of a Substantially Limiting Condition (56 Fed. Reg. 35735, Sec. 1630.2(k))

An individual with a record of an impairment that substantially limits a major life activity is an individual with a disability. (This provision also applies to individuals who have been misclassified as having a disability.) Because that is so, the fact that an individual has a record of being a disabled veteran, or of disability retirement, or is classified as disabled for other purposes, does not guarantee that the individual will satisfy the Title I definition of disability.

Regarded by the Local Government as Substantially Limited in a Major Life Activity (56 Fed. Reg. 35735, Sec. 1630.2(l))

An individual who is regarded as having an impairment that substantially limits a major life activity is an individual with a disability.

There are three ways in which an individual may satisfy the definition of "being regarded as having a disability".

- The individual may have an impairment which is not substantially limiting but is treated by the local government as constituting a substantially limiting impairment.
- The individual may have an impairment which is only substantially limiting because of the attitudes of others toward the impairment.

- Or the individual may have no impairment at all but is regarded by the local government as having a substantially limiting impairment.

If an individual who has no impairment can show that a local government made an employment decision because of a perception of disability based on "myth, fear, or stereotype," the individual will satisfy the "regarded as" part of the definition of disability.

Moreover, if the local government is unable to offer a nondiscriminatory reason for the employment action, it may be inferred that the local jurisdiction is acting on the basis of "myth, fear, or stereotype." For example, if a city employee were rumored to have AIDS and the individual's supervisor indicated that it would be inappropriate for someone with AIDS to remain employed in the department, the individual is covered under the ADA. The city employee could file a grievance as a disabled person under the condition of "being perceived as having a disability."

Reasonable Accommodation

Reasonable Accommodation (56 Fed. Reg. 35737, Sec. 1630.9)

It is unlawful for a local government not to make a reasonable accommodation to the known physical or mental limitations of an otherwise qualified applicant or employee with a disability, unless the local government can demonstrate that the accommodation would impose an undue hardship on its business operations.

Reasonable Accommodation Categories (56 Fed. Reg. 35735-36, Sec. 1630.2(o))

There are three categories of reasonable accommodations:

- accommodations that are required to ensure equal opportunity in the application process;
- accommodations that enable the local government's employees with disabilities to perform the essential functions of the position held or desired; and
- accommodations that enable the local government's employees with disabilities to enjoy equal benefits and privileges of employment as are enjoyed by employees without disabilities.

A reasonable accommodation may include one (or more) of the following activities:

■ making existing facilities used by employees readily accessible to and usable by individuals with disabilities. Under this requirement, the local government must assure that both those areas that must be accessible for the employee to perform essential job functions, as well as non-work areas used by local government employees are accessible (i.e., break rooms, cafeterias, training rooms, restrooms, etc.);

■ job re-structuring, including part-time or modified work schedules or reassignment to a vacant position;

■ acquisition or modifications of equipment or devices;

■ appropriate adjustment or modification of examinations, training materials, or policies;

■ the provision of qualified readers or interpreters; and

■ other similar accommodations for individuals with disabilities.

Essential Function Restructuring Not Required

A local government is not required to reallocate essential functions (those functions that the individual would have to perform, with or without reasonable accommodation, in order to be considered qualified for the position). However, reasonable accommodation may result in a local government restructuring a job by reallocating or redistributing nonessential, marginal job functions.

Reassignment — When Permitted And When Prohibited (56 Fed. Reg. 35744-45)

Reassignment should be considered only when accommodation within the individual's current position would pose an undue hardship. In circumstances where, because of undue hardship, there is no alternative to reassignment, the local government should reassign the individual to an equivalent position (one with equivalent pay and status) if the individual is qualified, and if the position is vacant within a reasonable time based on the totality of the circumstances.

A local government may reassign an individual to a lower-graded position if there are no accommodations that would enable the employee to remain in the current position and there are no vacant equivalent positions for which the individual is qualified with or without reasonable accommodation. The municipality does not have to maintain the reassigned individual with a disability at the salary of the higher-graded position if it does not do the same for reassigned employees who are not disabled.

Reassignment may not be used to limit, segregate, or otherwise discriminate against employees with disabilities by forcing reassignments to undesirable positions or to designated offices or facilities.

It is important to note that reassignment is not available to applicants. An applicant for a position must be qualified for, and be able to perform the essential functions of, the position sought with or without reasonable accommodation.

Reasonable Accommodation Determination

At any time, a qualified applicant or employee may request provision of a reasonable accommodation and the local government must make a reasonable effort to determine the appropriate accommodation. Although cases will arise in which the appropriate reasonable accommodation is obvious to both the local government and the qualified applicant/employee, in some cases the accommodation will best be determined through a flexible, interactive process that involves both the local government and the qualified applicant/employee. there are four steps in the process.

Step 1: Assessment and Analysis of the Job

This is a three-part process under which the local jurisdiction (1) analyzes the particular job involved (including the work site and equipment used); (2) determines the purpose or object of the job; and (3) identifies the essential function(s) of the job.

Step 2: Consultation with the Qualified Applicant/Employee

In consultation with the qualified applicant/employee, the local government assesses the specific job-related limitations imposed by the applicant's or employee's disability.

Step 3: Identification of Potential Accommodation and Assessment of Its Effectiveness

The local government, in consultation with the qualified applicant/employee, identifies potential accommodations and assesses the effectiveness of each in enabling the applicant to perform the essential functions of the job.

If no potential appropriate accommodation is identified, local government officials may wish to seek technical assistance from the Equal Employment Opportunity Commission (EEOC), state or local rehabilitation agencies, or disability constituent organizations. It is important, however, to note that the failure to obtain or receive technical assistance from the EEOC does not excuse the local government from its reasonable accommodation obligation.

Step 4: Selection and Implementation of a Reasonable Accommodation

Once a reasonable accommodation has been identified, the local government must select and implement the accommodation that is most appropriate for both the local government and the qualified applicant/employee, giving primary consideration to the preference of the qualified applicant/employee.

Although the local government must give primary consideration to the qualified applicant's/employee's preference in selecting from among effective accommodations. the final choice is at the discretion of the local government, which may choose the less expensive accommodation or the accommodation that is easier to provide.

A qualified applicant/employee may provide his or her own accommodation. However, the local government is not relieved of the duty to provide the accommodation in the event the qualified applicant/employee is (for any reason) unwilling or unable to continue to provide the accommodation.

Undue Hardship as a Defense for Not Making a Reasonable Accommodation

**Undue Hardship Defined (56 Fed.
Reg. 35736, Sec. 1630.2(p))**

Undue hardship means any accommodation that would be unduly costly, extensive, substantial, disruptive, or that would fundamentally alter the nature or operation of the business in light the following factors:

- the nature and net cost of the accommodation needed under the ADA, taking into consideration the availability of outside funding;
- the overall financial resources of the facility or facilities involved in the provision of the reasonable accommodation, the number of persons employed at such facility, and the effect on expenses and resources;
- the overall financial resources of the local government, the overall number of local government employees, and the number, type and location of its facilities;
- the type of operation or operations of the local government, including the composition, structure and functions of its work force, the geographic separateness and administrative or fiscal relationship of the facility or facilities in question; and
- the impact of the accommodation upon the operation of the facility, including the impact on the ability of other employees to perform their duties and the impact on the facility's ability to conduct business.

**Factors to Consider When
Determining Undue Hardship (56
Fed. Reg. 35738, Sec. 1630.15(d))**

As a defense against alleged discrimination because of the failure to make a reasonable accommodation, a local government may offer that it would have been an undue hardship to make the accommodation. However, in circumstances where this defense is offered, the local government must both present evidence and demonstrate that the accommodation would, in fact, cause it undue hardship.

A Section 504 court case, *Nelson v. Thornburgh* (567F, Supp. 369 aff'd 732 F.2d 146 (1984) cert. den. 53 U.S.L.W. 3528(1985), set the precedent for assessing "undue hardship" in the context of public employment. In *Nelson v. Thornburgh*, the Department of

Public Welfare in the Commonwealth of Pennsylvania was required to provide part-time readers for several visually impaired staff at the cost of $7,000 to $10,000 per disabled employee per year. The court held that these were not "undue" costs given tye department's budget.

Cost Would Result In Undue Hardship

To demonstrate that the cost of an accommodation poses an undue hardship, a local government must show that the cost is undue compared to the local government's budget. It is not sufficient to compare the cost of the accommodation to the salary of the individual with a disability. Remember, the EEOC did not place a dollar limit on how much an employer must pay to provide a reasonable accommodation.

The ADA coordinator or personnel director can contact the state department of rehabilitative services to see if that agency can provide funding for the accommodation (e.g., equipment). In addition, many local nonprofit organizations that serve the disabled community can also provide funding or services to assist disabled individuals with job readiness skills or training.

Even if the cost of the accommodation would pose an undue hardship, the local government cannot avoid making the accommodation if the individual with a disability is able to arrange to cover that portion of the cost that rises to the undue hardship level, or can otherwise arrange to provide the accommodation.

Accommodation Would Be Unduly Disruptive

Undue disruption may form the basis of an undue hardship defense where the local government is able to demonstrate that the particular accommodation would be unduly disruptive to its other employees or to the functioning of its business. However, if there were an alternate accommodation that would not result in undue hardship, the local government would have to provide that accommodation.

Undue hardship does not exist where the disruption to its employees is the result of those employees' fears or prejudices toward the individual's disability and not the result of the provision of the accommodation.

Undue hardship does not exist where the only showing the local government is able to make is that the provision of the accommodation has a negative impact on the morale of its other employees but not on the ability of these employees to perform their jobs.

Qualified Applicant/Employee Does Not Request Accommodation or Refuses Accommodation (56 Fed. Reg. 35737, Sec. 1630.9(d))

A local government cannot compel a qualified applicant/employee to accept an accommodation that (1) is neither requested nor needed by the individual or (2) refused by the individual. If a qualified applicant/employee refuses a reasonable accommodation and is unable to perform an essential function of the job without such accommodation, the individual would not be qualified for the job.

For example, a qualified applicant/employee with a minimal hearing loss in one ear but who can hear unaided would not be required to accept an amplifier as an accommodation. However, if the qualified applicant/employee were unable to hear unaided and hearing was an essential function of the job, the individual would not be qualified for the job if he or she refused a reasonable accommodation that would enable him or her to hear.

Pre-Employment Activities and Requirements

Job Description (56 Fed. Reg. 35736, Sec. 1630.4)

A local government may not discriminate on the basis of disability against a qualified applicant with a disability in regard to job descriptions. The ADA does not expressly require that your jurisdiction have job descriptions.

Recruitment, Advertising, Applications

Recruitment, Advertising And Job Application Procedures (56 Fed. Reg. 35736, Sec. 1630.4)

A local government may not discriminate on the basis of disability against a qualified applicant with a disability in regard to recruitment, advertising and job application procedures.

The Title II regulations specifically provide that a local government must take steps to ensure that communications with applicants with disabilities are as effective as communications with others (56 *Fed. Reg.* 35736, Sec. 35.160). Moreover, those regulations require that a municipality furnish appropriate auxiliary aids and services where necessary to afford an individual an equal opportunity to participate in, and enjoy the benefits of, its activities. In determining what type of auxiliary aid and service is necessary, the local government must give primary consideration to the requests of the individual with a disability.

Compliance with the Title II requirements may result in a local government expanding the communication media it currently uses to advertise job vacancies and recruit qualified candidates for vacant positions. For example, if municipal job vacancy announcements are only available in written form (e.g., newspaper, posted at city hall, etc.) it is not unreasonable to assume that the announcement has not been effectively communicated to individuals with a sight loss.

It has been suggested that personnel departments send job vacancy announcements to local organizations serving disabled individuals to advise them of openings.

Application Procedures

In its employment application process, a local government may not:

- use an application form that lists a number of potentially disabling impairments and ask the applicant to check any of the impairments she or he may have of their own;
- ask how often an applicant will require leave for treatment or use leave as a result of incapacitation because of one's own disability or that of a relative or associate.

A local jurisdiction may:

- state the attendance requirements of the job and inquire whether the applicant is able to meet them;
- require applicants with disabilities to advise them in advance of an employment test that they will require a reasonable

accommodation and request that documentation of the need for the accommodation accompany the request; and

■ collect information and invite applicants to identify themselves as individuals with disabilities as required to satisfy the affirmative action requirements of Section 503 of the Rehabilitation Act.

Qualifications, Tests, Selection Criteria

Qualification Standards, Tests and Other Selection Criteria (56 Fed. Reg. 35737, Sec. 1630.10)

A local government may not use qualification standards, employment tests, or other selection criteria that screen out or tend to screen out (even unintentionally) an individual with a disability or a class of individuals with disabilities, on the basis of disability. However, there are several exceptions to this general prohibition.

An exception to the general prohibition exists if the local government can show that the standard, test, or other selection criteria, as used by the local government, is both job-related for the position in question and is consistent with business necessity. Under this exception, however, it would not be consistent with the business necessity condition, if an applicant were denied a job for failure to satisfy certain job criteria where such criteria do not concern an essential function of the job. Moreover, selection criteria that are related to an essential function of the job may not be used to exclude an individual with a disability if that individual could satisfy the criteria with reasonable accommodation.

Qualification Standards

"Qualification standards" are defined as personal and professional attributes deemed necessary to perform the job. They represent the skills, education, experience, or physical or licensing requirements that an individual must possess in order to meet the minimum requirement to qualify for the position. These standards are determined by the employer in advance of advertising for a vacant position.

Threats to Health and Safety

Individual Poses a Direct Threat
(56 Fed. Reg. 35736, Sec.
1630.2(r))

As a qualification standard, a local government may require that an individual not pose a direct threat to the health or safety of himself/herself or others. If the local government has such a qualification standard, it must apply equally to all applicants or employees (i.e., not just to individuals with a disability).

According to the EEOC regulations, a direct threat must pose a significant risk to the health or safety of the individual with a disability or others (i.e., high probability of substantial harm). In making a determination whether an individual poses a significant risk, a municipality should:

■ Identify the specific risk posed by the individual: In the case of individuals with mental or emotional disabilities, the municipality must identify the specific behavior on the part of the individual that would pose the direct threat. For individuals with physical disabilities, the employer must identify the aspect of the disability that would pose the direct threat.

■ Analyze and assess the evidence: Using objective, factual evidence, analyze and consider the duration of the risk; nature and severity of the potential harm; the likelihood that the potential harm will occur; and the imminence of the potential harm. Relevant evidence may include input from the individual with a disability, the experience of the individual with a disability in previous similar positions, and opinions of medical doctors, rehabilitation counselors or physical therapists who have expertise in the disability involved and/or direct knowledge of the individual with a disability.

The determination that there is a high probability of substantial harm to the individual with a disability or others must be based solely on valid medical analyses and/or other objective evidence. Generalized fears about risks from the employment environment or risks to individuals with disabilities in the event of an evacuation or other emergency may not be used by a local government to disqualify and individual with a disability.

■ Identify a reasonable accommodation that would reduce or eliminate the risk: Determine whether a reasonable accommodation would either eliminate or reduce the risk to an acceptable level. If no accommodation exists that would either eliminate or reduce the risk, the local government may refuse to hire an applicant or may discharge an employee who poses a direct threat.

Tests

Administration Of Tests (56 Fed. Reg. 35737, Sec. 1630.11)

A local government may select and administer employment tests in the most effective manner to ensure that, when a test is administered to a job applicant who has a disability that impairs sensory, manual, or speaking skills, the test results accurately reflect what the test purports to measure, rather than reflecting the impaired sensory, manual, or speaking skills of the applicant. An exception to the general rule exists where the test purports to measure such skills.

For example, when testing an individual with a known learning disability for a parks maintenance position, the test administrator should ask that individual if he needs more time to complete the test.

Pre-Employment Medical Examinations and Medical Inquiries (56 Fed. Reg. 35737-38, Sec. 1630.13)

A local government may not conduct a medical examination of an applicant or make inquiries as to whether an applicant is an individual with a disability or as to the nature or severity of such disability.

The EEOC regulations include a pre-employment inquiry exception clause (56 *Fed. Reg.* 35737-38, Sec. 1630.14) that allows local governments to make narrowly tailored pre-employment inquiries into the ability of an applicant to perform job-related functions.

For example, the interviewer may explain that the job requires moderate lifting and ask if the applicant will be able to perform that function, with or without reasonable accommodation.

An applicant may be asked to describe how, with or without reasonable accommodation, he or she will be able to perform job-related functions. An interviewer may not inquire as to the nature or severity of the disability.

An applicant may be asked to demonstrate how, with or without reasonable accommodation, he or she will be able to perform job-related functions. If the applicant is required to provide such a demonstration, the local government must either provide the reasonable accommodation the applicant needs to perform the function or permit the applicant to explain how, with accommodation, he or she will perform the function.

Known Disability that may Interfere or Prevent the Performance of Job-Related Functions

The request for a demonstration may be made of an applicant whose known disability may interfere with or prevent the performance of a job-related function, whether or not the local government routinely makes such a request of all applicants in the same job category.

For example, the interviewer may ask an applicant with one arm who applies for a position as a file clerk in a library to demonstrate or explain how, with or without reasonable accommodation, she would be able to transport books up a ladder. The interviewer may not ask how the applicant lost her arm or whether the loss of the arm is indicative of an underlying impairment.

Known Disability will Not Interfere with or Prevent the Performance of Job Related Functions

If the known disability of an applicant will not interfere with or prevent the performance of a job-related function, the employer may only request of the applicant a description or demonstration of how they would perform a job-related function, if it routinely makes such a request of all applicants in the same job category.

For example, an interviewer may not request that a hearing impaired applicant for a position as a library file clerk demonstrate his ability to carry books up a ladder, if all applicants are not requested to provide such a demonstration.

Nonessential Job Functions

If the job-related function is not essential, local government officials may not exclude the applicant with a disability because of his or her inability to perform that function.

Rather, the local government must

- provide an accommodation that will enable the applicant to perform the function,
- transfer the function to another position, or
- exchange the function for one the applicant is able to perform.

For example, a local government cannot routinely require all applicants for employment to possess a valid driver's license when driving is not an essential job function.

Employment Agencies, Labor Unions and other Agencies or Organizations (56 Fed. Reg., Sec. 1630.6)

A local government may not participate in a contractual or other relationship or arrangement that has the effect of subjecting the municipality's job applicants or employees with a disability to discrimination under the Act. The term "contractual or other arrangement" includes, but is not limited to, a relationship with an employment or referral agency; labor union, including collective bargaining agreements; an organization providing fringe benefits to an employee of the covered entity; or an organization providing training and apprenticeship programs.

Limiting, Segregating or Classifying Job Applicants (56 Fed. Reg. 35737, Sec. 1630.5)

A local government is prohibited from denying employment to an applicant with a disability based on generalized fears about the safety of an individual with such a disability, or based on generalized assumptions about the absenteeism rate of an individual with such a disability.

The Job Offer

A local government may not prefer or select a qualified applicant without a disability over an equally qualified applicant with a disability merely because the applicant with a disability will require a reasonable accommodation. The only exception to this general prohibition exists where the municipality is able to show that the accommodation would impose an undue hardship on the local government.

Employment Entrance Medical Examination Exception (56 Fed. Reg. 35737-38, Sec. 1630.14)

A local government may require a medical examination (and/or make an inquiry) after making an offer of employment to a job applicant and before the applicant begins his or her employment duties, if such an exam is required of all employees in that job classification. Moreover, the local government may condition an offer of employment on the results of such examination (and/or make an inquiry), if all entering employees in the same job category are subjected to such an examination (and/or make an inquiry) regardless of disability.

No Requirement that Exam be Job-Related

The employment entrance examination does not have to be job-related and consistent with business necessity. However, if the municipality withdraws an offer of employment because the examination reveals that the employee does not satisfy certain employment criteria, either (1) the exclusionary criteria must not screen out or tend to screen out an individual with a disability or a class of individuals with disabilities, or (2) they must be job-related and consistent with business necessity.

Information Obtained must be Treated as Confidential

Information obtained as a result of a permissible entrance examination or inquiry must be treated as a confidential medical record and may not be used in any manner that is inconsistent with the ADA. State workers' compensation laws are not preempted by the ADA and local governments may submit information to state workers' compensation offices or second injury funds in accordance with state workers' compensation laws without violating Title I.

Physical Agility Tests Not Considered Medical Examinations 56 Fed. Reg. Sec. 1630.9)

Physical agility tests are not considered medical examinations, and they may be given at any point in the application or employment process if they are given to all similarly situated employees regardless of disability. However, if such tests screen out or tend to screen out an individuals with a disability or a class of individuals with disabilities, the employer would have to demonstrate that the test is job-related and consistent with business necessity and that performance cannot be achieved even with a reasonable accommodation.

Post-Employment Activities and Requirements

Title I sets specific requirements for dealing with employees with disabilities.

Classifying Employees

Limiting, Segregating, and
Classifying (56 Fed. Reg.
35736-37, Sec. 1630.4 - 1630.5)

The capabilities of qualified individuals with disabilities must be determined on a case-by-case basis. A local jurisdiction may not restrict the employment opportunities of qualified individuals with disabilities on the basis of stereotypes and myths about the individual's disability or segregate such individuals into separate work areas or into separate lines of advancement.

Limitation of Duties

A local government may not limit the duties of an employee with a disability based on a presumption of what is best for an individual with such a disability, or on a presumption about the abilities of someone with such a disability.

Separate Employment Tracks

A municipality or county may not adopt a separate track of job promotion or progression for employees with disabilities based on a presumption that employees with disabilities are uninterested in, or incapable of, performing particular jobs.

Position Reassignment

A local government may not assign or reassign (as a reasonable accommodation) employees with disabilities to one particular office or installation or require that employees with disabilities only use particular employer provided nonwork facilities (such as segregated breaks, lunch rooms, or lounges).

Fears, Assumptions, and Prejudices

A municipality or county may not deny employment or a promotion to an employee with a disability based on generalized fears or prejudices about the safety of an individual with a disability, or based on generalized assumptions about the absenteeism rate of an individual with such a disability.

Equal Access to Health Care Insurance

A local government must accord all employees with disabilities equal access to whatever health insurance coverage the employer provides to other employees.

Pre-Existing Condition Clauses

The local government may continue to offer a health plan that contains a pre-existing condition clause, even if it adversely affects individuals with disabilities, so long as the clause is not used as a subterfuge to evade the purpose of the Act.

Limitations — Coverage and Reimbursements

The local government's health plan may limit coverage for certain procedures or treatments to a specified number a year. The plan may also impose limitations on reimbursements for certain procedures or on the types of drugs or procedures covered. However, any limitations must be applied equally to individuals with and without disabilities.

Employee Leave Policies and Specified Benefit Plans

Municipal leave policies and specified employee benefits plans that are uniformly applied do not violate the Act merely, because they do not address the special needs of every individual with a disability.

It is not a violation of the Act for a municipality to reduce the number of sick leave days or medical insurance coverage it will provide to all employees, even if the benefits reduction has an impact on employees with disabilities in need of greater sick leave and medical coverage. However, benefit reductions adopted for discriminatory reasons are a violation of the Act.

Contractual or Other Arrangements (56 Fed. Reg. 35737, Sec. 1630.6)

It is unlawful for a local government to participate in a contractual or other arrangement that has the effect of subjecting any of the local government's own qualified applicant or employee with a disability to discrimination. This is true whether the local government (1) offered the contract or initiated the relationship or (2) accepted the contract or acceded to the relationship.

"Contracting out" cannot be used to circumvent compliance with any employment provisions. For example, a local government cannot contract with a trainer to provide computer training skills at the trainer's facility that is inaccessible to physically disabled persons.

Medical Examination of Employees (56 Fed. Reg. 35738, Sec. 1630.14(c))

A local government may:

■ make inquiries or require medical examinations (fitness for duty exam) when there is a need to determine whether an employee is still able to perform the essential functions of his or her job;
■ make inquiries or require medical examinations necessary to the reasonable accommodation process; and
■ require periodic physicals to determine fitness for duty or other medical monitoring if such physicals or monitoring are required medical standards or requirements established by Federal, state, or local law that are consistent with the Act, are job-related and consistent with business necessity.

Other Acceptable Examinations and Inquiries (56 Fed. Reg. 35738, Sec. 1630.14(d))

Under the Act, voluntary medical examinations, including voluntary medical histories, as part of employee health and wellness programs are permitted.

Drug Testing (56 Fed. Reg. 35739, Sec. 1630.16(c))

For the purpose of Title I, drug tests are not considered medical tests and nothing in the Act encourages, authorizes, or prohibits testing for the illegal use of drugs. Drug tests may be used as a basis for disciplinary action. However, if the drug tests reveals information abount an individual's medical condition beyond whether the individual is currently engaging in the illegal use of drugs, this additional information must be treated as a confidential medical record.

Information obtained in the course of all medical examinations or inquiries and the medical records developed over the course of such activities are to be treated as confidential medical records and may only be used in a manner not inconsistent with the Act.

Specific Activities Permitted

The prohibition or imposition of restrictions on smoking in places of employment is not a violation of the Act.

A local government may:

■ prohibit the unlawful use of drugs and the use of alcohol at the workplace by all employees;
■ require that employees not be under the influence of alcohol or be engaging in the unlawful use of drugs at the workplace;

■ require that all employees behave in conformance with the requirements established under the Drug-Free Workplace Act of 1988;
■ hold an employee who engages in the unlawful use of drugs or who is an alcoholic to the same qualification standards for employment or job performance and behavior to which the local government holds other employees, even if any unsatisfactory performance or behavior is related to the employee's drug use of alcoholism.

Individuals disabled by alcoholism are entitled to the same protections accorded other individuals with disabilities under Title II, so long as they can safely perform the essential job functions. However, individuals currently engaging in the unlawful use of drugs are not individuals with disabilities for the purposes of Title II when the actions taken by the employer are based on such use.

A local government may refuse to assign or continue to assign a job involving food handling to an individual with a disability if (1) the individual is disabled by one of the infectious or communicable diseases included on the Secretary of Health and Human Services annual list of infectious and communicable diseases which was published in August 1991, and (2) the risk of transmitting the disease associated with the handling of food cannot be eliminated by reasonable accommodation.

If the individual with a disability is a current employee, the municipality, town, or county must consider whether he or she can be accommodated by reassignment to a vacant position that does not involve food handling.

Title II does not preempt, modify, or amend any state, county, or local law, ordinance or regulation applicable to food handling that is (1) in accordance with the annual list of infectious and communicable diseases and the modes of transmissibility published by the Secretary of Health and Human Services and (2) designed to protect the public health from individuals who pose a significant risk to the health or safety of others, where that risk cannot be eliminated by reasonable accommodation.

Transportation Employees (56 Fed. Reg. 35739, Sec. 1630.16(2))

The EEOC regulation does not prohibit or encourage public agencies which are subject to the U.S. Department of Transportation's (DOT) regulations from (1) testing employees involved in safety sensitive duties for the illegal use of drugs or alcohol impairment; and (2) removing employees from such safety-sensitive positions if they test positive for the illegal use of drugs or on-duty impairment by alcohol.

Record Keeping and Reporting Requirements

The record keeping and reporting provisions of Title I are codified in 29 CFR Parts 1602 and 1627. The requirements for local governments are outlined below.

Personnel and Employment Records

Retention of Personnel and
Employment Records (56 Fed.
Reg., Sec. 1602.14)

All public employees' personnel and employment records must be retained by the local jurisdiction for a period of one year from the date of the making of the record or of the personnel action involved, whichever is later. The record retention requirement applies to the records of all employees, including the records of seasonal and temporary employees that were previously exempt from the retention requirements.

Reporting

Reporting Requirements (56 Fed.
Reg., Sec. 1602.7 and 1602.10)

On or before September 30 of each year, each local government that employs 100 or more employees must file a copy of Standard Form 164 with the Equal Employment Opportunity Commission (EEOC).

A local government may seek an exemption from the reporting requirements if it is able to show that the preparation or filing of the report would create undue hardship. Moreover, a municipality may seek a change of the date for filing its Standard Form 164 or the period for which data are reported. If a local government seeks such a change, it should submit a specific written proposal to the EEOC for an alternative reporting system prior to the date on which the report is due.

What Should a Local Government Do to Prepare for Compliance with Titles I and II?

The self-evaluation checklist for Title I is found in the appendix and offers a more thorough review of questions to consider when complying with Title I. Listed below are a series of activities that the Human Resources or Personnel Director should review in order to begin to comply with the employment provisions of the ADA.

- Review all job descriptions to determine when they were last revised. Be sure that the "essential functions" are accurately described, and separate out the "nonessential functions." If your city or town does not have formal written job descriptions, you may want to create descriptions that meet the requirements of Title I. However, written job descriptions are not required under the ADA.

- Review your job application form to be sure that your EEO statement mentions that your local government does not discriminate on the basis of disability. Furthermore, be sure that your application does not ask questions regarding disabilities. All questions must be job-related. You may inquire into skill, education and experiential qualifications of applicants.

- When giving notice of job vacancies, be sure that your EEO statement mentions that your local government does not discriminate on the basis of disability and use a variety of formats and media to ensure that individuals with different types of disabilities will have access to the job announcements.

- In addition to your application form and job descriptions, review all your employment policies to be sure that they don't discriminate against applicants or employees with disabilities or their associates.

- If your local government requires a general medical examination once an offer of employment has been made, be sure that you know what is acceptable practice. Consult with your city attorney, departmental directors, and medical advisor to determine the relevancy and necessity of examinations.

- Review your drug testing requirements to ensure compliance with the EEOC and DOJ regulations.

■ Examine your existing leave policies and employee benefit packages to ensure that they do not discriminate against disabled employees, their relatives, or their associates. If your local government has a family leave policy, it is not necessarily preempted by ADA provisions.

■ Conduct sensitivity or attitudinal awareness training sessions for city employees who have direct contact with the general public and job applicants. Include training on appropriate interviewing questions and techniques for those employees who have hiring authority.

■ Consider establishing an ADA oversight committee with representatives from disabled organizations and other community leaders. The committee can help determine reasonable accommodations, draft a contagious disease policy, set priorities for making structural changes to public facilities, and offer suggestions on how to achieve program accessibility as well as other tasks.

■ Review any pre- and post-employment tests that you now administer to determine if they accurately measure skill level. You must be sure that these tests do not screen out (either intentionally or unintentionally) individuals with disabilities. If your personnel department contracts with a private firm to test or certify applicants, you must be sure that their testing process does not screen out otherwise qualified disabled applicants. Furthermore, you should require them to make reasonable accommodations to individuals with disabilities when conducting tests.

■ Develop some guidelines for making reasonable accommodations and share these, along with some examples, with department directors to increase their awareness. Remain flexible when determining the appropriate accommodation and take into consideration the provisions related to "undue hardship."

■ Review all contracts with private sector and nonprofit organizations to ensure that your jurisdiction requires them to comply with relevant provisions of the ADA.

■ Review all the social and recreational activities that are sponsored by your local government to be sure that they are accessible to individuals with disabilities.

4
PUBLIC ACCOMMODATIONS AND COMMERCIAL FACILITIES

By Kathryn Shane McCarty

No individual shall be discriminated against on the basis of disability ... in any place of public accommodation ..., requires that all new places be designed and constructed ... to be readily accessible to and usable by persons with disabilities and requires examinations or courses related to licensing or certification for professional or trade purposes to be accessible... (42 U.S.C. 12182 - 12189).

While Title III of the Americans with Disabilities Act of 1990 (ADA) is intended to prohibit discrimination on the basis of disability in public accommodations and commercial facilities, building code enforcement and architectural design review functions, carried out through local building, zoning, and planning departments, give local government an essential role in making sure that disabled individuals have access to the goods, services, facilities, and advantages these facilities offer.

Although the DOJ regulations do not delegate enforcement of the ADA to local officials, local government officials must ensure that their local code meets the minimum standards established under the ADA and then enforce their local building code. In addition, the personnel or human resources departments will have to review the procedures, policies, and practices of private contractors who provide certification or examinations for city employee positions to ensure that their services and test results do not discriminate on the basis of disability.

Who is Covered Under Title III?

Title III affects two types of private entities — "places of public accommodation" and "commercial facilities".

Public Accommodations

Places of Public Accommodation (56 Fed. Reg. 35551, Sec. 36.104)

A private business, individual, or corporation that owns, leases, or operates a facility whose operation is affected by commerce and that falls into one of the twelve specific categories is a place of public accommodation. The definition of "commerce" is derived from Title II of the Civil Rights Act of 1964, which prohibits racial discrimination in public accommodations.

Public accommodations include these categories of facilities:

- places of lodging,
- establishments serving food or drink,
- places of exhibition or entertainment,
- places of public gathering,
- sales or rental establishments,
- service establishments,
- stations used for specified public transportation,
- places of public display or collection,
- places of recreation,
- places of education,
- social service center establishments, and
- places of exercise or recreation.

Commercial Facilities

Commercial Facility (56 Fed. Reg. 35547, Sec. 36.104)

A business whose operations are available to the general public, even though its major function is not defined as promoting commerce, is a commercial facility. Examples of commercial facilities include factories, warehouses, office buildings, car repair garages, privately operated airports, and other buildings in which employment occurs. The legislative intent was to broadly define the term to include most enterprises.

In both instances, it is the public accommodation (e.g., eating food in a restaurant) or the commercial service (e.g., access to your private airplane) delivered to the public that is subject to the nondiscrimination requirements. The burden of ensuring a nondiscriminatory environment or delivery of services rests with the owner or operator of the facility.

Review of Business Operations and Policies

In order to achieve these objectives, owners/lessors and lessees of public accommodations must review their policies, practices, and procedures to determine if reasonable modifications can be made to ensure equitable service to disabled persons as required by Title III of ADA.

Auxiliary Aids and Services (56 Fed. Reg. 35597, Sec. 36.303)

In addition to reviewing operational policies, owners and operators of public accommodations must closely examine their use of auxiliary aids and services. Simply put, "auxiliary aids and services" are devices (some with human assistance) that permit the disabled individual to receive an equal level of service to nondisabled persons (see the Glossary for a more formal definition). Auxiliary aids and services should be provided, so that individuals with disabilities are not excluded, denied services, segregated, or otherwise treated differently than other participants.

The concept of "undue burden" (that is, significant difficulty or expense) is a factor to consider when providing auxiliary aids or services. The U.S. Department of Justice regulations offer four measures to consider when determining whether the provision of such an aid will impose an undue burden on the owner or operator of the facility (56 *Fed. Reg.* 35594, Sec. 36.104).

Effective Communication (56 Fed. Reg. 35597, Sec. 36.303(c) - 36.304(d))

The effective communication provision is briefly described but potentially may have an extensive effect on places of public accommodation. This section mandates that they furnish appropriate auxiliary aids and services to ensure effective communication with individuals who have disabilities.

It is subject to interpretation whether this means that sign language proficiency among hotel staff, for example, is required under this section. The implication is that when hiring personnel, human resource managers should now give special consideration to sign language, just as they may have done for bilingual applicants in the past.

As a resource, local government officials should contact their local deaf/hearing-impaired associations when seeking a sign language interpreter. There is a growing supply of individuals proficient in sign language, since many institutions of higher education now offer sign language as part of their foreign language curriculum.

Section 36.304(d) does state that telecommunications devices for the deaf (TDDs) should be made available when other public telephones are available for public use. Owners of facilities covered under Title III should review the scoping requirements of the ADA Accessibility Guidelines (ADAAG) to determine the number and location of text telephones for hearing- and speech-impaired individuals when considering barrier removal activities and undertaking new construction and alterations.

Existing Facilities

A public accommodation should remove architectural barriers in existing buildings where such barriers are readily removable without much difficulty or expense.

Access

Readily Achievable Access (56 Fed. Reg. 35594, Sec. 36.104)

The concept of "readily achievable" is essential to physical accessibility. In determining whether an action is readily achievable, the Act specifies four factors to consider (Sec. 301(9) of the Act):

- the nature and cost of the action needed;
- the overall financial resources of the facility involved in undertaking this action; the number of employees at that facility; the effect on the expenses and resource of the operation of the facility;
- the overall financial resources of the covered entity (not just the facility affected), including the overall size of the business, total number of employees, number, type and location of all facilities; and
- the type of operation(s) of the covered private entity, including the composition, structure, and functions of the work force, the geographic separateness, fiscal or administrative relationship of the facility or facilities in question to the covered entity.

Structural Modifications

Priorities For Making Structural Modifications (56 Fed. Reg. 35597, Sec. 36.304(c))

Once the owner or operator of the facility has determined that the removal of architectural barriers is necessary, then the owner or operator should consider the four priority areas of making structural changes as outlined in 28 CFR Part 36, issued by the U.S. Department of Justice on July 26, 1991.

- Provide access on public sidewalks, parking or public transportation. This provision requires local governments to provide or at least ensure that access to public accommodations meets the accessibility standards set forth by the Architectural and Transportation Barriers Compliance Board (ATBCB) as Appendix A to 28 CFR Part 36. This will require design review by city building, planning or zoning departments whichever is the designated department in your community.
- Provide access to those places ... where goods and services are made available to the public. Compliance with this section may be easily achieved by rearranging tables or lowering displays. It can also mean installing a ramp or tactile signage.
- Provide accessible restrooms to the physically impaired and add signage for individuals with disabilities.
- Provide access to the goods, services, facilities, privileges, advantages or accommodations of a place of public accommodation.

After January 26, 1992, all building modifications or alterations must be made readily accessible to and usable by disabled patrons to the maximum extent feasible. It is important to provide an accessible path of travel to altered, accessible space as well as accessible restrooms, telephones, drinking fountains, etc. serving the altered space. The additional cost of providing an accessible path of travel is not to exceed 20 percent of the total alteration cost.

Historic Buildings

Alterations to Historic Buildings
(56 Fed. Reg. 35601, Sec. 36.405)

Buildings that are listed on the National Register for Historic Places or are protected under either state or local historic preservation laws shall comply, to the maximum extent feasible, with Section 4.1.7 ("Accessible Buildings: Historic Preservation") of the ADA Accessibility Guidelines published by ATBCB. This section of the ADAAG guidelines for historic places (56 Fed. Reg. 35428) contains scoping provisions and alternative requirements for alterations to qualified historic properties.

If the State Historic Preservation Officer or certified local government historic preservation officer determines that it is not feasible to provide physical access to an historic structure covered under Title III, then alternative methods of access should be followed. The threat or destruction of the historic significance of the historic building is cited as a primary consideration in determining whether physical access can be accomplished.

New Construction

New Construction (56 Fed. Reg. 35599, Sec. 36.401)

Title III requires that all facilities occupied after January 26, 1993, be readily accessible and usable by individuals with disabilities. Two conditions affect this compliance date: (1) whether the building permit was issued by the state or local government after January 26, 1992; and (2) if the first certificate of occupancy is issued after January 26, 1993.

Accessibility Standards

Accessibility Standards (56 Fed. Reg. 35602, Sec. 36.406)

The new ADA Accessibility Guidelines (ADAAG) were prepared by the Architectural and Transportation Barriers Compliance Board (ATBCB) and mandated by the U.S. Department of Justice regulations implementing Title III as the official ADA accessibility guidelines. All new construction and modifications must conform to these building standards.

There are some distinctions between the existing ANSI A117.1-1980 accessibility standards and the ADAAG requirements, which are indicated by italicized text in the ADAAG. A more extensive discussion of the accessibility guidelines is found in Chapter 6.

An elevator exemption in the ADAAG requirements applies to most private facilities. Elevators are not required in facilities that are less than three stories or that are less than 3,000 square feet per story. This exemption, however, does not apply to shopping centers or malls or professional offices of health care providers. All publicly owned or leased buildings are also required to have elevators to all floors used by the general public. An extensive discussion of the

ADAAG standards, along with a description of the 1984 Uniform Federal Accessibility Standards (UFAS) can be found in Chapter Six.

Examinations and Courses

Examinations and Courses (56 Fed. Reg. 35598, Sec. 36.309)

Where local government personnel and human resource departments use private entities to conduct examinations or courses, city employees must ensure that these private entities are not discriminating against individuals with disabilities.

Factors to consider include:

- permitting more time to complete the examination,
- ensuring an accessible testing site or alternative accessible arrangements, like a proctor at home,
- providing the appropriate auxiliary aids, and
- ensuring that the results will accurately reflect one's aptitude.

Certification of State and Local Building Codes

The regulations implementing Title III (28 CFR Part 36) established procedures to certify state laws, local building codes or local ordinances related to accessibility. This section (56 *Fed. Reg.* 35603-04, Subpart F) is important to local government building and code enforcement personnel.

Process for Certifying State or Local Building Codes (56 Fed. Reg. 35603, Sec. 36.603)

A state or local government official with primary responsibility for administration of a code may file a request for certification with the Assistant Attorney General at DOJ. In order to do so, however, the state or local government official must comply with three requirements:

- provide adequate public notice of intent to file;
- make copies of the proposed request available for public examination and distribution; and
- hold a public hearing where an official transcript is produced.

Upon receiving the certification request, the DOJ personnel will determine if the state or local code is "equivalent" to the ADA requirements. If DOJ issues a certification of equivalency, then the state or local code meets or exceeds the minimum requirements of Title III for accessibility and usability. If the review yields a denial of certification, the notification will include specific recommendations on how the code must be amended to meet the equivalency certification standard.

Building Codes

Development of Model Building Codes by National Associations (56 Fed. Reg. 35604, Sec. 36.608)

Three organizations that now set building code standards in the United States are either reviewing or have already reviewed their model codes for compliance with ADAAG requirements.

Building Officials and Code Administrators

The Building Officials and Code Administrators has reviewed the ADA Accessibility Guidelines issued by ATBCB and is proposing some modifications to the BOCA code. The 1992 supplement to the BOCA code will reflect those changes. BOCA officials will accordingly also submit their 1992 supplement to the U.S. Department of Justice for an informal review on the model code section of the regulations.

BOCA, however, will continue to cite ANSI A117.1-1986 as the accessibility standard. The American National Standards Institute (ANSI) is expected to issue an updated ANSI standard within the next twelve months, and BOCA officials will review the ADAAG requirements in light of the revised ANSI standard once it is issued.

For further information:
Building Officials and Code Administrators International
4051 W. Flossmoor Road
Country Club Hills, Illinois 60477-5795
(708) 799-2300

Southern Building Code Congress

The Southern Building Code references accessibility in Appendix M of its code and cites the ANSI A117.1-1986 standard. SBCCI also expects to review and possibly revise its building code in light of the recently issued ADAAG standards.

For further information:
Code Department
Southern Building Code Congress, International
900 Montclair Road
Birmingham, Alabama 35213
(205) 591-1853

International Conference of Building Officials

The International Conference of Building Officials published changes to its code in April 1991. Chapter 31 of the code refers to accessibility and makes reference to the ANSI A117.1-1980 standards. ICBO expects subsequent modifications to be made during the 1994 review process.

For further information:
Engineering and Technical Services Staff
International Conference of Building Officials
5360 S. Wakeman Mill Road
Whittier, California 90601
(213) 699-0541

Other Information on Accessibility Standards

For further information on accessibility standards as they apply to building codes:

Architectural and Transportation Barriers Compliance Board
1111 18th Street, N.W., Suite 501
Washington, D.C. 20036
202-272-5434 (Voice/TDD)
800-USA-ABLE (TDD/Voice)

American National Standards Institute (ANSI)
1430 Broadway
New York, New York 10018
(212) 642-4975

Implications for State and Local Building Code Personnel

Here are some reminders about how Title III may impact the operations of a local government's permitting and code enforcement operations.

- Before January 26, 1992, state and local code enforcement officials should review their building code to determine whether it meets the accessibility standards established by the Architectural and Transportation Barriers Compliance Board (ATBCB). In many states, this review process is already underway. Check with your state building code official to determine what is happening in your state.

- Also review your state accessibility codes to determine the degree of variance between the state accessibility codes and new federal standards set by ATBCB.

- Remember that accessibility standards for theaters, restaurants, hotels and recreational facilities are relatively new. The original ANSI standards (1961) were designed for office building access. As local government officials, if you perform an architectural design review function, you may want to advised builders that they must comply with the ADA, since these standards may not be familiar to the architect or the builder.

- You should consult with your state code officials and determine if you want to submit your state or local building code to the U.S. Department of Justice (DOJ) for certification under Title III.

- You should consult with one or all of the national associations representing building officials to determine if they will be developing a model accessibility code for DOJ's review and the timeframe scheduled for that activity.

- Finally, keep in mind that accessibility standards are designed to assist all types of disabilities, not just the physically challenged. Check to see if the building design includes appropriate signage and signals for visually and hearing impaired persons, particularly in the areas of evacuation and egress.

- If your community uses a private firm to issue permits and enforce the state building code, it is your responsibility to make sure that their procedures, policies and general operation does not discriminate against disabled persons.

5 TRANSPORTATION PROVISIONS

By Ronald S. Cooper
and
David H. Coburn

Titles II and III of the ADA impose new obligations on providers of public transportation. Those obligations vary depending on whether the provider is a public or private entity and, in significant part, on whether the subject's public transportation is provided on a fixed-route basis — and therefore subject to a paratransit obligation except for commuter bus and commuter rail services — or a demand-responsive basis, for which there is no paratransit obligation. Both titles also impose requirements for accessibility to and use of stations and other transportation facilities by disabled individuals.

Title II applies to public entities and to private persons who provide transportation services under a contract or other arrangement with a public entity. This chapter will focus on the provision of mass transit bus and rail services by public entities, and will touch only briefly on commuter rail transportation, which is subject to somewhat different requirements. Reference is made throughout the chapter to the relevant sections of the statute and to the detailed implementing rules issued by the U.S. Department of Transportation (DOT) as cited in 49 CFR Parts 37 and 38. It bears note that DOT has also issued an appendix to its rules providing interpretive guidance to them.

Services operated by private entities are generally regulated by Title III. Their obligations depend in large measure on whether the provision of public transportation is the entity's primary business or is incidental to some other business. This chapter will not address in detail transportation provided by private entities.

Definitions of Key Terms

Titles II and III define several key terms (56 *Fed. Reg.* 45622, Sec. 37.3).

Bus: self-propelled vehicles, including mini-buses and electric powered trolleys.

Commuter Bus Service: A fixed route bus service characterized by service predominantly in one direction during peak periods, limited stops, use of multi-ride tickets and extended routes between a central business district and suburbs — often coordinated with other modes.

Commuter Rail Service: Short-haul rail passenger service operating in metropolitan and suburban areas, whether within or across the geographical boundaries of a state, usually characterized by reduced fare, multiple ride, and commutation tickets and by morning and evening peak period operations.

Demand-Responsive System: Any system of providing public transportation which is not a fixed route system (Secs. 221(1), 301(3). With demand responsive systems, a person must request transportation before it is rendered.

Disability: 1) A physical or mental impairment that substantially limits one or more of the major life activities of an individual; 2) a record of such impairment; or 3) being regarded as having such an impairment. The terms used in this definition are defined in Sec. 3(2) of the Act and then further defined in the DOT regulations. (See 49 CFR 37.3.) The definition of "physical or mental impairment" includes orthopedic, visual, speech or hearing impairments; cerebral palsy; epilepsy; muscular dystrophy; cancer; heart disease; diabetes; mental retardation; emotional illness; HIV disease; tuberculosis; drug addiction (not current users) and alcoholism.

Fixed-Route System: A system of providing public transportation, other than by aircraft, on which a vehicle is operated along a prescribed route according to a fixed schedule (Secs. 221(3), 301(4).

Paratransit: Comparable transportation service required by ADA for disabled individuals unable to use fixed transportation systems.

Private Entity: any entity other than a public entity. (Sec. 301(6).

Nondiscrimination Obligation and Accessibility Standards

Nondiscrimination Provisions (56 Fed. Reg. 45624, Sec. 37.5)

No public entity may discriminate against an individual with a disability in connection with providing transportation service nor deny a disabled person the opportunity to use the entity's transportation service provided for the general public if the person is capable of so doing.

Furthermore, an entity may not make use of designated priority seats mandatory; impose special charges in providing required services; require use of attendants by disabled persons; discriminate even if its insurance company imposes conditions on coverage or rates; or refuse service to an individual whose appearance or involuntary behavior may offend, annoy, or inconvenience employees or others. Persons who engage in violent,

---

Definitions of Key Terms, continued

Public Entity: 1) Any state or local government (Sec. 201(1)(A); 2) any department, agency, special purpose district, or other instrumentality thereof (Sec. 201(1)(B); 3) Amtrak, and any commuter authority (Sec. 201(1)(C).

Public Transportation: Transportation by bus, rail, or any other conveyance that provides the general public with general or special service (including charter service) on a regular and continuing basis. Secs. 221(2), 301(10). However, public school transportation and transportation by aircraft are not covered by the ADA. Public school transportation is already covered by the Rehabilitation Act and air transportation is covered by the Air Carrier Access Act 49 U.S.C. 1374(c) (Supp. V 1987). See House Committee on Education and Labor, Americans With Disabilities Act of 1009, H.R. Rep. No. 485, 101st Cong., 2d Sess., pt. 2, at 87 (1990) (hereinafter "Education Rep."); House Committee on Public Works and Transportation, Americans with Disabilities Act of 1990, H.R. Rep. No. 485, 101st Cong., 2d Sess., pt. 1, at 26-27 (1990) (hereinafter "Transportation Rep."). Note, however, that ground transportation services and fixed facilities associated with air travel are covered by the ADA.

seriously disruptive, or illegal conduct can be refused service or an attendant can be required for such persons.

Accessibility Standards

Accessibility standards cover both transit vehicles and facilities.

Vehicles (56 Fed. Reg. 45625, Sec. 37.7))

The detailed and technical accessibility standards for buses, rail cars, and other conveyances are set forth in the DOT rules at 49 CFR Part 38. These standards were established by the Architectural and Transportation Barriers Compliance Board (ATBCB); a detailed discussion of them is beyond the scope of this chapter.

All vehicles must comply with these standards to meet the statutory requirement found throughout the ADA of being "readily accessible to and usable by individuals with disabilities" (See 56 *Fed. Reg.* 45757, 38.2). Departures from Part 38 standards are permitted where alternative designs will provide "substantially equivalent or greater access." DOT regulations spell out a procedure for obtaining approval for deviations.

Facilities (56 Fed. Reg. 45625, Sec. 37.9))

The detailed and technical accessibility standards for transportation facilities are set forth in Appendix A to Part 37 of the DOT rules, a discussion of which is beyond the scope of this chapter. These standards were developed by ATBCB.

A public entity may depart from these standards provided that equivalent accessibility is provided and that UMTA or the Federal Railroad Administration, as applicable, approve an application for deviation.

Public Entities Under Title II

Covered Transportation (42 U.S.C. 12141)

Title II extends the protection of Section 504 of the Rehabilitation Act to all public entities regardless of whether they receive federal aid. With the exceptions noted above for public school and aircraft transportation (see definition of "public transportation"), it covers all types of fixed route and demand responsive transportation operated by public entities that service the general public on a continuing basis, including service provided by bus, rail, or other conveyances (Sec. 221(2). For entities receiving federal financial assistance, compliance with the ADA is a condition of such assistance and a condition of compliance with Section 504 of the Rehabilitation Act.

Transportation Provided Under Contract (56 Fed. Reg. 45626, Sec. 37.23)

Title II also covers a fixed route or demand-responsive system operated by a private person under a contractual or other arrangement or relationship with a public entity. Sec. 221(4). The public entity must ensure that the private entity provides service pursuant to all requirements that would apply if the public entity provided service directly.

Vanpools and Other Miscellaneous Systems (56 Fed. Reg. 45626, Sec.37.31-37.37)

Vanpools operated by public entities or in which such entities own, purchase or lease the vehicles are covered by demand responsive provisions of the ADA applicable to public entities. Transportation systems operated by public institutions of higher education; airport transportation systems operated by public entities; and bus or other vehicle service supplemental to rail service are also subject to the fixed route or demand responsive provisions governing public entities (See 49 CFR 37.25(b); 37.33 - 37.37).

Public Transportation Other Than By Commuter or Intercity Rail

Acquisition of New Vehicles (Fixed Route and Demand Responsive Systems) (56 Fed. Reg. 45630, Sec. 37.71)

After August 25, 1990, new buses, rapid rail vehicles, light rail vehicles, or other new vehicles to be used on a fixed route or demand responsive system must be readily accessible to and usable by individuals with disabilities pursuant to the accessibility standards set forth in Part 38 of the DOT rules. Temporary waivers are available from UMTA for buses where lifts were solicited but could not be timely supplied and further delay would impair transportation services to the community (Sec. 225). Waivers are subject to time limits, the requirement that buses obtained be capable of accepting lifts. Congressional notification of waivers is required.

If there is reasonable cause to believe that an entity fraudulently applied for such relief, the remaining period of relief will be canceled and DOT may take such other action as it deems appropriate. Sec. 225(c). For demand responsive system only, there is an exception to the requirements for new vehicle purchase where the system, when viewed in its entirety, provides a level of service equivalent to that provided to individuals without disabilities.

DOT regulations spell out the "equivalent service" concept in terms of various criteria, including fares, response times, and the area served. (56 *Fed. Reg.* 45631, Sec. 37.77(c)). The public entity must file with UMTA or retain in its files (if it receives no UMTA funds) a certificate of equivalent service.

Used Vehicles
(Fixed route systems only)

After August 25, 1990, a public entity must make demonstrated good faith efforts to purchase or lease used vehicles for use on fixed route systems that are readily accessible to and usable by individuals with disabilities. Sec. 222(b). Legislative history indicates that "demonstrated good faith effort" requires a nationwide search, and might include advertising in trade magazines and contacting trade organizations. See Senate Rep. at 49; Education Rep. at 90.

Remanufactured Vehicles
(Fixed Route systems only)

A remanufactured vehicle is one that has been stripped to its frame and rebuilt (See Transportation Rep. at 28). If the remanufacture of a vehicle for use on a fixed route system was begun after August 25, 1990 and will extend its usable life for five years or more, the vehicle must, to the maximum extent feasible, be readily accessible to and usable by individuals with disabilities (Sec. 222(c)(1)(A)). If a remanufactured vehicle for use on a fixed route system is purchased or leased after August 25, 1990 it must, to the maximum extent feasible, be readily accessible to and usable by individuals with disabilities (Sec. 222(c)(1)(B)). Special rules apply for historic vehicles (Sec. 222(c)(2).

One Car Per Train Rule
(56 Fed. Reg. 45633, Sec. 37.93)

By July 25, 1995, public entities providing light or rapid rail service must ensure that each train consisting of two or more cars has at least one accessible car (see also Sec. 228(b)).

Ferries

Accessibility rules for ferries are still in the development stage; a Notice of Proposed Rulemaking is likely in early 1992. Nondiscrimination obligations apply to ferry operations.

Paratransit as a Complement to Fixed Route System

Each public entity operating a fixed route system must provide complimentary paratransit or other special service to disabled individuals. Fixed route systems that provide only commuter bus and commuter rail service are not required to provide paratransit service.

Paratransit services must be comparable to transportation services provided to individuals without disabilities in terms of both the level of services provided and, to the extent practicable, response time (Sec. 223(a)). The legislative history suggests that "comparable level of services" means that when all aspects of the system are analyzed, all persons have an equal opportunity to use the system. The essential test is whether the system provides a level of service that meets the needs of persons with and without disabilities to a comparable extent. (See Senate Rep. at 52; Education Rep. at 92-93.)

Paratransit Eligibility Requirements

Eligibility Requirements for Paratransit Services (56 Fed. Reg. 45634, Sec. 37.123)

Complementary paratransit services must be provided to the following eligible individuals with disabilities:

■ Any disabled individual who is unable, without the assistance of another person (other than an operator of a lift or other boarding assistance device), to board, ride or disembark from any vehicle on the system which is readily accessible to and usable by individuals with disabilities (Sec. 223(c)(1)(A)(i); (56 Fed. Reg. 45634, Sec. 37.123(e)(1)).

■ Any disabled individual who needs the assistance of a wheelchair lift or boarding assistance device to board, ride or disembark from any vehicle which is readily accessible and usable by individuals with disabilities, during the hours of operation of the system at a time when such vehicle is not being used to provide public transportation on the route. An individual is also deemed eligible under this provision if a lift cannot be deployed, if the lift cannot accommodate a common wheelchair, or, for rail systems, there is not yet one accessible car per train or key stations are not yet accessible (Sec. 223(c)(1)(A)(ii); (56 *Fed. Reg.* 45634, Sec. 37.123(e)(2))).

- Any individual whose "specific impairment-related condition" (e.g., chronic fatigue, blindness, inability to follow directions, cardiopulmonary conditions) prevents him or her from traveling to a boarding or disembarking location on the system (Sec. 223(c)(1)(A)(iii); (56 *Fed. Reg.* 45634, Sec. 37.123(e)(3))). Except for this narrow requirement, "paratransit" does not encompass travel to and from boarding and disembarking locations. The legislative history indicates that architectural barriers, the removal of which is not the operator's responsibility, should not trigger paratransit eligibility (see Transportation Rep. at 29.) Environmental factors (distance, weather, terrain) may interact with disability to create eligibility (56 *Fed. Reg.* 45634, Sec. 37.123(e)(3)).

One additional person accompanying a disabled individual (same origin/destination) who is eligible for paratransit services. Sec. 223(c)(1)(B).

If the disabled person travels with a personal care attendant, one person accompanying the disabled person and the attendant must be accommodated. Additional persons accompanying the disabled individual are to be accommodated, provided that space for such additional persons is available and that transportation of such additional persons will not result in a denial of service to disabled individuals (Sec. 223(c)(1)(C)).

Eligibility procedures (56 Fed. Reg. 45635, Sec. 37.125).

Persons claiming eligibility for paratransit must be given access to materials needed to apply for eligibility in an accessible format. Public entities must make written decisions on applications for eligibility. An applicant is treated as eligible if no decision is issued within twenty-one days of submission of a completed application.

Persons denied eligibility are entitled to an administrative appeal. Persons found eligible must be provided with documentation of eligibility and the public entity may require recertification. Persons who regularly miss scheduled trips may be suspended following notification and hearing procedures. Visitors from other jurisdictions are eligible if they present eligibility documentation from their home jurisdictions. Public entity may require evidence of disability from visitors if documentation unavailable. Visitor eligibility expires after 21 days.

Paratransit must be demand responsive, origin-to-destination service (56 Fed. Reg. 45635, Sec. 37.129).

With limited exceptions spelled out in DOT regulations, paratransit must be demand-responsive, origin-to-destination service. Paratransit service criteria are prescribed in the regulations (56 *Fed. Reg.* 45635-36, Sec. 37.131).

Service Areas (Bus) (56 Fed. Reg. 45635, Sec. 37.131)

Basic bus service must be provided to origins and destinations in a corridor three-fourths of a mile wide on each side of a fixed route and within an area the radius of which is three-fourths of a mile from the route's end point.

Bus service must also be provided to all points in "core service area" — the area of heaviest bus route concentration, such as where service area corridors substantially overlap. Outside core areas, bus service area corridors of three-fourths of a mile to one and one-half miles wide may be designated.

Each public entity required to make efforts to resolve any legal problems in providing service in neighboring jurisdictions within service area corridor.

Service Areas (Rail) (56 Fed. Reg.45636, Sec. 37.131(2))

Rail service areas are defined by three-fourths mile radius circles around stations. Service must be provided from any point in one circle to a point in another circle, but not to points that fall outside the circles or from one point in a circle to a point in the same circle.

Reservations/Hours of Service

The general rule is that paratransit service must be provided if it has been reserved on the previous day. Reservation service must be available during at least normal business hours of public entity's administrative office and during comparable hours on a non-business day.

Reservations must be accepted up to fourteen days before the service date. "Real time" scheduling of service is permitted but the entity cannot require service more than one hour earlier or later than the individual desires.

Service must be available during the same hours as the fixed route service to which it is complementary. The regulations allow subscription service for regular repeat trips for up to 50 percent of paratransit system capacity, or more if capacity for non-subscription service is unused. Restrictions cannot be imposed based on purpose of trip, except for subscription service.

Capacity Constraints (56 Fed. Reg. 45636, Sec. 131(f))

Waiting lists are not permitted, except for subscription service, and no limit can be placed on the number of trips. DOT rules prohibit "operational pattern or practice that significantly limits" available service, e.g., missed trips, late arrivals or denials.

Fares (56 Fed. Reg. 45636, Sec. 131 (c))

Fares for eligible persons and persons accompanying eligible persons (other than personal care attendants) may not exceed twice the full fare (including any applicable extra charges) charged for a similar trip at the same time of day on a fixed route system. The fare may not vary depending on type of paratransit service used. Organizations such as social service agencies may be charged more than twice the applicable fares for group trips.

Additional Service (56 Fed. Reg. 45636, Sec. 131 (g))

An entity may offer service additional to that or better than that prescribed in the regulations, but the costs of additional service would not count toward undue financial burden waiver requests.

Paratransit Services Plan (56 Fed. Reg. 45637, Sec. 37.135)

Each public entity that operates a fixed route system must, by January 26, 1992, submit a plan for providing paratransit services. Sec. 223(c)(7)(A). On each January 26 thereafter, the public entity must submit an annual update to such a plan (Sec. 223(c)(7)(B)). Plans are to be submitted to administering state agencies if the entity is UMTA recipient or if the state administers plan (56 *Fed. Reg.* 45637, Sec. 37.135)).

States are to comment on plans prior to submission to UMTA (56 *Fed. Reg.* 45638, Sec. 37.145). The public entity must hold at least one public hearing, provide an opportunity for comment and consult with disabled individuals in preparing its plan (Sec. 223(c)(6)). DOT regulations provide for continuing public input into all phases of the plan, e.g., through an advisory committee (56 *Fed. Reg.* 45637, Sec.37.137(c)).

DOT Review and Approval

DOT Review and Approval (56 Fed. Reg. 45638, Sec. 37.147)

The regulations set forth criteria under which paratransit plans will be judged, including whether the plan provides for service that is in fact comparable and whether the public was given opportunity for adequate participation in plan development (56 *Fed. Reg.* 45638, Sec. 37.147). A disapproved plan must be modified and resubmitted within 90 days following receipt of a disapproval letter (Sec. 223(d)(3); (56 *Fed. Reg.* 45639, Sec. 37.149).

Plan Contents (56 Fed. Reg. 45637, Sec. 37.137)

The plan contents are specified in detail in the DOT regulations and must include, among other items, a description of the service plan, a process for certifying eligibility criteria, an implementation timetable and budget, and various required certifications.

DOT regulations provide that joint plans providing for regional service may be filed by more than public entities with overlapping contiguous service areas (56 *Fed. Reg.* 45638, Sec. 37.141).

Timetable (56 Fed. Reg. 45636, Sec. 37.135(d))

A paratransit plan must be fully implemented by January 26, 1997, unless a financial burden waiver is obtained. If the date for full compliance is after January 26, 1993, the plan must include milestones for measured implementation.

Undue Financial Burden (Sec. 223(c)(4))

Paratransit requirements may be avoided to the extent the public entity can demonstrate that their provision would impose an "undue financial burden." However, the public entity must still provide the level of paratransit services that would not impose such a burden. Although "undue financial burden" is not defined in the ADA, it is analogous to "undue hardship" provisions in the ADA's employment provisions (Title I). See Education Rep. at 106-07.

Undue hardship is defined as "an action requiring significant difficulty or expense. . . ." when considered in light of specified factors set forth in the ADA (Sec. 101(10)). DOT regulations set forth in detail the factors to be considered in making determinations on waiver requests (56 *Fed. Reg.* 45639, Sec. 37.155).

Waiver Requests (56 Fed. Reg. 45639, Secs. 37.151, 37.153, 37.155)

Waiver requests must be submitted to UMTA if the entity knows it cannot meet the five-year phase in period, cannot make measured implementation progress or is confronted with changed circumstances which make implementation unlikely (56 *Fed. Reg.* 45639, Sec. 37.151).

Waivers will be granted on case by case basis subject to conditions (56 *Fed. Reg.* 45639, Sec. 37.153). DOT regulations define costs to be considered in assessing applications for waiver (56 *Fed. Reg.* 45639, Sec. 37.155).

Exception to the Exception (56 Fed. Reg. 45638, Sec. 37.153)

DOT may require an entity to provide paratransit services along key routes in core areas beyond the level of service that would otherwise be exempted as imposing an undue burden.

General Provision of Service Rules — Fixed Route and Demand Responsive Systems

Maintenance (56 Fed. Reg. 45640, Sec. 37.161)

DOT regulations require that accessibility features be maintained in operable condition and be repaired promptly. Special rules are prescribed for public entities concerning maintenance schedules for lifts and removal of vehicles with inoperable lifts from service (56 *Fed. Reg.* 45640, Sec.37.163).

Alternative service must be provided where a vehicle with an inoperable lift is in use on a fixed route system and the wait for the next accessible vehicle exceeds 30 minutes (56 *Fed. Reg.* 45640, Sec. 37.163).

Use of Lifts and Securement Devices (56 Fed. Reg. 45640, Sec. 37.165)

All common wheelchairs and their users must be transported. The public entity may require use of securement device, but may not deny transportation if the wheelchair may not be secured or require user to transfer out of the wheelchair, although voluntary transferring can be recommended. Drivers are required to assist in the use of lifts, ramps, and securement devices, even if this means leaving the driver's seat.

Other Service Requirements

Other requirements for public and private entities include announcement of transfer points and other major intersections required on fixed route systems; providing means to identify proper vehicle to visually impaired persons where vehicles for more than one route serve a particular stop; allowing use of guide dogs and like animals; allowing individuals to disembark using a lift unless the lift is inoperable, would be damaged if used, or cannot be safely used because of temporary conditions at a particular stop; making communications and information available using accessible formats and technologies and providing sufficient time to embark and disembark (56 *Fed. Reg.* 45640, Sec. 37.167).

Training (56 Fed. Reg. 45641, Sec. 37.173)

Personnel also must be trained in a manner appropriate to their duties in the operation of equipment and in means of meeting needs of disabled passengers.

Transportation Facilities

Transportation Facilities (56 Fed. Reg. 45627, Sec.37.41-37.61)

The term "facility" is not defined in the ADA but a Senate Report defines "facility" to include "all or any portion of buildings, structures, sites, complexes, equipment, roads, walks, passageways, parking lots or other real or personal property or interest in such property, including the site where the building, property, structure or equipment is located" (see Senate Rep. at 67). The same definition is incorporated into the DOT regulations (56 *Fed. Reg.* 45623, Sec. 37.3). Detailed standards for accessibility are set forth in Appendix A to Part 37 of the DOT regulations (56 *Fed. Reg.* 45642). DOT regulations provide a procedure for requesting UMTA or FRA approval to deviate from the Appendix A standards upon a finding of "equivalent facilitation" (56 *Fed. Reg.* 45625, Sec. 37.9(d)).

New Facilities

New Facilities (56 Fed. Reg. 45738-39, Sec. 37.41)

New facilities must be readily accessible to and usable by individuals with disabilities (Sec. 226). This provision applies to facilities construction of which begins after January 25, 1992, or in the case of intercity or commuter rail stations, after October 7, 1991. Detailed standards for accessibility are set forth in Appendix A to Part 37 of the DOT regulations (56 *Fed. Reg.* 45642).

Existing Facilities

Alterations to Existing Facilities (56 Fed. Reg. 45627, 37.43)

If alterations made after January 25, 1992 affect or could affect the usability of a facility or part thereof used in the provision of public transportation, the altered portions must be readily accessible to and usable by individuals with disabilities to the maximum extent feasible (Sec. 227(a)). DOT regulations define the phrase "to the maximum extent feasible" (56 *Fed. Reg.* 45627, Sec. 37.43).

Except when cost would be "disproportionate," where alterations affect or could affect usability of or access to an area containing the major activity for which the facility is intended, the continuous, unobstructed path of travel to the altered area and bathrooms, telephones and drinking fountains serving the altered area must, to the maximum extent feasible, be readily accessible to and usable by individuals with disabilities, including persons in wheelchairs (Sec. 227(a)).

DOT regulations define "disproportionate" alterations as those whose cost exceed 20 percent of the cost of the alteration to the primary function area, without regard to the cost of the accessibility modifications (56 *Fed. Reg.* 45627, Sec. 37.43(e).

Alterations to Key Rail Stations

Alterations to Rail and Light Rail Key Stations (56 Fed. Reg. 45628, Sec. 37.47)

Rapid and Light Rail "Key" Stations are defined in regulations to include stations with characteristics such as high ridership, transfer points (including transfer points from other fixed route systems) and location at the end of a line or near a major activity center.

Such stations must be readily accessible to and usable by individuals with disabilities as soon as practicable but not later than July 26, 1993. This period may be extended for up to a total of 30 years if extraordinarily expensive structural changes or replacement of facilities must be made. At least two-thirds of such key stations must be readily accessible to and usable by individuals with disabilities by July 26, 2010 (Sec. 227(b)(2)(B)).

Public entities must submit a plan to UMTA by July 26, 1992 for compliance with these provisions. The plan must reflect consultation with disabled individuals and the results of a public hearing and public comments, and it must establish milestones for achievement of the requirements regarding accessibility of key stations. Sec. 227(b)(3).

A grandfather provision for key rail stations provides that alterations begun before January 26, 1992 in an effort to enhance accessibility may deviate from the accessibility standards set forth in Appendix A to Part 37 of the DOT regulations, provided that the alterations conform to either the Uniform Federal Accessibility

Standard (UFAS) or the applicable American National Standards Specification for Making Buildings and Facilities Accessible to and Usable by the Physically Handicapped (ANSI A-117.1) (*56 Fed. Reg.* 45625, Sec. 37.9). However, the public entity remains responsible for making any other modifications needed to comply with the Appendix A standards.

Special exceptions to key station rules apply in New York and Philadelphia (*56 Fed. Reg.* 45627, Sec. 37.53).

Programs and Activities in Existing Facilities

Public Transportation Programs and Activities In Existing Facilities (56 Fed. Reg. 45630, Sec.37.61)

Such programs or activities conducted in an existing facility must, when viewed in their entirety, be readily accessible to and usable by individuals with disabilities (Sec. 228(a)(1)).

This relates to programs or activities that do not rise to the level of an alteration, such as user-friendly fare cards, edge detection on rail platforms, TDD devices, and public address systems.

Intercity and Commuter Rail Transportation

One Car Per Train Rule (56 Fed. Reg. 45633, Sec. 37.93)

No later than July 25, 1995, intercity and commuter rail systems must have at least one passenger car per train that is readily accessible to and usable by disabled individuals.

Purchase and Lease of Cars (56 Fed. Reg. 45632, Secs.37.85-89)

Special rules apply to the purchase or lease of new, used, and remanufactured cars. Special accessibility standards also apply for intercity and commuter rail.

Facilities (56 Fed. Reg. 45629, Secs. 37.51, 37.53, 37.55)

Same construction and alteration rules apply to intercity and commuter rail facilities as to rapid rail facilities. Key commuter rail stations must be made accessible by July 26, 1993. Extensions may be granted to July 2010.

Special rules are prescribed for designating responsibility for intercity and commuter rail stations (*56 Fed. Reg.* 45628, Sec.37.49).

Special provisions require cooperation of owners or persons in control of stations with responsible persons in efforts to comply with ADA. Sec. 242(e)(2)(C).

No Paratransit Obligation

Providers of commuter or intercity rail transportation are not required to provide paratransit services.

Enforcement

Remedies, procedures and rights in Section 505 of the Rehabilitation Act, 29 U.S.C. 794(a) (1988).

These include a private right of action, without necessity of exhausting administrative remedies. The legislative history indicates that the Justice Department will identify federal agencies to oversee compliance activities for state and local governments. These agencies, including DOJ, will receive, investigate, and attempt to resolve complaints. Unresolved complaints will be referred to DOJ, which may bring an action in federal court (See 28 CFR Part 35)

Violations of Title II

Violations of Title II are also violations of the Rehabilitation Act. (See, for example, Secs. 222(a), 223(a), 242(a)).

DOT's Administrative Enforcement Procedures (49 CFR Part 27, Subpart F)

Administrative enforcement procedures available through the U.S. Department of Transportation against recipients of federal financial assistance are found in 49 CFR Part 27, Subpart F.

Public Accommodations Operated by Private Entities

Title III applies to transportation provided by private entities, both those primarily engaged in providing public transportation (taxi services) and those primarily engaged in other businesses. The provisions address, among other matters, purchase or lease of vehicles, alteration of facilities, and provision of special services.

DOT has issued extensive regulations concerning private transportation systems. Where the regulations are identical to requirements imposed on public entities, they have been noted above. A discussion of requirements unique to private systems is beyond the scope of this chapter.

6
ACCESSIBILITY
STANDARDS

By Kathryn Shane McCarty

Two accessibility standards apply to new construction and modifications to existing buildings — the 1984 Uniform Federal Accessibility Standard (UFAS) and the Americans with Disabilities Act Accessibility Guidelines (ADAAG).

Local governments have the option of following either the UFAS standards or the recently released ADA guidelines established by the Architectural and Transportation Barriers Compliance Board (ATBCB) on July 26, 1991. A brief description of each of the federal accessibility standards is outlined below.

Uniform
Federal Accessibility Standards

The Uniform Federal Accessibility Standards (UFAS) was published in the *Federal Register* on August 7, 1984 (49 CFR 31528). The UFAS presents uniform standards for the design, construction and alterations of buildings, so that individuals with disabilities will have ready access to and use of these facilities in accordance with the Architectural Barriers Act, 42 U.S.C. 4151-4157.

The UFAS standards were agreed to by the four federal agencies authorized to issue standards under the Architectural Barriers Act: General Services Administration, Department of Defense, Department of Housing and Urban Development, and U.S. Postal Service.

To ensure compliance, Congress established the Architectural and Transportation Barriers Compliance Board (ATBCB) in Section 502 of the Rehabilitation Act of 1973, 29 U.S.C. 792. Members of eleven federal agencies and eleven members appointed by the President comprise the governing board of ATBCB. The 1978 amendments to the Rehabilitation Act gave the ATBCB the additional responsibility to issue minimum guidelines and requirements for the standards established by the four standard-setting agencies.

The American National Standards Institute, a non-governmental agency located in New York City, has published accessibility standards for the past thirty years. Many state and local building codes reference either the ANSI A117.1-1980 or the revised 1986 standard as the basis for the technical specifications related to handicapped access.

In order to maintain uniformity with existing accessibility standards, the Uniform Federal Accessibility Standards follow the ANSI A117.1-1980.

ADA Accessibility Guidelines

28 CFR Part 36, Appendix A

The Americans with Disabilities Accessibility Guidelines (ADAAG) were issued in conjunction with the ADA regulations for Titles II and III which the U.S. Department of Justice issued on July 26, 1991. The issuing federal agency for the guidelines is the Architectural and Transportation Barriers Compliance Board (ATBCB), which maintains oversight over architectural barrier standards.

General Provisions

The ADA accessibility guidelines contain general design standards for building and site elements, such as accessible entrances and routes, ramps, parking spaces, stairs, elevators, restrooms, signage, etc. Also included are specific standards for restaurants, medical care facilities, libraries and transportation facilities and vehicles, and places of lodging.

The guidelines also include "scoping" requirements that outline the necessary features or appropriate quantity for achieving ready access. For example, at least 50 percent of all public entrances to buildings must be accessible with an accessible path of travel. In public restrooms, at least one bathroom stall must be accessible, unless there are more than six stalls, in which case two stalls must be accessible to physically disabled persons.

It was not the objective of ATBCB to create confusion or conflict over the ADAAG guidelines. ATBCB is committed to working cooperatively with the ANSI A117 Committee in the hopes of achieving a single accessibility standard for the future.

Yet the ADAAG guidelines differ from the ANSI A117.1-80 standards (amended in 1986) and the UFAS standards. The difference between the ADAAG and the ANSI standards are noted in italics in the ADA-AG standards issued by the ATBCB.

Elevator Exemption

The ADAAG guidelines include an elevator exemption for newly constructed or altered facilities that are less than three stories or have less than 3,000 square feet per story. (Note: There are some instances in which places of public accommodation are required to have an elevator even if the exemption criteria is met.)

ATBCB staff have clearly stated in the preamble (56 *Fed. Reg.* 35412) that all state and local government buildings must install an elevator regardless of the size of the facility when the facility is newly constructed or when alterations are being made. The so-called elevator exemption does not exist for local governments. The rationale is that disabled citizens must have ready access to such public places as jury boxes, witness stands, detention facilities.

Implications for Local Governments

There are important implications for municipal building department personnel. Although local building inspectors are not required to enforce or monitor ADA compliance, they may play an advisory role to owners of public accommodations and commercial facilities. If the local government's building code is not fully in compliance with ADA standards, the local government may leave itself open to torts liability.

The number of businesses affected by Title III compliance is enormous. In their September issue of the AIA *Memo*, the American Institute of Architects estimated that more than five million places of public accommodation and commercial facilities will be affected by Title III accessibility requirements.[1] Indeed, many small, family owned and operated enterprises that have traditionally been exempt from Federal civil rights laws must now comply. Without direct communication from their local governments and oversight by building inspectors, they may unwittingly fail to undertake compliance activities when they are making modifications or constructing new facilities.

As noted earlier, the requirements of ADA do not supersede state or local building codes or accessibility laws if the state or local laws are more stringent. The ADA accessibility guidelines should be viewed as a minimum standard for achieving accessibility.

1   Stephanie Stubbs, "Justice Dept. Releases ADA Regs", *Memo* (Washington, D.C.: The American Institute of Architects, September, 1991), pp. 10-11.

7
ACTION STEPS TOWARDS COMPLIANCE

By Kathryn Shane McCarty

Local governments must take five key action steps to assess and then to ensure compliance with ADA:

- designate an ADA coordinator;
- provide public notice about compliance actions;
- conduct a self-evaluation process;
- prepare a transition plan, if structural changes are needed; and
- produce a grievance procedure for handling complaints.

Designating an ADA Coordinator

Designation of Responsible Employee (56 Fed. Reg. 35718, Sec. 35.107)

The Title II regulations issued by the U.S. Department of Justice require that all public entities with fifty or more employees must designate at least one employee to coordinate compliance with ADA. In fact, it is advisable, and in practical terms probably necessary, for all local governments to identify a lead staff person to coordinate and/or implement ADA compliance.

The larger jurisdictions that are required to designate an ADA coordinator, must also notify all interested individuals, parties, and organizations of the name, address, and phone number of this employee. It is essential that the notice provisions are adequately followed. It is advisable to install an accessible telecommunications device (TDD or text telephone) in the office of the ADA coordinator, so that hearing and speech impaired citizens can reach the ADA coordinator.

Public Notice

Notice Provision
(56 Fed. Reg. 35718, Sec 35.106)

All local governments, regardless of size, must advise all applicants, participants, beneficiaries and other interested persons that information is available on how government programs are complying with ADA. All public services contracted to another entity, either private or non-profit, must still meet all the nondiscrimination provisions of ADA.

It is important to mention your nondiscrimination on the basis of disability clause on all employment-related documents, all program applications, and all policy statements.

All local governments should be sensitive to the limitations of those individuals with sensory impairments when providing public notice. It will be necessary to use a wide range of media to ensure easy access by all citizens. Be sure to use newspapers, radio, and closed caption television to ensure that individuals with different disabilities will have ready access to the information. Remember to provide information in Braille or on audio-cassettes for vision impaired citizens and to hire sign language interpreters for hearing impaired persons when holding public hearings.

The Self-Evaluation Process

Self-Evaluation Process
(56 Fed. Reg. 35718, Sec 35.105)

The self-evaluation process should be viewed as the starting point towards achieving compliance. It permits local government officials to assess whether potential or existing compliance problems exist. The appendices include a series of sample self-evaluation checklists. Please copy them and distribute them to relevant city departments and programs.

If a local government has already conducted a self-evaluation while implementing Section 504 compliance, then the self-evaluation requirement under ADA only affects those programs and policies that were not evaluated under the existing Section 504 compliance checklist.

Effective Compliance Deadline

The compliance deadline for completing one's self-evaluation is January 26, 1993. But don't delay. The ADA Coordinator should begin undertaking the self-evaluation process immediately. Since the self-evaluation is the logical first step towards compliance, you should start your assessment as soon as possible.

Even though the self-evaluation deadline is January 1993, the effective date for program compliance is January 26, 1992. Potential compliance problems may surface in the course of completing the self-evaluation exercise. The self-evaluation process will review program and service access. Some nonstructural modifications may be necessary, along with staff training on how to make reasonable modifications to achieve program accessibility. Finally, some structural modifications may be necessary. These should be identified early on, so that the modifications can be budgeted for and completed as quickly as possible.

Furthermore, if a disabled individual were to file a lawsuit alleging discrimination, the affected local government officials would certainly want to demonstrate their "good faith intent" to comply with the provisions of ADA, and the self-evaluation checklist would be proof to that effect.

The self-evaluation checklist should be a comprehensive assessment of all current services, policies and practices, and the effects thereof, that do not or may not meet the requirements of ADA compliance. Once identified, local government officials must begin to make modifications to ensure compliance.

Key Steps for Conducting a Self-Evaluation Process

The self-evaluation should include the following important elements:

■ a list of the interested persons consulted;

- a description of areas examined and any problems identified; and
- a description of any modifications made.

Additional Requirements for Larger Jurisdictions

In addition, the DOJ regulations require all local governments with 50 or more employees to include the following two steps in their self-evaluation process. Please note that we are advising all local governments regardless of employee size to include these two steps in their review process:

Involve Interested and Potentially Affected Individuals in an Advisory Role

We recommend that all local governments contact organizations representing individuals with disabilities to solicit their participation in the self-evaluation process. These individuals can often identify problem areas and offer cost-effective solutions that might not be readily apparent to those responsible for conducting the self-evaluation.

Retain the Self-Evaluation Checklist on File in a Public Place for at least Three Years

The self-evaluation should be made available for public inspection. It is advisable for all local governments to conduct a self-evaluation and all local governments should retain a copy of their effort.

The Transition Plan

Transition Plan
(56 Fed. Reg. 35720, Sec. 35.150(d))

The DOJ regulations ask local governments to remember that their service delivery goal should be to provide government services in the most integrated setting possible while recognizing that structural modifications to achieve such a goal may or may not be necessary.

When structural changes to public facilities are needed, alterations must meet one of the two federal accessibility standards. A transition plan is the document that specifies the modifications to be made, the standards to be used, and the timeframe for changes.

While the DOJ regulations only require those public entities with 50 or more employees to complete and retain a transition plan, any jurisdiction that will be making structural changes should take the time to document the changes to be made and their timing. This can serve as a proactive step to diffuse concerns and/or legal actions that otherwise might result if a public facility is presently inaccessible.

A sample architectural barriers checklist and transition plan are included in the appendices. These tools are designed to be straightforward and easy to use. You can copy these forms or use any other transition plan form that you find serves your needs.

Remember that when structural changes are being made, they must comply with either of two federal standards — the Uniform Federal Accessibility Standards (UFAS) and the Americans with Disabilities Act Accessibility Guidelines for Buildings and Facilities (ADAAG) — or your state building code standard, whichever is more stringent. Both of these accessibility guidelines are discussed in more detail in Chapter 6.

Complaint Procedures

Complaint Procedure (56 Fed. Reg. 35718, Sec 35.107)

A complaint procedure to resolve grievances in a prompt and equitable manner is required of all those jurisdictions employing 50 or more employees. The grievance procedure must be formally adopted and published.

It's important to note that the DOJ regulations strongly encourage the use of alternative means of dispute resolution as a way to resolve ADA complaints.

A sample generic complaint procedure has been prepared by the legal staff of the Municipal Technical Advisory Service at the University of Tennessee. A copy of this procedure is included as an appendix.

The specific steps on how to file a grievance under ADA are found in Chapter 8. Once again, it seems advisable that all jurisdictions develop a complaint procedure now, before it is ever needed.

It should be noted that a local government does not necessarily have to establish a separate complaint procedure to handle all ADA complaints. Local jurisdictions may prefer to modify existing grievance procedures established by city departments to ensure compliance with ADA.

8
COMPLAINTS, ENFORCEMENT, AND REMEDIES

By Katharine L. Herber
and
Kathryn Shane McCarty

The remedies, procedures, and rights of individuals under Title II of the ADA are clarified in Subpart F (Sections 35.170 - 35177) of 28 CFR Part 35. An individual who believes that he or she has been discriminated against on the basis of disability (or the individual's authorized representative) may file a complaint with the federal agency responsible for enforcement.

The complaint must be filed within 180 days from the date of the alleged discrimination, unless a good cause for the delay can be shown. If, for example, the individual decided to pursue some form of informal dispute resolution or followed a local government's grievance procedure before filing a formal complaint, this would meet the "good cause shown" clause.

Under Title II, once the appropriate federal agency has received a complaint of discrimination, that agency will promptly review the complaint to determine whether it has jurisdiction over the complaint under Section 504. If the federal agency does not have jurisdiction over the complaint, then the complaint will be referred to the appropriate federal agency overseeing ADA compliance. It is important to note that eight federal agencies, in addition to the Equal Employment Opportunity Commission (EEOC), have been designated as having ADA compliance oversight. (See Subpart G, Section 35.190, 56 *Fed. Reg.* 35722). The Department of Justice is the lead agency for enforcing compliance under Title II as it relates to state and local governments.

The appropriate federal agency will attempt to resolve the complaint informally. If it does not meet with success, the agency will issue a Letter of Findings outlining the corrective action that must be taken within the specified timeframe. If the local government fails to comply with these findings, the complaint will be referred to the Department of Justice for further action, including filing for damages and equitable relief. State and local government immunity under the 11th amendment of the U.S. Constitution has been waived under ADA.

In addition, individuals still have the option to file suit in federal court to seek remedies. Generally, the prevailing party may be granted reasonable attorney's fees, including litigation expenses, and related costs.

The following outline provides a detailed summary of the administrative enforcement provisions of Subtitle A of Title II and how it specifically addresses the nondiscrimination requirements in all state and local government services and programs.

Administrative Enforcement Provisions

Administrative enforcement provisions are spelled out in the regulations for Title II (56 *Fed. Reg.* Sections 35.165 -35.169).

Who May File

Filing of Complaints (56 Fed. Reg. 35721, Sec. 35.170)

Any individual who believes that he or she (or a specific class of individuals) has been subjected to unlawful discrimination on the basis of disability by a municipality may file a complaint by himself, herself or by an authorized representative.

Filing Deadline

A complaint must be filed no later than 180 days from the date of the alleged discrimination. The filing deadline may be extended upon a showing of good cause. A complaint will be treated as filed on the date it is first filed with any Federal agency.

Where to File

An individual may file a complaint with:

- any Federal agency that he or she believes is the appropriate designated Federal agency,
- any Federal agency that provides funding to the municipality that is the subject of the complaint; or
- the Department of Justice for referral to the appropriate designated Federal agency.

Federal Agency Action on Complaints

Acceptance of Complaints (56 Fed. Reg. 35721, Sec. 35.171)

Title II spells out procedures for Federal agency actions on complaints.

Section 504 Jurisdiction Determination

When a Federal agency receives a complaint of discrimination on the basis of disability by a municipality it must promptly review the complaint to determine whether it has jurisdiction over the complaint under Section 504.

If the agency has Section 504 jurisdiction, it must process the complaint according to its procedures for enforcement of Section 504. If the agency determines that it does not have Section 504 jurisdiction, it must promptly determine if it is the designated agency for complaints filed against that municipality or, that component of municipal government.

Designated Agency Determination (56 Fed. Reg. 35722, Sec. 35.190)

An agency is the "designated agency" for the local government (or component of local government) that exercises responsibility for, regulates, or administers services, programs, or activities in the following areas:

Department of Agriculture: All programs, services, and regulatory activities relating to farming and the raising of livestock, including extension services.

Department of Education: All programs, services, and regulatory activities relating to the operation of public elementary and secondary education systems and institutions, institutions of higher education and vocational education (other than schools of medicine, dentistry, nursing, and other health-related schools), and libraries.

Department of Health and Human Services: All programs, services, and regulatory activities relating to the provision of health care and social services, including schools of medicine, dentistry, nursing, and other health-related schools, the operation of health care and social service providers and institutions, including "grass-roots" and community services organizations and programs, and preschool and day care programs.

Department of Housing and Urban Development: All programs, services, and regulatory activities relating to state and local public housing, and housing assistance and referral.

Department of Interior: All programs, services, and regulatory activities relating to lands and natural resources, including parks and recreation, water and waste management, environmental protection, energy, historic and cultural preservation, and museums.

Department of Justice: All programs, services, and regulatory activities relating to law enforcement, public safety, and the administration of justice, including courts and correctional institution; commerce and industry, including general economic development, banking and finance, consumer protection, insurance, and small business; planning, development and regulation (unless assigned to other designated agencies); state and local government support services (e.g., audit, personnel, comptroller, administrative services); all other government functions not assigned to other designated agencies.

Department of Labor: All programs, services, and regulatory activities relating to labor and the work force.

Department of Transportation: All programs, services, and regulatory activities relating to transportation, including highways, public transportation, traffic management (non-law enforcement), automobile licensing and inspection, and driver licensing.

Agency Action When It Neither Has Section 504 Jurisdiction Nor Qualifies As a Designated Agency

When an agency (other than the Department of Justice) determines that it neither has Section 504 jurisdiction nor qualifies as a designated agency, it must promptly refer the complaint to the Department of Justice and notify the complainant of such referral.

When the Department of Justice determines that it neither has Section 504 jurisdiction nor qualifies as a designated agency, it must refer the complaint to:

- an agency that has Section 504 jurisdiction;
- an agency that is a designated agency; or
- in the case of an employment complaint that is also subject to Title I, to the Equal Employment Opportunity Commission.

Resolving Complaints

Resolution of Complaints (56 Fed. Reg. 35722, Sec. 35.172)

The agency with jurisdiction over the complaint must:

- investigate each complete complaint;
- attempt informal resolution; and
- if resolution is not achieved, issue to the complainant and the local government a Letter Of Findings.

The Letter of Findings must include:

- findings of fact and conclusions of law;
- a description of a remedy for each violation found; and
- notice of the rights available to both the municipality and the complainant, including the complainant's right to file a private suit (whether or not the agency finds a violation of the Act).

Voluntary Compliance Agreements (56 Fed. Reg. 35723, Sec. 35.173)

After the agency issues a noncompliance Letter of Findings, it must:

- notify the Assistant Attorney General by forwarding a copy of the Letter of Findings to the Assistant Attorney General and

■ initiate negotiations with the public entity to secure compliance by voluntary means.

A voluntary compliance agreement must:

■ be in writing and signed by the parties;
■ address each cited violation;
■ specify the corrective or remedial action to be taken by the local government to come into compliance with the Act;
■ establish a compliance schedule for the corrective or remedial action;
■ provide assurance that the discrimination will not recur; and
■ provide for enforcement of the voluntary compliance agreement by the Attorney General.

Referral (56 Fed. Reg. 35722, Sec. 35.174)

If a local government refuses to enter into a voluntary compliance agreement or if negotiations are unsuccessful, the agency must refer the complaint to the Attorney General with a recommendation for appropriate action.

Attorney's Fees (56 Fed. Reg. 35722, Sec. 35.175)

In any action or administrative proceeding brought pursuant to the Act, the court or agency may, in its discretion, award the prevailing party, reasonable attorney's fees (including litigation expenses and costs).

Alternative Dispute Resolution (56 Fed. Reg. 35722, Sec. 35.176)

Alternative means of dispute resolution, including settlement negotiations, conciliation, facilitation, mediation, fact finding, minitrials, and arbitration, is encouraged to resolve discrimination complaints under ADA.

Summary of Title III Enforcement

Under 28 CFR Part 36, which mandates nondiscrimination in places of public accommodation and in commercial facilities, the consequences of noncompliance are significantly greater than under Subtitle A of Title II, as it now stands. In this case, monetary damages may be awarded to the aggrieved party.

Subpart E is the enforcement section of the promulgating regulations for Title III. Individuals have the right to file a civil law suit for preventive relief, including an injunction, restraining order, etc., without exhausting their administrative remedies. This is a significant change from the Section 504 regulations in this area.

If the U.S. Attorney General intervenes and brings suit in federal district court, then the remedies may include monetary damages and/or a civil penalty in an amount up to $50,000 for the first violation and up to $100,000 for any subsequent violation.

Effect Of Civil Rights Amendments

Public Law #102-166—the 1991 amendments to the Civil Rights Act of 1964—expands the rights and remedies available to plaintiffs who prevail in a cause of action filed pursuant to the Americans With Disabilities Act of 1990. A summary of those amendments is detailed below.

Damages

Under Public Law #102-166, plaintiffs who prevail in court cases brought pursuant to the Americans With Disabilities Act may recover compensatory damages for unlawful and intentional discrimination.

Damage Limitations

The total amount of compensatory damages may not exceed:

- $50,000 in the case of a municipality with more than 15 and fewer than 101 employees;
- $100,000 in the case of a municipality with more than 100 and fewer than 201 employees;
- $200,000 in the case of a municipality with more than 200 and fewer than 501 employees; and
- $300,000 in the case of a municipality with more than 500 employees.

Trial by Jury Available

If a plaintiff seeks compensatory or punitive damages, either party may demand a trial by jury, although the court may not inform the jury of any damage limitations.

Expert Witness Fees

The 1991 amendment to the Civil Rights Act clarifies that successful plaintiffs may recover fees paid to expert witnesses, in addition to attorney's fees.

A

GLOSSARY

Prepared by
Florence K. Stewart

Accessible: Describes a site, building, facility or portion thereof that complies with the ADAAG guidelines.

Accessible Element: An element specified by the ADAAG guidelines (e.g., text telephone, controls, curb ramps, and the like).

Accessible Route: A continuous unobstructed path connecting all accessible elements and spaces of a building or facility. Interior accessible routes may include corridors, floors, ramps, elevators, lifts and clear floor space at fixtures. Exterior accessible routes may include parking access isles, curb ramps, crosswalks at vehicular ways, walks, ramps and lifts.

Access Aisle: An accessible pedestrian space between elements, such as parking spaces, seating and desks, that provides clearances appropriate for use of the elements.

Accessibility Standards: Two accessibility standards apply to new construction and/or modifications to existing buildings. They are the 1984 Uniform Federal Accessibility Standards (UFAS) and the Americans with Disabilities Act Accessibility Guidelines (ADAAG). Local governments are given the option of following either the UFAS standards or the newly released ADA guidelines established by the Architectural and Transportation Barriers Compliance Board (ATBCB) on July 26, 1991.

ADA Accessibility Guidelines (ADAAG): The ADAAG, issued in conjunction with Titles II and III DOJ regulations on July 26, 1991, contain general design standards for building and site elements, such as accessible entrances, routes, ramps, parking spaces, stairs, elevators, restrooms, signage, etc. Specific standards for restaurants, medical care facilities, places of lodging, libraries and transportation facilities and vehicles are also included.

Adaptability: The ability of certain building spaces and elements, such as kitchen counters, sinks and grab bars, to be added or altered so as to accommodate the needs of individuals with or without disabilities or to accommodate the needs of persons with different types or degrees of disability.

Administrative Authority: A governmental agency that adopts or enforces regulations and guidelines for the design, construction or alteration of buildings and facilities.

Alteration: An alteration is a change to a building or facility, made by, on behalf of, or for the use of a public accommodation or commercial facility, that affects or could affect the usability of the building or facility or part thereof. Normal maintenance, reroofing, painting, wallpapering or changes to mechanical and electrical systems are not alterations, unless they affect the usability of the building or facility.

Architectural and Transportation Barriers Compliance Board (ATBCB): Section 502 of the Rehabilitation Act of 1973, as amended, established the ATBCB as a regulatory, monitoring, reporting and investigative body operating under the Architectural Barriers Act. It enforces compliance with accessibility standards developed in response to the Architectural Barriers Act, examines and determines ways to eliminate barriers — physical and attitudinal — and makes reports and recommendations to Congress.

Area of Rescue Assistance: An area, which has direct access to an exit, where people who are unable to use stairs may remain temporarily in safety to await further instructions or assistance during emergency evacuation.

Auxiliary Aids and Services: Auxiliary aids and services are generally divided into four major categories:

■ qualified interpreters, note takers, transcription services, written materials, telephone handset amplifiers, assistive listening devices and systems, telephones compatible with hearing aids, closed caption decoders, open and closed captioning, telecommunications devices for deaf persons (TDDs), videotext displays, or other effective methods of making aurally delivered materials available to individuals with hearing impairments.

■ qualified readers, taped texts, audio recordings, materials in Braille, large print materials, or other effective methods of making visually delivered materials available to individuals with visual impairments.

■ acquisition or modification of equipment or devices; and:

■ other similar services and actions. (Referenced in DOJ Titles II and III regulations).

Circulation Path: An exterior or interior way of passage from one place to another for pedestrians, including, but not limited to, walks, hallways, courtyards, stairways and stair landings.

Clear Floor Space: The minimum unobstructed floor or ground space required to accommodate a single, stationary wheelchair and occupant.

Commission (EEOC): Equal Employment Opportunity Commission (EEOC) established by Section 705 of the Civil Rights Act of 1964. (Referenced in EEOC regulations.)

Complete Complaint: A written statement that contains the complainant's name and address and describes the public entity's alleged discriminatory action in sufficient detail to inform the agency of the nature and date of the alleged violation of this part. It shall be signed by the complainant or by someone authorized to do so on his or her behalf. Complaints filed on behalf of classes or third parties shall describe or identify (by name, if possible) the alleged victims of discrimination. (Referenced in DOJ Title II regulations.)

Commerce: Refers to travel, trade, traffic, commerce, transportation, or communication among states, between any foreign country or between points in the same state. (Same definition as included in the Civil Rights Act of 1964.)

Commercial Facilities: Refers to facilities whose operations will affect commerce and that are intended for nonresidential use by a private entity. Does not include facilities expressly exempted from coverage under the Fair Housing Act of 1968, aircraft, rail or railroad vehicles.

Covered Entity: An employer, employment agency, labor organization or joint labor management committee (Referenced in EEOC regulations.)

Cross Slope: The slope that is perpendicular to the direction of travel.

Curb Ramp: A short ramp cutting through a curb or built up to it.

Current Illegal Use of Drugs: Illegal use of drugs that occurred recently enough to justify a reasonable belief that a person's drug use is current or that continuing use is a real and ongoing problem (Referenced in DOJ Titles II and III regulations.)

Designated Agency: This refers to the Federal agency designated under Subpart G of the regulations to oversee compliance activities under this part for particular components of State and local governments (Referenced in DOJ Title II Regulations).

Detectable Warning: A standardized surface feature built in or applied to walking surfaces or other elements to warn visually impaired people of hazards on a circulation path.

Direct Threat: Significant risk of substantial harm to the health or safety of the individual or others, based on an individualized assessment of the individual's present ability to safely perform the essential functions of the job; including the duration of the risk, the nature and severity of the potential harm, likelihood that the potential harm will occur, and the imminence of the potential harm (Referenced in EEOC regulations.)

Disability: In reference to an individual, a physical or mental impairment that substantially limits one or more of the major life activities of such individual; a record of such an impairment; or being regarded as having an impairment.

Does not include transvestism, transsexualism, pedophilia, exhibitionism, voyeurism, gender identity disorders not resulting from physical impairments, or other sexual behavior disorders; compulsive gambling, kleptomania, pyromania; or psychoactive substance use disorders resulting from current illegal use of drugs.

Drug: A controlled substance, as defined in schedules I through V of Section 202 of the Controlled Substances Act.

Dwelling Unit: A single unit which provides a kitchen or food preparation area in addition to rooms and spaces for living, bathing, sleeping and the like. For purposes of these guidelines, "Dwelling Unit" does not imply that the unit is used as a residence.

Egress, Means of: A continuous and unobstructed way of exit travel from any point in a building or facility to a public way. A means of egress comprises vertical and horizontal travel and may include:

■ intervening room spaces, doorways, hallways, corridors, passageways, balconies, ramps, stairs, enclosures, lobbies, horizontal exits, courts and yards. An accessible means of egress is one that complies with these guidelines, and does not include stairs, steps, or escalators. Areas of rescue assistance or evacuation elevators may be included as part of an accessible means of egress.

Element: An architectural or mechanical component of a building, facility, space or site (e.g. telephone, curb ramp, door, drinking fountain, seating or water closet).

Employee: Individual employed by an employer (Referenced in EEOC regulations.)

Employer: A person engaged in an industry affecting commerce who has 15 or more employees for each working day in each of 20 or more calendar weeks in the current or preceding year, and any agent of such person, except that, from July 26, 1992 through July 25, 1994, an employer means a person engaged in an industry affecting commerce who has 25 or more employees for each working day in each of 20 or more calendar weeks in the current or preceding year and any agent of such person. (Referenced in EEOC regulations.)

Essential Functions: Fundamental job duties of the employment position the individual with the disability holds or desires. (Referenced in EEOC regulations.)

Facility: All or any portion of buildings, structures, sites, complexes, equipment, rolling stock or other conveyances, roads, walks, passageways, parking lots, other real or personal property, including the site where the building, property, structure or equipment is located (Referenced in ATBCB guidelines, DOJ Titles II and III regulations.)

Has a Record of Such Impairment: Has a history of, or has been misclassified as having, a mental or physical impairment that substantially limits one or more major life activities.

Historic Properties: Properties that are listed or eligible for listing in the National Register of Historic Places or properties designated as historic under state or local law. (Referenced in DOJ Titles II and III regulations.)

Historic Preservation Programs: Programs conducted by a public entity that have preservation of historic properties as a primary purpose. (Referenced in DOJ Title III regulations.)

Illegal Use Of Drugs The use of one or more drugs, the possession or distribution of which is unlawful under the Controlled Substances Act. Does not include the use of a drug taken under the supervision of a licensed health care professional or other drugs authorized by the Controlled Substances Act or other provisions of Federal Law.

Individual With A Disability: A person who has a disability. Does not include an individual who is currently engaging in the illegal use of drugs, when the public entity acts on the basis of such use (Referenced in DOJ Title II regulations.)

Is Regarded As Having An Impairment: Has a physical or mental impairment that does not substantially limit major life activities but that is treated by a public entity as constituting such a limitation; has a physical or mental impairment that substantially limits major life activities only as a result of the attitudes of others towards such impairment; has none of the impairments defined above in Physical or Mental Impairment, but is treated as having such an impairment (Referenced in EEOC and DOJ Titles II and III regulations.)

Major Life Activities: Functions such as caring for one's self, performing manual tasks, walking, seeing hearing, breathing, learning, and working (Referenced in EEOC and DOJ Titles II and III regulations.)

Mezzanine or Mezzanine Floor: That portion of a story that is an intermediate floor level placed within the story and having occupiable space above and below its floor.

Non-essential Functions: Those job duties and assignments which are marginal. These duties are not a measure of whether an applicant is qualified to perform the job. Indeed, these functions might be shared with another staff member as a reasonable accommodation to an employee with a disability. (Referenced in EEOC regulations.) :

Notice: Refers to the requirement of a local government to provide information to applicants, participants and other interested persons to inform them of the rights and protections set forth in the ADA.

Occupiable: A room or enclosed space designed for human occupancy in which individuals congregate for amusement, educational or similar purposes, or in which occupants are engaged at labor, and which is equipped with means of egress, light and ventilation.

Operable Part: A part or a piece of equipment or appliance used to insert or withdraw objects, or to activate, deactivate or adjust the equipment or appliance (e.g., coin slot, push-button, handle).

Physical or Mental Impairment: Any physiological disorder or condition, cosmetic disfigurement or anatomical loss affecting one or more of the following body systems:

- Neurological, musculoskeletal, special sense organs, respiratory (including speech organs), cardiovascular, reproductive, digestive, genitourinary, hemic and lymphatic, skin, and endocrine.
- Any mental or psychological disorder such as mental retardation, organic brain syndrome, emotional or mental illness, and specific learning disabilities.

Includes, but is not limited to such contagious and noncontagious diseases and conditions as orthopedic, visual, speech and hearing impairments, cerebral palsy, epilepsy, muscular dystrophy, multiple sclerosis, cancer, heart disease, diabetes, HIV disease (whether symptomatic or asymptomatic), tuberculosis, drug addiction and alcoholism.

Does not include homosexuality or bisexuality. (Referenced in EEOC and DOJ Titles II and III regulations.)

Power-assisted Door: A door used for human passage with a mechanism that helps to open the door, or relieves the opening resistance of a door, upon the activation of a switch or continued force applied to the door itself.

Program Accessibility: Refers to ensuring nondiscrimination and equal opportunities for disabled persons to utilize and participate in programs and activities. Compliance activities, whether taken as a result of your self-evaluation or in response to requests, must ensure access via modifications and adjustments to procedures, practices and/or policies, with barrier removal efforts as appropriate, when undertaking building renovation and/or new construction. (Referenced in DOJ Title II regulations.):

Public Accommodation: Refers to a private entity that owns, leases, or operates a place of public accommodation (that is included in one of the 12 categories). (Referenced in DOJ Title III regulations.)

Public Entity: Any State or local government; any department, agency, special purpose district, or other instrumentality of a state or states or local government; The National Railroad Passenger Corporation and any commuter authority (as defined in Sec 103(8) of the Rail Passenger Service Act (Referenced in DOJ Title II and DOT regulations.)

Qualification Standards: Personal and professional attribute, including the skill, experience, education, physical, medical, safety and other requirements established by a covered entity as requirements that an individual must meet in order to be eligible for the position held or desired. (Referenced in EEOC regulations.)

Qualified Interpreter: An interpreter who is able to interpret effectively, accurately, and impartially both receptively and expressively, using any necessary specialized vocabulary. (Referenced in DOJ Title II regulations.)

Qualified Individual with a Disability: An individual with a disability who, with or without reasonable modifications to rules, policies or practices, the removal of architectural, communication or transportation barriers, or the provision of auxiliary aids and services, meets the essential eligibility requirements for the receipt of services or the participation in programs or activities provided by a public entity. (Referenced in DOJ Title II regulations.)

Ramp: A walking surface that has a running slope greater than 1:20.

Readily Achievable: Easily accomplishable and able to be carried out without much difficulty or expense. There are four factors to consider:

- the nature and cost of the action needed;
- the overall financial resources of the facility involved; the number of employees at the facility; the effect on the expenses and resources or impact of such action upon the operation of the facility;
- the overall financial resources of the covered entity; and
- the type of operation(s) of the covered entity, including the composition, structure and functions of the workforce; the

geographic separateness, administrative, or fiscal relationship of the facility in question to the covered entity. (Referenced in DOJ Title III regulations.)

Reasonable Accommodations: The definition as set forth in Sec. 101(9) of the Act states:

■ making existing facilities readily accessible to and usable by individuals with disabilities; and

■ job restructuring, part-time or modified work schedules, reassignment to a vacant position, acquisition or modifications of equipment or devices, appropriate adjustment or modifications of examinations, training materials or policies; the provision of qualified readers or interpreters; and other similar accommodations for individuals with disabilities. (Referenced in EEOC regulations.)

The EEOC regulations provide additional insight into the definition and how it can be applied:

■ modifications or adjustments to a job application process that enable a qualified applicant with a disability to be considered for the position he/she desires; or

■ modifications or adjustments to the work environment, or to the manner or circumstances under which the position held or desired is customarily performed, that enable a qualified individual with a disability to perform the essential functions of that position; or

■ modifications or adjustments that enable a covered entity's employee with a disability to enjoy equal benefits and privileges of employment as are enjoyed by its other similarly situated employees without disabilities.

Running Slope: The slope that is parallel to the direction of travel.

Section 504: Refers to Section 504 of the Rehabilitation Act of 1973 (Pub. L. 93-112, 87 Stat. 394 (29 U.S.C. 794, as amended).

Self-Evaluation: Section 504 requires that the local government evaluate its current policies and practices to identify and correct those which do not comply with the accessibility guidelines. Local governments with 50 or more employees must maintain the self-evaluation on file and make it available for public inspection for three years.

Site Improvement: Landscaping, paving for pedestrian and vehicular ways, outdoor lighting, recreational facilities, and the like, added to a site.

State: Each of the several states, the District of Columbia, the Commonwealth of Puerto Rico, Guam, American Samoa, the Virgin Islands, the Trust Territory of the Pacific Islands, and the Commonwealth of the Northern Mariana Island (Referenced in EEOC and DOJ Title III regulations.)

Structural Frame: The structural frame shall be considered to be the columns and the girders, beams, trusses and spandrels having direct connections to the columns and all other members that are essential to the stability of the building as a whole.

Substantially Limited: Unable to perform a major life activity that the average person in the general population can perform; or

Significantly restricted as to the condition, manner or duration under which an individual can perform a particular major life activity as compared to the condition, manner or duration under which the average person in the general population can perform that same major life activity.

Regarding the major life activity of working, significantly restricted in the ability to perform either a class of jobs in various classes as compared to the average person having comparable training skills and abilities. (Referenced in EEOC regulations.)

Tactile: Describes an object that can be perceived using the sense of touch.

Telecommunications devices of deaf persons (TDD/TTYs) Equipment that displays type in order to telecommute with deaf and hearing impaired.

Text Telephone Machinery or equipment that employs interactive graphic (i.e., typed) communications through the transmission of coded signals across the standard telephone network. Text telephones can include, for example, devices known as TDDs (telecommunications display devices or telecommunications devices for deaf persons) or computers.

Transient Lodging: A building, facility, or portion thereof, excluding inpatient medical care facilities, that contains one or more dwelling units or sleeping accommodations. Transient lodging may include, but is not limited to, resorts, group homes, hotels, motels, and dormitories.

Transition Plan: When structural changes to facilities will be undertaken to achieve program accessibility, a government that employs 50 or more persons will complete a plan by July 26, 1992, specifying the steps scheduled to facilitate the changes.

Undue Hardship: Regarding the provision of an accommodation, significant difficulty or expense incurred by a covered entity when considered in light of the factors set forth as follows:

- nature and net cost of the accommodations needed;
- overall financial resources of the facility or facilities involved in providing reasonable accommodations, the number of persons employed at the facility, and the effect on expenses and resources;
- overall financial resources of the covered entity, overall size of the business of the covered entity with respect to the number of employees and the number, type, and location of its facilities;
- type of operation or operations of the covered entity; and
- impact of the accommodation upon the operation of the facility, including the impact on the ability of other employees to perform their duties and the impact on the facility's ability to conduct business. (Referenced in EEOC regulations.)

Uniform Federal Accessibility Standards (UFAS): The UFAS (49 CFR 31528) presents uniform standards for the design, construction and alterations of buildings, so individuals with disabilities will have ready access to and use of facilities in accordance with the Architectural Barriers Act, 42 U.S.C. 4151-4157.

Legal Action Center
236 Massachusetts Avenue, NE
Suite 510
Washington, D.C. 20002
(202) 544-5478

National AIDS Information Clearinghouse
P.O. Box 6003
Rockville, MD
(800) 458-5231

National Alliance for the Mentally Ill
2101 Wilson Blvd.
Suite 302
Arlington, VA 22201
(703) 524-7600

National Association for the Deaf
814 Thayer Avenue
Silver Spring, MD 20910-4500
(301) 587-1788 (Voice)
(301) 587-1789 (TDD)

National Association for the Physically Handicapped
4230 Emerick Street
Saginaw, MI 48602
(517) 799-3060

National Association for Retarded Citizens
1522 K Street, NW
Suite 516
Washington, D.C. 20005
(202) 785-3388 (Voice)
(202) 785-3411 (TDD)

National Center For Access Unlimited
155 N. Wacker Drive, Ste. 315
Chicago, IL 60606
(312) 368-0380 (Voice)
(312) 368-0179 (TDD)

National Center for Law and Deafness
Gallaudet University
800 Florida Avenue, NE
Ely Center, Rm. 326
Washington, D.C. 20002
(202) 651-5373

National Council on Independent Living
Troy Atrium
Fourth and Broadway
Troy, N.Y. 12180
(518) 274-1979 (Voice)
(518) 274-0701 (TDD)

National Easter Seals Society
1350 New York Ave, NW
Suite 915
Washington, D.C. 20005
(202) 347-3066 (Voice)
(202) 347-7385 (TDD)
(For technical/legal info)

National Easter Seals Society
70 E. Lake Street
Chicago, IL 60601
(312) 726-6200 (Voice)
(312) 4258 (TDD)
(For training, videos, publications, etc.)

National Federation of the Blind
1800 Johnson Street
Baltimore, Md 21230
(301) 659-9314

National Head Injury Foundation
1140 Connecticut Avenue, NW
Suite 812
Washington, D.C.20036
(202) 296-6443
1 800 444-6443 (Families, consumers)

National Information Center on Deafness

Gallaudet University
800 Florida Avenue, NE
Washington, D.C. 20002
(202) 651-5051 (Voice)
(202) 651-5052 (TDD)

National Mental Health Consumers' Association

311 South Juniper Street
Room 902
Philadelphia, PA 19107
(215) 735-2465 (Voice)
(215) 735-1273 (TDD)
1 800 688-4226 (Voice)

National Mental Health Law Project

1101 15th Street, NW
Suite 1212
Washington, D.C. 20005
(202) 467-5730 (Voice)
(202) 467-4232 (TDD)

National Multiple Sclerosis Society

205 E. 42nd Street
New York, NY 10017
(212) 986-3240

National Organization for Rare Disorders

Fairwood Professional Building
P.O. Box 8923
New Fairfield, Connecticut 06812-1783
1 800 999-6673
(203) 746-6518

National Organization on Disability

910 16th Street NW, Ste. 600
Washington, D.C. 20006
(202) 293-5960
(800) 248-ABLE (Voice/TDD)

National Spinal Cord Injury Association
600 West Cummings Park
Suite 2000
Woburn, Massachusetts 01801
(617) 935-2722

Paralyzed Veterans of America
801 18th Street, NW
Washington, D.C. 20006
(202) 872-1300

President's Committee on Employment of People with Disabilities
1331 F Street, NW
Washington, D.C. 20004-1107
(202) 376-6200

Rochester Institute of Technology
National Center on Employment for the Deaf
Lyndon Baines Johnson Building
P.O. Box 9887
Rochester NY 14623-0887
(716) 475-6219 (Voice)
(716) 475-6205 (TDD)

Self-Help for Hard of Hearing People
7800 Wisconsin Avenue
Bethesda, MD 20814
(301) 657-2248 (Voice)
(301) 657-2249 (TDD)

Standing Committee on Dispute Resolution
American Bar Association
1800 M Street, N.W.
Washington, D.C. 20036
(202) 331-2258

Telecommunications for the Deaf, Inc.
8719 Colesville Road
Suite 300
Silver Spring, MD 20910
(301) 589-3786 (Voice)
(301) 589-3006 (TDD)

United Cerebral Palsy Associations
Community Services Division 1522 K Street, NW,#1112
Washington, D.C. 20005
(202) 842-1266
(800) USA-5UPC

U.S. Department of Transportation
Urban Mass Transit Administration
400 7th Street, SW
Washington, D.C. 20590
(202) 366-9305 (Voice)
(202) 755-7607 (TDD)

U.S. Department of Justice
Office on the American Disabilities Act
ADA Information Line
Washington, D.C. 20530
(202) 514-0301 (Voice)
(202) 514-0381 (TDD)
(202) 514-6193 (Electronic Bulletin Board)

Western Law Center for the Handicapped
1441 West Olympic Blvd.
Los Angeles, CA 90015
(213) 736-1031

World Institute on Disability
510-16th Street
Oakland, CA 94612
(510) 763-4100 (Voice/TDD)

C

ADA ACTION PLAN

Prepared by the National League of Cities' Center for Education and Information Resources.

This action plan outline will assist you in identifying the steps and resources needed to comply with the Americans with Disabilities Act of 1990.

Beginning Date: _____

Participant's Name: _____

Title: _____

Agency/Dept: _____

City: _____ State: _____ Zip: _____

Telephone #: _____ Fax #: _____

I. Background Information To Determine Compliance

	Yes	No
1. Does your local government have more than 50 employees?	☐	☐
2. Does your local government operate a public transit or paratransit service?	☐	☐
3. Have you complied with Section 504 to the best of your knowledge?	☐	☐

4. Name of ADA Coordinator: _____
Telephone Number: _____

II. Coordination of ADA Compliance

List persons of influence:

Name	Position	Agency/Dept	Date Contacted
_____	_____	_____	_____
_____	_____	_____	_____
_____	_____	_____	_____
_____	_____	_____	_____
_____	_____	_____	_____
_____	_____	_____	_____
_____	_____	_____	_____
_____	_____	_____	_____

III. Disabled Resource Persons who can Assist

Name	Position	Phone #	Date Contacted
_____	_____	_____	_____
_____	_____	_____	_____
_____	_____	_____	_____
_____	_____	_____	_____
_____	_____	_____	_____
_____	_____	_____	_____
_____	_____	_____	_____

IV. Action Steps

	Exists?	Date In Place	Reexamine?
1. Self-Evaluation Plan	_____	_____	_____
2. Transition Plan	_____	_____	_____
3. Grievance Procedure	_____	_____	_____
4. S ensitivity Training	_____	_____	_____
5. Public Notice Procedures	_____	_____	_____
6. Review of Building Code/ State Statutes	_____	_____	_____
7. Auxiliary Aids	_____	_____	_____
8. Review of employment policies and practices	_____	_____	_____

V. Problem Identification (List and check one category)

As a result of completing the self-evaluation checklist and/or the transition plan, you may have identified some problem areas that you may want to summarize in this section provided below.

	Current Problem	Potential Problem
_____	☐	☐
_____	☐	☐
_____	☐	☐
_____	☐	☐
_____	☐	☐

VI. Resource Identification

_____

_____

_____

_____

_____

_____

_____

_____

_____

_____

_____

_____

_____

_____

_____

_____

If you have not already do so, your next step is to complete the series of self-evaluation checklists and the architectural barriers checklist found as appendices to the guidebook in order to determine any potential problem areas. You may wish to summarize your findings in the space provided on this Action Plan.

D
OUTLINE FOR JOB DESCRIPTION DEVELOPMENT

Prepared by Leslie Shechter, Legal Consultant, Municipal Technical Advisory Service, and Marie Allen Murphy, Legal Services Coordinator, County Technical Assistance Service at the Institute for Public Service, University of Tennessee, Knoxville, Tennessee.

Job Title: This is a description of the job title or classification.

Definition: This section should contain a brief description of the position, the level and/or type of supervision received by the employee, an identification of who the employee is responsible to, and the type and/or level of independent judgment used by the employee when performing tasks.

Equipment/Job Location: This section should describe the type of equipment used by the employee, the location and environment in which the job is usually undertaken, and any special environmental conditions or physical requirements the employee may encounter.

Essential Functions of the Job: This section should identify "essential functions" of the job — basic duties for which the job was created which cannot normally be transferred to another position without disruption in the flow or process of work.

Additional Examples of Work Performed: Here you may want to list the duties that are not "essential functions", but are typically undertaken or expected of the employee.

Required Knowledge and Abilities: List the basic abilities and knowledge the employee will need to adquately perform the job. These may be both specific and broad-based requirements. They should definitely be job-related.

Qualifications: List the basic or minimum qualifications every employee in this position must have to be considered for employment.

E

SAMPLE GRIEVANCE PROCEDURE

Prepared by Leslie Shechter, Legal Consultant, Municipal Technical Advisory Service and Marie Allen Murphy, Legal Services Coordinator, County Technical Assistance Service at the University of Tennessee, Knoxville, Tennessee.

1. Submit all complaints regarding access or alleged discrimination in writing to the designated official (such as the ADA Coordinator, city manager, mayor or county executive) for resolution. A record of the complaint and action taken will be maintained. A decision by the designated official will be rendered within fifteen working days.

2. If the complaint cannot be resolved to the satisfaction of the complainant by the designated local government official, it will be forwarded to an ADA compliance committee composed of representatives from elected officials, the disabled community, business or non-profit sectors, education and the health/medical profession. The committee will be appointed by the city council or board of supervisors.

3. The committee should be charged to establish ground rules or procedures for hearing complaints, requests or suggestions from disabled persons regarding access to and participation in public facilities, services, activities and functions in the community. Further, the committee should be directed to hear such complaints in public, after adequate public notice is given, in an unbiased, objective manner. The committee should issue a written decision within 30 days of notification. All proceedings of the committee should be recorded, transcripted and maintained.

4. If the complaint cannot be resolved to the complainant's satisfaction by the committee, the complaint will be heard by the city council or board of supervisors. An open, public meeting of the governing board will precede the vote. A determination must be made within 30 days of the hearing. The decision of the governing board is final.

5. A record of action taken on each request or complaint must be maintained as a part of the records or minutes at each level of the grievance process.

6. The individual's right to prompt and equitable resolution of the complaint must be not impaired by his/her pursuit of other remedies, such as the filing of a complaint with the U.S. Department of Justice or any other appropriate federal agency. Furthermore, the filing of a lawsuit in state or federal district court can occur at any time. The use of this grievance procedure is not a prerequisite to the pursuit of other remedies.

F

SELF-EVALUATION CHECKLIST
Employment Provisions (Titles I, II)

Developed by the Texas
Governor's Committee for Disabled Persons, in conjunction with the Office for Civil Rights at the U.S. Department of Health and Human Services, Region IV.

The questions included in this self-evaluation checklist were designed to help employers, both public and private, come into compliance with Title I of the ADA.

1. Have you reviewed your employment policies (recruiting, hiring, upgrading, promotion, award of tenure, demotion, transfer, layoff, termination, right of return from layoff, and rehiring) to be sure that you and your employees are giving nondiscriminatory treatment to applicants and employees with disabilities?

Yes ☐ No ☐ Action/Due Date: _____

2. Have you reviewed your employment practices to make sure that they do not limit, segregate or classify job applicants or employees in ways that adversely affect their opportunities or status because of the disability of the applicant or employee.

Yes ☐ No ☐ Action/Due Date: _____

3. Have you reviewed your employment practices to make sure that you are not participating in a contractual or other arrangement or relationship that subjects your qualified applicant or employee with a disability to discrimination (i.e., relationships with employment or referral agencies, labor unions or organizations that provide fringe benefits, training or apprenticeship programs.

Yes ☐ No ☐ Action/Due Date: _____

4. Have you reviewed your employment practices to make sure that you are not using standards, criteria or methods of administration that have the effect of discriminating on the basis of disability or that perpetuate the discrimination of others who are subject to common administrative control?

Yes ☐ No ☐ Action/Due Date: _____

5. Have you reviewed your employment practices to make sure that you are giving nondiscriminatory treatment to applicants and employees who have a friend, associate or family member with a disability?

Yes ☐ No ☐ Action/Due Date: _____

6. Have you determined the process you will use to decide at which point "reasonable accommodation" causes an "undue hardship"?

Yes ☐ No ☐ Action/Due Date: _____

7. Do you have a policy concerning "reasonable accommodation"?

Yes ☐ No ☐ Action/Due Date: _____

8. Do you have a procedure to document decisions not to hire or promote because of "undue hardship"?

Yes ☐ No ☐ Action/Due Date: _____

9. Have you reviewed the requirements of your jobs (job descriptions, employment tests, or other selection criteria) to be sure that no criteria are included that would discriminate against an individual with a disability unless such criteria are job-related and consistent with business necessity?

Yes ☐ No ☐ Action/Due Date: _____

10. Are your hiring procedures (applying, testing and interviewing for a job) carried out in wheelchair accessible locations using accessible formats, such as a reader, tactile information, Braille, audio cassette for vision impaired people, written materials, sign language interpreters for hearing impaired people, and personal assistance for people with manual impairments?

Yes ☐ No ☐ Action/Due Date: _____

11. Have you made sure that employment tests are selected and administered in a way to ensure that test results accurately reflect the skills or aptitude necessary to perform the job rather than reflect the impaired sensory, manual or speaking skills of the applicant or employee, unless the sensory, speaking, or manual ability is necessary to perform critical element(s) of the job?

Yes ☐ No ☐ Action/Due Date: _____

12. Have you made sure that your employment application forms do not contain questions as to whether an applicant is an individual with a disability?

Yes ☐ No ☐ Action/Due Date: _____

13. If your business conditions an offer of employment based upon the job applicant's satisfactory completion of a medical examination, do your procedures conform to the requirements of the law prohibiting inquiries as to the nature and severity of disabilities except as they are job-related?

Yes ☐ No ☐ Action/Due Date: _____

14. Have you reviewed your personnel policies and practices to be sure that an applicant or employee who is a recovering alcohol or drug abuser (not currently using alcohol or drugs) is included in accordance with the law?

Yes ☐ No ☐ Action/Due Date: _____

15. Have you posted equal employment opportunity notices in an accessible format (e.g., in large print, Braille, and audio cassette)?

Yes ☐ No ☐ Action/Due Date: _____

16. Have you reviewed medical, hospital, accident, life insurance, and retirement fringe benefits to ensure that they give nondiscriminatory treatment to people with disabilities?

Yes ☐ No ☐ Action/Due Date: _____

17. Are your social and recreational activities accessible to all employees and their relatives and associates?

Yes ☐ No ☐ Action/Due Date: _____

18. Do you have a policy on how to handle contagious diseases?

Yes ☐ No ☐ Action/Due Date: _____

19. Have you considered the creation of an ADA employment committee to assist you in making policy decisions?

Yes ☐ No ☐ Action/Due Date: _____

20. Have you reviewed your interview questions and techniques to determine whether they are nondiscriminatory?

Yes ☐ No ☐ Action/Due Date: _____

G
SELF-EVALUATION CHECKLIST
Local Government ADA Adminstration

Prepared by the National League of Cities' Center for Education and Information Resources.

The following self-evaluation checklist was to assist local government officials ensure that they have met the administrative requirements of Subtitle A of Title II.

1. Have you designated someone to coordinate your efforts to comply with ADA?

Yes ☐ No ☐ Action/Due Date: _____

2. Have you established grievance procedures that incorporate due process standards and that provide for the prompt and equitable solution of complaints of discrimination against an individual with a disability, including job applicants, employees, citizens, and other visitors?

Yes ☐ No ☐ Action/Due Date: _____

3. Do your written materials (publications) include a notice of nondiscrimination?

Yes ☐ No ☐ Action/Due Date: _____

4. When you provide public notices, including employment notices, do your procedures utilize all types of media and displays, e.g., print media, radio/television and other alternatives, such as taped job announcements available over the phone?

Yes ☐ No ☐ Action/Due Date: _____

5. Have you reviewed policies related to hiring, upgrading, promotion, award of tenure, demotion, transfer, layoff, termination, right of return from layoff and rehiring to ensure they are not discriminatory?

Yes ☐　No ☐　Action/Due Date: _____

6. Have you reviewed medical, hospital, accident, life insurance and retirement fringe benefits to ensure that they give nondiscriminatory treatment to people with disabilities?

Yes ☐　No ☐　Action/Due Date: _____

7. Are the social and recreational activities offered by your local government accessible to all employees and their friends and relatives with disabilities?

Yes ☐　No ☐　Action/Due Date: _____

8. Have you notified unions and professional organizations with whom you have collective bargaining or other professional agreements of your nondiscrimination policy?

Yes ☐　No ☐　Action/Due Date: _____

9. Have you made sure that individuals with disabilities are allowed the opportunity to participate as members of your planning or advisory boards?

Yes ☐　No ☐　Action/Due Date: _____

H
SELF-EVALUATION CHECKLIST
Title III (Public Accommodations)

Developed by the Texas Governor's Committee for Disabled Persons, in conjunction with the Office for Civil Rights at the U.S. Department of Health and Human Services, Region IV.

The questions in the following self-evaluation guide were designed to help places of public accommodation come into compliance with Title III of the ADA.

As a local government official, you may wish to determine if your current building code requires places of public accommodation and commercial facilities to meet these ADA requirements. You can also share a copy of this self-evaluation checklist with businesses trying to comply with Title III of the Act.

1. Is nondiscriminatory treatment given directly or through contractual licensing or other arrangements to people with disabilities that affords them full and equal enjoyment of the goods, services, facilities, privileges, advantages or accommodations as are afforded to other as individuals? Are you sure that the goods, services, etc. are not provided differently or separately unless such action is necessary to ensure that they are as effective as those provided to others?

Yes ☐ No ☐ Action/Due Date: _____

2. Are the goods, services, facilities, privileges, advantages, and accommodations of all private entities covered by Title III are offered and provided to an individual with a disability in the most integrated setting (same settingoffered to others) appropriate to the needs of the individual?

Yes ☐ No ☐ Action/Due Date: _____

3. Even if separate or different programs or activities are provided for individuals with disabilities, are you sure that they are not denied the opportunity to participate in those that are not separate or different if they so choose?

Yes ☐ No ☐ Action/Due Date: _____

4. Have business entities and contractors utilized, directly and/or through contractual or other arrangements, use only standards or criteria or methods of administration that do not have the effect of discrimination by others that are subject to common administrative control?

Yes ☐ No ☐ Action/Due Date: _____

5. Are you sure that people with friends, associates or relative with a disability are provided goods, services, facilities, privileges, advantages, accommodations and other opportunities on a nondiscriminatory basis?

Yes ☐ No ☐ Action/Due Date: _____

6. Are you confident that eligibility criteria screen in, not out, individuals with disabilities (unless such criteria can be shown to be necessary for the provision of the goods, services, etc...being offered)?

Yes ☐ No ☐ Action/Due Date: _____

7. Have private entities made reasonable modifications to policies, practices or procedures, when such modifications are necessary to offer goods or services, etc., to individuals with disabilities, unless doing so would fundamentally alter the goods or services, etc.?

Yes ☐ No ☐ Action/Due Date: _____

8. Are people with disabilities included, allowed services, integrated and otherwise treated the same as others through the provision of auxiliary aids and services, unless doing so would fundamentally alter the nature of the goods or services?

Yes ☐   No ☐   Action/Due Date: _____

9. Have architectural barriers and communication barriers that are structural in nature, including permanent, temporary or movable structures, such as furniture, equipment and display racks, been removed from existing facilities where such removal is "readily achievable"?

Yes ☐   No ☐   Action/Due Date: _____

10. Where removal of a barrier is not "readily achievable," have goods, services, etc., been made available through alternative methods if such methods are "readily achievable"?

Yes ☐   No ☐   Action/Due Date: _____

11. All new construction with a first occupancy date after January 26, 1993 (and a permit issuance date after January 26, 1992) must be accessible. Have your building codes and permitting process been changed to reflect this new requirement? Do builders know that all new construction must be readily accessible to and usable by individuals with disabilities?

Yes ☐   No ☐   Action/Due Date: _____

12. If a building owner or leasor is altering a facility, alterations must be made in such a manner that, to the maximum extent feasible, the altered portions of the facility are readily accessible to and usable by individuals with disabilities, including individuals who use wheelchairs. Have you changed your building code to reflect this change, subject to the "not to exceed 20 percent of the total alteration cost" provision?

Yes ☐   No ☐   Action/Due Date: _____

Resource for ADA Accessibility Guidelines:

For more information on accessibility guidelines for businesses and local governments, you can contact:

Architectural and Transportation Barriers Compliance Board (ATBCB)
1111 18th Street NW, Suite 50
Washington, DC 20036-3894
(800) 872-2253

The ATBCB published the ADA Accessibility Guidelines in conjunction with the U.S. Department of Justice regulations implementing Title III in the *Federal Register* on Friday, July 26, 1991.

Note: The Texas Governor's Committee for Disabled Persons is not a regulatory or enforcement body for the Americans with Disabilities Act. This self-evaluation guide developed by the Governor's Committee is a tool for identifying and eliminating potential problem areas identified in the law.

I
ARCHITECTURAL
BARRIERS CHECKLIST

This checklist is designed to give local governments a very quick appraisal of potential problem areas for achieving accessibility and when making structural changes.

Building Access	**Yes**	**No**
1. Are 96" wide parking spaces designated with a 60" access aisle?	☐	☐
2. Are accessible parking spaces near the main building entrance?	☐	☐
3. Is there a "drop off" zone at building entrance?	☐	☐
4. Is the gradient from parking to building entrance 1:20 or less?	☐	☐
5. Is the clearance of the entrance doorway at least 32" wide?	☐	☐
6. Is door handle easy to grasp?	☐	☐
7. Is door easy to open (less than 8 lbs. pressure)?	☐	☐
8. Are other than revolving doors available?	☐	☐

Building Corridors	**Yes**	**No**
1. Is path of travel free of obstruction and wide enough for a wheelchair?	☐	☐

2. Is floor surface hard and not slippery? ☐ ☐

3. Do obstacles (phones, fountains) protrude no more than 4"? ☐ ☐

4. Are elevator controls low enough (48") to be reached from a wheelchair? ☐ ☐

5. Are elevator markings in Braille for the blind? ☐ ☐

6. Does elevator provide audible signals for the blind? ☐ ☐

7. Does elevator interior provide a turning area of 51" for wheelchair? ☐ ☐

Restrooms   Yes   No

1. Are restrooms near building entrance and/or personnel office? ☐ ☐

2. Do doors have lever handles? ☐ ☐

3. Are doors at least 32" wide? ☐ ☐

4. Is restroom large enough for wheelchair turnaround (51" minimum)? ☐ ☐

5. Are stall doors at least 32" wide? ☐ ☐

6. Are grab bars provided in toilet stalls? ☐ ☐

7. Are sinks at least 30" high with room for a wheelchair to roll under? ☐ ☐

8. Are sink handles easily reached and used? ☐ ☐

9. Are soap dispensers, towels, etc. no more than 48" from floor? ☐ ☐

10. Are exposed hot water pipes located under sinks wrapped in insulation to avoid injury to those individuals using a wheelchair? ☐ ☐

City Departments that Serve the General Public

Yes No

1. Are doors at least 32" wide? ☐ ☐

2. Is the door easy to open? ☐ ☐

3. Is the threshold no more than 1/2" high? ☐ ☐

4. Is the path of travel between desk, tables, etc. wide enough for wheelchairs? ☐ ☐

5. Do you have a counter that is too high to serve individuals in wheelchairs? ☐ ☐

J

CALENDAR OF EFFECTIVE DATES

August 26, 1990

Title II B — All buses and other some other transit vehicles ordered on or after that date must be accessible.

January 26, 1992

Title II A — Public employers with 25 or more employees must follow Section 504 rule (28 CFR Part 41) until July 26, 1992 (then they follow EEOC rule).

Title II A — Public employers with 15 - 24 employees must follow Section 504 rule until January 26, 1994 (then they follow EEOC rule).

Title II A — All public employers with less than 15 employees must comply with the Section 504 rule, as it pertains to employment.

Title II A — State and local government programs must be accessible to disabled persons.

Title II A — Emergency systems (911) must have equipment for hearing and speech impaired persons in place.

Titles II & III — Public bldgs. and places of public accommodation must be accessible, if nonstructural changes are required.

Title III — Public accommodations cannot discriminate against persons with disabilities in access to goods, services, facilities, etc.

July 26, 1992

Title I — Employers with 25 or more employees must follow EEOC requirements for employment.

	Title II A — Transition plan must be completed if structural changes are needed.
January 26, 1993	Title II A — Self-evaluation plan must be completed.
	Title III — Public accommodations designed for first occupancy on or after this date must be accessible.
July 26, 1993	Title IV — Telecommunication relay services must be in place.
July 26, 1994	Title I — All employers with 15 or more employees must follow EEOC rules regarding employment.
January 26, 1995	Title III — Public accommodations that required structural changes must be accessible.
July 26, 1995	Title II B — Rail systems must have at least one accessible car per train.

K

ADA TRANSITION PLAN

Prepared by the National League of Cities' Center for Education and Information Services

Use this transition plan to document those architectural barriers that need to be removed. The deadline for completing this plan, not the changes, is July 26, 1992. After you have completed your self-evaluation checklists and architectural barriers checklist, you are now ready to prepare your transition plan. Use this form for each facility that needs structural modification. If your local government employs more than fifty people, you must retain this transition plan for three years and make it available for public inspection.

Date: _____

Name of person completing the plan: _____

Name of the ADA coordinator: _____

Address of the facility: _____

List public services offered at this location:

_____

_____

_____

_____

_____

_____

_____

_____

List all structural modifications to be made and their location:

Modification	Location	Complete By:
_____	_____	_____
_____	_____	_____
_____	_____	_____
_____	_____	_____
_____	_____	_____
_____	_____	_____
_____	_____	_____

List the names, organizations and phone nubmers of the disabled persons who served as advisors:

Name/Organization	Phone
_____	_____
_____	_____
_____	_____
_____	_____
_____	_____
_____	_____
_____	_____
_____	_____
_____	_____

L
AMERICANS WITH DISABILITIES ACT OF 1990

This appendix presents the full text of the Americans with Disabilities Act of 1990 (42 U.S.C. Sec. 12101 Note).

SECTION 1. SHORT TITLE; TABLE OF CONTENTS.

(a) SHORT TITLE. - This Act may be cited as the "Americans with Disabilities Act of 1990."

(b) TABLE OF CONTENTS. - The table of contents is as follows:

SEC. 2. FINDINGS AND PURPOSES.

(a) FINDINGS. - The Congress finds that -

(1) some 43,000,000 Americans have one or more physical or mental disabilities, and this number is increasing as the population as a whole is growing older;

(2) historically, society has tended to isolate and segregate individuals with disabilities, and, despite some improvements, such forms of discrimination against individuals with disabilities continue to be a serious and persuasive social problem;

(3) discrimination against individuals with disabilities persists in such critical area as employment, housing, public accommodations, eduction, transportation, communication, recreation, institutionalization, health services, voting, and access to public services;

(4) unlike individuals who have experience discrimination on the basis of race, color, sex, national origin, religion, or age, individuals who have experience discrimination on the basis of disability have often had no legal recourse to redress such discrimination;

(5) individuals with disabilities continually encounter various forms of discrimination, including outright intentional exclusion, the discriminatory effects of architectural, transportation, and communication barriers, overprotective rules and policies, failure to make modifications to existing facilities and practices, exclusionary qualification standards and criteria, segregation, and relegation to lesser services, programs, activities, benefits, jobs, or other opportunities;

(6) census data, national polls, and other studies have documented that people with disabilities, as a group, occupy an inferior status in our society, and are severely disadvantage socially, vocationally, economically, and educationally;

(7) individuals with disabilities are a discrete and insular minority who have been faced with restrictions and limitations, subjected to a history of purposeful unequal treatment, and related to a position of political powerlessness in our society, based on characteristics that are beyond the control of such individuals and resulting from stereotypic assumptions not truly indicative of the individual ability of such individuals to participate in, and contribute to, society;

(8) the Nation's proper goals regarding individuals with disabilities are to assure equality of opportunity, full participation, independent living, and economic self - sufficiency for such individuals; and

(9) the continuing existence of unfair and unnecessary discrimination and prejudice denies people with disabilities the opportunity to compete on an equal basis and to pursue those opportunities for which our free society is justifiably famous, and costs the United States billions of dollars in unnecessary expenses resulting from dependency and nonproductivity.

(b) **PURPOSE.** - It is the purpose of this Act -

(1) to provide a clear and comprehensive national mandate for the elimination of discrimination against individuals with disabilities;

(2) to provide clear, strong, consistent, enforceable standards addressing discrimination against individuals with disabilities;

(3) to ensure that the Federal Government plays a central role in enforcing the standards established in this Act on behalf of individuals with disabilities; and

(4) to invoke the sweep of congressional authority, including the power to enforce the fourteenth amendment and to regulate commerce, in order to address the major areas of discrimination faced day-to-day by people with disabilities.

SEC. 3. DEFINITIONS.

As used in this Act:
(1) AUXILIARY AIDS AND SERVICES. - The term "auxiliary aid and services: includes -
(A) qualified interpreters or other effective methods of making aurally delivered materials available to individuals with hearing impairments;
(B) qualified readers, taped texts, or other effective methods of making visually delivered materials available to individuals with visual impairments;
(C) acquisition or modification of equipment or devices; and
(D) other similar services and actions.
(2) DISABILITY. - The term "disability" means, with respect to an individual
(A) a physical or mental impairment that substantially limits one or more of the major life activities of such individual;
(B) a record of such an impairment; or
(C) being regarded as having such an impairment
(3) STATE. - The term "State means each of the several States, the District of Columbia, the Commonwealth of Puerto Rico, Guam, American Samoa, the Virgin Islands, the Trust Territory of the Pacific Islands and the Commonwealth of the Northern Mariana Islands.

TITLE I EMPLOYMENT

SEC. 101. DEFINITIONS.

As used in this title:
(1) COMMISSION. - The term "Commission" means the Equal Employment Opportunity Commission established by section 705 of the Civil Rights Act of 1964 (42 U.S.C. 2000e - 4).
(2) COVERED ENTITY. - The term "covered entity" means an employer, employment agency, labor organization, or joint labor - management committee.
(3) DIRECT THREAT. - The term "direct threat" means a significant risk to the health or safety of others that cannot be eliminated by reasonable accommodation.
(4) EMPLOYEE. - The term "employee" means an individual employed by an employer.
(5) EMPLOYER. -
(A) IN GENERAL. - The term "employer means a person engaged in an industry affecting commerce who has 15 or more employees for each working day in each of 20 or more calendar weeks in the current or preceding calendar year, and any agency of such person, except that, for two years following the effective date of this title, an employer means a person engaged in an industry affecting commerce who has 25 or more employees for each working day in each of 20 or more calendar weeks in the current or preceding year, and any agent of such person.
(B) EXCEPTIONS. - The term "employer does not include -
i) the United States, a corporation wholly owned by the government of the United States, or an Indian tribe; or

(ii) a bona fide private membership club (other than a labor organization) that is exempt from taxation under section 501(c) of the Internal Revenue Code of 1986.

(6) ILLEGAL USE OF DRUGS. -

(A) IN GENERAL. - The term "illegal use of drugs" means the use of drugs, the possession or distribution of which is unlawful under the Controlled Substances Act (21 U.S.C. 812). Such term does not include the use of a drug taken under supervision by a licensed health care professional, or other uses authorized by the Controlled Substances Act or other provisions of Federal law.

(B) DRUGS. - The term "drug" means a controlled substance, as defined in schedules I through V of section 202 of the Controlled Substances Act.

(7) PERSON, ETC. - The terms "person," "labor organization," "employment agency," "commerce," and "industry affecting commerce" shall have the same meaning given such terms in section 701 of the Civil Rights Act of 1964 (42 U.S.C. 2000e).

(8) QUALIFIED INDIVIDUAL WITH A DISABILITY. - The term "qualified individual with a disability" means an individual with a disability who, with or without reasonable accommodation, can perform the essential functions of the employment position that such individual holds or desires. For the purposes of this title, consideration shall be given to the employer's judgment as to what functions of a job are essential, and if an employer has prepared a written description before advertising or interviewing applicants for the job, this description shall be considered evidence of the essential functions of the job.

(9) REASONABLE ACCOMMODATION. - The term "reasonable accommodation" may include -

(A) making existing facilities used by employees readily accessible to and usable by individuals with disabilities; and

(B) job restructuring, part - time or modified work schedules, reassignment to a vacant position, acquisition or modification of equipment or devises, appropriate adjustment or modifications of examinations training materials or policies, the provision of qualified readers or interpreters, and other similar accommodations for individuals with disabilities.

(10) UNDUE HARDSHIP. -

(A) IN GENERAL. - The term "undue hardship" means an action requiring significant difficulty or expense, when considered in light of the factors set forth in subparagraph (B).

(B) FACTORS TO BE CONSIDERED. - In determining whether an accommodation would impose an undue hardship on a covered entity, factors to be considered include -

(i) the nature and cost of the accommodation needed under this Act;

(ii) the overall financial resources of the facility or facilities involved in the provision of the reasonable accommodation; the number of persons employed at such facility; the effect on expenses and resources, or the impact otherwise of such accommodation upon the operation of the facility;

(iii) the overall financial resources of the covered entity; the overall size of the business of a covered entity with respect to the number of its employees; the number, type, and location of its facilities; and

(iv) the type of operation or operations of the covered entity, including the composition, structure, and functions of the workforce of such entity; the geographic separateness. administrative, or fiscal relationship of the facility or facilities in question to the covered entity.

SEC. 102. DISCRIMINATION.

(a) GENERAL RULE. - No covered entity shall discriminate against a qualified individual with a disability because of the disability of such individual in regard to job application procedures, the hiring, advancement, or discharge of employees, employee compensation, job training, and other terms, conditions, and privileges of employment.

(b) CONSTRUCTION. - As used in subsection (a), the term "discriminate" includes -

(1) limiting, segregating, or classifying a job applicant or employee in a way that adversely affects the opportunities or status of such applicant or employee because of the disability of such applicant or employee;

(2) participating in a contractual or other arrangement or relationship that has the effect of subjecting a covered entity's qualified applicant or employee with a disability to the discrimination prohibited by this title (such relationship includes a relationship with an employment or referral agency, labor union, an organization providing fringe benefits to an employee of the covered entity, or an organization providing training and apprenticeship programs);

(3) utilizing standards, criteria, or methods of administration -

(A) that have the effect of discrimination on the basis of disability; or

(B) that perpetuate the discrimination of others who are subject to common administrative control;

(4) excluding or otherwise denying equal jobs or benefits to a qualified individual because of the known disability of an individual with whom the qualified individual is known to have a relationship or association;

(5)(A) not making reasonable accommodations to the known physical or mental limitations of an otherwise qualified individual with a disability who is an applicant or employee, unless such covered entity can demonstrate that the accommodation would impose an undue hardship or the operation of the business of such covered entity; or

(B) denying employment opportunities to a job applicant or employee who is an otherwise qualified individual with a disability, if such denial is based on the need of such covered entity to make reasonable accommodation to the physical or mental impairments of the employee or applicant;

(6) using qualification standards, employment tests or other selection criteria that screen out or tend to screen out an individual with a disability or a class of individuals with disabilities unless the standard, test or other selection criteria, as used by the covered entity, is shown to be job - related for the position in question and is consistent wit business necessity; and

(7) failing to select and administer tests concerning employment in the most effective manner to ensure that, when such test is administered to a job applicant or employee who has a disability that impairs sensor,

manual, or speaking skills, such tests results accurately reflect the skills, aptitude or whatever other factor os such applicant or employee that such test purports to measure, rather than reflecting the impaired sensory, manual, or speaking skills of such employee or applicant (except where such skills are the factors that the test purports to measure).

(c) MEDICAL EXAMINATIONS AND INQUIRIES. -

(1) IN GENERAL. - The prohibition against discrimination as referred to in subsection (a) shall include medical examinations and inquiries.

(2) PREEMPLOYMENT. -

(A) PROHIBITED EXAMINATION OR INQUIRY. - Except as provided in paragraph (3), a covered entity shall not conduct a medical examination or make inquiries of a job applicant as to whether such applicant is an individual with a disability or as to the nature or severity of such disabilities

(B) ACCEPTABLE INQUIRY. - A covered entity may make preemployment inquiries into the ability of an applicant to perform job - related functions.

(3) EMPLOYMENT ENTRANCE EXAMINATION. - A covered entity may require a medical examination after an offer of employment has been made to a job applicant and prior to the commencement of the employment duties of such applicant, and may condition an offer of employment on the results of such examination, if -

(A) All entering employees are subjected to such an examination regardless of disability;

(B) information obtained regarding the medical condition or history of the applicant is collected and maintained on separate forms and in separate medical files and is treated as a confidential medical record, except that -

(i) Supervisors and managers may be informed regarding necessary restrictions on the work or duties of the employee and necessary accommodations;

(ii) first aid and safety personnel may be informed, when appropriate, if the disability might require emergency treatment; and

(iii) government officials investigating compliance with this Act shall be provided relevant information on request; and

(C) the results of such examination are used only in accordance with this title.'

(4) EXAMINATION AND INQUIRY. -

(A) PROHIBITED EXAMINATIONS AND INQUIRIES. - A covered entity shall not require a medical examination and shall not make inquiries of an employee as to whether such employee is an individual with a disability or as to the nature or severity of the disability, unless such examination or inquiry is shown to be job - related and consistent with business necessity.

(B) ACCEPTABLE EXAMINATIONS AND INQUIRIES. - A covered entity may conduct voluntary medical examinations, including voluntary medical histories, which are part of an employee health program and available to employees at the work site. A| covered entity may make inquiries into the ability of an employee to perform job - related functions.

(C) REQUIREMENT. - Information obtained under subparagraph (B) regarding the medical condition or history of any employee are subject to the requirements of subparagraphs (B) and (C) of paragraph (3).

SEC. 103. DEFENSES.

(a) IN GENERAL. - It may be a defense to a charge of discrimination under this Act that an alleged application of qualification standards, tests, or selection criteria that screen out or tend to screen out or otherwise deny a job or benefit to an individual with a disability has been shown to be job - related and consistent with business necessity, and such performance cannot be accomplished by reasonable accommodation, as required under this title.

(b) QUALIFICATION STANDARDS. - The term "qualification standards" may include a requirement that an individual shall not pose a direct threat to the health or safety of other individuals in the workplace.

(c) RELIGIOUS ENTITIES. -

(1) IN GENERAL. - This title shall not prohibit a religious corporation, association,educational institution, or society from giving preference in employment to individuals of a particular religion to perform work connected with the carrying on by such corporation, association, educational institution, or society of its activities.

(2) RELIGIOUS TENETS REQUIREMENTS. - Under this title, a religious organization may require that all applicants and employees conform to the religious tenets of such organization.

(b) LIST OF INFECTIOUS AND COMMUNICABLE DISEASES. -

(1) IN GENERAL. - The Secretary of Health and Human Services, not later than 6 months after the date of enactment of this Act, shall -

(A) review all infectious and communicable diseases which may be transmitted through handling the food supply;

(B) publish a list of infectious and communicable diseases which are transmitted through handling the food supply;

(C) publish the methods by which such diseases are transmitted; and

(D) widely disseminate such information regarding the list of diseases and their modes of transmissibility to the general public.

Such list shall be updated annually.

(2) APPLICATIONS. - In any case in which an individual has an infectious or communicable disease that is transmitted to others through the handling of food, that is included on the list developed by the Secretary of health and Human Services under paragraph (1), and which cannot be eliminated by reasonable accommodation, a covered entity may refuse to assign or continue to assign such individual to a job involving food handling.

(3) CONSTRUCTION. - Nothing in this Act shall be construed to preempt, modify, or amend any State, county, or local law, ordinance, or regulation applicable to food handling which is designed to protect the public health from individuals who pose a significant risk to the health or safety of others, which cannot be eliminated by reasonable accommodation, pursuant to the list of infectious or communicable diseases and the modes of transmissibility published by the Secretary of Health and Human Services.

SEC. 104. ILLEGAL USE OF DRUGS AND ALCOHOL

(a) QUALIFIED INDIVIDUAL WITH A DISABILITY. - For purposes of this title, the term "qualified individual with a disability" shall not include any employee or applicant who is currently engaged in the illegal use of drugs, when the cored entity acts on the basis of such use.

(b) RULES OF CONSTRUCTION. - Nothing in subsection (a) shall be construed to exclude as a qualified individual with a disability an individual who -

(1) has successfully completed a supervised drug rehabilitation program and is no longer engaging in the illegal use of drugs, or has otherwise been rehabilitated successfully and is no longer engaging in such use;

(2) is participating in a supervised rehabilitation program and is no longer engaging in such use; or

(3) is erroneously regarded as engaging in such use, but is not engaging in such use;

except that it shall not be a violation of this Act for a covered entity to adopt or administer reasonable policies or procedures, including but not limited to drug testing, designed to ensure that an individual described in paragraph (1) or (2) is no longer engaging in the illegal use of drugs.

(c) AUTHORITY OF COVERED ENTITY. - A covered entity -

(1) may prohibit the illegal use of drugs and the use of alcohol at the workplace by all employees;

(2) may require that employees shall not be under the influence of alcohol or be engaging in the illegal use of drugs at the workplace;

(3) may require that employees behave in conformance with the requirements established under the Drug - Free Workplace Act of 1988 (41 U.S.C. 701 et seq.);

(4) may hold an employee who engages in the illegal use of drugs or who is an alcoholic to the same qualification standards for employment or job performance and behavior that such entity holds other employees, even if any unsatisfactory performance or behavior is related to the drug use or alcoholism of such employee; and

(5) may, with respect to federal regulations regarding alcohol and the illegal use of drugs, require that

(A) employees comply with the standards established in such regulations of the |department of Defense, if the employees of the covered entity are employed in an industry subject to such regulations, including complying with regulations (if any) that apply to employment in sensitive positions in such an industry, in the case of employees of the covered entity who are employed in such positions (as defined in the regulations of the Department of Defense);

(B) employees comply with the standards established in such regulations of the nuclear Regulatory Commission, if the employee of the covered entity are employed in an industry subject to sucn rugulations, including complying with regulation (if any) that apply to employment in sensitive positions in such an industry, in the case of employees of the covered entity who are employed in such positions (as defined in the regulations of the Nuclear Regulatory Commission); and

(C) employees comply with the standards established in such regulations of the Department of Transportation, if the employees of the covered entity are employed in a transportation industry subject to such regulations, including complying with such regulations (if any) that apply to employment in sensitive positions in such an industry, in the case of employees of the covered entity who are employed in such positions (as defined in the regulations of the d = Department of Transportation).

(d) DRUG TESTING. -

(1) IN GENERAL. - For purposes of this title, a test to determine the illegal use of drugs shall not be considered a medical examination.

2 CONSTRUCTION. - Nothing in this title shall be construed to encourage, prohibit, or authorize the conducting of drug testing for the illegal use of drugs by job applicants or employees or making employment decisions based on such test results.

(e) TRANSPORTATION EMPLOYEES. - Nothing in this title shall be construed to encourage, prohibit, restrict, or authorize the otherwise lawful exercise by entities subject t the jurisdiction of the Department of Transportation of authority to -

(1) test employees or such entities in, and applicants for, positions involving safety - sensitive duties for the illegal use of drugs nd for on - duty impairment by alcohol; and

(2) remove such persons who test positive for illegal use of drugs and on - duty impairment by alcohol pursuant to paragraph (1) from safety - sensitive duties in implementing subsection (c).

SEC. 105. POSTING NOTICES.

Every employer, employment agency, labor organization, or joint labor - management committee covered under this title shall post notices in an accessible format to applicants, employees, and members describing the applicable provisions of this Act, in the manner prescribed by section 711 of the Civil Rights Act of 1964 (42 U.S.C. 2000e - 10).

SEC. 106 REGULATIONS.

Not later than 1 year after the date of enactment of this Act, the Commission shall issue regulations in an accessible format to carry out this title in accordance with subchapter II of chapter 5 of title 4, United States Code.

SEC. 107. ENFORCEMENT.

(a) POWERS, REMEDIES, AND PROCEDURES. - The powers, remedies, and procedures set forth in sections 705, 706, 707, 709, and 710 of the Civil Rights Act of 1964 (42 U.S.C. 2000e - 4, 2000e - 5, 2000e - 6, 2000e - 8, and 2000e - 9) shall be the powers, remedies, and procedures this title provides to the Commission, to the Attorney general, or to any person alleging discrimination on the basis of disability in violation of any provision of this Act, or regulations promulgated under section 106, concerning employment.

(b) COORDINATION. - The agencies with enforcement authority for actions which allege employment discrimination under this title and under the Rehabilitation Act of 1973 shall develop procedures to ensure that administrative complaints filed under this title and under the Rehabilitation Act of 1973 are dealt with in a manner that avoids duplication of effort and prevents imposition of inconsistent or conflicting standards for the same requirements under this title and the Rehabilitation Act of 1973. The Commission, the Attorney General, and the Office of Federal Contract Compliance Programs shall establish such coordinating mechanisms similar to provisions contained in the joint regulations promulgated by the Commission and the Attorney General at part 42 of title 28 and part 1691 of title 29, Code of Federal Regulations, and the Memorandum of Understanding between the Commission and the Office of Federal Contract Compliance Programs dated January 16, 1981 (46 Fed. Reg. 7435, January 23, 1981) in regulations implementing this title and the Rehabilitation Act of 1973 not later than 18 months after the date of enactment of this Act.

SEC. 108. EFFECTIVE DATE.

This title shall become effective 24 months after the date of enactment.

TITLE II - PUBLIC SERVICES

Subtitle A - Prohibition Against Discrimination and Other Generally Applicable Provisions

SEC. 201. DEFINITION.

As used in this title:
(1) PUBLIC ENTITY. - The term "public entity" means -
(A) any state or local government;
(B) any department, agency, special purpose district, or other instrumentality of a State or States or local government; and
(C) the National Railroad Passenger Corporation, and any commuter authority (as defined in section 103(8) of the Rail Passenger Service Act).
(2) QUALIFIED INDIVIDUAL WITH A DISABILITY. - The term "qualified individual with a disability" means an individual with a disability who, with or without reasonable modifications to rules, policies, or practices, the removal of architectural, communication, or transportation barriers, or the provision of auxiliary aids and services, meets the essential eligibility requirements for the receipt of services or the participation in programs or activities provided by a public entity.

SEC. 202. DISCRIMINATION.

Subject to the provisions of this title, no qualified individual with a disability shall, by reason of such disability, be excluded from participation in or be denied the benefits of the services, programs, or activities of a public entity, or be subjected to discrimination by any such entity.

SEC. 203. ENFORCEMENT.

The remedies, procedures, and rights set forth in section 505 of the Rehabilitation Ac of 1973 929 U.S.C. 794a) shall be the remedies, procedures and rights this title provides to any person alleging discrimination no the basis of disability in violation of section 202.

SEC. 204. REGULATIONS.

(a) IN GENERAL. - Not later than 1 year after the date of enactment of this Act, the Attorney General shall promulgate regulations in an accessible format that implement this subtitle. Such regulations shall not include any matter within the scope o the authority of the Secretary of Transportation under section 223, 229, or 244.
(b) RELATIONSHIP TO OTHER REGULATIONS. - Except for "program accessibility, existing facilities" and communications," regulations under subsection (a) shall be consistent with this Act and with the coordination regulations under part 41 of title 28, Code of Federal Regulations (as promulgated by the Department of Health, Education, and Welfare on January 13, 1978), applicable to recipients of Federal financial assistance under section 504 of the Rehabilitation Act of 1973 929 U.S.C. 794). With respect to "program accessibility, existing facilities" and "communications" such regulations shall be consistent with regulations and analysis as in part 39 of title 28 of the Code of Federal Regulations, applicable to federally conducted activities under such section 504.
(c) STANDARDS. - Regulations under subsection (a) shall include standards applicable to facilities and vehicles covered by this subtitle, other than facilities, stations, rail passenger cars, and vehicles covered by subtitle . Such standards shall be consistent with the minimum guidelines and requirements issued by the Architectural and Transportation Barriers Compliance Board in accordance with section 504(a) of this Act.

SEC. 205. EFFECTIVE DATE.

(a) GENERAL RULE. - Except as provided in subsection (b), this subtitle shall become effective 18 months after the date of enactment of this Act.
(b) EXCEPTION. - Section 204 shall become effective on the date of the enactment of this Act.

Subtitle B - Actions Applicable to Public Transportation Provided by Public Entities Considered Discriminatory

PART I - PUBLIC TRANSPORTATION OTHER THAN BY AIRCRAFT OR CERTAIN RAIL OPERATIONS

SEC. 221. DEFINITIONS.

(1) DEMAND RESPONSIVE SYSTEM. - The term "demand responsive system" means any system of providing designated public transportation which is not a fixed route system.

(2) DESIGNATED PUBLIC TRANSPORTATION. - The term "designated public transportation" means transportation (other than public school transportation) by bus, rail, or any other conveyance (other than transportation by aircraft or intercity or commuter rail transportation (as defined in section 241) that provides the general public with general or special service (including charter service) on a regular and continuing basis.

(3) FIXED ROUTE SYSTEM. - The term "fixed - route system" means a system of providing designated public transportation on which a vehicle is operated along a prescribed route according to a fixed schedule.

(4) OPERATIONS. - The term "operations", as used with respect to a fixed route system or demand responsive system, includes operation of such system by a person under a contractual or other arrangement or relationship with a public entity.

(5) PUBLIC SCHOOL TRANSPORTATION. - The term "public school transportation" means transportation by schoolbus vehicles of schoolchildren, personnel, and equipment to and from a public elementary or secondary school and school - related activities.

(6) SECRETARY. - The term "Secretary" means the Secretary of Transportation.

SEC.222. PUBLIC ENTITIES OPERATING FIXED ROUTE SYSTEMS.

(a) PURCHASE AND LEASE OF NEW VEHICLES. - It shall be considered discrimination for purposes of section 202 of this Act and section 504 of the Rehabilitation Act of 1973 (29 U.S.C. 794) for a public entity which operates a fixed route system to purchase or lease a new bus, a new rapid rail vehicle, new light rail vehicle, or any other new vehicle to be used on such system, if the solicitation for such purchase or else is made after the 30th day following the effective date of this subsection and if such bus, rail vehicle, or other vehicle is not readily accessible to and usable by individuals with disabilities, including individuals who use wheelchairs.

(b) PURCHASE AND LEASE OF USED VEHICLES. - Subject to subsection (c)(1), it shall be considered discrimination for purposes of section 202 of this Act and section 504 of the Rehabilitation Act of 1973 (29 U.S.C. 794) for a public entity which operates a fixed route system to purchase or lease, after the 30th day following the effective date of this subsection, a used vehicle for use on such system unless such entity makes demonstrated good faith efforts to purchase or lease a used vehicle for use on such system that is readily accessible to and usable by individuals with disabilities, including individuals who use wheelchairs.

(c) REMANUFACTURED VEHICLES. -

(1) GENERAL RULE. - Except as provided in paragraph (2), it shall be considered discrimination for purposes of section 202 of this Act and section 504 of the Rehabilitation Act of 1973 (29 U.S.C. 794) for a public entity which operates a fixed route system -

(A) to remanufacture a vehicle for use on such system so as to extent its usable life for 5 years or more, which remanufacture begins (or for which the solicitation is made) after the 30th day following the effective date of this subsection; or

(B) to purchase or lease for use on such system a remanufactured vehicle which has been remanufactured so as to extend its usable life for 5 years or more, which purchase or lease occurs after such 30th day and during the period in which the usable life is extended;

unless, after remanufacture, the vehicle is, to the maximum extent feasible, readily accessible to and usable by individuals with disabilities, including individuals who use wheelchairs.

(2) EXCEPTION FOR HISTORIC VEHICLES. -

(A) GENERAL RULE. - If a public entity operates a fixed route system any segment of which is included on the national Register of Historic Places and if making a vehicle of historic character to used solely on such segment readily accessible to and usable by individuals with disabilities would significantly alter the historic character of such vehicle, the public entity only has to make (or to purchase or lease a remanufactured vehicle with) those modifications which are necessary to meet the requirements of paragraph (1) and which do not significantly alter the historic character of such vehicle.

(B) VEHICLES OF HISTORIC CHARACTER DEFINED BY REGULATIONS. - For purposes of this paragraph and section 228(b), a vehicle of historic character shall be defined by the regulations issued by the Secretary to carry out this subsection.

SEC. 223. PARATRANSIT AS A COMPLEMENT TO FIXED ROUTE SERVICE.

(a) GENERAL RULE. - It shall be considered discrimination for purposes of section 202 of this Act and section 504 of the Rehabilitation Act of 1973 (29 U.S.C. 794) for a public entity which operates a fixed route system (other than a system which provides solely commuter bus service) to fail to provide with respect to the operations of its fixed route system, in accordance with this section, paratransit and other special transportation services to individuals with disabilities, including individuals who use wheelchairs, that are sufficient to provide to such individuals a level of service (1) which is comparable to the level of designated public transportation services provided to individuals without disabilities using such system; or (2) in the case of response time, which is comparable, to the extent practicable, to the level of designated public transportation services provided to individuals without disabilities using such system.

(b) ISSUANCE OF REGULATIONS. - Not later than 1 year after the effective date of this subsection, the Secretary shall issue final regulations to carry out this section.

(c) REQUIRED CONTENTS OF REGULATIONS. -

(1) ELIGIBLE RECIPIENTS OF SERVICE. - The regulations issued under this section shall require Each public entity which operates a fixed route system to provide the

(A)(i) to any individual with a disability who is unable, as a result of a physical or mental impairment (including a vision impairment) and without the assistance of another individual (except an operator of a wheelchair lift or other boarding assistance device), to board, ride, or disembark from any vehicle on the system which is readily accessible to and usable by individuals with disabilities;

(ii) to any individual with a disability who needs the assistance of a wheelchair lift or other boarding assistance device (and is able with such assistance) to board, ride, and disembark from any vehicle which is readily accessible to and usable by individuals with disabilities if the individual wants to travel on a route on the system during the hours of operation of the system at a time (or within a reasonable period of such time) when such a vehicle is not being used to provide designated public transportation on the route; and

(iii) to any individual with a disability who has a specific impairment - related condition which prevents such individual from traveling to a boarding location or from a disembarking location on such system;

(B) to 1 other individual accompanying the individual with the disability; and

(C) to other individuals, in addition to the one individual described in subparagraph (B), accompanying the individual with a disability provided that space for these additional individuals is available on the paratransit vehicle carrying the individual with a disability and that the transportation of such additional individuals will not result in a denial of service to individuals with disabilities. For purposes of clauses (i) and (ii) of subparagraph (A), boarding or disembarking from a vehicle does not include travel to the boarding location or from the disembarking location.

(2) SERVICE AREA. - The regulations issued under this section shall require the provision of paratransit and special transportation services required under this section in the service area of each public entity which operates a fixed route system, other than any portion of the service in which the public entity solely provides commuter bus service.

(3) SERVICE CRITERIA. - Subject to paragraphs (1) and (2), the regulations issued under this section shall establish minimum service criteria for determining the level of services to be required under this section.

(4) UNDUE FINANCIAL BURDEN LIMITATION. - The regulations issued under this section shall provide that, if the public entity is able to demonstrate to the satisfaction of the Secretary that the provision of paratransit and other special transportation services otherwise required under this section would impose an undue financial burden on the public entity, notwithstanding any other provision of this section (other than paragraph (5)), shall only be required to provide

such services to the extent that providing such services would not impose such a burden.

(5) ADDITIONAL SERVICES. - The regulations issued under this section shall establish circumstances under which the Secretary may require a public entity to provide, notwithstanding paragraph (4), paratransit and other special transportation services under this section beyond the level of paratransit and other special transportation services which would otherwise be required under paragraph (4).

(6) PUBLIC PARTICIPATION. - The regulations issued under this section shall require that each public entity which operates a fixed route system hold a public hearing, provide an opportunity for public comment, and consult with individuals with disabilities in preparing its plan under paragraph (7).

(7) PLANS. - The regulations issued under this section shall require that each public entity which operates a fixed route system -

(A) within 18 month's after the effective date of this subsection, submit to the Secretary, and commence implementation of, a plan for providing paratransit and other special transportation services which meet the requirements of this section; and

(B) on an annual basis thereafter, submit to the Secretary, and commence implementation of a plan for providing such services.

(8) PROVISION OF SERVICES BY OTHERS. - The regulations issued under this section shall -

(A) require that a public entity submitting a plan to the Secretary under this section identify in the plan any person or other public entity which is providing a paratransit or other special transportation service for individuals with disabilities in the service area to which the plan applies; and

(B) provide that the public entity submitting the plan does not have to provide under the plan such service for individuals with disabilities.

(9) OTHER PROVISIONS. - The regulations issued under this section shall include such other provisions and requirements as the Secretary determines are necessary to carry out the objectives of this section.

(d) REVIEW OF PLAN. -

(1) GENERAL RULE. - The Secretary shall review a plan submitted under this section for the purpose of determining whether or not such plan meets the requirements of this section, including the regulations issued under this section.

(2) DISAPPROVAL. - If the Secretary determines that a plan reviewed under this subsection fails to meet the requirements of this section, the Secretary shall disapprove the plan and notify the public entity which submitted the plan of such disapproval and the reasons therefor.

(3) MODIFICATION O DISAPPROVED PLAN. - Not later than 90 days after the date of disapproval of a plan under this subsection, the public entity which submitted the plan shall modify the plan to meet the requirements of this section and shall submit to the Secretary, and commence implementation of, such modified plan.

(e) DISCRIMINATION DEFINED. - As used in subsection (a), the term "discrimination" includes -

(1) a failure of a public entity to which the regulations issued under this section apply to submit, or

commence implementation of, a plan in accordance with subsections (c)(6) and (c)(7);

(2) a failure of such entity to submit, or commence implementation of, a modified plan in accordance with subsection (d)(3);

(3) submission to the Secretary of a modified plan under subsection (d)(3) which does not meet the requirements of this section; or

(4) a failure of such entity to provide paratransit or other special transportation services in accordance with the plan or modified plan the public entity submitted to the Secretary under this section.

(f) STATUTORY CONSTRUCTION. - Nothing in this section shall be construed as preventing a public entity -

(1) from providing paratransit or other special transportation services at a level which is greater than the level of such services which are required by this section,

(2) from providing paratransit or other special transportation services in addition to those paratransit and special transportation services required by this section, or

(3) from providing such services to individuals in addition to those individuals to whom such services are required to be provided by this section.

SEC. 224. PUBLIC ENTITY OPERATING A DEMAND RESPONSIVE SYSTEM.

If a public operates a demand responsive system, it shall be considered discrimination, for purposes of section 202 of this Act and section 504 of the Rehabilitation Act of 1973 (29 U.S.C. 794) for such entity to purchase or lease a new vehicle for use on such system, for which a solicitation is made after the 30th day following the effective date of this section, that is not readily accessible to and usable by individuals with disabilities, including individuals who use wheelchairs, unless such system, when viewed in its entirety, provides a level of service to such individuals equivalent to the level of service such system provides to individuals without disabilities.

SEC. 225. TEMPORARY RELIEF WHERE LIFTS ARE UNAVAILABLE.

(a) GRANTING. - With respect to the purchase of new buses, a public entity may apply for, and the Secretary may temporary relieve such public entity from the obligation under section 222(a) or 224 to purchase new buses that are readily accessible to and usable by individuals with disabilities if such public entity demonstrates to the satisfaction of the Secretary -

(1) that the initial solicitation for new buses made by the public entity specified that all new buses were to be lift - equipped and were to be otherwise accessible to and usable by individuals with disabilities;

(2) the unavailability from any qualified manufacturer of hydraulic, electromechanical, or other lifts for such new buses;

(3) that the public entity seeking temporary relief has made good faith efforts to locate a qualified manufacturer to supply the lifts to the manufacturer of

such buses in sufficient time to comply with such solicitation; and

(4) that any further delay in purchasing new buses necessary to obtain such lifts would significantly impair transportation services in the community served by the pubic entity.

(b) DURATION AND NOTICE TO CONGRESS. - Any relief granted under subsection (a) shall be limited in duration by a specified date, and the appropriate committees of Congress shall be notified of any such relief granted.

(c) FRAUDULENT APPLICATION. - If, at any time, the Secretary has reasonable cause to believe that any relief granted under subsection (a) was fraudulently applied for, the Secretary shall -

(1) cancel such relief if such relief is still in effect; and

(2) take such other action as the Secretary considers appropriate.

SEC. 226. NEW FACILITIES.

For purposes of section 202 of this Act and section 504 of the Rehabilitation Act of 1973 (29 U.S.C. 794), it shall be considered discrimination for a public entity to construct a new facility to be used in the provision of designated public transportation services unless such facility is readily accessible to and usable by individuals with disabilities, including individuals who use wheelchairs.

SEC. 227. ALTERATIONS OF EXISTING FACILITIES.

(a) GENERAL RULE. - With respect to alterations of an existing facility or part thereof used in the provision of designated public transportation services that affect or could affect the usability of the facility or part thereof, it shall be considered discrimination, for purposes of section 2020 of this Act and section 504 of the Rehabilitation Act off 1973 (29 U.S.C. 794), for a public entity to fail to make such alterations (or to ensure that the alterations are made) in such a manner that, to the maximum extent feasible, the altered portions of the facility are readily accessible to and usable by individuals with disabilities, including individuals who use wheelchairs, upon the completion of such alterations. Where the public entity is undertaking an alteration that affects or could affect usability of or access to an area of the facility containing a primary function, the entity, shall also make the alterations in such a manner that, to the maximum extent feasible, the path of travel to the altered area and the bathrooms, telephone, and drinking fountains serving the altered area, are readily accessible to and usable by individuals with disabilities, including individuals who use wheelchairs, upon completion of such alterations, where such alterations to the path of travel or the bathrooms, telephones and drinking fountain serving the altered area are not disproportionate to the overall alterations in terms of cost and scope (as determined under criteria established by the Attorney General).

(b) SPECIAL RULE FOR STATIONS. -

(1) GENERAL RULE. - For purposes os section 202 of this Act and section 504 of the Rehabilitation Act of 1973 (29 U.S.C. 794), it shall be considered discrimination for a public entity that provides designated public transportation to fail , in accordance with the provisions of this subsection, to make key stations, (as determined under criteria established by the Secretary by regulation) in rapid rail and light rail systems readily accessible to and usable by individuals with disabilities, including individuals who use wheelchairs.

(2) RAPID RAIL AND LIGHT RAIL KEY STATIONS. -

(A) ACCESSIBILITY. - Except as otherwise provided in this paragraph, all key stations (as determined under criteria established by the Secretary by regulation) in rapid rail and light rail systems shall be made readily accessible to and usable by individuals with disabilities, including individuals who use wheelchairs, as soon as practicable but in no event later than the last day of the 3 - year period beginning on the effective date of this paragraph.

(B) EXTENSION FOR EXTRAORDINARILY EXPENSIVE STRUCTURAL CHANGES. - The Secretary may extend the 3 - year period under subparagraph (A) up to a 30 - year period for key stations in a rapid rail or light rail system which stations need extraordinarily expensive structural changes to, or replacement of, existing facilities; except that by the last day of the 20th year following the date of the enactment of this Act at least two - thirds of such key stations must be readily accessible to and usable by individuals with disabilities.

(3) PLANS AND MILESTONES. - The Secretary shall require the appropriate public entity to develop and submit to the Secretary a plan for compliance with this subsection -

(A) that reflects consultation with individuals with disabilities affected by such plan and the results of a public hearing and public comments on such plan, and

(B) that established milestones for achievement of the requirements of this subsection.

SEC. 228. PUBLIC TRANSPORTATION PROGRAMS AND ACTIVITIES IN EXISTING FACILITIES AND ONE CARE PER TRAIN RULE.

(a) PUBLIC TRANSPORTATION PROGRAMS AND ACTIVITIES IN EXISTING FACILITIES. -

(1) IN GENERAL. - With respect to existing facilities used in the provision of designated public transportation services, it shall be considered discrimination , for purposes of section 202 of this Act and section 504 of the Rehabilitation Act of 1973 (29 U.S.C. 794), for a public entity to operate a designated public transportation program or activity conducted in such facilities so that, when viewed in the entirety, the program or activity is readily accessible to and usable by individuals with disabilities.

(2) EXCEPTION. - Paragraph (1) shall not require a public entity to make structural changes to existing facilities in order to make such facilities accessible to individuals who use wheelchairs, unless and to the extent required by section 227(a) (relating to alterations) or section 227(b) (relating to key stations).

(3) UTILIZATION. - Paragraph (1) shall not require a public entity to which paragraph (2) applies, to provide to individuals who use wheelchairs services made available to the general public at such facilities when such individuals could not utilize or benefit from such services provided at such facilities.

(b) ONE CAR PER TRAIN RULE. -

(1) GENERAL RULE. - Subject to paragraph 92), with respect to 2 or more vehicles operated as a train by a light or rapid rail system, for purposes of section 202 of this Act and section 504 of the Rehabilitation Act of 1973 (u.S.C. 794) it shall be considered discrimination for a public entity to fail to have at least 1 vehicle per train that is accessible to individuals with disabilities, including individuals who use wheelchairs, as soon as practicable but in no event later than the last day of the 5-year period beginning on the effective date of this section.

(2) HISTORIC TRAINS. - In order to comply with paragraph (1) with respect to the remanufacture of a vehicle of historic character which is to be used on a segment of a light or rapid rail system which is included on the National Register of Historic Places, if making such vehicle readily accessible to and usable by individuals with disabilities would significantly alter the historic character of such vehicle, the public entity which operates such system only has to make (or to purchase or lease a manufactured vehicle with) those modifications which are necessary to meet the requirements of section 222(c)(1) and which do not significantly alter the historic character of such vehicle.

SEC. 229. REGULATIONS.

(a) IN GENERAL. - Not later than 1 year after the date of enactment of this Act, the Secretary of Transportation shall issue regulations, in an accessible format, necessary for carrying out this part (other than section 223).

(b) STANDARDS. - The regulations issued under this section and section 223 shall include standards applicable to facilities and vehicles covered by this subtitle. The standards shall be consistent with the minimum guidelines and requirements issued by the Architectural and Transportation Barriers Compliance Board in accordance with section 504 of this Act.

SEC. 230. INTERIM ACCESSIBILITY REQUIREMENTS.

If financial regulation shave not been issued pursuant to section 229, for new construction or alterations for which a valid and appropriate State or local building permit is obtained prior to the issuance of final regulations under such section, and for which the construction or alteration authorized by such permit begins within one year of the receipt of such permit and is completed under the terms of such permit, compliance with the Uniform Federal Accessibility Standards in effect at the time the building permit is issued shall suffice to satisfy the requirements that facilities be readily accessible to and usable by persons with disabilities as required under sections 226 and 227, except that, if such final regulations have not been issued one year after the Architectural and Transportation Barriers Compliance Board has issued the supplemental minimum guidelines required under section 504(a) of this Act, compliance with such supplement minimum guidelines shall be necessary to satisfy the requirement that facilities be readily accessible to and usable by persons with disabilities prior to issuance of the final regulations.

SEC. 231 EFFECTIVE DATE

(a) GENERAL RULE. - Except as provided in subsection (b), this part shall become effective 18 months after the date of enactment of this Act.

(b) EXCEPTION. - Sections 222, 223 (other than subsection (a)), 224, 225, 227(b), 228(b), and 229 shall become effective on the date of enactment of this Act.

PART II - PUBLIC TRANSPORTATION BY INTERCITY AND COMMUTER RAIL

SEC. 241. DEFINITIONS.

As used in this part:

(1) COMMUTER AUTHORITY. - The term "commuter authority" has the meaning given such term in section 103(8) of the Rail Passenger Service Act (45 U.S.C. 503(8)).

(2) COMMUTER RAIL TRANSPORTATION. - The term "commuter rail transportation" has the meaning given the term "commuter service" in section 103(9) of the Rail Passenger Service Act (45 U.S.C. 502(9)).

(3) INTERCITY RAIL TRANSPORTATION. - The term "intercity rail transportation" means transportation provided by the National Railroad Passenger Corporation.

(4) RAIL PASSENGER CAR. - The term "rail passenger car" means, with respect to intercity rail transportation, single - level and bi - level coach cars, single - level and bi - level dining cars, single - level and bi - lever sleeping cars, single - level and bi - level lounge cars, and food service cars.

(5) RESPONSIBLE PERSON. - The term "responsible person" means -

(A) in the case of a station more than 50 percent of which is owned by a public entity, such public entity;

(B) in the case of a station more than 50 percent of which is owned by private party, the persons providing intercity or commuter rail transportation to such station, as allocated on an equitable basis by regulation by the Secretary of Transportation; and

(C) in a case where no party owns more than 50 percent of a station, the persons providing intercity or commuter rail transportation to such station and the owners of the station, other than private party owners, as allocated on an equitable basis by regulation by the Secretary of Transportation.

(6) STATION. - The term "station" means the portion of a property located appurtent to a right - of - way on which intercity or commuter rail transportation is operated, where such portion is used by the general public and is related to the provision of such transportation, including passenger platforms, designated waiting areas, ticketing areas, restrooms, and where a public entity providing rail transportation owns the property, concession area, to the extent that such public entity exercises control over the selection, design, construction, or alterations of the property, but such term does not include flag stops.

SEC. 242. INTERCITY AND COMMUTER RAIL ACTIONS CONSIDERED DISCRIMINATORY.

(a) INTERCITY RAIL TRANSPORTATION -

(1) ONE CAR PER TRAIN RULE. - It shall be considered discrimination for purposes of section 202 of this Act and section 504 of the Rehabilitation Act of 1973 (29 U.S.C. 794) for a person who provides intercity rail transportation to fail to have at least one passenger car per taint that is readily accessible to and usable by individuals with disabilities, including individuals who use wheelchairs, in accordance with regulations issued under section 2444, as soon as practicable, but in no event later than 5 years after the date of enactment of this Act.

(2) NEW INTERCITY CARS. -

(A) GENERAL RULE. - Except as otherwise provided in this subsection with respect to individual who use wheelchairs, it shall be considered discrimination for purposes of section 202 of this Act and section 504 of the Rehabilitation Act of 1973 (29 U.S.C. 794) for a person to purchase or lease any new rail passenger cars for use in intercity rail transportation, and for which a solicitation is made later than 30 days after the effective date of this section, unless all such rail cards, are readily accessible to and usable by individuals with disabilities, including individuals who use wheelchairs, as prescribed by the Secretary of Transportation in regulations issued under section 244.

(B) SPECIAL RULE FOR SINGLE - LEVEL PASSENGER COACHES FOR INDIVIDUALS WHO USE WHEELCHAIRS. - Single - level passenger coaches shall be required to -

(i) be able to be entered by an individual who uses a wheelchair;

(ii) have space to park and secure a wheelchair;

(iii) have a seat to which a passenger in a wheelchair can transfer, and a space to fold and store such passenger's wheelchair; and

(iv) have a restroom usable by an individual who uses a wheelchair,

only to the extent provided in paragraph (3).

(C) SPECIAL RULE FOR SINGLE - LEVEL DINING CARDS FOR INDIVIDUALS WHO USE WHEELCHAIRS. - Single - level dining cars shall not be required to -

(i) be able to be entered from the station platform by an individual who uses a wheelchair; or

(ii) have a restroom usable by an individual who uses a wheelchair if no restroom is provided in such car for any passenger.

(D) SPECIAL RULE FOR BI - LEVEL DINING CARDS FOR INDIVIDUALS WHO USE WHEELCHAIRS. - Bi - level dining cars shall not be required to -

(i) be able to be entered by an individual who uses a wheelchair;

(ii) have space to park and secure a wheelchair;

(iii) have a seat to which a passenger in a wheelchair can transfer, and a space to fold and store such passenger's wheelchair; or

(iv) have a restroom usable by an individual who uses a wheelchair.

(3) ACCESSIBILITY OF SINGLE - LEVEL COACHES. -

(A) GENERAL RULE. - It shall be considered discrimination for purposes of section 202 of this Act and section 504 of the Rehabilitation Act of 1973 (29 U.S.C. 794) for a person who provides intercity rail transportation to fail to have on each train which includes one or more single - level rail passenger coaches

(i) a number of spaces -

(I) to park and secure wheelchairs (to accommodate individuals who wish to remain in their wheelchairs) equal to not less than one - half of the number of single - level rail passenger coaches in such train; and

(II) to fold and store wheelchairs (to accommodate individuals who wise to transfer to coach seats) equal to not less than one - half of the number of single - level rail passenger coaches in such train, as soon as practicable, but in no event later than 5 years after the date of enactment of this Act; and

(ii) a number of spaces -

(I) to park and secure wheelchairs (to accommodate individuals who wish to remain in their wheelchairs equal to not less than the total number of single - level rail passenger coaches in such train; and

(II) to park and secure wheelchairs (to accommodate individuals who wish to transfer to coach seats) equal to not less than the total number of single - level rail passenger coaches in such train, as soon aa practicable, but in no event later than 10 years after the date of enactment of this Act.

(B) LOCATION. - Spaces required by subparagraph (A) shall be located in single - level rail passenger coaches or food serve cars.

(C) LIMITATION. - Of the number of spaces required on a train by subparagraph (A), not more than two spaces to park and secure wheelchairs not more than two spaces to fold and store wheelchairs shall be located in any one coach or food service car.

(D) OTHER ACCESSIBILITY FEATURES. - Single - level rail passenger coaches and food service cards on which the spaces required by subparagraph (A) are located shall have a restroom usable by an individual who uses a wheelchair and shall be able to be entered from the station platform by an individual who uses a wheelchair.

(4) FOOD SERVICE. -

(A) SINGLE - LEVEL DINING CARS. - On any train in which a single - level dining car is used to provide food service -

(i) if such single - level dining car was purchased after the date of enactment of this Act, table service in such car shall be provided to a passenger who uses a wheelchair if -

(I)the car adjacent to the end of the dining care through which a wheelchair i y enter is itself accessible to a wheelchair;

(II)such passenger can exit to the platform from the car such passenger occupies, move down the platform, and enter the adjacent accessible car described in subclause (I) without the necessity of the train being moved within the station; and

(III) space to park and secure a wheelchair is available in the dining car at the time such passenger wishes to eat (if such passenger wishes to remain in a wheelchair), or space to store and fold a wheelchair is available in the dining car at the time such passenger wishes to each (if such passenger wishes to transfer to a dining car seat); and

(ii) appropriate auxiliary aids and services, including a hard surface on which to each, shall be provided to ensure that other equivalent food service is available to individuals with disabilities, including individuals who use wheelchairs, and to passengers traveling with such individuals.

Unless not practicable, a person providing intercity rail transportation shall place an accessible car adjacent to the end of a dining car described in clause (i) through which an individual who uses a wheelchair may enter.

(B) BI - LEVEL DINING CARS. - On any train in which a bi - level dining car is used to provide food service -

(i) if such train includes a bi - level lounge car purchased after the date of enactment of this Act, table service in such car shall be provided to individuals who use wheelchairs and to other passengers, and

(ii) appropriate auxiliary aids and services, including a hard surface on which to each, shall be provided to ensure that other equivalent food service is available to individuals with disabilities, including individuals who use wheelchairs, and to passengers traveling with such individuals.

(b) COMMUTER RAIL TRANSPORTATION. -

(1) ONE CAR PER TRAIN RULE. - It shall be considered discrimination for purposes of section 202 of this Act and section 504 of the Rehabilitation Act of 1973 (29 U.S.C. 794) for person who provides commuter rial transportation to fail to have at lease one passenger car per train that is readily accessible to and usable by individuals with disabilities, including individuals who use wheelchairs, in accordance with regulations issued under section 244, as soon as practicable, but in no event later than 5 years after the date of enactment of this Act.

(2) NEW COMMUTER RAIL CARS. -

(A) GENERAL RULE. - It shall be considered discrimination for purposes of section 202 of this Act and section 504 of the Rehabilitation Act of 1973 (29 U.S.C. 794) for a person to purchase or lease any new rail passenger cars for use in commuter rail transportation, and for which a solicitation is made later than 30 days after the effective date of this section, unless all such rails cars are readily accessible to and usable by individuals with disabilities, including individuals who use wheelchairs, as prescribed by the Secretary of Transportation in regulations issued under section 244.

(B) ACCESSIBILITY. - For purposes of section 202 of this Act and section 504 of the Rehabilitation Act of 1973 (29 U.S.C. 794), a requirement that a rail passenger car used in commuter rail transportation be accessible to or readily accessible to and usable by individuals with disabilities, including individuals who use wheelchairs, shall not be construed to require -

(i) a restroom usable by an individual who uses a wheelchair if not restroom is provided in such car for any passenger;

(ii) space to fold and store a wheelchair; or

(iii) a seat to which a passenger who uses a wheelchair can transfer.

(c) USED RAIL CARS. - It shall be considered discrimination for purposes of section 202 of this Act and section 504 of the Rehabilitation Act of 1973 (29 U.S.C. 794) for a person to purchase or lease a used rail passenger car for use in intercity or commuter rail transportation, unless such person makes demonstrated good faith efforts to purchase or lease a used rail car that is readily accessible to and usable by individuals with disabilities, including individuals who use wheelchairs, as prescribed by the Secretary of Transportation in regulations issued under section 244.

(d) REMANUFACTURED RAIL CARS. -

(1) REMANUFACTURING. - It shall be considered discrimination for purposes of section 202 of this Act and section 504 of the Rehabilitation Act of 1973 (29 U.S.C. 794) for a person to remanufacture a rail passenger car for use in intercity or commuter rail transportation so as to extent is usable life for 10 years or more, unless the rail car, to the maximum extent feasible, is made readily accessible to and usable by individuals with disabilities, including individuals who use wheelchairs, as prescribed by the Secretary of Transportation in regulations issued under section 244.

(2) PURCHASE OR LEASE. - It shall be considered discrimination for purposes of section 202 of this Act and section 504 of the Rehabilitation Act of 1973 (29 U.S.C. 794) for a person to purchase or lease a remanufactured rail passenger car for use in intercity or commuter rail transportation unless such car was remanufactured in accordance with paragraph (1).

(e) STATIONS. -

(1) NEW STATIONS. - It shall be considered discrimination for purposes of section 202 of this Act and section 504 of the Rehabilitation Act of 1973 (29 U.S.C. 794) for a person to build a new station for use in intercity or commuter rail transportation that is not readily accessible to and usable by individuals with disabilities, including individuals who use wheelchairs, as prescribed by the Secretary of Transportation in regulations issued under section 244.

(2) EXISTING STATIONS. -

(A) FAILURE TO MAKE READILY ACCESSIBLE. -

(i) GENERAL RULE. - It shall be considered discrimination for purposes of section 202 of this Act and section 504 of the Rehabilitation Act of 1973 (29 U.S.C. 794) for a responsible person to fail to make existing stations in the intercity rail transportation system, and existing key stations in commuter rail transportation systems, readily accessible to and usable by individuals with disabilities, including individuals who use wheelchairs, as prescribed by the Secretary of Transportation in regulations issued under section 244.

(ii) PERIOD FOR COMPLIANCE

(I) INTERCITY RAIL. - All stations in the intercity rail transportation system shall be made readily accessible to and usable by individuals with disabilities, including individuals who use wheelchairs, as soon as practicable, but in no event later than 20 years after the date of enactment of this Act.

(II) COMMUTER RAIL. - Key stations in commuter rail transportation system shall be made readily accessible to and usable by individuals with disabilities,

including individuals who use wheelchairs, as soon as practicable but in no event later than 3 years after the date of enactment of this Act, except that the time limit may be extended by the Secretary of Transportation up to 20 years after the date of enactment of this Act in a case where the raising of the entire passenger platform is the only means available of attaining accessibility or where other extraordinarily expensive structural changes are necessary to attain accessibility.

(iii) DESIGNATION OF KEY STATIONS. - Each commuter authority shall designate the key stations in its commuter rail transportation system, in consultation with individuals with disabilities and organizations representing such individuals, taking into consideration such factors as high ridership and whether such station serves s a transfer or feeder station. Before the final designation of key stations under this clause, a commuter authority shall hold a public hearing.

(iv) PLANS AND MILESTONES. - The Secretary of Transportation shall require the appropriate person to develop a plan for carrying out this subparagraph that reflects consultation with individuals with disabilities affected by such plan and that establishes milestones for achievement of the requirements of this subparagraph.

(B) REQUIREMENT WHEN MAKING ALTERATIONS. -

(i) GENERAL RULE. - It shall be considered discrimination for purposes of section 202 of this Act and section 504 of the Rehabilitation Act of 1973 (29 U.S.C. 794), with respect to alterations of an existing station or part thereof in the intercity or commuter rail transportation systems that affect or could affect the usability of the station or part thereof, for the responsible person, owner, or person in control of the station to fail to make the necessary alterations in such a manner that, to the maximum extent feasible, the altered portions of the station are readily accessible to and usable by individuals with disabilities, including individuals who use wheelchairs, upon completion of such alterations.

(ii) ALTERATIONS TO A PRIMARY FUNCTION AREA. - It shall be considered discrimination for purposes of section 202 of this Act and section 504 of the Rehabilitation Act of 1973 (29 U.S.C. 794), with respect to alterations that affect or could affect the usability of or access to an area of the station containing a primary function, for the responsible person, owner, or person in control of the station to fail to make the alterations in such a manner that, to the maximum extent feasible, the path of travel to the altered area, and the bathrooms, telephones, and drinking fountains serving the altered area, are readily accessible to and usable by individuals with disabilities, including individuals who use wheelchairs,upon completion of such alterations where such alterations to the path of travel or the bathrooms, telephones, and drinking fountains serving the altered area are not disproportionate to the overall alterations in terms of cost and scope (as determined under criteria established by the Attorney General).

(C) REQUIRED COOPERATION. - It shall be considered discrim action for purposes of section 202 of this Act and section 504 of the Rehabilitation Act of 1973 (29 U.S.C. 794) for an owner, or person in control, of a station governed by subparagraph (A) or (B) to fail to provide reasonable cooperation to a responsible person with respect to such station in that responsible person's efforts to comply with such subparagraph. An owner, or person in control, of a station shall be liable to a responsible person for any failure to provide reasonable cooperation as required by this subparagraph. Failure to receive reasonable cooperation required by this subparagraph. Failure to receive reasonable cooperation required by this subparagraph shall not be a defense to a claim of discrimination under this Act.

SEC. 243. CONFORMANCE OF ACCESSIBILITY STANDARDS.

Accessibility standards included in regulations issued under this part shall be consistent with the minimum guidelines issued by the Architectural and Transportation Barriers Compliance Board under section 504(a) of this Act.

SEC. 244. REGULATIONS.

Not later than 1 year after the date of enactment of this Act, the Secretary of Transportation shall issue regulations, in an accessible format, necessary for carrying out this part.

SEC. 245. INTERIM ACCESSIBILITY REQUIREMENTS.

(a) STATIONS. - If final regulations have not been issued pursuant to section 244, for new construction or alterations for which a valid and appropriate State or local building permit is obtained prior to the issuance of final regulations under such section, and for which the construction or alteration authorized by such permit begins within one year of the receipt of such permit and is completed under the terms of such permit, compliance with the Uniform Federal Accessibility Standards in effect at the time the building permit is issued shall suffice to satisfy the requirements that stations be readily accessible to and usable by persons with disabilities as required under section 242(e), except that, if such final regulations have not been issued one year after the Architectural and Transportation Barriers Compliance Board has issued the supplemental minimum guidelines required under section 504(a) of this Act, compliance with such supplemental minimum guidelines shall be necessary to satisfy the requirement that stations be readily accessible to and usable by persons with disabilities prior to issuance of the final regulations.

(b) RAIL PASSENGER CARS. - If final regulations have not been issued pursuant to section 244, a person shall be considered to have complied with the requirements of section 242(a) through (d) that a rail passenger car be readily accessible to and usable by individuals with disabilities, if the design for such car complies with the laws and regulations (including the Minimum Guidelines and Requirements for Accessible Design and supplemental minimum guidelines as are issued under section 504(a) of this Act) governing accessibility of such cars, to the extent that such laws and regulations are not inconsistent with this part and are in effect at the time such design is substantially completed.

SEC. 246. EFFECTIVE DATE

(a) GENERAL RULE. - Except as provided in subsection (b), this part shall become effective 18 months after the date of enactment of this Act.

(b) EXCEPTION. - Sections 242 and 244 shall become effective on the date of enactment of this Act.

TITLE III - PUBLIC ACCOMMODATIONS AND SERVICES OPERATED BY PRIVATE ENTITIES

SEC. 301. DEFINITIONS.

As used in this title:

(1) COMMERCE. - The term "commerce" means travel, trade, trade, commerce, transportation, or communication -

(A) among the several States;

(B) between any foreign country or any territory or possession and any State; or

(C) between points in the same State but through another State or foreign country.

(2) COMMERCIAL FACILITIES. - The term "commercial facilities" means facilities -

(A) that are intended for nonresidential use; and

(B) whose operations will affect commerce.

Such term shall not include railroad locomotives, railroad freight cars, railroad cabooses, railroad care described in section 242 or covered under this title, railroad rights-of-way, or facilities that are covered or expressly exempted from coverage under the Fair Housing Act of 1968 (42 U.S.C. 3601 et seq.).

(3) DEMAND RESPONSIVE SYSTEM. - The term "demand responsive system" means any system of providing transportation of individuals by a vehicle, other than a system which is a fixed route system.

(4) FIXED ROUTE SYSTEM. - The term "fixed route system" means a system of providing transportation of individuals (other than by aircraft) on which a vehicle is operated along a prescribed route according to a fixed schedule.

(5) OVER-THE-ROAD BUS. - The term "over-the-road bus" means a bus characterized by an elevated passenger deck located over a baggage compartment.

(6) PRIVATE ENTITY. - The term "private entity" means any entity other than a public entity (as defined in section 201(1)).

(7) PUBLIC ACCOMMODATION. - The following private entities are considered public accommodations for purposes of this title, if the operations of such entities affect commerce -

(A) an inn, hotel, motel, or other place of lodging, except for an establishment located within a building that contains not more than five rooms for rent or hire and that is actually occupied by the proprietor of such establishment s the residence of such proprietor;

(B) a restaurant, bar, or other establishment serving food or drink;

(C) a motion picture house, theater, concert hall, stadium, or other place of exhibition of entertainment;

(D) an auditorium, convention center, lecture hall, or other place of public gathering;

(E) a bakery, grocery store, clothing store, hardware store, shopping center, or other sales or rental establishment;

(F) a laundromat, dry-cleaner, bank, barber shop, beauty shop, travel service, shoe repair service, funeral parlor, gas station, office of an accountant or lawyer, pharmacy, insurance office, professional office of a health care provider, hospital, or other secure establishment;

(G) a terminal, depot, or other station used for specified public transportation;

(H) a museum, library, gallery, or other place of public display or collection;

(I) a park, zoo, amusement park, or other place of recreation;

(J) a nursery, elementary, secondary, undergraduate, or postgraduate private school, or other place of education;

(K) a day care center, senior citizen center, homeless shelter, food bank, adoption agency, or other social service center establishment; and

(L) a gymnasium, health spa, bowling alley, golf course, or other place of exercise or recreation.

(8) RAIL AND RAILROAD. - The terms "rail" and railroad" have the meaning given the term "railroad" in section 202(e) of the Federal Railroad Safety Act of 1970 (45 U.S.C. 431(e).

(9) READILY ACHIEVABLE. - The term "readily achievable" means easily accomplishable and able to be carried out without much difficulty or expense. In determining whether an actin is readily achievable, factors to be considered include -

(A) the nature and cost of the action needed under this Act;

(B) the overall financial resources of the facility or facilities involved in the action; the number of persons employed at such facilities; the effect on expenses and resources, or the impact otherwise of such action upon the operation of the facility;

(C) the overall financial resources of the covered entity; the overall size of the business of a covered entity with respect to the number of its employees; the number, type and location of its facilities; and

(D) the type of operation or operations of the covered entity, including the composition, structure, and functions of the workforce of such entity; the geographic separateness, administrative or fiscal relationship of the facility or facilities in question to the covered entity.

(10) SPECIFIED PUBLIC TRANSPORTATION. - The term "specified public transportation" means transportation by bus, rail, or any other conveyance (other than by aircraft) that provides the general public a = with general or special service (including charter service) on a regular or continuing basis.

(11) VEHICLE. - The term "vehicle" does not include a rail passenger car, railroad locomotive, railroad freight car, railroad caboose, or a railroad car described in section 242 or covered under this title.

SEC. 302. PROHIBITION OF DISCRIMINATION BY PUBLIC ACCOMMODATIONS.

(a) GENERAL RULE. - No individual shall be discriminated against on the basis of disability in the full and equal enjoyment of the goods, services, facilities, privileges, advantages, or accommodations of any place of public accommodation by any person who owns, leases (or leases to), or operates a place of public accommodation.

(b) CONSTRUCTION. -

(1) GENERAL PROHIBITION. -

(A) ACTIVITIES. -

(i) DENIAL OF PARTICIPATION. - It shall be discriminatory to subject an individual or class of individuals on the basis of a disability or disabilities of such individual or class, directly, or though contractual, licensing, o other arrangement, to a denial of the opportunity of the individual or class to participate in or benefit from the goods, services, facilities, privileges, advantages, or accommodations of an entity.

(ii) PARTICIPATION IN UNEQUAL BENEFIT. - It shall be discriminatory to afford an individual or class of individuals, on the basis of a disability or disabilities of such individual or class, directly, or through contractual licensing, or other arrangements with the opportunity to participate in or benefit from good, service, facility, privilege, advantage, or accommodation that is not equal to that afforded to other individuals.

(iii) SEPARATE BENEFIT. - It shall be discriminatory to provide an individual or class of individuals, on the basis of a disability or disabilities of such individual or class, directly, or through contractual, licensing, or other arrangements with a good, service, facility, privilege, advantage, or accommodation that is different or separate from that provided to other individuals, unless such action is necessary to provide the individual or class of individuals with a good, service, facility, privilege, advantage, or accommodation, or other opportunity that is as effective as that provided to others.

(iv) INDIVIDUAL OR CLASS OF INDIVIDUALS. - For purposes of clauses (i) through (iii) of this subparagraph, the term "individual or class of individuals" refers to the clients or customers of the covered public accommodation that enters into the contractual, licensing or other arrangement.

(B) INTEGRATED SETTINGS. - - Goods, services, facilities, privileges, advantages, and accommodations shall be afforded to an individual with a disability in the most integrated setting appropriate to the needs of the individual.

(C) OPPORTUNITY TO PARTICIPATE. - Notwithstanding the existence of separate or different programs or activities provided in accordance with this section, an individual with a disability shall not be denied the opportunity to participate in such programs or activities that are not separate or different.

(D) ADMINISTRATIVE METHODS. - An individual or entity shall not, directly or through contractual or other arrangement, utilize standards or criteria or methods of administration -

(i) that have the effect of discriminating on the basis of disability; or

(ii) that perpetuate the discrimination of others who are subject to common administrative control.

(E) ASSOCIATION. - It shall be discriminatory to exclude or otherwise deny equal goods, services, facilities, privileges, advantages, accommodations, or other opportunities to an individual or entity because of the known disability of an individual with whom the individual or entity is known to have a relationship or association.

(2) SPECIFIC PROHIBITIONS. -

(A) DISCRIMINATION. - For purposes of subsection(a), discrimination includes -

(i) the imposition or application of eligibility criteria that screen out or tend to screen out an individual with a disability or any class of individuals with disabilities from fully and equally enjoying any goods, services, facilities, privileges, advantages, or accommodations, unless such criteria can be shown to be necessary for the provision of the goods, services, facilities privileges, advantages, or accommodations being offered;

(ii) a failure to make reasonable modifications in policies, practices, or procedures, when such modifications are necessary to afford such goods, services, facilities, privileges, advantages, or accommodations to individuals with disabilities, unless the entity can demonstrate that making such modifications would fundamentally alter the nature of such goods, service, facilities, privileges, advantages, or accommodations;

(iii) a failure to take such steps as may be necessary to ensure that no individual with a disability is excluded, denied services, segregated or otherwise treated differently than other individuals because of the absence of auxiliary aids and services, unless the entity can demonstrate that taking such steps would fundamentally alter the nature of the good, service, facility, privilege, advantage, or accommodation being offered or would result in an undue burden;

(iv) a failure to remove architectural barriers, and communication barriers that are structural in nature, in existing facilities, and transportation barriers in existing vehicles and rail passenger cars used by an establishment for transporting individuals (not including barriers that can only be removed through the retrofitting of vehicles or rail passenger cars by the installation of a hydraulic or other lift), where such removal is readily achievable; and

(v) where an entity can demonstrate that the removal of a barrier under clause (iv) is not readily achievable, a failure to make such goods, services, facilities, privileges, advantages, or accommodations available through alternative methods if such methods are readily achievable.

(B) FIXED ROUTE SYSTEM. -

(i) ACCESSIBILITY. - It shall be considered discrimination for a private entity which operates a fixed route system and which is not subject to section 304 to purchase or lease a vehicle with a seating capacity in excess of 16 passengers (including the driver) for use on such system, for which a solicitation is made after the 30th day following the effective date of this subparagraph, that is not readily accessible to and usable by individuals with disabilities, including individuals who use wheelchairs.

(ii) EQUIVALENT SERVICE. - If a private entity which operates a fixed route system and which is not subject to section 304 purchases or leases a vehicle with a seating capacity of 16 passengers of less (including the driver) for use on such system after the effective date of this subparagraph that is not readily accessible to or usable by individuals with disabilities, it shall be

considered discrimination for such entity to fail to operate such system so that, when viewed in its entirety, such system ensures a level of service to individuals with disabilities, including individuals who use wheelchairs, equivalent to the level of service provided to individuals without disabilities.

(C) DEMAND RESPONSIVE SYSTEM. - For purposes of subsection (a), discrimination includes -

(i) a failure of a private entity which operates a demand responsive system and which is not subject to section 304 to operate such system so that, when viewed in its entirety, such systems ensures a level of service to individuals with disabilities, including individuals who use wheelchairs, equivalent to the level of service provided to individuals without disabilities; and

(ii) the purchase or lease by such entity for use on such system of a vehicle with a seating capacity in excess of 16 passengers (including the driver), for which solicitations are made after the 30th day following the effective date of this subparagraph, that is not readily accessible to and usable by individuals with disabilities (including individuals who use wheelchairs) unless such entity can demonstrate that such system, when viewed in its entirety, provides a level of service to individuals with disabilities equivalent to that provided to individuals without disabilities.

(D) OVER - THE - ROAD BUSES. -

(i) LIMITATION ON APPLICABILITY. - Subparagraphs (B) and (C) do not apply to over - the - road buses.

(ii) ACCESSIBILITY REQUIREMENTS. - For purposes of subsection (a), discrimination includes (I) the purchase or lease of an over - the - road bus which does not comply with the regulations issued under section 306(a)(2) by a private entity which provides transportation of individuals and which is not primarily engaged in the business of transporting people, and (II) any other failure of such entity to comply with such regulations.

(3) SPECIFIC CONSTRUCTION. - Nothing in this title shall require an entity to permit an individual to participate in or benefit from the goods, services, facilities, privileges,. advantages and accommodations of such entity where such individual poses a direct threat to the health or safety of others. The term "direct threat" means a significant risk to the health or safety of others that cannot be eliminated by a modification of policies, practices, or procedures or by the provision of auxiliary aids or services.

SEC. 303 NEW CONSTRUCTION AND ALTERATIONS IN PUBLIC ACCOMMODATIONS AND COMMERCIAL FACILITIES.

(a) APPLICATION OF TERM. - Except s provided in subsection (b), as applied to public accommodations and commercial facilities, discrimination for purposes of section 302(a) includes -

(1) a failure to design and construct facilities for first occupancy later than 30 months after the date of enactment of this Act that are readily accessible to and usable by individuals with disabilities, except where an entity can demonstrate that it is structurally impracticable to meet the requirements of such subsection in accordance with standards set forth or incorporated by reference in regulations issued under this title; and

(2) with respect to a facility or part thereof that is altered by, on behalf of, or for the use of an establishment in a manner that affects or could affect the usability of the facility or part thereof, a failure to make alterations in such a manner that, to the maximum extent feasible, the altered portions of the facility are readily accessible to and usable by individuals with disabilities, including individuals who use wheelchairs. Where the entity is undertaking an alteration that affects or could affect usability of or access to an area of the facility containing a primary function, the entity shall also make the alterations in such a manner that, to the maximum extent feasible, the path of travel to the altered area and the bathrooms, telephones, and drinking fountains serving the altered area are not disprotionate to the overall alterations in terms of cost and scope (as determined under criteria established by the Attorney General).

(b) ELEVATOR. - Subsection (a) shall not be construed to require the installation of an elevator for facilities that are less than three stories or have less than 3,000 square feet per story unless the building is a shopping center, a shopping mall, or the professional office of a health care provided or unless the Attorney General determines that a particular category of such facilities requires the installation of elevators based on the usage of such facilities.

SEC. 304. PROHIBITION OF DISCRIMINATION IN SPECIFIED PUBLIC TRANSPORTATION SERVICES PROVIDED BY PRIVATE ENTITIES.

(a) GENERAL RULE. - No individual shall be discriminated against on the basis of disability in the full and equal enjoyment of specified public transportation services provided by a private entity that is primarily engaged in the business of transporting people and whose operations affect commerce.

(b) CONSTRUCTION. - For purposes of subsection (a) discrimination includes -

(1) the imposition of application by an entity described in subsection (a) of eligibility criteria that screen out or tend to screen out an individual with a disability or any class of individuals with disabilities from fully enjoying the specified public transportation services provided by the entity, unless such criteria can be shown to be necessary for the provision of the services being offered;

(2) the failure of such entity to -

(A) make reasonable modifications consistent with those required under section 302(b)(2)(A)(ii);

(B) provide auxiliary aids and services consistent with the requirements of section 302(b)(2)(A)(iii); and

(C) remove barriers consistent with the requirement of section 302(b)(2)(A) and with the requirements of section 303(a)(2);

(3) the purchase or lease by such entity of a new vehicle (other than an automobile, a van with a seating capacity of less than 8 passengers, including the driver, or an over - the - road bus) which is to be used to provide specified public transportation and for which a solicitation is made after the 30th day following the effective date of this section that is not readily accessible to and usable by individuals with disabilities, including individuals who use wheelchairs; except that the new vehicle need not be readily accessible to and usable by

such individuals if the new vehicles is to be used solely in a demand responsive system and if the entity can demonstrate that such system, when viewed in its entirety, provides a level of service to such individuals equivalent to the level of service provided to the general public;

(4)(A) the purchase or lease by such entity of an over - the - road bus which does not comply with the regulations issued under section 306(a)(2); and

(B) any other failure of such entity to comply with such regulations; and

(5) the purchase or lease by such entity of a new van with a seating capacity of less than 8 passengers, including the driver, which is to be used to provide specified public transportation and for which a solicitation is made after the 30th day following the effective date of this section that is not readily accessible to or usable by individuals with disabilities, including individuals who use wheelchairs; except that the new van need not be readily accessible to and usable by such individuals of the entity can demonstrate that the system for which the van is being purchased or leased, when viewed in its entirely, provides a level of service to such individuals equivalent to the level of service provided to the general public;

(6) the purchase or lease by such entity of a new rail passenger car that is to be used to provide specified public transportation, and for which a solicitation is made later than 30 days after the effective date of this paragraph, that is not readily accessible to and usable by individuals with disabilities, including individuals who use wheelchairs; and

(7) the remanufacture by such entity of a rail passenger car that is to be used to provide specified pubic transportation so as to extend its usable life for 10 years or more, or the purchase or lease by such entity of such a rail car, unless the rail car, to the maximum extent feasible, is made readily accessible to and usable by individuals with disabilities, including individuals who use wheelchairs.

(c) HISTORICAL OR ANTIQUATED CARS. -

(1) EXCEPTION. - To the extent that compliance with subsection (b)(2)(C) or (b)(7) would significantly alter the historic or antiquated character of a historical or antiquated rail passenger car, or a rail station served exclusively by such car, or would result in violation of any rule, regulation, standard, or order issued by the Secretary of Transportation under the Federal Railroad Safety Act of 1970, such compliance shall not be required.

(2) DEFINITION. - As used in this subsection, the term "historical or antiquated rail passenger car" means a rail passenger car -

(A) which is not less than 30 years old at the time of its use for transporting individuals;

(B) the manufacturer of which is no longer in the business of manufacturing rail passenger cars; and

(C) which -

(i)has a consequential association with events of persons significant to the past; or

(ii) embodies, or is being restored to embody, the distinctive characteristics of a type of rail passenger car used in the past, or to represent a time period which has passed.

SEC. 305. STUDY.

(a) PURPOSES. - The Office of Technology Assessment shall undertake a study to determine -

(1) the access needs of individuals with disabilities to over - the - road buses and over - the - road bus service; and

(2) the most cost - effective methods of providing access to over - the - road buses and over - the - road bus service to individuals with disabilities, particularly individuals who use wheelchairs, through all forms of boarding options.

(b) CONTENTS. - The study shall include, at a minimum, an analysis of the following:

(1) The anticipated demand by individual with disabilities for accessible over - the - road buses and over - the - road bus service.

(20 The degree to which such buses and service, including any service required under sections 304(b)(4) and 306(a)(2), are readily accessible to and usable by individuals with disabilities.

(3) The effectiveness of various methods of providing accessibility to such buses and service to individuals with disabilities.

(4) The cost of providing accessible over - the - road buses and bus service to individuals with disabilities, including consideration of recent technological and cost saving developments in equipment and devices.

(5) Possible design changes in over - the - road buses that could enhance accessibility, including the installation f accessible restrooms which do not result in a loss of seating capacity.

(6) ADVISORY COMMITTEE. - In conducting the study required by subsection (a), the Office of Technology Assessment shall establish an advisory committee, which shall consist of -

(1) members selected from among private operators and manufacturers of over - the - road buses;

(2) members selected from among individuals with disabilities, particularly individuals who use wheelchairs, who are potential riders of such buses;; and

(3) members selected for their technical expertise on issues included in the study, including manufacturers of boarding assistance equipment and devices.

The number of members selected under each of paragraphs (1) and (2) shall be equal, and the total number of members selected under paragraphs (1) and (2) shall exceed the number of members selected under paragraph (3).

(d) DEADLINE. - The study required by subsection (a), along with recommendations by the Office of Technology Assessment, including any policy options for legislative action, shall be submitted to the President and Congress within 36 months after the date of the enactment of this Act. If the President determines that compliance with the regulations issued pursuant to section 306(a)(2)(B) on or before the applicable deadlines specified in section 306(a)(2)(B) will result in a significant reduction in intercity over - the - road bus service, the President shall extend each such deadline by 1 year.

(e) REVIEW. - In developing the study required by subsection (a), the Office of Technology Assessment shall provide a preliminary draft of such study to the Architectural and Transportation Barriers Compliance

Board established under section 502 of the Rehabilitation Act of 1973 (20 U.S.C. 792). The Board shall have an opportunity to comment on such draft study, and any such comments by the Board made in writing within 120 days after the Board's receipt of the draft study shall be incorporated as part of the final study required to be submitted under subsection (d).

SEC. 306. REGULATIONS.

(a) TRANSPORTATION PROVISIONS. -

(1) GENERAL RULE. - Not later than 1 year after the date of the enactment of this Act, the Secretary of Transportation shall issue regulations in an accessible format to carry out sections 302(b)(2)(B) and (C) and to carry out section 304 (other than subsection (b)(4).

(2) SPECIAL RULES FOR PROVIDING ACCESS TO OVER - THE - ROAD BUSES. -

(A) INTERIM REQUIREMENTS -

(i) ISSUANCE. - Not later than 1 year after the date of enactment of this Act, the Secretary of Transportation shall issue regulations in an accessible format to carry out sections 304(b)(4) and 302(b)(2)(D)(ii) that require each private entity which uses an over - the - road bus to provide transportation of individuals to provide accessibility to such bus; except that such regulations shall not require any structural changes in over - the - road buses in order to provide access to individuals who use wheelchairs during the effective period of such regulations and shall not require the purchase of boarding assistance devices to provide access to such individuals.

(ii) EFFECTIVE PERIOD. - The regulations issued pursuant to this subparagraph shall be effective until the effective date of the regulations issued under subparagraph (B).

(B) FINAL REQUIREMENT. -

(i) REVIEW OF STUDY AND INTERIM REQUIREMENTS. - The Secretary shall review the study submitted under section 305 and the regulations issued pursuant to subparagraph (A).

(ii) ISSUANCE. - Not later than 1 year after the date of the submission of the study under section 305, the Secretary shall issue in an accessible format new regulations to carry out sections 304(b)(4) and 302(b)(2)(D)(ii) that require, taking into account the purposes of the study under section 305 and any recommendations regulating from such study, each private entity which uses an over - the - road bus to provide transportation to individuals to provide accessibility to such bus to individuals with disabilities, including individuals who use wheelchairs.

(iii) EFFECTIVE PERIOD. - Subject to section 305(d), the regulations issued pursuant to this subparagraph shall take effect -

(I) with respect to small provides of transportation (as defined by the Secretary), 7 years after the date of the enactment of this Act; and

(II) with respect to other providers of transportation, 6 years after such date of enactment.

(C) LIMITATION ON REQUIRING INSTALLATION OF ACCESSIBLE RESTROOMS. - The regulations issued pursuant to this paragraph shall not require the installation of accessible restrooms in over - the - road buses if such installation would result in a loss of seating capacity.

(3) STANDARDS. - The regulations issued pursuant to this subsection shall include standards applicable to facilities and vehicles covered by sections 302(b)(2)and 304.

(b) OTHER PROVISIONS. - Not later than 1 year after the date of the enactment of this Act, the Attorney General shall issue regulations in an accessible format to carry out the provisions of this title not referred to in subsection (a) that include standards applicable to facilities and vehicles covered under section 302.

(c) CONSISTENCY WITH ATBCB GUIDELINES. - Standards included in regulations issued under subsections (a) and (b) shall be consistent with the minimum guidelines and requirements issued by the Architectural and Transportation Barriers Compliance board in accordance with section 504 of this Act.

(d) INTERIM ACCESSIBILITY STANDARDS. -

(1) FACILITIES. - If final regulations have not been issued pursuant to this section, for new construction or alterations for which a valid and appropriate State or local building permit is obtained prior to the issuance of final regulations under this section, and for which the construction or alteration authorized by such permit begins within one year of the receipt of such permit and is completed under the terms of such permit, compliance with the Uniform Federal Accessibility Standards in effect at the time the building permit is issued shall suffice to satisfy the requirement that facilities be readily accessible to and usable by persons with disabilities as required under section 303, except that, if such final regulations have not been issued one year after the Architectural and Transportation Barriers Compliance Board has issued the supplemental minimum guidelines required under section 504(a) of this Act, compliance with such supplemental minimum guidelines shall be necessary to satisfy the requirement that facilities be readily accessible to and usable by persons with disabilities prior to issuance of the final regulations.

(2) VEHICLES AND RAIL PASSENGER CARS. - If final regulations have not been issued pursuant to this section, a private entity shall be considered to have complied with the requirements of this title, if any, that a vehicle or rail passenger car be readily accessible to and usable by individuals with disabilities, if the design for such vehicle or car complies with the laws and regulations (including the Minimum Guidelines and Requirements for Accessible Design and such supplemental minimum guidelines as are issued under section 504(a) of this Act) governing accessibility of such vehicles or cars, to the extent that such laws and regulations are not inconsistent with this title and are in effect at the time such design is substantially completed.

SEC. 307. EXEMPTIONS FOR PRIVATE CLUBS AND RELIGIOUS ORGANIZATIONS.

The provisions of this title shall not apply to private clubs or establishments exempted from coverage under title II of the Civil Rights Act of 1964 (42 U.S.C. 2000 - a(e)) or to religious organizations or entities controlled by religious organizations, including places of worship.

SEC. 308. ENFORCEMENT.

(a) IN GENERAL. -
(1) AVAILABILITY OF REMEDIES ND PROCEDURES. - The remedies and procedures set forth in section 204(a) of the Civil Rights Act of 1964 (42 U.S.C. 2000a - 3(a)) are the remedies and procedures this title provides to any person who is being subjected to discrimination on the basis of disability in violation of this title or who has reasonable grounds for believing that such person is about to be subjected to discrimination in violation of section 303. Nothing in this section shall require a person with a disability to engage in a futile gesture if such person has actual notice that a person or organization covered by this title does not intent to comply with its provisions.

(2) INJUNCTIVE RELIEF. - In the case of violations of section 302(b)(2)(A)(iv) and section 303(a), injunctive relief shall include an order to alter facilities to make such facilities readily accessible to and usable by individuals with disabilities to the extent required by this title. Where appropriate, injunctive relief shall also include requiring the provision of an auxiliary aid or service, modification of a policy, or provision of alternative methods, to the extent required by this title.

(b) ENFORCEMENT BY THE ATTORNEY GENERAL. -
(1) DENIAL OF RIGHTS. -
(A) DUTY TO INVESTIGATE. -
(i) IN GENERAL. - The Attorney General shall investigate alleged violations of this title, and shall undertake periodic reviews of compliance of covered entities under this title.

(ii) ATTORNEY GENERAL CERTIFICATION. - On the application of a State or local government, the Attorney General may, in consultation with the Architectural and Transportation Barriers Compliance Board, and after prior notice and a public hearing at which persons, including individuals with disabilities, are provided an opportunity to testify against such certification, certify that a state law or local building code or similar ordinance that establishes accessibility requirements meets or exceeds the minimum requirements of this Act for the accessibility and usability of covered facilities under this title. At any enforcement proceeding under this section, such certification by the Attorney General shall be rebuttable evidence that such state law or local ordinance does meet or exceed the minimum requirements of this Act.

(B) POTENTIAL VIOLATION. - If the Attorney General has reasonable cause to believe that -
(i) any person or group of persons is engaged in a pattern of practice of discrimination under this title; or
(ii) any person or group of persons has been discriminated against under this title and such discrimination raises an issue of general public importance,
the Attorney General may commence a civil action in any appropriate United States court.

(2) AUTHORITY OF COURT. - In a civil action under paragraph (1)(B) the court -
(A) may grant any equitable relief that such court considers to be appropriate, including, to the extent required by this title -

(i) granting temporary, preliminary or permanent relief;
(ii) providing an auxiliary aid or service, modification of policy, practice, or procedure, or alternative method; and
(iii) making facilities readily accessible to and usable by individuals with disabilities;
(B) may award such other relief as the court consider to be appropriate, including monetary damages to persons aggrieved when requested by the Attorney General; and
(C) may, to vindicate the public interest, assess a civil penalty against the entity in an amount -
(i) not exceeding $50,000 for a first violation; and
(ii) not exceeding $100,000 for any subsequent violation.

(3) SINGLE VIOLATION. - For purposes of paragraph (2)(C), in determining whether a first or subsequent violation has occurred, a determination in a single action, by judgment or settlement, that the covered entity has engaged in more than one discriminatory act shall be counted as a single violation.

(4) PUNITIVE DAMAGES. - For purposes of subsection (b)(2)(B), the term "monetary damages" and "such other relief" does not include punitive damages.

(5) JUDICIAL CONSIDERATION. - In a civil action under paragraph (1)(B), the court, when considering what amount of civil penalty, if any, is appropriate, shall give consideration to any good faith effort or attempt to comply with this Act by the entity. In evaluating good faith, the court shall consider, among other factors it deems relevant, whether the entity could have reasonably anticipated the need for an appropriate type of auxiliary aid needed to accommodate the unique needs of a particular individual with a disability.

SEC. 309. EXAMINATIONS AND COURSES.

Any person that offers examinations or courses related to applications, licensing, certification, or credentialing for secondary or post - secondary education, professional, or trade purposes shall offer such examinations or courses in a place and manner accessible to persons with disabilities or offer alternative accessible arrangements for such individuals.

SEC. 310. EFFECTIVE DATE.

(a) GENERAL RULE. - Except provided in subsections (b) and (c), this title shall become effective 18 months after the date of the enactment of this Act.

(b) CIVIL ACTIONS. - Except for any civil action brought for a violation of section 303, no civil action shall be brought for any act or omission described in section 302 which occurs -
(1) during the first 6 months after the effective date, against businesses that employ 25 or fewer employees , ⁴ have gross receipts of $1,000,000 or less; and
(2) during the first year after the effective date, against businesses that employ 10 or fewer employees and have gross receipts of $500,000 or less.

(c) EXCEPTION. - Sections 302(a) for purposes of section 302(b)(2)(B)(C) only, 304(a) for purposes of section 304(b)(3) only, 304(b)(3) and 306 shall take effect on the date of the enactment of this Act.

TITLE IV TELECOMMUNICATIONS

SEC. 401. TELECOMMUNICATIONS RELAY SERVICES FOR HEARING - IMPAIRED AND SPEECH - IMPAIRED INDIVIDUALS.

(a) TELECOMMUNICATIONS. - Title II of the Communications Act of 1934 (47 U.S.C. 21 et seq.) is amended by adding at the end thereof the following new section:

SEC 225. TELECOMMUNICATIONS SERVICES FOR HEARING IMPAIRED AND SPEECH IMPAIRED INDIVIDUALS.

"(a) DEFINITIONS. - As used in this section -

"(1) COMMON CARRIER OR CARRIER. - The term 'common carrier' or 'carrier' includes any common carrier engaged in interstate communication by wire or radio as defined in section 3(h) and any common carrier engaged in intrastate communication by wire or radio, notwithstanding sections 2(b) and 221(b).

"(2) TDD. - The term 'TDD' means a Telecommunications Device for the Deaf, which is a machine that employs graphic communication in the transmission of coded signals through a wire or radio communication system.

"(3) TELECOMMUNICATIONS RELAY SERVICES. - The term 'telecommunications relay service'" means telephone transmission services that provide the ability for an individual who has a hearing impairment or speech impairment to engage in communication by wire or radio with a hearing individual in a manner that is functionally equivalent to the ability of an individual who does not have a hearing impairment or speech impairment to communicate using voice communication services by wire or radio. Such term includes services that enable two - way communication between an individual who uses a TDD or other nonvoice terminal device and an individual who does not use such a device.

(b) AVAILABILITY OF TELECOMMUNICATIONS RELAY SERVICES. -

(1) IN GENERAL. - In order to carry out the purposes established under section 1, to make available to all individuals in the United States a rapid, efficient nationwide communication service, and to increase the utility of the telephone system of the nation, the commission shall ensure that interstate and intrastate telecommunications relay services are available, to the extent possible and in the most efficient manner, to hearing - impaired and speech - impaired individuals in the United States.

(2) USE OF GENERAL AUTHORITY AND REMEDIES. - For the purposes of administering and enforcing the provisions of this section and the regulations prescribed thereunder, the commission shall have the same authority, power, and function with respect to common carriers engaged in intrastate communication as the commission has in administering and enforcing the provisions of this title with respect to all common carrier

engaged in interstate communication. Any violation of this section by any common carrier engaged in intrastate communication shall be subject to the same remedies, penalties, and procedures as are applicable to a violation of this act by a common carrier engaged in interstate communication.

(c) PROVISION OF SERVICES. - Each common carrier providing telephone voice transmission services shall, not later than 3 years after the date of enactment of this section, provide in compliance with the regulations prescribed under this section, throughout the area in which it offers service, telecommunications relay services, individually, through designees, through a competitively selected vendor, or in concert with other carriers. A common carrier shall be considered to be in compliance with regulations -

"(1) with respect to intrastate telecommunications relay services in any state that does not have a certified program under subsection (f) and with respect to interstate telecommunications relay services, if such common carrier (or other entity through which the carrier is providing such relay services) is in compliance with the program certified under subsection (f) for such state.

(d) REGULATIONS. -

"(1) IN GENERAL. - The commission shall, not later than 1 year after the date of enactment of this section, prescribe regulations to implement this section, including regulations that -

"(A) establish functional requirements, guidelines, and operations procedures for telecommunications relay services;

"(B) establish minimum standards that shall be met in carrying out subsection (c);

"(C) require that telecommunications relay services operate every day for 24 hour per day;

"(D) require that users of telecommunications relay services pay rates no greater than the rates paid for functionally equivalent voice communication services with respect to such factors as the duration of the call, the time of day, and the distance from point of origination to point of termination.

"(E) prohibit relay operators from failing to fulfill the obligations of common carriers by refusing calls or limiting the length of calls that use telecommunications relay services;

"(F) prohibit relay operators from disclosing the content of any relayed conversation and from keeping records of the content of any such conversation beyond the duration of the call; and

"(G) prohibit relay operators from intentionally altering a relayed conversation.

"(2) TECHNOLOGY. - The commission shall ensure that regulations prescribed to implement this section encourage, consistent with section 7(a) of this act, the use of existing technology and do not discourage or impair the development of improve technology.

"(3) JURISDICTIONAL SEPARATION OF COSTS. -

"(A) IN GENERAL. - Consistent with the provisions of section 410 of this act, the commission shall prescribe regulations governing the jurisdictional separation of costs for the services provided pursuant to this section.

"(B) RECOVERING COSTS. - Such regulations shall generally provide that costs caused by interstate telecommunications relay services shall be recovered from all subscribers for every interstate service and costs caused by intrastate telecommunications relay services shall be recovered from the intrastate jurisdiction. In a state that has a certified program under subsection (f), a state commission shall permit a common carrier to recover the costs incurred in providing intrastate telecommunications relay services by a method consistent with the requirements of this section.

"(e) ENFORCEMENT. -

"(1) IN GENERAL. - Subject to subsections (f) and (g), the commission shall enforce this section.

"(2) COMPLAINT. - The commission shall resolve, by final order, a complaint alleging a violation of this section within 180 days after the date such complaint is filed.

"(f) CERTIFICATION. -

"(1) STATE DOCUMENTATION. - Any state desiring to establish a state program under this section shall submit documentation to the commission that describes the program of such state for implementing intrastate telecommunications relay services and the procedures and remedies available for enforcing any requirements imposed by the state program.

"(2) REQUIREMENTS FOR CERTIFICATION. - After review of such document, the commission shall certify the state program if the commission determines that -

"(A) the program makes available to hearing impaired and speech - impaired individuals, either directly , through designates, through a competitively selected vendor, or through regulation of intrastate common carriers, intrastate telecommunications relay services in such state in a manner that meets or exceeds the requirements of regulations prescribed by the commission under subsection (d); and

"(B) the program makes available adequate procedures and remedies for enforcing the requirements of the state program.

"(3) METHOD OF FUNDING. - Except as provided in subsection (d), the commission shall not refuse to certify a state program based solely on the method such state will implement for funding intrastate telecommunication relay services.

"(4) SUSPENSION OF REVOCATION OF CERTIFICATION. - The commission may suspend or revoke such certification if, after notice and opportunity for hearing, the commission determines that such certification is no longer warranted. In a state whose program has been suspended or revoked, the commission shall take such steps as may be necessary, consistent with this section, to ensure continuity of telecommunications relay services.

"(g) COMPLAINT. -

"(1) REFERRAL OF COMPLAINT. - If a complaint to the commission alleges a violation of this section with respect to intrastate telecommunications relay services within a state and certification of the program of such state under subsection (f) is in effect, the commission shall refer such complaint to such state.

"(2) JURISDICTION OF COMMISSION. - After referring a complaint to a state under paragraph (1), the commission shall exercise jurisdiction over such complaint only if -

"(A) final action under such state program has not been taken on such complaint by such state -

"(i) within 180 days after the complaint is filed with such state; or

"(ii) within a shorter period as prescribed by the regulations of such state; or

"(B) the commission determines that such state program is no longer qualified for certification under subsection (f)."

(b) CONFORMING AMENDMENTS. - The Communications Act of 1934 (47 U.S.C. 151 et seq.0 is amended -

(1) in section 2(b) (47 U.S.C. 152(b)), by striking "section 224" and inserting "sections 224 and 225"; and

(2) in section 221(b) (47 U.S.C. 221(b)), by striking "section 301" and inserting "sections 225 and 301".

SEC. 402. CLOSED - CAPTIONING OF PUBLIC SERVICE ANNOUNCEMENTS.

Section 711 of the Communications Act of 1934 is amended to read as follows:

"SECTION 711. CLOSED - CAPTIONING OF PUBLIC SERVICE ANNOUNCEMENTS.

"Any television public service announcement that is produced or funded in whole or in part by any agency or instrumentality of federal government shall include closed captioning of the verbal content of such announcement. A television broadcast station licensee -

"(1) shall not be required to supply closed captioning for any such announcement that fails to include it; and

"(2) shall not be liable for broadcasting any such announcement without transmitting a closed caption unless the licensee intentionally fails to transmit the closed caption that was included with the announcement."

TITLE V - MISCELLANEOUS PROVISIONS

SEC. 501. CONSTRUCTION.

(a) IN GENERAL. - Except as otherwise provided in this act, nothing in this act shall be construed to apply a lesser standard than the standards applied under title V of the Rehabilitation Act of 1973 (29 U.S.C. 790 et seq.) or the regulations issued by federal agencies pursuant to such title.

(b) RELATIONSHIP TO OTHER LAWS. - Nothing in this act shall be construed to invalidate or limit the remedies, rights, and procedures of any federal law or law of any state or political subdivision of any state or jurisdiction that provides greater or equal protection for the rights of individuals with disabilities than are afforded by this act. Nothing in this act shall be construed to preclude the prohibition of, or the imposition of restrictions on, smoking in places of employment covered by title I, in transportation covered by title II or III, or in places of public accommodation covered by title III.

(c) INSURANCE. - Titles I through IV of this act shall not be construed to prohibit or restrict -

(1) an insurer, hospital or medical service company, health maintenance organization, or any agent, or entity that administers benefit plans, or similar organizations from underwriting risks, classifying risks, or administering

such risks that are based on or not inconsistent with state law; or

(2) a person or organization covered by this act from establishing, sponsoring, observing or administering the terms of a bona fide benefit plan that are based on underwriting risks, classifying risks, or administering such risks that are based on or not inconsistent with state law; or

(3) a person or organization covered by this act from establishing, sponsoring, observing or administering the terms of a bona fide benefit plan that is not subject to state laws that regulate insurance.

Paragraphs (1), (2), and (3) shall not be used as a subterfuge to evade the purposes of titles I and III.

(d) ACCOMMODATIONS AND SERVICES. - Nothing in this act shall be construed to require an individual with a disability to accept an accommodation, aid, service, opportunity, or benefit which such individual chooses not to accept.

SEC. 502. STATE IMMUNITY.

A state shall not be immune under the eleventh amendment to the Constitution of the United States from an action in federal or state court of competent jurisdiction for a violation of this act. In any action against a state for a violation of the requirements of this act, remedies (including remedies both at law and in equity) are available for such a violation to the same extent as such remedies are available for such a violation in an action against any public or private entity other than a state.

SEC. 503. PROHIBITION AGAINST RETALIATION AND COERCION.

(a) RETALIATION. - No person shall discriminate against any individual because such individual has opposed any act or practice made unlawful by this act or because such individual made a charge, testified, assisted, or participated in any manner in an investigation, proceeding, or hearing under this act.

(b) INTERFERENCE, COERCION, OR INTIMIDATION. - It shall be unlawful to coerce, intimidate, threaten, or d with any individual in the exercise of enjoyment of, or on account of his or her having exercised or enjoyed, or an account of his or her having aided or encouraged any other individual in the exercise of enjoyment of, any right granted or protected by this act.

(c) REMEDIES AND PROCEDURES. - The remedies and procedures available under sections 107, 203, and 308 of this act shall be to aggrieved persons for violations of subsections (a) and (b), with respect to title I title I and title III, respectively.

SEC. 504. REGULATIONS BY THE ARCHITECTURAL AND TRANSPORTATION BARRIERS COMPLIANCE BOARD.

(a) ISSUANCE OF GUIDELINES. - Not later than 9 months after the date of enactment of this act, the Architectural and Transportation barriers Compliance Board shall issue minimum guidelines that shall supplement the existing Minimum Guidelines and

Requirements for Accessible Design for purposes of titles II and III of this act.

(b) CONTENTS OF GUIDELINES. - The supplemental guidelines issued under subsection (a) shall establish additional requirements, consistent with this act, to ensure that buildings, facilities, rail passenger cars, and vehicles are accessible, in terms of architecture and design, transportation and communication, to individuals with disabilities.

(c) QUALIFIED HISTORIC PROPERTIES. -

(1) IN GENERAL. - The supplemental guidelines issued under subsection (a) shall include procedures and requirements for alterations that will threaten or destroy the historic significance of qualified historic buildings and facilities as defined in 4.17(1)(a) of the Uniform Federal Accessibility Standards.

(2) SITES ELIGIBLE FOR LISTING IN NATIONAL REGISTER. - With respect to alterations of buildings or facilities that are eligible for listing in the National Register of Historic Places under the National Historic Preservation Act (16 U.S.C. 470 et seq.), the guidelines described in paragraph (1) shall, at a minimum, maintain the procedures and requirements established in 4.17(1) and (2) of the Uniform Federal Accessibility Standards.

(3) OTHER SITES. - With respect to alterations of buildings or facilities designated as historic under state or local law, the guidelines described in paragraph (1) shall establish procedures equivalent to those established by 417(1)(b) and (c) of the Uniform Federal Accessibility Standards, and shall require, at a minimum, compliance with the requirements established in 4.17(2) of such standards.

SEC. 505. ATTORNEY FEES.

In any action or administrative proceeding commenced pursuant to this act, the court or agency, in its discretion, may allow the prevailing party, other than the United States, a reasonable attorney's fee, including litigation expenses, and costs, and the United States shall be liable for the foregoing the same as a private individual.

SEC. 506. TECHNICAL ASSISTANCE.

(a) PLAN FOR ASSISTANCE. -

(1) IN GENERAL. - Not later than 180 days after the date of enactment of this act, the Attorney General, in consultation with the Chair of the Equal Employment Opportunity Commission, the Secretary of Transportation, the Chair of the Architectural and Transportation Barriers Compliance Board, and the Chairman of the Federal Communications Commission, shall develop a plan to assist entities covered under this Act, and other Federal agencies, in understanding the responsibility of such entities and agencies under this act.

(2) PUBLICATION OF PLAN. - The Attorney General shall publish the plan referred to in paragraph (1) for public comment in accordance with subchapter II of chapter 5 of title 5, United States Code (commonly known as the Administrative Procedure Act).

(b) AGENCY AND PUBLIC ASSISTANCE. - The Attorney General may obtain the assistance of other federal agencies in carrying out subsection (a), including the National Council on Disability, the President's Committee on Employment of People with Disabilities, the Small Business Administration, and the Department of Commerce.

(c) IMPLEMENTATION. -

(A) RENDERING ASSISTANCE. - Each federal agency that has responsibility under paragraph (2) for implementing this act may render technical assistance to individuals and institutions that have rights or duties under the respective title or titles for which such agency has responsibility.

(2) IMPLEMENTATION OF TITLES. -

(A) TITLE I. - The Equal Employment Opportunity Commission and the Attorney General shall implement the plan for assistance developed under subsection (a), for title I.

(B) TITLE II. -

(i) SUBTITLE A. - The Attorney General shall implement such plan for assistance for subtitle A of title II.

(ii) SUBTITLE B. - The Secretary of Transportation shall implement such plan for assistance for subtitle B.

(C) TITLE III. - The Attorney General, in coordination with the Secretary of Transportation and the chair of the Architectural Transportation Barriers Compliance Board shall implement such plan for assistant for title III, except for section 304, the plan for assistance for which shall be implemented by the Secretary of Transportation.

(D) TITLE IV. - The chairman of the Federal Communications Commission, in coordination with the Attorney General, shall implement such plan for assistance for title IV.

(3) TECHNICAL ASSISTANCE MANUALS. - Each federal agency that has responsibility under paragraph (2) for implementing this act shall, as part of its implementation responsibilities, ensure the availability and provision of appropriate technical assistance manuals to individuals or entities with rights or duties under this act no later than six months after applicable final regulations are published under titles I, II, III, and IV.

(d) GRANTS AND CONTRACTS. -

(1) IN GENERAL. - Each federal agency that has responsibility under subsection (c) for implementing this Act may make grants or awards contracts to effectuate the purposes of this section, subject to the availability of appropriations. Such grants and contracts may be awarded to individuals, institutions not organized for profit and no part of the net earnings of which inures to the benefit of any private shareholder or individual (including educational institutions), and associations representing individuals who have rights or duties under this act. Contracts may be awarded to entities organized for profit, but such entities may not be the recipients of grants described in this paragraph.

(2) DISSEMINATION OF INFORMATION. - Such grants and contracts, among other uses, may be designed to ensure wide dissemination of information about the rights and duties established by this act and to provide information and technical assistance about techniques for effective compliance with this act.

(e) FAILURE TO RECEIVE ASSISTANCE. - An employer, public accommodation, or other entity covered under this act shall not be excused from compliance with the requirements of this act because of any failure to receive technical assistance under this section, including the development or dissemination of any technical assistance manual authorized by this section.

SEC. 507. FEDERAL WILDERNESS AREAS.

(a) STUDY. - The National Council on Disability shall conduct a study and report on the effect that wilderness designation as and wilderness land management practices have on the ability of individuals with disabilities to use and enjoy the National Wilderness Preservation System as established under the Wilderness Act (16 U.S.C. 1131 et seq.).

(b) SUBMISSION OF REPORT. - Not later than 1 year after the enactment of this Act, the National Council on Disability shall submit the report required under subsection (a) to Congress.

(c) SPECIFIED WILDERNESS ACCESS. -

(1) IN GENERAL. - Congress reaffirms that nothing in the Wilderness Act is to be construed as prohibiting the use of a wheelchair in a wilderness area by an individual whose disability requires use of a wheelchair, and consistent with the Wilderness Act no agency is required to provide any form of special treatment or accommodation, or to construct any facilities or modify any conditions of lands within a wilderness are in order to facilitate such use.

(2) DEFINITION. - For purposes of paragraph (1), the term "wheelchair" means a device designed solely for use by a mobility - impaired person for locomotion, that is suitable for use in an indoor pedestrian area.

SEC. 508. TRANSVESTITES.

For the purpose of this Act, the term "disabled" or "disability" shall not apply to an individual solely because that individual is a transvestite.

SEC. 509. COVERAGE OF CONGRESS AND THE AGENCIES OF THE LEGISLATIVE BRANCH

(a) COVERAGE OF THE SENATE. -

(1) COMMITMENT TO RULE XLII. - The Senate reaffirms its commitment to rule XLII of the Standing Rules of the Senate which provi   as follows:

"No member, officer, or employee of the Senate shall, with respect to employment by the Senate or any office thereof -

"(a) fail to refuse to hire an individual;

"(b) discharge an individual; or

"(c) otherwise discriminate against an individual

with respect to promotion, compensation, or terms, conditions, or privileges of employment on the basis of such individuals race, color, religion, sex, national origin, age, or state of physical handicap.".

(2) APPLICATION TO SENATE EMPLOYMENT. - The rights and protections provided pursuant to this Act, the Civil Rights Act of 1990 (S.2104, 101st Congress), the Civil Rights Act of 1964, the Age Discrimination in Employment Act of 1967, and the Rehabilitation Act of 1973 shall apply with respect to employment by the United States Senate.

(3) INVESTIGATION AND ADJUDICATION OF CLAIMS. - All claims raised by an individual with respect to Senate employment, pursuant to the Acts referred to in paragraph (2), shall be investigated and adjudicated by the Select Committee on Ethics, pursuant to S. Res. 338, 88th Congress, as amended, so such other entity as the Senate may designate.

(4) RIGHTS OF EMPLOYEES. - The Congress on rules and Administration shall ensure that Senate employees are informed of their rights under the Acts referred to in paragraph (2).

(5) APPLICABLE REMEDIES. - When assigning remedies to individuals found to have a valid claim under the Acts referred to in paragraph (2), the Select Committee on Ethics, or such other entity as the Senate may designate, should to the extent practicable apply the same remedies applicable to all other employees covered by the Acts referred to in paragraph (2). Such remedies shall apply exclusively.

(6) MATTERS OTHER THAN EMPLOYMENT. -

(A) IN GENERAL. - The rights and protections under this Act shall, subject to subparagraph (B), apply with respect to the conduct of the Senate regarding matters other than employment.

(B) REMEDIES. - The Architect of the Capital shall establish remedies and procedures to be utilized with respect to the rights and protections provided pursuant to subparagraph (A). Such remedies and procedures shall apply exclusively, after approval in accordance with subparagraph (C).

(C) PROPOSED REMEDIES AND PROCEDURES. - For purposes of subparagraph (B), the Architect of the Capitol shall submit proposed remedies and procedures to the Senate Committee on Rules and Administration. The remedies and procedures shall be effective upon the approval of the Committee on Rules and Administration.

(7) EXERCISE OF RULEMAKING POWER. - Notwithstanding any other provision of law, enforcement and adjudication of the rights and protections referred to in paragraphs (2) and (6)(A) shall be within the exclusive jurisdiction of the United States Senate. The provisions of paragraphs (1), (3), (4), (5), (6)(B), and (6)(C) are enacted by the Senate as an exercise of the rulemaking power of the Senate, with full recognition of the right of the Senate to change its rules, in the same manner, and to the same extent, as in the case of any other rule of the Senate.

(b) COVERAGE OF THE HOUSE OF REPRESENTATIVES. -

(1) IN GENERAL. - Notwithstanding any other provision of this Act or of law, the purposes of this Act shall, subject to paragraphs (2) and (3), apply in their entirety to the House of Representatives.

(2) EMPLOYMENT IN THE HOUSE. -

(A) APPLICATION. - The rights and protections under this Act shall, subject to subparagraph (B), apply with respect to any employee in an employment position in the House of Representatives and any employing authority of the House of Representatives.

(B) ADMINISTRATION. -

(i) IN GENERAL. - In the administration of this paragraph, the remedies and procedures made applicable pursuant to the resolution described in clause (ii) shall apply exclusively.

(ii) RESOLUTION. - The resolution referred to in clause (i) is House Resolution 15 of the One Hundredth First Congress, as agreed to January 3, 1989, or any other provision that continues in effect the provisions of, or is a successor to, the Fair Employment Practices Resolution (House Resolution 558 of the One Hundredth Congress, as agreed to October 4, 1988).

(C) EXERCISE OF RULEMAKING POWER. - The provisions of subparagraph (B) are enacted by the House of Representatives as an exercise of the rulemaking power of the House of Representatives, with full recognition of the right of the House to change its rules, in the same manner, and to the same extent as in the case of any other rule of the House.

(3) MATTERS OTHER THAN EMPLOYMENT. -

(A) IN GENERAL. - The rights and protections under this Act shall, subject to subparagraph (B), apply with respect to the conduct of the House of Representatives regarding matters other than employment.

(B) REMEDIES. - The Architect of the Capitol shall establish remedies and procedures to be utilized with respect to the rights and protections provided pursuant to subparagraph (A). Such remedies and procedures shall apply exclusively after approval in accordance with subparagraph (C).

(C) APPROVAL. - For purposes of subparagraph (B), the Architect of the Capitol shall submit proposed remedies and procedures to the Speaker of the House of Representatives. The remedies and procedures shall be effective upon the approval of the Speaker, after consultation with the House Office Building Commission.

(c) INSTRUMENTALITIES OF CONGRESS. -

(1) IN GENERAL. - The rights and protections under this Act shall, subject to paragraph (8), apply with respect to the conduct of each instrumentality of t he Congress.

(2) ESTABLISHMENT OF REMEDIES AND PROCEDURES BY INSTRUMENTALITIES. - The chief official of each instrumentality of the Congress shall establish remedies and procedures to be utilized with respect to the rights and protections provided pursuant to paragraph (1)., Such remedies and procedures shall apply exclusively.

(3) REPORT TO CONGRESS. - The chief official of each instrumentality of the Congress shall, after establishing remedies and procedures for purposes of paragraph (2), submit to the Congress a report describing the remedies and procedures.

(4) DEFINITION OF INSTRUMENTALITIES. - For purposes of this section, instrumentalities of the Congress include the following: the Architect of the Capitol, the Congressional Budget Office, the General Accounting Office, the Government Printing Office, the Library of Congress, the Office of Technology Assessment, and the United States Botanic Garden.

(5) CONSTRUCTION. - Nothing in this section shall alter the enforcement procedures for individuals with disabilities provided in the General Accounting Office Personnel Act of 1980 and regulations promulgated pursuant to that Act.

SEC. 510. ILLEGAL USE OF DRUGS

(a) IN GENERAL. - For purposes of this Act, the terms "individual with a disability" does not include an individual who is currently engaged in the illegal use of drugs, when the covered entity acts on the basis of such use.

(b) RULES OF CONSTRICTION. - Nothing in subsection (a) shall be construed to exclude as an individual with a disability an individual who -

(1) has successfully completed a supervised drug rehabilitation program and is no longer engaging in the illegal use of drugs, or has otherwise been rehabilitated successfully and is no longer engaging in such use;

(2) is participating in a supervised rehabilitation program and is no longer engaging in such use; or

(3) is erroneously regarded as engaging in such use, but is not engaging in such use;

except that it shall not be a violation of this Act for a covered entity to adopt or administer reasonable policies or procedures including but not limited to drug testing, designed to ensure that n individual described in paragraph (1) or (2) is no longer engaging in the illegal use of drugs; however, nothing in this section shall be construed to encourage, prohibit, restrict, or authorize the conducting of testing for the illegal use of drugs.

(c) HEALTH AND OTHER SERVICES. - Notwithstanding subsection (a) and section 511(b)(3) an individual shall not be denied health services, or services provided in connection with drug rehabilitation, on the basis of the current illegal use of drugs if the individual is otherwise entitled to such services.

(d) DEFINITION OF ILLEGAL USE OF DRUGS. -

(1) IN GENERAL. - The term "illegal use of drugs" means the use of drugs, the possession or distribution of which is unlawful under the Controlled Substances Act (21 U.S.C. 812). Such term does not include the use of a drug taken under supervision by a licensed health care professional, or other uses authorized by the Controlled Substances Act or other provisions of Federal law.

(2) DRUGS. - The term "drug" means a controlled substance, as defined in schedules I through V of section 202 of the Controlled Substances Act.

SEC. 511. DEFINITIONS.

(a) HOMOSEXUALITY AND BISEXUALITY. - For purposes of the definition of "disability" in section 3(2). homosexuality and bisexuality are not impairments and as such are not disabilities under this Act.

(b) CERTAIN CONDITIONS. - Under this Act, the term "disability" shall not include -

(1) transvestism, transsexualism, pedophilia, exhibitionism, voyeurism, gender identity disorders not resulting from physical impairments, or other sexual behavior disorders;

(2) compulsive gambling, kleptomania, or pyromania; or

(3) psychoactive substance use disorders resulting from current illegal use of drugs.

SEC. 512. AMENDMENTS TO THE REHABILITATION ACT.

(a) DEFINITION OF HANDICAPPED INDIVIDUAL. - Section 7(8) of the Rehabilitation Act of 1973 (29 U.S.C. 706(8)) is amended by redesignating subparagraph (C) as subparagraph (D), and by inserting after subparagraph (B) the following subparagraph:

"(C)(i) For purposes of title V, the term 'individual with handicaps' does not include an individual who is currently engaging in the illegal use of drugs, when a covered entity acts on the basis of such use.

"(ii) Nothing in clause (i) shall be construed to exclude as an individual with handicaps an individual who

"(I) has successfully completed a supervised drug rehabilitation program and is no longer engaging in the illegal use of drugs, or has otherwise been rehabilitated successfully and is no longer engaging in such use;

("II) is erroneously regarding as engaging in such use, but is not engaging in such use; except that it shall not be a violation of this Act for a covered entity to adopt or administer reasonable policies or procedures, including but not limited to drug testing, designed to ensure that an individual described in subclause (I) or (II) is no longer engaging in the illegal use of drugs.

"(iii) Notwithstanding clause (i) for purposes of programs and activities providing health services and services provided under titles I, II, and III, an individual shall not be excluded from the benefits of such programs or activities on the basis of his or her current illegal use of drugs if he or she is otherwise entitled to such services.

"(iv) For purposes of programs and activities providing educational services, local educational agencies may take disciplinary action pertaining to the use or possession of illegal drugs or alcohol against any handicapped student who currently is engaging in the illegal use of drugs or in the use of alcohol to the same extent that such disciplinary action is taken against nonhandicapped students. Furthermore, the due process procedures at 34 CFR 104.36 shall not apply to such disciplinary actions.

"(v) For purposes of sections 503 and 504 as such sections relate to employment, the term 'individual with handicaps' does not include any individual who is an alcoholic whose current use of alcohol prevents such individual from performing the duties of the job in question or whose employment, by reason of such current alcohol abuse, would constitute a direct threat to property or the safety of others.".

(b) DEFINITION OF ILLEGAL DRUGS. - Section 7 of the Rehabilitation Act of 1973 (29 U.S.C. 706) is amended by adding at the end the following new paragraph:

"(22)(A) The term 'drug' means a controlled substance, as defined in schedules I through V of section 202 of the Controlled Substances Act (21 U.S.C. 812).

"(B) The term 'illegal use of drugs' means the use of drugs, the possession or distribution of which is unlawful under the Controlled Substances Act. Such term does not include the use of a drug taken under supervision by a licensed health care professional, or other uses authorized by the Controlled Substances Act or other provisions of Federal law.".

(c) CONFORMING AMENDMENTS. - Section 7(8)(B) of the Rehabilitation Act of 1973 (29 U.S.C. 706(8)(B)) is amended -

(1) in the first sentence, by striking "Subject to the second sentence of this subparagraph," and inserting "Subject to subparagraphs (C) and (D),"' and

(2) by striking the second sentence.

SEC.. 513. ALTERNATIVE MEANS OF DISPUTE RESOLUTION.

Where appropriate and to the extent authorized by law, the use of alternative means of dispute resolution, including settlement negotiations, conciliation, facilitation, mediation, factfinding, minitrials, and arbitration, is encouraged to resolve disputes arising under this Act.

SEC. 514. SEVERABILITY.

. Should any provision in this Act be found to be unconstitutional by a court of law, such provision shall be severed from the remainder of the Act, and such action shall not affect the enforceability of the remaining provisions of the Act.

M
REHABILITATION ACT OF 1973, AS AMENDED

This appendix presents the full text of the Rehabilitation Act of 1973, as amended (29 U.S.C. Sec. 791 et seq.).

DEFINITIONS
****

Sec. 7(8)(A) Except as otherwise provided in subparagraph (B), the term "handicapped individual" means any individual who (i) has a physical or mental disability which for such individual constitutes or results in a substantial handicap to employment and (ii) can reasonably be expected to benefit in terms of employability from vocational rehabilitation services provided pursuant to title I and III of this Act.

(B) Subject to subparagraphs (C) and (D), the term "handicapped individual" means, for purposes of titles IV and V of this Act, any person who (i) has a physical or mental impairment which substantially limits one or more of such person's major life activities, (ii) has a record of such an impairment, or (iii) is regarded as having such an impairment.

(C)(i) For purposes of title V, the term "individual with handicaps' does not include an individual who is currently engaging in the illegal use of drugs, when a covered entity acts on the basis of such use.

(ii) Nothing in clause (i) shall be construed to exclude as an individual with handicaps an individual who-

(I) has successfully completed a supervised drug rehabilitation program and is no longer engaging in the illegal use of drugs, or has otherwise been rehabilitated successfully and is no longer engaging in such use;

(II) is participating in a supervised rehabilitation program and is no longer engaging in such use; or

(III) is erroneously regarded as engaging in such use, but is not engaging in such use;

except that it shall not be a violation of this Act for a covered entity to adopt or administer reasonable policies or procedures, including but not limited to drug testing, designed to ensure that an individual described in subclause (I) or (II) is no longer engaging in the illegal use of drugs.

(iii) Notwithstanding clause (i) for purposes of programs and activities providing health services and services provided under titles I, II, and III, an individual shall not be excluded from the benefits of such programs or activities on the basis of his or her current illegal use of drugs if he or she is otherwise entitled to such services.

(iv) For purposes of programs and activities providing educational services, local educational agencies may take disciplinary action pertaining to the use or possession of illegal drugs or alcohol against any handicapped student who currently is engaging in the illegal use of drugs or in the use of alcohol to the same extent that such disciplinary action is taken against nonhandicapped students. Furthermore, the due process procedures at 34 CFR 104.36 shall not apply to such disciplinary actions.

(v) For purposes of sections 503 and 504 as such sections relate to employment, the term "individual with handicaps" does ont include any individual who is an alcoholic whose current use of alcohol prevents such individual from performing the duties of the job in question or whose employment , by reason of such current alcohol abuse, would constitute a direct threat to property or the safety of others.

(D) For the purpose of sections 503 and 504, as such sections relate to employment, such term does not include an individual who has a currently contagious disease or infection and who, by reason of such disease or infection, would constitute a direct threat to the health or safety of other individuals or who, by reason of the currently contagious disease or infection, is unable to perform the duties of the job.

* * *

Sec. 7(22)(A). The term "drug" means a controlled substance, as defined in schedules I through V of section 202 of the Controlled Substances Act (21 U.S.C. 812).

(B) The term "illegal use of drugs" means the use of drugs, the possession or distribution of which is unlawful under the Controlled Substances Act. Such term does not include the use of a drug taken under supervision by a licensed health car professional, or other uses authorized by the Controlled Substances Act or other provisions of federal law.

* * *

EMPLOYMENT OF HANDICAPPED INDIVIDUALS

Sec. 501 (a) There is established within the Federal Government an Interagency Committee on Handicapped Employees (hereinafter in this section referred to as the "Committee"), comprised of such members as the President may select, including the following (or their designees whose positions are Executive Level IV or higher): the Chairman of the Civil Service Commission, the Administrator of Veterans' Affairs, and the Secretaries of Labor and Health, Education, and Welfare. The Secretary of Health, Education, and Welfare and the Chairman of the Civil Service Commission shall serve as co-chairman of the Committee. The resources of the President's Committees on Employment of the Handicapped and on Mental Retardation shall be made fully available to the Committee. It shall be the purpose and function of the Commission (1) to provide a focus for Federal and other employment of handicapped individuals, and to review, on a period basis, in cooperation with the Civil Service Commission, the adequacy of hiring, placement, and advancement practices with respect to handicapped individuals, by each department, agency and instrumentality in the executive branch of Government, and to insure that the special needs of such individuals are being met; and (2) to consult with the Civil Service Commission to assist the Commission to carry out its responsibilities under subsections (b), (c), and (d) of this section. On the basis of such review and consultation, the Committee shall periodically make to the Civil Service Commission such recommendations for legislative and administrative changes as it deems necessary or desirable. The Civil Service Commission shall timely transmit to the appropriate committees of Congress any such recommendations.

(b) Each department, agency, and instrumentality (including the United States Postal Service and the Postal Rate Commission) in the executive branch shall, within one hundred and eight days after the date of enactment of this Act, submit to the Civil Service Commission and to the Committee an affirmative action program plan for the hiring, placement, and advancement of handicapped individuals in such department, agency, or instrumentality. Such plan shall include a description of the extent to which and methods whereby the special needs of handicapped employees are being met. Such plan shall be updated annually, and shall be reviewed annually and approved by the Commission, if the Commission determines, after consultation with the Committee, that such plan provides sufficient assurances, procedures and commitments to provide adequate hiring, placement, and advancement opportunities for handicapped individuals.

(c) The Civil Service Commission, after consultation with the Committee, shall develop and recommend to the Secretary for referral to the appropriate State agencies, policies and procedures which will facilitate the hiring, placement, and advancement in employment of individuals who have received rehabilitation services under State vocational rehabilitation programs, veterans' programs, or any other program for handicapped individuals, including the promotion of job opportunities for such individuals. The Secretary shall encourage such State agencies to adopt and implement such policies and procedures.

(d) The Civil Service Commission, after consultation with the Committee, shall, on June 30, 1974, and at the end of each subsequent fiscal year, make a complete report to the appropriate committees of the Congress with respect to the practices of an achievements in hiring, placement, and advancement of handicapped individuals by each department, agency, and instrumentality and the effectiveness of the affirmative action programs required by subsection (b) of this section, together with recommendations as to legislation which have been submitted to the Civil Service Commission under subsection (a) of this section, or other appropriate action to insure the adequacy of such practices. Such report shall also include an evaluation by the Committee of the effectiveness of the Civil Service Commission's activities under subsection (b) and (c) of this section.

(e) An individual who, as a part of his individualized written rehabilitation program under a State plan approved under this Act, participates in a program of unpaid work experience in a Federal agency, shall not, by reason thereof, be considered to be a Federal employee or to be subject to the provisions of law relating to Federal employment, including those relating to hours of work, rates of compensation, leaves, unemployment compensation, and Federal employee benefits.

(f)(1) The Secretary of Labor and the Secretary of Health, Education, and Welfare are authorized and directed to cooperate with the President's Committee on Employment of the Handicapped in carrying out its functions.

(2) In selecting personnel to fill all positions on the President's Committee on Employment of the Handicapped, special consideration shall be given to qualified handicapped individuals.

ARCHITECTURAL AND TRANSPORTATION BARRIERS COMPLIANCE BOARD

Sec. 502(a)(1) There is established within the Federal Government the Architectural and Transportation Barriers Compliance Board (hereinafter referred to as the "Board") which shall be composed as follows:

(A) Eleven members shall be appointed by the President from among members of the general public of whom five shall be handicapped individuals.

(B) The remaining members shall be the heads of each of the following departments or agencies (or their designees whose positions are executive level IV or higher);

(i) Department of Health, Education, and Welfare.
(ii) Department of Transportation.
(iii) Department of Labor.
(iv) Department of Interior.
(v) Department of Defense.
(vi) Department of Justice.
(vii) General Services Administration.
(viii) Veterans' Administration.
(ix) United States Postal Service.

The President shall appoint the first Chairman of such Board who shall serve for a term of not more than two years; thereafter, the Chairman shall be elected by a vote of a majority of the Board for a term of one year.

(2) The term office of each appointed member of the Board shall be three years; except that (i) the members first taking office shall serve, as designated by the President at the time of appointment, four for a term of one year, four for a terms of two years, and three for a term of three years, and (ii) any member appointed to fill a vacancy shall service for the remainder of the term for which his predecessor was appointed.

(3) If any appointed member of the Board becomes a Federal employee, such member may continue as a member of the Board for not longer than the sixty-day period being on the date he becomes such an employee.

(4) No individual appointed under paragraph (1)(A) of this subsection who has serviced as a member of the Board may be reappointed to the Board more than once unless such individual has not served on the Board for a period of two years prior to the effective date of such individual's appointment.

(5)(A) Members of the board who are not regular fulltime employees of the United States shall, while servicing on the business of the Board, be entitled to receive compensation at rates fixed by the President, but not to exceed the daily rate prescribed for GS-18 under section 5332 of title 5, United States Code, including traveltime, for each day they are engaged in the performance of their duties as members of the Board; and shall be entitled to reimbursement for travel, subsistence, and other necessary expenses incurred by them in carrying out their duties n'under this section.

(B) Members of the Board who are employed by the Federal Government shall serve without compensation, but shall be reimbursed for travel, subsistence, and other necessary expenses incurred by them in carrying out their duties under this section.

It shall be the function of the Board to:

(1) insure compliance with the standards prescribed pursuant to the Act of August 12, 1968, commonly known as the Architectural Barriers Act of 1968 (including the application of that Act to the United States Postal Service) including but not limited to enforcing all standards under that Act, and insuring that all waivers and modifications of standards are based upon findings of fact and are not inconsistent with the provisions of such Act and this section; (2) investigate and examine alternative approaches to the architectural, transportation, communication, and attitudinal barriers confronting handicapped individuals, particularly with respect to telecommunication devices, public building and monuments, parks and parklands, public transportation (including air, water, and surface transportation whether interstate, foreign, intrastate, or local), and residential and institutional housing; (3) determine what measures are being taken by Federal, State, and local governments and by other public or nonprofit agencies to eliminate the barriers described in clause (2) of this subsection; (4) promote the use of the International Accessibility Symbol in all public facilities that are in compliance with the standards prescribed by the Administrator of the General Services Administration, the Secretary of Defense, and the Secretary of Housing and Urban Development pursuant to the Architectural Barriers Act of 1968; (5) make to the President and to Congress reports which shall describe in detail the results to its investigations under clauses (2) and (3) of this subsection; (6) make to the President and to Congress such recommendations for legislation and administration as it deems necessary or desirable to eliminate the barriers described in clause (2) of this subsection; (7) establish minimum guidelines and requirements for the standards issued pursuant to the Act of August 12, 1968, as amended, commonly known as the Architectural Barriers Act of 1968; and (8) insure that public conveyances, including rolling stock, are readily accessible to, and usable by, physically handicapped persons.

The Board shall also

(1)(A) determine how and to what extent transportation barriers impede the mobility of handicapped individuals and aged handicapped individuals and consider ways in which travel expenses in connection with transportation to and from work for handicapped individuals can be met or subsidized when such individuals are unable to use mass transit systems or need special equipment in private transportation, and (B) consider the housing needs of handicapped individuals; (2) determine what measures are being taken, especially by public and other nonprofit agencies and groups having an interest in and a capacity to deal with such problems. (A) to eliminate barriers from public transportation systems and (B) to make housing available and accessible to handicapped individuals or to meet sheltered housing needs; and (3) prepare plans and proposal for such further actions as may be necessary to the goals of adequate transportation and housing for handicapped individuals, including proposals for bringing together in a cooperative effort, agencies, organizations, and groups already working toward such goals or whose cooperation is essential to effective and comprehensive action.

(1) In carrying out its functions under this chapter, the Board shall, directly or through grants to public or private nonprofit organizations or contracts with private nonprofit or for profit organizations, carry out its functions under subsections (b) and (c) of this section, and shall conduct investigations, hold public hearings, and issue such orders as it deems necessary to insure compliance with the provisions of the Acts cited in subsection (8b) of this section. Except as provided in paragraph (3) of subsection (e) of this section, the provisions of subchapter II of chapter 5, and chapter 7 of Title 5 shall apply to procedures under this section, and an order of compliance issued by the Board shall be a final order for purposes of judicial review. Any such order affecting any Federal department, agency, or instrumentality of the United States shall be final and binding on such department, agency, or instrumentality. An order of compliance may include the withholding or suspension of Federal funds with respect to any building or public conveyance or rolling stock found not to be in compliance with standard enforced under this section. Pursuant to chapter 7 of title 5, United States Code, any complainant or participant in a proceeding under this subsection may obtain review of a final order issued in such proceeding.

(2) The executive director is authorized, at the direction of the Board

(A) to bring a civil action in any appropriate United States district court to enforce, in whole or in part, any final order of the Board under this subsection; and

(B) to intervene, appear, and participate, or to appear as amicus curiae, in any court of the United States or in any court of a State in civil actions which relates to this section or to the Architectural Barriers Act of 1958. Except as provided in section 518(a) of title 28, United States Code, relating to litigation before the Supreme Court, the executive director may appear for and represent the Board in any civil litigation brought under this section.

(3) The Board, in consultation and coordination with other concerned Federal departments and agencies; and agencies within the Departments of health, Education, and Welfare, shall develop standards and provide appropriate technical assistance to any public or private activity, person, or entity, affected by regulations prescribed pursuant to this title with respect to overcoming architectural, transportation, and communications barriers. Any funds appropriated to any such department or agency for the purpose of providing such assistance may be transferred to the Board for the purpose of carrying out this paragraph. The Board may arrange to carry out its responsibilities under this paragraph through such other departments and agencies for such periods as the Board determines is appropriate. In carrying out its technical assistance responsibilities under this paragraph, the Board shall establish a procedure to insure separation of its compliance and technical assistance responsibilities under this section.

(e)(1) There shall be appointed by the Board an executive director and such other professional and clerical personnel as are necessary to carry out its functions under this Act. The Board is authorized to appoint as many hearing examiners as are necessary for proceedings required to be conducted under this section. The provisions applicable to hearing examiners appointed under section 3105 of title 5, United States Code, shall apply to hearing examiners appointed under this subsection.

(2) The executive Director shall exercise general supervision over all personnel employed by the Board (other

than hearing examiners and their assistants). The Executive Director shall have final authority on behalf of the Board, with respect to the investigation of alleged noncompliance in the issuance of formal complaints before the Board, and shall have such duties as the Board may prescribe.

(3) For the purpose of this section, an order of compliance issued by a hearing examiner shall be deemed to be an order of the Board and shall be the final order for the purpose judicial review.

(f) The departments or agencies specified in subsection (a) of this section shall make available to the Board such technical, administrative, or other assistance as it may require to carry out its functions under this section, and the Board may appoint such other advises, technical experts, and consultants as it deems necessary to assist in carrying out its functions under this section. Special advisory and technical experts and consultants appointed pursuant to this subsection shall, while performing their functions under this section, be entitled to receive compensation at rates fixed by the Secretary, but not exceeding the daily pay rate, for a person employed as a GS-18 under section 5332 of title 45, United States Code, including travel time, and while servicing away from their homes or regular places of business they may be allowed travel expenses, including per diem in lieu of subsistence, as authorized by section 5703 of such title 5 for persons in the Government service employed intermittently.

(g) The Board shall, at the end of each fiscal year, report its activities during the preceding fiscal year to the Congress. Such report shall include an assessment of the extent of compliance with the Acts cited in subsection (b) of this section, along with a description and analysis of investigations made and actions taken by the Board, and the reports and recommendations described in clauses (5) and (6) of subsection (b) of this section. The Board shall prepare two final reports of its activities under subsection (c). One such report shall be on its activities in the field of transportation barriers to handicapped individuals, while performing their and the other such report shall be on its activities in the field of the housing needs of handicapped individuals. The Board shall, not later than September 30, 1975, submit each such report, together with its recommendations, to the President and the Congress. Thee Board shall also prepare for such submission an interim report of its activities in each such filed within 18 months after the date of enactment of this Act.

(h)(1) Within one year following the enactment of this subsection, the Board shall submit to the President and the Congress a report containing an assessment of the amounts required to be expended by States and by political subdivisions thereof to provide handicapped individuals with full access to all program and activities receiving Federal assistance.

(2) The Board may make grants to, or enter into contracts with, public or private organizations to carry out its duties under subsections (b) and (c). The Board may also make grants to provide the cost assessments required by paragraph (1). Before including in such report the findings of any stu   onducted by the Board under a grant or contract to provide the Board with such cost assessments, the Board shall take all necessary steps to validate the accuracy of any such findings.

(i) There are authorized to be appropriate for the purpose of carrying out the duties and functions of the Board under this section such sums as may be necessary for each fiscal year ending before October 1, 1982, but in no event shall the amount appropriated for any one fiscal year exceed 3,000,000.

EMPLOYMENT UNDER FEDERAL CONTRACTS

Sec. 503 (a) Any contract in excess of $2,500 entered into by any Federal department or agency for the procurement of personal property and nonpersonal services (including construction) for the United States shall contain a provision requiring that, in employing persons to carry out such contract the party contracting with the United States shall take affirmative action to employ and advance in employment qualified handicapped individuals as defined in section 7(6). The provisions of this section shall apply to any subcontract in excess of $2,500 entered into by a prime contractor in carrying out any contract fore the procurement of personal property and nonpersonal services (including construction) for the United States. The President shall implement the provisions of this section by promulgating regulations within ninety days after the date of enactment of this section.

(b) If any handicapped individual believes any contractor has failed or refuses to comply with the provisions of his contract with the United States, relating to employment of handicapped individuals, such individual may file a complaint with the Department of Labor. The Department shall promptly investigate such complaint and shall take such action thereon as the facts and circumstances warrant, consistent with the terms of such contract and the laws and regulations applicable thereto.

(c) The requirements of this section may be waived, in whole or in part, by the President with respect to a particular contract or subcontract, in accordance with guidelines set forth in regulations which he shall prescribe, when he determines that special circumstances in the national interest so require and states in writing his reasons for such determination.

NONDISCRIMINATION UNDER FEDERAL GRANTS AND PROGRAMS

Sec. 504. (a) No otherwise qualified handicapped individual in the United States, as defined in section 7(8), shall solely by reason of his handicap, be excluded from the participation in, be denied the benefits of, or be subjected to discrimination under any program or activity receiving Federal financial assistance or under any program or activity conducted by any Executive agency or by the United States Postal Service. The head of each such agency shall promulgate such regulations as may be necessary to carry out the amendments to this section made by the Rehabilitation, Comprehensive Services, and Developmental Disabilities Act of 1978. Copies of any proposed regulations shall be submitted to appropriate authorizing committees of the Congress, and such regulation may take effect no earlier than the thirtieth day after the date on which such regulation is so submitted to such committees.

(a) For the purposes of this section, the term "program or activity" means all the operations of

(1)(A) a department, agency, special purpose district, or other instrumentality of a State or local government; or

    (B) the entity of such State or local government that distributes slow assistance (and each other State or local government entity) to which the assistance is extended, in the case of assistance to a State or local government;

    (2)(A) a college, university, of other post-secondary institution, or a public system of higher education; or

    (B) a local educational agency (as defined in section 198(a)(10) of the Elementary and Secondary Education Act of 1965), system of vocational education, or other school system;

    (3)(A) an entire corporation, partnership, or other private organization, or an entire sole proprietorship-

    (i) if assistance is extended to such corporation, partnership, private organization, or sole proprietorship as a whole; or

    (ii) which is principally engaged in the business of providing education, health care, housing, social services, or parks and recreation; or

    (b) the entire plant or other comparable, geographically separate facility to which Federal financial aid is extended, in the case of any other corporation, partnership, private organization, or sole proprietorship; or

    (4) any other entity which is established by two or more of the entities described in paragraph (1), (2), or (3);

    (c) Small providers are not required by subsection (a) to make significant structural alterations to their existing facilities for the purpose of assuring program accessibility, if alternative means of providing the services are available. The terms used in this subsection shall be constructed with reference to the regulations existing on the date of the enactment of this subsection.

REMEDIES AND ATTORNEY'S FEES

    Sec. 505. (a)(1) The remedies, procedures, and rights set forth in section 717 of the Civil Rights Act of 1964 (42 U.S.C. 2000e-16), including the application of sections 706(f) through 706(k) (42 U.S.C. 2000e-5(f) through (k)) shall be available, with respect to any complaint under section 501 of this Act, to any employee or applicant for employment aggrieved by the final disposition of such complaint, or by the failure to take final action on such complaint. In fashioning an equitable or affirmative action remedy under such section, a court may take into account the reasonableness of the cost of any necessary work place accommodation, and the availability of alternatives therefor or other appropriate relief in order to achieve an equitable and appropriate remedy.

    (2) The remedies, procedures and rights set forth in title VI of the Civil Rights Act of 1964 shall be available to any person aggrieved by any act or failure to act by any recipient of Federal assistance or Federal provider of such assistance under section 504 of this Act.

    (b) In any action or proceeding to enforce or charge a violation of a provision of this title, the court, in its discretion, may allow the prevailing party, other than the United States, a reasonable attorney's fee as part of the costs.

INTERAGENCY COORDINATING COUNCIL

    Sec/ 507. There shall be established an Interagency Coordinating Council (hereinafter referred to in this section as the "Council") composed of the Secretary of Health, Education, and Welfare, the Secretary of Labor, the Attorney General, the Chairman of the United States Civil Service Commission, the Chairman of the Equal Employment Opportunity Commission and the Chairman of the Architectural and Transportation Barriers Compliance Board. The Council shall have the responsibility for developing and implementing agreements, policies, and practices designed to maximize effort, promote efficiency, and eliminate conflict, competition, duplication, and inconsistencies among the operations, functions, and jurisdictions of the various departments, agencies, and branches of the Federal Government responsible for the implementation and enforcement of the provisions of this title and the regulations prescribed thereunder. On or before July 1 of each year, the Council shall transmit to the President and to the Congress a report of its activities, together with such recommendations for legislative or administrative changes as it concludes are desirable to further promote the purposes of this section. Nothing in this section shall impair any responsibilities assigned by any Executive Order to any Federal department, agency, or instrumentality to act as a lead Federal agency with respect to any provisions of this title.

N
EEOC REGULATIONS
IMPLEMENTING TITLE I OF THE ADA

This appendix presents the full text of the regulations implementing Title I of the Americans with Disabilities Act.

Friday
July 26, 1991

Part V

Equal Employment Opportunity Commission

29 CFR Part 1630
Equal Employment Opportunity for Individuals With Disabilities; Final Rule

29 CFR Parts 1602 and 1627
Recordkeeping and Reporting Under Title VII of the Civil Rights Act of 1964 and the Americans With Disabilities Act (ADA); Final Rule

Equal Employment Opportunity Commission

29 CFR Part 1630

Equal Employment Opportunity for Individuals With Disabilities

AGENCY: Equal Employment Opportunity Commission.

ACTION: Final rule.

SUMMARY: On July 26, 1990, the Americans With Disabilities Act (ADA) was signed into law. Section 106 of the ADA requires that the Equal Employment Opportunity Commission (EEOC) issue substantive regulations implementing title I (Employment) within one year of the date of enactment of the Act. Pursuant to this mandate, the Commission is publishing a new part 1630 to its regulations to implement title I and sections 3(2), 3(3), 501, 503, 506(e), 508, 510, and 511 of the ADA as those sections pertain to employment. New part 1630 prohibits discrimination against qualified individuals with disabilities in all aspects of employment.

EFFECTIVE DATE: July 26, 1992.

FOR FURTHER INFORMATION CONTACT: Elizabeth M. Thornton, Deputy Legal Counsel, (202) 663–4638 (voice), (202) 663–7026 (TDD) or Christopher G. Bell, Acting Associate Legal Counsel for Americans With Disabilities Act Services, (202) 663–4679 (voice), (202) 663–7026.

Copies of this final rule and interpretive appendix may be obtained by calling the Office of Communications and Legislative Affairs at (202) 663–4900. Copies in alternate formats may be obtained from the Office of Equal Employment Opportunity by calling (202) 663–4398 or (202) 663–4395 (voice) or (202) 663–4399 (TDD). The alternate formats available are: Large print, braille, electronic file on computer disk, and audio-tape.

SUPPLEMENTARY INFORMATION:

Rulemaking History

The Commission actively solicited and considered public comment in the development of part 1630. On August 1, 1990, the Commission published an advance notice of proposed rulemaking (ANPRM), 55 FR 31192, informing the public that the Commission had begun the process of developing substantive regulations pursuant to title I of the ADA and inviting comment from interested groups and individuals. The comment period ended on August 31, 1990. In response to the ANPRM, the Commission received 138 comments from various disability rights organizations, employer groups, and individuals. Comments were also solicited at 62 ADA input meetings conducted by Commission field offices throughout the country. More than 2400 representatives from disability rights organizations and employer groups participated in these meetings.

On February 28, 1991, the Commission published a notice of proposed rulemaking (NPRM), 56 FR 8578, setting forth proposed part 1630 for public comment. The comment period ended April 29, 1991. In response to the NPRM, the Commission received 697 timely comments from interested groups and individuals. In many instances, a comment was submitted on behalf of several parties and represented the views of numerous groups, employers, or individuals with disabilities. The comments have been analyzed and considered in the development of this final rule.

Overview of Regulations

The format of part 1630 reflects congressional intent, as expressed in the legislative history, that the regulations implementing the employment provisions of the ADA be modeled on the regulations implementing section 504 of the Rehabilitation Act of 1973, as amended, 34 CFR part 104. Accordingly, in developing part 1630, the Commission has been guided by the section 504 regulations and the case law interpreting those regulations.

It is the intent of Congress that the regulations implementing the ADA be comprehensive and easily understood. Part 1630, therefore, defines terms not previously defined in the regulations implementing section 504 of the Rehabilitation Act, such as "substantially limits," "essential functions," and "reasonable accommodation." Of necessity, many of the determinations that may be required by this part must be made on a case-by-case basis. Where possible, part 1630 establishes parameters to serve as guidelines in such inquiries.

The Commission is also issuing interpretive guidance concurrently with the issuance of part 1630 in order to ensure that qualified individuals with disabilities understand their rights under this part and to facilitate and encourage compliance by covered entities. Therefore, part 1630 is accompanied by an appendix. This appendix represents the Commission's interpretation of the issues discussed, and the Commission will be guided by it when resolving charges of employment discrimination. The appendix addresses the major provisions of part 1630 and explains the major concepts of disability rights. Further, the appendix cites to the authority, such as the legislative history of the ADA and case law interpreting section 504 of the Rehabilitation Act, that provides the basis and purpose of the rule and interpretive guidance.

More detailed guidance on specific issues will be forthcoming in the Commission's Compliance Manual. Several Compliance Manual sections and policy guidances on ADA issues are currently under development and are expected to be issued prior to the effective date of the Act. Among the issues to be addressed in depth are the theories of discrimination; definitions of disability and of qualified individual with a disability; reasonable accommodation and undue hardship, including the scope of reassignment; and pre-employment inquiries.

To assist us in the development of this guidance, the Commission requested comment in the NPRM from disability rights organizations, employers, unions, state agencies concerned with employment or workers compensation practices, and interested individuals on specific questions about insurance, workers' compensation, and collective bargaining agreements. Many commenters responded to these questions, and several commenters addressed other matters pertinent to these areas. The Commission has considered these comments in the development of the final rule and will continue to consider them as it develops further ADA guidance.

In the NPRM, the Commission raised questions about a number of insurance-related matters. Specifically, the Commission asked commenters to discuss risk assessment and classification, the relationship between "risk" and "cost," and whether employers should consider the effects that changes in insurance coverage will have on individuals with disabilities before making those changes. Many commenters provided information about insurance practices and explained some of the considerations that affect insurance decisions. In addition, some commenters discussed their experiences with insurance plans and coverage. The commenters presented a wide range of opinions on insurance-related matters, and the Commission will consider the comments as it continues to analyze these complex matters.

The Commission received a large number of comments concerning inquiries about an individual's workers' compensation history. Many employers asserted that such inquiries are job related and consistent with business necessity. Several individuals with disabilities and disability rights organizations; however, argued that such inquiries are prohibited pre-employment inquiries and are not job related and consistent with business necessity. The Commission has addressed this issue in the interpretive guidance accompanying § 1630.14(a) and will discuss the matter further in future guidance.

There was little controversy about the submission of medical information to workers' compensation offices. A number of employers and employer groups pointed out that the workers' compensation offices of many states request medical information in connection with the administration of second-injury funds. Further, they noted that the disclosure of medical information may be necessary to the defense of a workers' compensation claim. The Commission has responded to these comments by amending the interpretive guidance accompanying § 1630.14(b). This amendment, discussed below, notes that the submission of medical information to workers' compensation offices in accordance with state workers' compensation laws is not inconsistent with § 1630.14(b). The Commission will address this area in greater detail and will discuss other issues concerning workers' compensation matters in future guidances, including the policy guidance on pre-employment inquiries.

With respect to collective bargaining agreements, the Commission asked commenters to discuss the relationship between collective bargaining agreements and such matters as undue hardship, reassignment to a vacant position, the determination of what constitutes a "vacant" position, and the confidentiality requirements of the ADA. The comments that we received reflected a wide variety of views. For example, some commenters argued that it would always be an undue hardship for an employer to provide a reasonable accommodation that conflicted with the provisions of a collective bargaining agreement. Other commenters, however, argued that an accommodation's effect on an agreement should not be considered when assessing undue hardship. Similarly, some commenters stated that the appropriateness of reassignment to a vacant position should depend upon the provisions of a collective bargaining agreement while others asserted that an agreement cannot limit the right to reassignment. Many commenters discussed the relationship between an agreement's seniority provisions and an employer's reasonable accommodation obligations.

In response to comments, the Commission has amended § 1630.2(n)(3) to include "the terms of a collective bargaining agreement" in the types of evidence relevant to determining the essential functions of a position. The Commission has made a corresponding change to the interpretive guidance on § 1630.2(n)(3). In addition, the Commission has amended the interpretive guidance on § 1630.15(d) to note that the terms of a collective bargaining agreement may be relevant to determining whether an accommodation would pose an undue hardship on the operation of a covered entity's business.

The divergent views expressed in the public comments demonstrate the complexity of employment-related issues concerning insurance, workers' compensation, and collective bargaining agreement matters. These highly complex issues require extensive research and analysis and warrant further consideration. Accordingly, the Commission has decided to address the issues in depth in future Compliance Manual sections and policy guidances. The Commission will consider the public comments that it received in response to the NPRM as it develops further guidance on the application of title I of the ADA to these matters.

The Commission has also decided to address burdens-of-proof issues in future guidance documents, including the Compliance Manual section on the theories of discrimination. Many commenters discussed the allocation of the various burdens of proof under title I of the ADA and asked the Commission to clarify those burdens. The comments in this area addressed such matters as determining whether a person is a qualified individual with a disability, job relatedness and business necessity, and undue hardship. The Commission will consider these comments as it prepares further guidance in this area.

A discussion of other significant comments and an explanation of the changes made in part 1630 since publication of the NPRM follows.

Section-by-Section Analysis of Comments and Revisions

Section 1630.1   Purpose, Applicability, and Construction

The Commission has made a technical correction to § 1630.1(a) by adding section 506(e) to the list of statutory provisions implemented by this part. Section 506(e) of the ADA provides that the failure to receive technical assistance from the federal agencies that administer the ADA is not a

defense to failing to meet the obligations of title I.

Some commenters asked the Commission to note that the ADA does not preempt state claims, such as state tort claims, that confer greater remedies than are available under the ADA. The Commission has added a paragraph to that effect in the appendix discussion of §§ 1630.1 (b) and (c). This interpretation is consistent with the legislative history of the Act. See H.R. Rep. No. 485 part 3, 101st Cong., 2d Sess. 69–70 (1990) (hereinafter referred to as House Judiciary Report).

In addition, the Commission has made a technical amendment to the appendix discussion to note that the ADA does not automatically preempt medical standards or safety requirements established by Federal law or regulations. The Commission has also amended the discussion to refer to a direct threat that cannot be eliminated "or reduced" through reasonable accommodation. This language is consistent with the regulatory definition of direct threat. (See § 1630.2(r), below.)

Section 1630.2   Definitions

Section 1630.2(h)   Physical or Mental Impairment

The Commission has amended the interpretive guidance accompanying § 1630.2(h) to note that the definition of the term "impairment" does not include characteristic predisposition to illness or disease.

In addition, the Commission has specifically noted in the interpretive guidance that pregnancy is not an impairment. This change responds to the numerous questions that the Commission has received concerning whether pregnancy is a disability covered by the ADA. Pregnancy, by itself, is not an impairment and is therefore not a disability.

Section 1630.2(j)   Substantially Limits

The Commission has revised the interpretive guidance accompanying § 1630.2(j) to make clear that the determination of whether an impairment substantially limits one or more major life activities is to be made without regard to the availability of medicines, assistive devices, or other mitigating measures. This interpretation is consistent with the legislative history of the ADA. See S. Rep. No. 116, 101st Cong., 1st Sess. 23 (1989) (hereinafter referred to as Senate Report); H.R. Rep. No. 485 part 2, 101st Cong., 2d Sess. 52 (1990) (hereinafter referred to as House Labor Report); House Judiciary Report at 28. The Commission has also revised the examples in the third paragraph of this section's guidance. The examples now focus on the individual s capacity to perform major life activities rather than on the presence or absence of mitigating measures. These revisions respond to comments from disability rights groups, which were concerned that the discussion could be misconstrued to exclude from ADA coverage individuals with disabilities who function well because of assistive devices or other mitigating measures.

In an amendment to the paragraph concerning the factors to consider when determining whether an impairment is substantially limiting, the Commission has provided a second example of an impairment's "impact." This example notes that a traumatic head injury's affect on cognitive functions is the "impact" of that impairment.

Many commenters addressed the provisions concerning the definition of "substantially limits" with respect to the major life activity of working (§ 1630.2(j)(3)). Some employers generally supported the definition but argued that it should be applied narrowly. Other employers argued that the definition is too broad. Disability rights groups and individuals with disabilities, on the other hand, argued that the definition is too narrow, unduly limits coverage, and places an onerous burden on individuals seeking to establish that they are covered by the ADA. The Commission has responded to these comments by making a number of clarifications in this area.

The Commission has revised § 1630.2(j)(3)(ii) and the accompanying interpretive guidance to note that the listed factors "may" be considered when determining whether an individual is substantially limited in working. This revision clarifies that the factors are relevant to, but are not required elements of, a showing of a substantial limitation in working.

Disability rights groups asked the Commission to clarify that "substantially limited in working" applies only when an individual is not substantially limited in any other major life activity. In addition, several other commenters indicated confusion about whether and when the ability to work should be considered when assessing if an individual has a disability. In response to these comments, the Commission has amended the interpretive guidance by adding a new paragraph clarifying the circumstances under which one should determine whether an individual is substantially limited in the major life activity of working. This paragraph makes clear that a determination of whether an individual is substantially limited in the

ability to work should be made only when the individual is not disabled in any other major life activity. Thus, individuals need not establish that they are substantially limited in working if they already have established that they are, have a record of, or are regarded as being substantially limited in another major life activity.

The proposed interpretive guidance in this area provided an example concerning a surgeon with a slight hand impairment. Several commenters expressed concern about this example. Many of these comments indicated that the example confused, rather than clarified, the matter. The Commission, therefore, has deleted this example. To explain further the application of the "substantially limited in working" concept, the Commission has provided another example (concerning a commercial airline pilot) in the interpretive guidance.

In addition, the Commission has clarified that the terms "numbers and types of jobs" (see § 1630.2(j)(3)(ii)(B)) and "numbers and types of other jobs" (see § 1630.2(j)(3)(ii)(C)) do not require an onerous evidentiary showing.

In the proposed Appendix, after the interpretive guidance accompanying § 1630.2(l), the Commission included a discussion entitled "Frequently Disabling Impairments." Many commenters expressed concern about this discussion. In response to these comments, and to avoid confusion, the Commission has revised the discussion and has deleted the list of frequently disabling impairments. The revised discussion now appears in the interpretive guidance accompanying § 1630.2(j).

Section 1630.2(l) Is Regarded as Having Such an Impairment

Section 1630.2(l)(3) has been changed to refer to "a substantially limiting impairment" rather than "such an impairment." This change clarifies that an individual meets the definition of the term "disability" when a covered entity treats the individual as having a substantially limiting impairment. That is, § 1630.2(l)(3) refers to any substantially limiting impairment, rather than just to one of the impairments described in §§ 1630.2(l) (1) or (2).

The proposed interpretive guidance on § 1630.2(l) stated that, when determining whether an individual is regarded as substantially limited in working, "it should be assumed that all similar employers would apply the same exclusionary qualification standard that the employer charged with discrimination has used." The Commission specifically requested

comment on this proposal, and many commenters addressed this issue. The Commission has decided to eliminate this assumption and to revise the interpretive guidance. The guidance now explains that an individual meets the "regarded as" part of the definition of disability if he or she can show that a covered entity made an employment decision because of a perception of a disability based on "myth, fear, or stereotype." This is consistent with the legislative history of the ADA. See House Judiciary Report at 30.

Section 1630.2(m) Qualified Individual With a Disability

Under the proposed part 1630, the first step in determining whether an individual with a disability is a qualified individual with a disability was to determine whether the individual "satisfies the requisite skill, experience and education requirements of the employment position" the individual holds or desires. Many employers and employer groups asserted that the proposed regulation unduly limited job prerequisites to skill, experience, and education requirements and did not permit employers to consider other job-related qualifications. To clarify that the reference to skill, experience, and education requirements was not intended to be an exhaustive list of permissible qualification requirements, the Commission has revised the phrase to include "skill, experience, education, and other job-related requirements." This revision recognizes that other types of job-related requirements may be relevant to determining whether an individual is qualified for a position.

Many individuals with disabilities and disability rights groups asked the Commission to emphasize that the determination of whether a person is a qualified individual with a disability must be made at the time of the employment action in question and cannot be based on speculation that the individual will become unable to perform the job in the future or may cause increased health insurance or workers' compensation costs. The Commission has amended the interpretive guidance on § 1630.2(m) to reflect this point. This guidance is consistent with the legislative history of the Act. See Senate Report at 26, House Labor Report at 55, 136; House Judiciary Report at 34, 71.

Section 1630.2(n) Essential Functions

Many employers and employer groups objected to the use of the terms "primary" and "intrinsic" in the definition of essential functions. To avoid confusion about the meanings of "primary" and "intrinsic," the Commission has deleted these terms from the definition. The final regulation defines essential functions as "fundamental job duties" and notes that essential functions do not include the marginal functions of a position.

The proposed interpretive guidance accompanying § 1630.2(n)(2)(ii) noted that one of the factors in determining whether a function is essential is the number of employees available to perform a job function or among whom the performance of that function can be distributed. The proposed guidance explained that "(t)his may be a factor either because the total number of employees is low, or because of the fluctuating demands of the business operations." Some employers and employer groups expressed concern that this language could be interpreted as requiring an assessment of whether a job function could be distributed among all employees in any job at any level. The Commission has amended the interpretive guidance on this factor to clarify that the factor refers only to distribution among "available" employees.

Section 1630.2(n)(3) lists several kinds of evidence that are relevant to determining whether a particular job function is essential. Some employers and unions asked the Commission to recognize that collective bargaining agreements may help to identify a position's essential functions. In response to these comments, the Commission has added "(t)he terms of a collective bargaining agreement" to the list. In addition, the Commission has amended the interpretive guidance to note specifically that this type of evidence is relevant to the determination of essential functions. This addition is consistent with the legislative history of the Act. See Senate Report at 32; House Labor Report at 63.

Proposed § 1630.2(n)(3) referred to the evidence on the list as evidence "that may be considered in determining whether a particular function is essential." The Commission has revised this section to refer to evidence "of" whether a particular function is essential. The Commission made this revision in response to concerns about the meaning of the phrase "may be considered." In that regard, some commenters questioned whether the phrase meant that some of the listed evidence might not be considered when determining whether a function is essential to a position. This revision clarifies that all of the types of evidence on the list, when available, are relevant

to the determination of a position's essential functions. As the final rule and interpretive guidance make clear, the list is not an exhaustive list of all types of relevant evidence. Other types of available evidence may also be relevant to the determination.

The Commission has amended the interpretive guidance concerning § 1630.2(n)(3)(ii) to make clear that covered entities are not required to develop and maintain written job descriptions. Such job descriptions are relevant to a determination of a position's essential functions, but they are not required by part 1630.

Several commenters suggested that the Commission establish a rebuttable presumption in favor of the employer's judgment concerning what functions are essential. The Commission has not done so. On that point, the Commission notes that the House Committee on the Judiciary specifically rejected an amendment that would have created such a presumption. See House Judiciary Report at 33–34.

The last paragraph of the interpretive guidance on § 1630.2(n) notes that the inquiry into what constitutes a position's essential functions is not intended to second guess an employer's business judgment regarding production standards, whether qualitative or quantitative. In response to several comments, the Commission has revised this paragraph to incorporate examples of qualitative production standards.

Section 1630.2(o)   Reasonable Accommodation

The Commission has deleted the reference to undue hardship from the definition of reasonable accommodation. This is a technical change reflecting that undue hardship is a defense to, rather than an aspect of, reasonable accommodation. As some commenters have noted, a defense to a term should not be part of the term's definition. Accordingly, we have separated the concept of undue hardship from the definition of reasonable accommodation. This change does not affect the obligations of employers or the rights of individuals with disabilities. Accordingly, a covered entity remains obligated to make reasonable accommodation to the known physical or mental limitations of an otherwise qualified individual with a disability unless to do so would impose an undue hardship on the operation of the covered entity's business. See § 1630.9.

With respect to § 1630.2(o)(1)(i), some commenters expressed confusion about the use of the phrase "qualified individual with a disability." In that

regard, they noted that the phrase has a specific definition under this part (see § 1630.2(m)) and questioned whether an individual must meet that definition to request an accommodation with regard to the application process. The Commission has substituted the phrase "qualified applicant with a disability" for "qualified individual with a disability." This change clarifies that an individual with a disability who requests a reasonable accommodation to participate in the application process must be eligible only with respect to the application process.

The Commission has modified § 1630.2(o)(1)(iii) to state that reasonable accommodation includes modifications or adjustments that enable employees with disabilities to enjoy benefits and privileges that are "equal" to (rather than "the same" as) the benefits and privileges that are enjoyed by other employees. This change clarifies that such modifications or adjustments must ensure that individuals with disabilities receive equal access to the benefits and privileges afforded to other employees but may not be able to ensure that the individuals receive the same results of those benefits and privileges or precisely the same benefits and privileges.

Many commenters discussed whether the provision of daily attendant care is a form of reasonable accommodation. Employers and employer groups asserted that reasonable accommodation does not include such assistance. Disability rights groups and individuals with disabilities, however, asserted that such assistance is a form of reasonable accommodation but that this part did not make that clear. To clarify the extent of the reasonable accommodation obligation with respect to daily attendant care, the Commission has amended the interpretive guidance on § 1630.2(o) to make clear that it may be a reasonable accommodation to provide personal assistants to help with specified duties related to the job.

The Commission also has amended the interpretive guidance to note that allowing an individual with a disability to provide and use equipment, aids, or services that an employer is not required to provide may also be a form of reasonable accommodation. Some individuals with disabilities and disability rights groups asked the Commission to make this clear.

The interpretive guidance points out that reasonable accommodation may include making non-work areas accessible to individuals with disabilities. Many commenters asked the Commission to include rest rooms in the examples of accessible areas that may be required as reasonable accommodations. In response to those comments, the Commission has added rest rooms to the examples.

In response to other comments, the Commission has added a paragraph to the guidance concerning job restructuring as a form of reasonable accommodation. The new paragraph notes that job restructuring may involve changing when or how an essential function is performed.

Several commenters asked the Commission to provide additional guidance concerning the reasonable accommodation of reassignment to a vacant position. Specifically, commenters asked the Commission to clarify how long an employer must wait for a vacancy to arise when considering reassignment and to explain whether the employer is required to maintain the salary of an individual who is reassigned from a higher-paying position to a lower-paying one. The Commission has amended the discussion of reassignment to refer to reassignment to a position that is vacant "within a reasonable amount of time * * * in light of the totality of the circumstances." In addition, the Commission has noted that an employer is not required to maintain the salaries of reassigned individuals with disabilities if it does not maintain the salaries of individuals who are not disabled.

Section 1630.2(p)   Undue Hardship

The Commission has substituted "facility" or "facilities" for "site." or "sites" in § 1630.2(p)(2) and has deleted the definition of the term "site" Many employers and employer groups expressed concern about the use and meaning of the term "site." The final regulation's use of the terms "facility" and "facilities" is consistent with the language of the statute.

The Commission has amended the last paragraph of the interpretive guidance accompanying § 1630.2(p) to note that, when the cost of a requested accommodation would result in an undue hardship and outside funding is not available, an individual with a disability should be given the option of paying the portion of the cost that constitutes an undue hardship. This amendment is consistent with the legislative history of the Act. See Senate Report at 36; House Labor Report at 69.

Several employers and employer groups asked the Commission to expand the list of factors to be considered when determining if an accommodation would impose an undue hardship on a covered entity by adding another factor: The

relationship of an accommodation's cost to the value of the position at issue, as measured by the compensation paid to the holder of the position. Congress, however, specifically rejected this type of factor. See House Judiciary Report at 41 (noting that the House Judiciary Committee rejected an amendment proposing that an accommodation costing more than ten percent of the employee's salary be treated as an undue hardship). The Commission, therefore, has not added this to the list.

Section 1630.2(q)   Qualification Standards

The Commission has deleted the reference to direct threat from the definition of qualification standards. This revision is consistent with the revisions the Commission has made to §§ 1630.10 and 1630.15(b). (See discussion below.)

Section 1630.2(r)   Direct Threat

Many disability rights groups and individuals with disabilities asserted that the definition of direct threat should not include a reference to the health or safety of the individual with a disability. They expressed concern that the reference to "risk to self" would result in direct threat determinations that are based on negative stereotypes and paternalistic views about what is best for individuals with disabilities. Alternatively, the commenters asked the Commission to clarify that any assessment of risk must be based on the individual's present condition and not on speculation about the individual's future condition. They also asked the Commission to specify evidence other than medical knowledge that may be relevant to the determination of direct threat.

The final regulation retains the reference to the health or safety of the individual with a disability. As the appendix notes, this is consistent with the legislative history of the ADA and the case law interpreting section 504 of the Rehabilitation Act.

To clarify the direct threat standard, the Commission has made four revisions to § 1630.2(r). First, the Commission has amended the first sentence of the definition of direct threat to refer to a significant risk of substantial harm that cannot be eliminated "or reduced" by reasonable accommodation. This amendment clarifies that the risk need not be eliminated entirely to fall below the direct threat definition; instead, the risk need only be reduced to the level at which there no longer exists a significant risk of substantial harm. In addition, the Commission has rephrased the second sentence of § 1630.2(r) to

clarify that an employer's direct threat standard must apply to all individuals, not just to individuals with disabilities. Further, the Commission has made clear that a direct threat determination must be based on "an individualized assessment of the individual's present ability to safely perform the essential functions of the job." This clarifies that a determination that employment of an individual would pose a direct threat must involve an individualized inquiry and must be based on the individual's current condition. In addition, the Commission has added "the imminence of the potential harm" to the list of factors to be considered when determining whether employment of an individual would pose a direct threat. This change clarifies that both the probability of harm and the imminence of harm are relevant to direct threat determinations. This definition of direct threat is consistent with the legislative history of the Act. See Senate Report at 27, House Labor Report at 56–57, 73–75, House Judiciary Report at 45–46.

Further, the Commission has amended the interpretive guidance on § 1630.2(r) to highlight the individualized nature of the direct threat assessment. In addition, the Commission has cited examples of evidence other than medical knowledge that may be relevant to determining whether employment of an individual would pose a direct threat.

Section 1630.3   Exceptions to the Definitions of "Disability" and "Qualified Individual With a Disability"

Many commenters asked the Commission to clarify that the term "rehabilitation program" includes self-help groups. In response to these comments, the Commission has amended the interpretive guidance in this area to include a reference to professionally recognized self-help programs.

The Commission has added a paragraph to the guidance on § 1630.3 to note that individuals who are not excluded under this provision from the definitions of the terms "disability" and "qualified individual with a disability" must still establish that they meet those definitions to be protected by part 1630. Several employers and employer groups asked the Commission to clarify that individuals are not automatically covered by the ADA simply because they do not fall into one of the exclusions listed in this section.

The proposed interpretive guidance on § 1630.3 noted that employers are entitled to seek reasonable assurances that an individual is not currently engaging in the illegal use of drugs. In that regard, the guidance stated, "It is essential that the individual offer evidence, such as a drug test, to prove that he or she is not currently engaging" in such use. Many commenters interpreted this guidance to require individuals to come forward with evidence even in the absence of a request by the employer. The Commission has revised the interpretive guidance to clarify that such evidence is required only upon request.

Section 1630.6   Contractual or Other Arrangements

The Commission has added a sentence to the first paragraph of the interpretive guidance on § 1630.6 to clarify that this section has no impact on whether one is a covered entity or employer as defined by § 1630.2.

The proposed interpretive guidance on contractual or other relationships noted that § 1630.6 applied to parties on either side of the relationship. To illustrate this point, the guidance stated that "a copier company would be required to ensure the provision of any reasonable accommodation necessary to enable its copier service representative with a disability to service a client's machine." Several employers objected to this example. In that respect, the commenters argued that the language of the example was too broad and could be interpreted as requiring employers to make all customers premises accessible. The Commission has revised this example to provide a clearer, more concrete indication of the scope of the reasonable accommodation obligations in this area.

In addition, the Commission has clarified the interpretive guidance by noting that the existence of a contractual relationship adds no new obligations "under this part."

Section 1630.8   Relationship or Association With an Individual With a Disability

The Commission has added the phrase "or otherwise discriminate against" to § 1630.8. This change clarifies that harassment or any other form of discrimination against a qualified individual because of the known disability of a person with whom the individual has a relationship or an association is also a prohibited form of discrimination.

The Commission has revised the first sentence of the interpretive guidance to refer to a person's relationship or association with an individual who has a "known" disability. This revision makes the language of the interpretive guidance consistent with the language of

the regulation. In addition, to reflect current, preferred terminology, the Commission has substituted the term "people who have AIDS" for the term "AIDS patients." Finally, the Commission has added a paragraph to clarify that this provision applies to discrimination in other employment privileges and benefits, such as health insurance benefits.

Section 1630.9   Not Making Reasonable Accommodation

Section 1630.9(c) provides that "(a) covered entity shall not be excused from the requirements of this part because of any failure to receive technical assistance * * *." Some employers asked the Commission to revise this section and to state that the failure to receive technical assistance is a defense to not providing reasonable accommodation. The Commission has not made the requested revision. Section 1630.9(c) is consistent with section 506(e) of the ADA, which states that the failure to receive technical assistance from the federal agencies that administer the ADA does not excuse a covered entity from compliance with the requirements of the Act.

The first paragraph of the interpretive guidance accompanying § 1630.9 notes that the reasonable accommodation obligation does not require employers to provide adjustments or modifications that are primarily for the personal use of the individual with a disability. The Commission has amended this guidance to clarify that employers may be required to provide items that are customarily personal-use items where the items are specifically designed or required to meet job-related needs.

In addition, the Commission has amended the interpretive guidance to clarify that there must be a nexus between an individual's disability and the need for accommodation. Thus, the guidance notes that an individual with a disability is "otherwise qualified" if he or she is qualified for the job except that, "because of the disability," the individual needs reasonable accommodation to perform the essential functions of the job. Similarly, the guidance notes that employers are required to accommodate only the physical or mental limitations "resulting from the disability" that are known to the employer.

In response to commenters' requests for clarification, the Commission has noted that employers may require individuals with disabilities to provide documentation of the need for reasonable accommodation when the need for a requested accommodation is not obvious.

In addition, the Commission has amended the last paragraph of the interpretive guidance on the "Process of Determining the Appropriate Reasonable Accommodation." This amendment clarifies that an employer must consider allowing an individual with a disability to provide his or her own accommodation if the individual wishes to do so. The employer, however, may not require the individual to provide the accommodation.

Section 1630.10   Qualification Standards, Tests, and Other Selection Criteria

The Commission has added the phrase "on the basis of disability" to § 1630.10(a) to clarify that a selection criterion that is not job related and consistent with business necessity violates this section only when it screens out an individual with a disability (or a class of individuals with disabilities) on the basis of disability. That is, there must be a nexus between the exclusion and the disability. A selection criterion that screens out an individual with a disability for reasons that are not related to the disability does not violate this section. The Commission has made similar changes to the interpretive guidance on this section.

Proposed § 1630.10(b) stated that a covered entity could use as a qualification standard the requirement that an individual not pose a direct threat to the health or safety of the individual or others. Many individuals with disabilities objected to the inclusion of the direct threat reference in this section and asked the Commission to clarify that the direct threat standard must be raised by the covered entity as a defense. In that regard, they specifically asked the Commission to move the direct threat provision from § 1630.10 (qualification standards) to § 1630.15 (defenses). The Commission has deleted the direct threat provision from § 1630.10 and has moved it to § 1630.15. This is consistent with section 103 of the ADA, which refers to defenses and states (in section 103(b)) that the term "qualification standards" may include a requirement that an individual not pose a direct threat.

Section 1630.11   Administration of Tests

The Commission has revised the interpretive guidance concerning § 1630.11 to clarify that a request for an alternative test format or other testing accommodation generally should be made prior to the administration of the test or as soon as the individual with a disability becomes aware of the need for accommodation. In addition, the Commission has amended the last paragraph of the guidance on this section to note that an employer can require a written test of an applicant with dyslexia if the ability to read is "the skill the test is designed to measure." This language is consistent with the regulatory language, which refers to the skills a test purports to measure.

Some commenters noted that certain tests are designed to measure the speed with which an applicant performs a function. In response to these comments, the Commission has amended the interpretive guidance to state that an employer may require an applicant to complete a test within a specified time frame if speed is one of the skills being tested.

In response to comments, the Commission has amended the interpretive guidance accompanying § 1630.14(a) to clarify that employers may invite applicants to request accommodations for taking tests. (See § 1630.14(a), below.)

Section 1630.12 Retaliation and Coercion

The Commission has amended § 1630.12 to clarify that this section also prohibits harassment.

Section 1630.13 Prohibited Medical Examinations and Inquiries

In response to the Commission's request for comment on certain workers' compensation matters, many commenters addressed whether a covered entity may ask applicants about their history of workers' compensation claims. Many employers and employer groups argued that an inquiry about an individual's workers' compensation history is job related and consistent with business necessity. Disability rights groups and individuals with disabilities, however, asserted that such an inquiry could disclose the existence of a disability. In response to comments and to clarify this matter, the Commission has amended the interpretive guidance accompanying § 1630.13(a). The amendment states that an employer may not inquire about an individual's workers' compensation history at the pre-offer stage.

The Commission has made a technical change to § 1630.13(b) by deleting the phrase "unless the examination or inquiry is shown to be job-related and consistent with business necessity" from the section. This change does not affect the substantive provisions of § 1630.13(b). The Commission has incorporated the job-relatedness and

business-necessity requirement into a new § 1630.14(c), which clarifies the scope of permissible examinations or inquiries of employees. (See § 1630.14(c), below.)

Section 1630.14 Medical Examinations and Inquiries Specifically Permitted

Section 1630.14(a) Acceptable Pre-employment Inquiry

Proposed § 1630.14(a) stated that a covered entity may make pre-employment inquiries into an applicant's ability to perform job-related functions. The interpretive guidance accompanying this section noted that an employer may ask an individual whether he or she can perform a job function with or without reasonable accommodation.

Many employers asked the Commission to provide additional guidance in this area. Specifically, the commenters asked whether an employer may ask how an individual will perform a job function when the individual's known disability appears to interfere with or prevent performance of job-related functions. To clarify this matter, the Commission has amended § 1630.14(a) to state that a covered entity "may ask an applicant to describe or to demonstrate how, with or without reasonable accommodation, the applicant will be able to perform job-related functions." The Commission has amended the interpretive guidance accompanying § 1630.14(a) to reflect this change.

Many commenters asked the Commission to state that employers may inquire, before tests are taken, whether candidates will require any reasonable accommodations to take the tests. They asked the Commission to acknowledge that such inquiries constitute permissible pre-employment inquiries. In response to these comments, the Commission has added a new paragraph to the interpretive guidance on § 1630.14(a). This paragraph clarifies that employers may ask candidates to inform them of the need for reasonable accommodation within a reasonable time before the administration of the test and may request documentation verifying the need for accommodation.

The Commission has received many comments from law enforcement and other public safety agencies concerning the administration of physical agility tests. In response to those comments, the Commission has added a new paragraph clarifying that such tests are not medical examinations.

Many employers and employer groups have asked the Commission to discuss whether employers may invite applicants to self-identify as individuals

with disabilities. In that regard, many of the commenters noted that section 503 of the Rehabilitation Act imposes certain obligations on government contractors. The interpretive guidance accompanying § 1630.1(b) and (c) notes that "title I of the ADA would not be a defense to failing to collect information required to satisfy the affirmative action requirements of section 503 of the Rehabilitation Act." To reiterate this point, the Commission has amended the interpretive guidance accompanying § 1630.14(a) to note specifically that this section does not restrict employers from collecting information and inviting individuals to identify themselves as individuals with disabilities as required to satisfy the affirmative action requirements of section 503 of the Rehabilitation Act.

Section 1630.14(b) Employment Entrance Examinations

Section 1630.14(b) has been amended to include the phrase "(and/or inquiry)" after references to medical examinations. Some commenters were concerned that the regulation as drafted prohibited covered entities from making any medical inquiries or administering questionnaires that did not constitute examinations. This change clarifies that the term "employment entrance examinations" includes medical inquiries as well as medical examinations.

Section 1630.14(b)(2) has been revised to state that the results of employment entrance examinations "shall not be used for any purpose inconsistent with this part." This language is consistent with the language used in § 1630.14(c)(2).

The second paragraph of the proposed interpretive guidance on this section referred to "relevant" physical and psychological criteria. Some commenters questioned the use of the term "relevant" and expressed concern about its meaning. The Commission has deleted this term from the paragraph.

Many commenters addressed the confidentiality provisions of this section. They noted that it may be necessary to disclose medical information in defense of workers' compensation claims or during the course of other legal proceedings. In addition, they pointed out that the workers' compensation offices of many states request such information for the administration of second-injury funds or for other administrative purposes.

The Commission has revised the last paragraph of the interpretive guidance on § 1630.14(b) to reflect that the information obtained during a permitted employment entrance examination or inquiry may be used only "in a manner not inconsistent with this part." In addition, the Commission has added language clarifying that it is permissible to submit the information to state workers' compensation offices.

Several commenters asked the Commission to clarify whether information obtained from employment entrance examinations and inquiries may be used for insurance purposes. In response to these comments, the Commission has noted in the interpretive guidance that such information may be used for insurance purposes described in § 1630.16(f).

Section 1630.14(c) Examination of Employees

The Commission has added a new § 1630.14(c), Examination of employees, that clarifies the scope of permissible medical examinations and inquiries. Several employers and employer groups expressed concern that the proposed version of part 1630 did not make it clear that covered entities may require employee medical examinations, such as fitness-for-duty examinations, that are job related and consistent with business necessity. New § 1630.14(c) clarifies this by expressly permitting covered entities to require employee medical examinations and inquiries that are job-related and consistent with business necessity. The information obtained from such examinations or inquiries must be treated as a confidential medical record. This section also incorporates the last sentence of proposed § 1630.14(c). The remainder of proposed § 1630.14(c) has become § 1630.14(d).

To comport with this technical change in the regulation, the Commission has made corresponding changes in the interpretive guidance. Thus, the Commission has moved the second paragraph of the proposed guidance on § 1630.13(b) to the guidance on § 1630.14(c). In addition, the Commission has reworded the paragraph to note that this provision permits (rather than does not prohibit) certain medical examinations and inquiries.

Some commenters asked the Commission to clarify whether employers may make inquiries or require medical examinations in connection with the reasonable accommodation process. The Commission has noted in the interpretive guidance that such inquiries and examinations are permissible when they are necessary to the reasonable accommodation process described in this part.

Section 1630.15 Defenses

The Commission has added a sentence to the interpretive guidance on § 1630.15(a) to clarify that the assertion that an insurance plan does not cover an individual's disability or that the disability would cause increased insurance or workers' compensation costs does not constitute a legitimate, nondiscriminatory reason for disparate treatment of an individual with a disability. This clarification, made in response to many comments from individuals with disabilities and disability rights groups, is consistent with the legislative history of the ADA. See Senate Report at 85; House Labor Report at 136; House Judiciary Report at 71.

The Commission has amended § 1630.15(b) by stating that the term "qualification standard" may include a requirement that an individual not pose a direct threat. As noted above, this is consistent with section 103 of the ADA and responds to many comments from individuals with disabilities.

The Commission has made a technical correction to § 1630.15(c) by changing the phrase "an individual or class of individuals with disabilities" to "an individual with a disability or a class of individuals with disabilities."

Several employers and employer groups asked the Commission to acknowledge that undue hardship considerations about reasonable accommodations at temporary work sites may be different from the considerations relevant to permanent work sites. In response to these comments, the Commission has amended the interpretive guidance on § 1630.15(d) to note that an accommodation that poses an undue hardship in a particular job setting, such as a temporary construction site, may not pose an undue hardship in another setting. This guidance is consistent with the legislative history of the ADA. See House Labor Report at 69–70; House Judiciary Report at 41–42.

The Commission also has amended the interpretive guidance to note that the terms of a collective bargaining agreement may be relevant to the determination of whether a requested accommodation would pose an undue hardship on the operation of a covered entity's business. This amendment, which responds to commenters' requests that the Commission recognize the relevancy of collective bargaining agreements, is consistent with the legislative history of the Act. See Senate Report at 32; House Labor Report at 63.

Section 1630.2(p)(2)(v) provides that the impact of an accommodation on the ability of other employees to perform their duties is one of the factors to be considered when determining whether the accommodation would impose an undue hardship on a covered entity. Many commenters addressed whether an accommodation's impact on the morale of other employees may be relevant to a determination of undue hardship. Some employers and employer groups asserted that a negative impact on employee morale should be considered an undue hardship. Disability rights groups and individuals with disabilities, however, argued that undue hardship determinations must not be based on the morale of other employees. It is the Commission's view that a negative effect on morale, by itself, is not sufficient to meet the undue hardship standard. Accordingly, the Commission has noted in the guidance on § 1630.15(d) that an employer cannot establish undue hardship by showing only that an accommodation would have a negative impact on employee morale.

Section 1630.16 Specific Activities Permitted

The Commission has revised the second sentence of the interpretive guidance on § 1630.16(b) to state that an employer may hold individuals with alcoholism and individuals who engage in the illegal use of drugs to the same performance and conduct standards to which it holds "all of its" other employees. In addition, the Commission has deleted the term "otherwise" from the third sentence of the guidance. These revisions clarify that employers may hold all employees, disabled (including those disabled by alcoholism or drug addiction) and nondisabled, to the same performance and conduct standards.

Many commenters asked the Commission to clarify that the drug testing provisions of § 1630.16(c) pertain only to tests to determine the illegal use of drugs. Accordingly, the Commission has amended § 1630.16(c)(1) to refer to the administration of "such" drug tests and § 1630.16(c)(3) to refer to information obtained from a "test to determine the illegal use of drugs." We have also made a change in the grammatical structure of the last sentence of § 1630.16(c)(1). We have made similar changes to the corresponding section of the interpretive guidance. In addition, the Commission has amended the interpretive guidance to state that such tests are neither encouraged, "authorized," nor prohibited. This amendment conforms the language of the guidance to the language of § 1630.16(c)(1).

The Commission has revised § 1630.16(e)(1) to refer to communicable diseases that "are" (rather than "may be") transmitted through the handling of food. Several commenters asked the Commission to make this technical change, which adopts the statutory language.

Several commenters also asked the Commission to conform the language of proposed § 1630.16(f) (1) and (2) to the language of sections 501(c) (1) and (2) of the Act. The Commission has made this change. Thus, § 1630.16(f) (1) and (2) now refer to risks that are "not inconsistent with State law."

Executive Order 12291 and Regulatory Flexibility Act

The Commission published a Preliminary Regulatory Impact Analysis on February 28, 1991 (56 FR 8578). Based on the Preliminary Regulatory Impact Analysis, the Commission certifies that this final rule will not have a significant economic impact on a substantial number of small business entities. The Commission is issuing this final rule at this time in the absence of a Final Regulatory Impact Analysis in order to meet the statutory deadline. The Commission's Preliminary Regulatory Impact Analysis was based upon existing data on the costs of reasonable accommodation. The Commission received few comments on this aspect of its rulemaking. Because of the complexity inherent in assessing the economic costs and benefits of this rule and the relative paucity of data on this issue, the Commission will further study the economic impact of the regulation and intends to issue a Final Regulatory Impact Analysis prior to January 1, 1992. As indicated above, the Preliminary Regulatory Impact Analysis was published on February 28, 1991 (56 FR 8578) for comment. The Commission will also provide a copy to the public upon request by calling the Commission's Office of Communications and Legislative Affairs at (202) 663-4900. Commenters are urged to provide additional information as to the costs and benefits associated with this rule. This will further facilitate the development of a Final Regulatory Impact Analysis. Comments must be received by September 26, 1991. Written comments should be submitted to Frances M. Hart, Executive Officer, Executive Secretariat, Equal Employment Opportunity Commission, 1801 "L" Street, NW., Washington, DC 20507.

As a convenience to commenters, the Executive Secretariat will accept public comments transmitted by facsimile ("FAX") machine. The telephone number of the FAX receiver is (202) 663-4114. (This is not a toll-free number). Only public comments of six or fewer pages will be accepted via FAX transmittal. This limitation is necessary in order to assure access to the equipment. Comments sent by FAX in excess of six pages will not be accepted. Receipt of FAX transmittals will not be acknowledged, except that the sender may request confirmation of receipt by calling the Executive Secretariat Staff at (202) 663-4078. (This is not a toll-free number).

Comments received will be available for public inspection in the EEOC Library, room 6502, by appointment only, from 9 a.m. to 5 p.m., Monday through Friday except legal holidays from October 15, 1991, until the Final Regulatory Impact Analysis is published. Persons who need assistance to review the comments will be provided with appropriate aids such as readers or print magnifiers. To schedule an appointment call (202) 663-4630 (voice), (202) 663-4630 (TDD).

List of Subjects in 29 CFR Part 1630

Equal employment opportunity, Handicapped, Individuals with disabilities.

For the Commission,

Evan J. Kemp, Jr.,

Chairman.

Accordingly, 29 CFR chapter XIV is amended by adding part 1630 to read as follows:

PART 1630—REGULATIONS TO IMPLEMENT THE EQUAL EMPLOYMENT PROVISIONS OF THE AMERICANS WITH DISABILITIES ACT

Sec.
1630.1 Purpose, applicability, and construction.
1630.2 Definitions.
1630.3 Exceptions to the definitions of "Disability" and "Qualified Individual with a Disability."
1630.4 Discrimination prohibited.
1630.5 Limiting, segregating, and classifying.
1630.6 Contractual or other arrangements.
1630.7 Standards, criteria, or methods of administration.
1630.8 Relationship or association with an individual with a disability.
1630.9 Not making reasonable accommodation.
1630.10 Qualification standards, tests, and other selection criteria.
1630.11 Administration of tests.
1630.12 Retaliation and coercion.
1630.13 Prohibited medical examinations and inquiries.
1630.14 Medical examinations and inquiries specifically permitted.
1630.15 Defenses.
1630.16 Specific activities permitted.

Appendix to Part 1630—Interpretive Guidance on Title I of the Americans with Disabilities Act

Authority: 42 U.S.C. 12116.

§ 1630.1 Purpose, applicability, and construction.

(a) *Purpose.* The purpose of this part is to implement title I of the Americans with Disabilities Act (42 U.S.C. 12101, *et seq.*) (ADA), requiring equal employment opportunities for qualified individuals with disabilities, and sections 3(2), 3(3), 501, 503, 506(e), 508, 510, and 511 of the ADA as those sections pertain to the employment of qualified individuals with disabilities.

(b) *Applicability.* This part applies to "covered entities" as defined at § 1630.2(b).

(c) *Construction.*—(1) *In general.* Except as otherwise provided in this part, this part does not apply a lesser standard than the standards applied under title V of the Rehabilitation Act of 1973 (29 U.S.C. 790-794a), or the regulations issued by Federal agencies pursuant to that title.

(2) *Relationship to other laws.* This part does not invalidate or limit the remedies, rights, and procedures of any Federal law or law of any State or political subdivision of any State or jurisdiction that provides greater or equal protection for the rights of individuals with disabilities than are afforded by this part.

§ 1630.2 Definitions.

(a) *Commission* means the Equal Employment Opportunity Commission established by section 705 of the Civil Rights Act of 1964 (42 U.S.C. 2000e-4).

(b) *Covered Entity* means an employer, employment agency, labor organization, or joint labor management committee.

(c) *Person, labor organization, employment agency, commerce and industry affecting commerce* shall have the same meaning given those terms in section 701 of the Civil Rights Act of 1964 (42 U.S.C. 2000e).

(d) *State* means each of the several States, the District of Columbia, the Commonwealth of Puerto Rico, Guam, American Samoa, the Virgin Islands, the Trust Territory of the Pacific Islands, and the Commonwealth of the Northern Mariana Islands.

(e) *Employer.*—(1) *In general.* The term employer means a person engaged in an industry affecting commerce who has 15 or more employees for each working day in each of 20 or more calendar weeks in the current or preceding calendar year, and any agent of such person, except that, from July 26,

1992 through July 25, 1994, an employer means a person engaged in an industry affecting commerce who has 25 or more employees for each working day in each of 20 or more calendar weeks in the current or preceding year and any agent of such person.

(2) *Exceptions.* The term employer does not include—

(i) The United States, a corporation wholly owned by the government of the United States, or an Indian tribe; or

(ii) A bona fide private membership club (other than a labor organization) that is exempt from taxation under section 501(c) of the Internal Revenue Code of 1986.

(f) *Employee* means an individual employed by an employer.

(g) *Disability* means, with respect to an individual—

(1) A physical or mental impairment that substantially limits one or more of the major life activities of such individual;

(2) A record of such an impairment; or

(3) being regarded as having such an impairment.

(See § 1630.3 for exceptions to this definition).

(h) *Physical or mental impairment* means:

(1) Any physiological disorder, or condition, cosmetic disfigurement, or anatomical loss affecting one or more of the following body systems: neurological, musculoskeletal, special sense organs, respiratory (including speech organs), cardiovascular, reproductive, digestive, genito-urinary, hemic and lymphatic, skin, and endocrine; or

(2) Any mental or psychological disorder, such as mental retardation, organic brain syndrome, emotional or mental illness, and specific learning disabilities.

(i) *Major Life Activities* means functions such as caring for oneself, performing manual tasks, walking, seeing, hearing, speaking, breathing, learning, and working.

(j) *Substantially limits*—(1) The term *substantially limits* means:

(i) Unable to perform a major life activity that the average person in the general population can perform; or

(ii) Significantly restricted as to the condition, manner or duration under which an individual can perform a particular major life activity as compared to the condition, manner, or duration under which the average person in the general population can perform that same major life activity.

(2) The following factors should be considered in determining whether an individual is substantially limited in a major life activity:

(i) The nature and severity of the impairment;

(ii) The duration or expected duration of the impairment; and

(iii) The permanent or long term impact, or the expected permanent or long term impact of or resulting from the impairment.

(3) With respect to the major life activity of *working*—

(i) The term *substantially limits* means significantly restricted in the ability to perform either a class of jobs or a broad range of jobs in various classes as compared to the average person having comparable training, skills and abilities. The inability to perform a single, particular job does not constitute a substantial limitation in the major life activity of working.

(ii) In addition to the factors listed in paragraph (j)(2) of this section, the following factors may be considered in determining whether an individual is substantially limited in the major life activity of "working":

(A) The geographical area to which the individual has reasonable access;

(B) The job from which the individual has been disqualified because of an impairment, and the number and types of jobs utilizing similar training, knowledge, skills or abilities, within that geographical area, from which the individual is also disqualified because of the impairment (class of jobs); and/or

(C) The job from which the individual has been disqualified because of an impairment, and the number and types of other jobs not utilizing similar training, knowledge, skills or abilities, within that geographical area, from which the individual is also disqualified because of the impairment (broad range of jobs in various classes).

(k) *Has a record of such impairment* means has a history of, or has been misclassified as having, a mental or physical impairment that substantially limits one or more major life activities.

(l) *Is regarded as having such an impairment* means:

(1) Has a physical or mental impairment that does not substantially limit major life activities but is treated by a covered entity as constituting such limitation;

(2) Has a physical or mental impairment that substantially limits major life activities only as a result of the attitudes of others toward such impairment; or

(3) Has none of the impairments defined in paragraphs (h) (1) or (2) of this section but is treated by a covered entity as having a substantially limiting impairment.

(m) *Qualified individual with a disability* means an individual with a disability who satisfies the requisite skill, experience, education and other job-related requirements of the employment position such individual holds or desires, and who, with or without reasonable accommodation, can perform the essential functions of such position. (See § 1630.3 for exceptions to this definition).

(n) *Essential functions.*—(1) *In general.* The term *essential functions* means the fundamental job duties of the employment position the individual with a disability holds or desires. The term "essential functions" does not include the marginal functions of the position.

(2) A job function may be considered essential for any of several reasons, including but not limited to the following:

(i) The function may be essential because the reason the position exists is to perform that function;

(ii) The function may be essential because of the limited number of employees available among whom the performance of that job function can be distributed; and/or

(iii) The function may be highly specialized so that the incumbent in the position is hired for his or her expertise or ability to perform the particular function.

(3) Evidence of whether a particular function is essential includes, but is not limited to:

(i) The employer's judgment as to which functions are essential;

(ii) Written job descriptions prepared before advertising or interviewing applicants for the job;

(iii) The amount of time spent on the job performing the function;

(iv) The consequences of not requiring the incumbent to perform the function;

(v) The terms of a collective bargaining agreement;

(vi) The work experience of past incumbents in the job; and/or

(vii) The current work experience of incumbents in similar jobs.

(o) *Reasonable accommodation.* (1) The term *reasonable accommodation* means:

(i) Modifications or adjustments to a job application process that enable a qualified applicant with a disability to be considered for the position such qualified applicant desires; or

(ii) Modifications or adjustments to the work environment, or to the manner or circumstances under which the position held or desired is customarily performed, that enable a qualified individual with a disability to perform the essential functions of that position; or

(iii) Modifications or adjustments that enable a covered entity's employee with a disability to enjoy equal benefits and privileges of employment as are enjoyed by its other similarly situated employees without disabilities.

(2) *Reasonable accommodation* may include but is not limited to: .

(i) Making existing facilities used by employees readily accessible to and usable by individuals with disabilities; and

(ii) Job restructuring; part-time or modified work schedules; reassignment to a vacant position; acquisition or modifications of equipment or devices; appropriate adjustment or modifications of examinations, training materials, or policies; the provision of qualified readers or interpreters; and other similar accommodations for individuals with disabilities.

(3) To determine the appropriate reasonable accommodation it may be necessary for the covered entity to initiate an informal, interactive process with the qualified individual with a disability in need of the accommodation. This process should identify the precise limitations resulting from the disability and potential reasonable accommodations that could overcome those limitations.

(p) *Undue hardship*—(1) *In general.* Undue hardship means, with respect to the provision of an accommodation, significant difficulty or expense incurred by a covered entity, when considered in light of the factors set forth in paragraph (p)(2) of this section.

(2) *Factors to be considered.* In determining whether an accommodation would impose an undue hardship on a covered entity, factors to be considered include:

(i) The nature and net cost of the accommodation needed under this part, taking into consideration the availability of tax credits and deductions, and/or outside funding;

(ii)The overall financial resources of the facility or facilities involved in the provision of the reasonable accommodation, the number of persons employed at such facility, and the effect on expenses and resources;

(iii) The overall financial resources of the covered entity, the overall size of the business of the covered entity with respect to the number of its employees, and the number, type and location of its facilities;

(iv) The type of operation or operations of the covered entity, including the composition, structure and functions of the workforce of such entity, and the geographic separateness and administrative or fiscal relationship of the facility or facilities in question to the covered entity; and

(v) The impact of the accommodation upon the operation of the facility, including the impact on the ability of other employees to perform their duties and the impact on the facility's ability to conduct business.

(q) *Qualification standards* means the personal and professional attributes including the skill, experience, education, physical, medical, safety and other requirements established by a covered entity as requirements which an individual must meet in order to be eligible for the position held or desired.

(r) *Direct Threat* means a significant risk of substantial harm to the health or safety of the individual or others that cannot be eliminated or reduced by reasonable accommodation. The determination that an individual poses a "direct threat" shall be based on an individualized assessment of the individual's present ability to safely perform the essential functions of the job. This assessment shall be based on a reasonable medical judgment that relies on the most current medical knowledge and/or on the best available objective evidence. In determining whether an individual would pose a direct threat, the factors to be considered include:

(1) The duration of the risk;

(2) The nature and severity of the potential harm;

(3) The likelihood that the potential harm will occur; and

(4) The imminence of the potential harm.

§ 1630.3 Exceptions to the definitions of "Disability" and "Qualified individual with a Disability."

(a) The terms *disability* and *qualified individual with a disability* do not include individuals currently engaging in the illegal use of drugs, when the covered entity acts on the basis of such use.

(1) *Drug* means a controlled substance, as defined in schedules I through V of Section 202 of the Controlled Substances Act (21 U.S.C 812)

(2) *Illegal use of drugs* means the use of drugs the possession or distribution of which is unlawful under the Controlled Substances Act, as periodically updated by the Food and Drug Administration. This term does not include the use of a drug taken under the supervision of a licensed health care professional, or other uses authorized by the Controlled Substances Act or other provisions of Federal law.

(b) However, the terms *disability* and *qualified* individual with a disability may not exclude an individual who:

(1) Has successfully completed a supervised drug rehabilitation program and is no longer engaging in the illegal use of drugs, or has otherwise been rehabilitated successfully and is no longer engaging in the illegal use of drugs; or

(2) Is participating in a supervised rehabilitation program and is no longer engaging in such use; or

(3) Is erroneously regarded as engaging in such use, but is not engaging in such use.

(c) It shall not be a violation of this part for a covered entity to adopt or administer reasonable policies or procedures, including but not limited to drug testing, designed to ensure that an individual described in paragraph (b)·(1) or (2) of this section is no longer engaging in the illegal use of drugs. (See § 1630.16(c) Drug testing).

(d) *Disability* does not include:

(1) Transvestism, transsexualism, pedophilia, exhibitionism, voyeurism, gender identity disorders not resulting from physical impairments, or other sexual behavior disorders;

(2) Compulsive gambling, kleptomania, or pyromania; or

(3) Psychoactive substance use disorders resulting from current illegal use of drugs.

(e) *Homosexuality and bisexuality* are not impairments and so are not disabilities as defined in this part.

§ 1630.4 Discrimination prohibited.

It is unlawful for a covered entity to discriminate on the basis of disability against a qualified individual with a disability in regard to:

(a) Recruitment, advertising, and job application procedures;

(b) Hiring, upgrading, promotion, award of tenure, demotion, transfer, layoff, termination, right of return from layoff, and rehiring;

(c) Rates of pay or any other form of compensation and changes in compensation;

(d) Job assignments, job classifications, organizational structures, position descriptions, lines of progression, and seniority lists;

(e) Leaves of absence, sick leave, or any other leave;

(f) Fringe benefits available by virtue of employment, whether or not administered by the covered entity;

(g) Selection and financial support for training, including: apprenticeships, professional meetings, conferences and other related activities, and selection for leaves of absence to pursue training;

(h) Activities sponsored by a covered entity including social and recreational programs; and

(i) Any other term, condition, or privilege of employment.

The term *discrimination* includes, but is not limited to, the acts described in §§ 1630.5 through 1630.13 of this part.

§ 1630.5 Limiting segregating, and classifying.

It is unlawful for a covered entity to limit, segregate, or classify a job applicant or employee in a way that adversely affects his or her employment opportunities or status on the basis of disability.

§ 1630.6 Contractual or other arrangements.

(a) *In general.* It is unlawful for a covered entity to participate in a contractual or other arrangement or relationship that has the effect of subjecting the covered entity's own qualified applicant or employee with a disability to the discrimination prohibited by this part.

(b) *Contractual or other arrangement defined.* The phrase *contractual or other arrangement or relationship* includes, but is not limited to, a relationship with an employment or referral agency; labor union, including collective bargaining agreements; an organization providing fringe benefits to an employee of the covered entity; or an organization providing training and apprenticeship programs.

(c) *Application.* This section applies to a covered entity, with respect to its own applicants or employees, whether the entity offered the contract or initiated the relationship, or whether the entity accepted the contract or acceded to the relationship. A covered entity is not liable for the actions of the other party or parties to the contract which only affect that other party's employees or applicants.

§ 1630.7 Standards, criteria, or methods of administration.

It is unlawful for a covered entity to use standards, criteria, or methods of administration, which are not job-related and consistent with business necessity, and:

(a) That have the effect of discriminating on the basis of disability; or

(b) That perpetuate the discrimination of others who are subject to common administrative control.

§ 1630.8 Relationship or association with an individual with a disability.

It is unlawful for a covered entity to exclude or deny equal jobs or benefits to, or otherwise discriminate against, a qualified individual because of the known disability of an individual with whom the qualified individual is known

to have a family, business, social or other relationship or association.

§ 1630.9 Not making reasonable accommodation.

(a) It is unlawful for a covered entity not to make reasonable accommodation to the known physical or mental limitations of an otherwise qualified applicant or employee with a disability, unless such covered entity can demonstrate that the accommodation would impose an undue hardship on the operation of its business.

(b) It is unlawful for a covered entity to deny employment opportunities to an otherwise qualified job applicant or employee with a disability based on the need of such covered entity to make reasonable accommodation to such individual's physical or mental impairments.

(c) A covered entity shall not be excused from the requirements of this part because of any failure to receive technical assistance authorized by section 506 of the ADA, including any failure in the development or dissemination of any technical assistance manual authorized by that Act.

(d) A qualified individual with a disability is not required to accept an accommodation, aid, service, opportunity or benefit which such qualified individual chooses not to accept. However, if such individual rejects a reasonable accommodation, aid, service, opportunity or benefit that is necessary to enable the individual to perform the essential functions of the position held or desired, and cannot, as a result of that rejection, perform the essential functions of the position, the individual will not be considered a qualified individual with a disability.

§ 1630.10 Qualification standards, tests, and other selection criteria.

It is unlawful for a covered entity to use qualification standards, employment tests or other selection criteria that screen out or tend to screen out an individual with a disability or a class of individuals with disabilities, on the basis of disability, unless the standard, test or other selection criteria, as used by the covered entity, is shown to be job-related for the position in question and is consistent with business necessity.

§ 1630.11 Administration of tests.

It is unlawful for a covered entity to fail to select and administer tests concerning employment in the most effective manner to ensure that, when a test is administered to a job applicant or employee who has a disability that

impairs sensory, manual or speaking skills, the test results accurately reflect the skills, aptitude, or whatever other factor of the applicant or employee that the test purports to measure, rather than reflecting the impaired sensory, manual, or speaking skills of such employee or applicant (except where such skills are the factors that the test purports to measure).

§ 1630.12 Retaliation and coercion.

(a) *Retaliation.* It is unlawful to discriminate against any individual because that individual has opposed any act or practice made unlawful by this part or because that individual made a charge, testified, assisted, or participated in any manner in an investigation, proceeding, or hearing to enforce any provision contained in this part.

(b) *Coercion, interference or intimidation.* It is unlawful to coerce, intimidate, threaten, harass or interfere with any individual in the exercise or enjoyment of, or because that individual aided or encouraged any other individual in the exercise of, any right granted or protected by this part.

§ 1630.13 Prohibited medical examinations and inquiries.

(a) *Pre-employment examination or inquiry.* Except as permitted by § 1630.14, it is unlawful for a covered entity to conduct a medical examination of an applicant or to make inquiries as to whether an applicant is an individual with a disability or as to the nature or severity of such disability.

(b) *Examination or inquiry of employees.* Except as permitted by § 1630.14, it is unlawful for a covered entity to require a medical examination of an employee or to make inquiries as to whether an employee is an individual with a disability or as to the nature or severity of such disability.

§ 1630.14 Medical examinations and inquiries specifically permitted.

(a) *Acceptable pre-employment inquiry.* A covered entity may make pre-employment inquiries into the ability of an applicant to perform job-related functions, and/or may ask an applicant to describe or to demonstrate how, with or without reasonable accommodation, the applicant will be able to perform job-related functions.

(b) *Employment entrance examination.* A covered entity may require a medical examination (and/or inquiry) after making an offer of employment to a job applicant and before the applicant begins his or her employment duties, and may condition an offer of employment on the results of such examination (and/or inquiry), if all entering employees in the same job category are subjected to such an examination (and/or inquiry) regardless of disability.

(1) Information obtained under paragraph (b) of this section regarding the medical condition or history of the applicant shall be collected and maintained on separate forms and in separate medical files and be treated as a confidential medical record, except that:

(i) Supervisors and managers may be informed regarding necessary restrictions on the work or duties of the employee and necessary accommodations;

(ii) First aid and safety personnel may be informed, when appropriate, if the disability might require emergency treatment; and

(iii) Government officials investigating compliance with this part shall be provided relevant information on request.

(2) The results of such examination shall not be used for any purpose inconsistent with this part.

(3) Medical examinations conducted in accordance with this section do not have to be job-related and consistent with business necessity. However, if certain criteria are used to screen out an employee or employees with disabilities as a result of such an examination or inquiry, the exclusionary criteria must be job-related and consistent with business necessity, and performance of the essential job functions cannot be accomplished with reasonable accommodation as required in this part. (See § 1630.15(b) Defenses to charges of discriminatory application of selection criteria.)

(c) *Examination of employees.* A covered entity may require a medical examination (and/or inquiry) of an employee that is job-related and consistent with business necessity. A covered entity may make inquiries into the ability of an employee to perform job-related functions.

(1) Information obtained under paragraph (c) of this section regarding the medical condition or history of any employee shall be collected and maintained on separate forms and in separate medical files and be treated as a confidential medical record, except that:

(i) Supervisors and managers may be informed regarding necessary restrictions on the work or duties of the employee and necessary accommodations;

(ii) First aid and safety personnel may be informed, when appropriate, if the

disability might require emergency treatment; and

(iii) Government officials investigating compliance with this part shall be provided relevant information on request.

(2) Information obtained under paragraph (c) of this section regarding the medical condition or history of any employee shall not be used for any purpose inconsistent with this part.

(d) *Other acceptable examinations and inquiries.* A covered entity may conduct voluntary medical examinations and activities, including voluntary medical histories, which are part of an employee health program available to employees at the work site.

(1) Information obtained under paragraph (d) of this section regarding the medical condition or history of any employee shall be collected and maintained on separate forms and in separate medical files and be treated as a confidential medical record, except that:

(i) Supervisors and managers may be informed regarding necessary restrictions on the work or duties of the employee and necessary accommodations;

(ii) First aid and safety personnel may be informed, when appropriate, if the disability might require emergency treatment; and

(iii) Government officials investigating compliance with this part shall be provided relevant information on request.

(2) Information obtained under paragraph (d) of this section regarding the medical condition or history of any employee shall not be used for any purpose inconsistent with this part.

§ 1630.15 Defenses.

Defenses to an allegation of discrimination under this part may include, but are not limited to, the following:

(a) *Disparate treatment charges.* It may be a defense to a charge of disparate treatment brought under §§ 1630.4 through 1630.8 and 1630.11 through 1630.12 that the challenged action is justified by a legitimate, nondiscriminatory reason.

(b) *Charges of discriminatory application of selection criteria*—(1) *In general.* It may be a defense to a charge of discrimination, as described in § 1630.10, that an alleged application of qualification standards, tests, or selection criteria that screens out or tends to screen out or otherwise denies a job or benefit to an individual with a disability has been shown to be job-related and consistent with business necessity, and such performance cannot

be accomplished with reasonable accommodation, as required in this part.

(2) *Direct threat as a qualification standard.* The term "qualification standard" may include a requirement that an individual shall not pose a direct threat to the health or safety of the individual or others in the workplace. (See § 1630.2(r) defining direct threat.)

(c) *Other disparate impact charges.* It may be a defense to a charge of discrimination brought under this part that a uniformly applied standard, criterion, or policy has a disparate impact on an individual with a disability or a class of individuals with disabilities that the challenged standard, criterion or policy has been shown to be job-related and consistent with business necessity, and such performance cannot be accomplished with reasonable accommodation, as required in this part.

(d) *Charges of not making reasonable accommodation.* It may be a defense to a charge of discrimination, as described in § 1630.9, that a requested or necessary accommodation would impose an undue hardship on the operation of the covered entity's business.

(e) *Conflict with other federal laws.* It may be a defense to a charge of discrimination under this part that a challenged action is required or necessitated by another Federal law or regulation, or that another Federal law or regulation prohibits an action (including the provision of a particular reasonable accommodation) that would otherwise be required by this part.

(f) *Additional defenses.* It may be a defense to a charge of discrimination under this part that the alleged discriminatory action is specifically permitted by §§ 1630.14 or 1630.16.

§ 1630.16 Specific activities permitted.

(a) *Religious entities.* A religious corporation, association, educational institution, or society is permitted to give preference in employment to individuals of a particular religion to perform work connected with the carrying on by that corporation, association, educational institution, or society of its activities. A religious entity may require that all applicants and employees conform to the religious tenets of such organization. However, a religious entity may not discriminate against a qualified individual, who satisfies the permitted religious criteria, because of his or her disability.

(b) *Regulation of alcohol and drugs.* A covered entity:

(1) May prohibit the illegal use of drugs and the use of alcohol at the workplace by all employees;

(2) May require that employees not be under the influence of alcohol or be engaging in the illegal use of drugs at the workplace;

(3) May require that all employees behave in conformance with the requirements established under the Drug-Free Workplace Act of 1988 (41 U.S.C. 701 et seq.);

(4) May hold an employee who engages in the illegal use of drugs or who is an alcoholic to the same qualification standards for employment or job performance and behavior to which the entity holds its other employees, even if any unsatisfactory performance or behavior is related to the employee's drug use or alcoholism:

(5) May require that its employees employed in an industry subject to such regulations comply with the standards established in the regulations (if any) of the Departments of Defense and Transportation, and of the Nuclear Regulatory Commission, regarding alcohol and the illegal use of drugs; and

(6) May require that employees employed in sensitive positions comply with the regulations (if any) of the Departments of Defense and Transportation and of the Nuclear Regulatory Commission that apply to employment in sensitive positions subject to such regulations.

(c) *Drug testing*—(1) *General policy.* For purposes of this part, a test to determine the illegal use of drugs is not considered a medical examination. Thus, the administration of such drug tests by a covered entity to its job applicants or employees is not a violation of § 1630.13 of this part. However, this part does not encourage, prohibit, or authorize a covered entity to conduct drug tests of job applicants or employees to determine the illegal use of drugs or to make employment decisions based on such test results.

(2) *Transportation Employees.* This part does not encourage, prohibit, or authorize the otherwise lawful exercise by entities subject to the jurisdiction of the Department of Transportation of authority to:

(i) Test employees of entities in, and applicants for, positions involving safety sensitive duties for the illegal use of drugs or for on-duty impairment by alcohol; and

(ii) Remove from safety-sensitive positions persons who test positive for illegal use of drugs or on-duty impairment by alcohol pursuant to paragraph (c)(2)(i) of this section.

(3) *Confidentiality.* Any information regarding the medical condition or history of any employee or applicant obtained from a test to determine the illegal use of drugs, except information

regarding the illegal use of drugs, is subject to the requirements of § 1630.14(b) (2) and (3) of this part.

(d) *Regulation of smoking.* A covered entity may prohibit or impose restrictions on smoking in places of employment. Such restrictions do not violate any provision of this part.

(e) *Infectious and communicable diseases; food handling jobs*—(1) *In general.* Under title I of the ADA, section 103(d)(1), the Secretary of Health and Human Services is to prepare a list, to be updated annually, of infectious and communicable diseases which are transmitted through the handling of food. (Copies may be obtained from Center for Infectious Diseases, Centers for Disease Control, 1600 Clifton Road, NE., Mailstop C09, Atlanta, GA 30333.) If an individual with a disability is disabled by one of the infectious or communicable diseases included on this list, and if the risk of transmitting the disease associated with the handling of food cannot be eliminated by reasonable accommodation, a covered entity may refuse to assign or continue to assign such individual to a job involving food handling. However, if the individual with a disability is a current employee, the employer must consider whether he or she can be accommodated by reassignment to a vacant position not involving food handling.

(2) *Effect on state or other laws.* This part does not preempt, modify, or amend any State, county, or local law, ordinance or regulation applicable to food handling which:

(i) Is in accordance with the list, referred to in paragraph (e)(1) of this section, of infectious or communicable diseases and the modes of transmissibility published by the Secretary of Health and Human Services; and

(ii) Is designed to protect the public health from individuals who pose a significant risk to the health or safety of others, where that risk cannot be eliminated by reasonable accommodation.

(f) *Health insurance, life insurance, and other benefit plans*—(1) An insurer, hospital, or medical service company, health maintenance organization, or any agent or entity that administers benefit plans, or similar organizations may underwrite risks, classify risks, or administer such risks that are based on or not inconsistent with State law.

(2) A covered entity may establish, sponsor, observe or administer the terms of a bona fide benefit plan that are based on underwriting risks, classifying risks, or administering such risks that

are based on or not inconsistent with State law.

(3) A covered entity may establish, sponsor, observe, or administer the terms of a bona fide benefit plan that is not subject to State laws that regulate insurance.

(4) The activities described in paragraphs (f) (1), (2), and (3) of this section are permitted unless these activities are being used as a subterfuge to evade the purposes of this part.

Appendix to Part 1630—Interpretive Guidance on Title I of the Americans with Disabilities Act

Background

The ADA is a federal antidiscrimination statute designed to remove barriers which prevent qualified individuals with disabilities from enjoying the same employment opportunities that are available to persons without disabilities.

Like the Civil Rights Act of 1964 that prohibits discrimination on the bases of race, color, religion, national origin, and sex, the ADA seeks to ensure access to equal employment opportunities based on merit. It does not guarantee equal results, establish quotas, or require preferences favoring individuals with disabilities over those without disabilities.

However, while the Civil Rights Act of 1964 prohibits any consideration of personal characteristics such as race or national origin, the ADA necessarily takes a different approach. When an individual's disability creates a barrier to employment opportunities, the ADA requires employers to consider whether reasonable accommodation could remove the barrier.

The ADA thus establishes a process in which the employer must assess a disabled individual's ability to perform the essential functions of the specific job held or desired. While the ADA focuses on eradicating barriers, the ADA does not relieve a disabled employee or applicant from the obligation to perform the essential functions of the job. To the contrary, the ADA is intended to enable disabled persons to compete in the workplace based on the same performance standards and requirements that employers expect of persons who are not disabled.

However, where that individual's functional limitation impedes such job performance, an employer must take steps to reasonably accommodate, and thus help overcome the particular impediment, unless to do so would impose an undue hardship. Such accommodations usually take the form of adjustments to the way a job customarily is performed, or to the work environment itself.

This process of identifying whether, and to what extent, a reasonable accommodation is required should be flexible and involve both the employer and the individual with a disability. Of course, the determination of whether an individual is qualified for a particular position must necessarily be made on a case-by-case basis. No specific form of accommodation is guaranteed for all individuals with a particular disability.

Rather, an accommodation must be tailored to match the needs of the disabled individual with the needs of the job's essential functions.

This case-by-case approach is essential if qualified individuals of varying abilities are to receive equal opportunities to compete for an infinitely diverse range of jobs. For this reason, neither the ADA nor this part can supply the "correct" answer in advance for each employment decision concerning an individual with a disability. Instead, the ADA simply establishes parameters to guide employers in how to consider, and take into account, the disabling condition involved.

Introduction

The Equal Employment Opportunity Commission (the Commission or EEOC) is responsible for enforcement of title I of the Americans with Disabilities Act (ADA), 42 U.S.C. 12101 *et seq.* (1990), which prohibits employment discrimination on the basis of disability. The Commission believes that it is essential to issue interpretive guidance concurrently with the issuance of this part in order to ensure that qualified individuals with disabilities understand their rights under this part and to facilitate and encourage compliance by covered entities. This appendix represents the Commission's interpretation of the issues discussed, and the Commission will be guided by it when resolving charges of employment discrimination. The appendix addresses the major provisions of this part and explains the major concepts of disability rights.

The terms "employer" or "employer or other covered entity" are used interchangeably throughout the appendix to refer to all covered entities subject to the employment provisions of the ADA.

Section 1630.1 Purpose, Applicability and Construction

Section 1630.1(a) Purpose

The Americans with Disabilities Act was signed into law on July 26, 1990. It is an antidiscrimination statute that requires that individuals with disabilities be given the same consideration for employment that individuals without disabilities are given. An individual who is qualified for an employment opportunity cannot be denied that opportunity because of the fact that the individual is disabled. The purpose of title I and this part is to ensure that qualified individuals with disabilities are protected from discrimination on the basis of disability.

The ADA uses the term "disabilities" rather than the term "handicaps" used in the Rehabilitation Act of 1973, 29 U.S.C. 701–796. Substantively, these terms are equivalent. As noted by the House Committee on the Judiciary, "[t]he use of the term 'disabilities' instead of the term 'handicaps' reflects the desire of the Committee to use the most current terminology. It reflects the preference of persons with disabilities to use that term rather than 'handicapped' as used in previous laws, such as the Rehabilitation Act of 1973 * * *." H.R. Rep. No. 485 part 3, 101st Cong., 2d Sess. 26–27 (1990) [hereinafter House Judiciary Report]; see also S. Rep. No. 116, 101st Cong., 1st Sess. 21 (1989) [hereinafter Senate Report]; H.R. Rep. No. 485 part 2, 101st Cong., 2d Sess. 50–51 (1990) [hereinafter House Labor Report].

The use of the term "Americans" in the title of the ADA is not intended to imply that the Act only applies to United States citizens. Rather, the ADA protects all qualified individuals with disabilities, regardless of their citizenship status or nationality.

Section 1630.1(b) and (c) Applicability and Construction

Unless expressly stated otherwise, the standards applied in the ADA are not intended to be lesser than the standards applied under the Rehabilitation Act of 1973.

The ADA does not preempt any Federal law, or any state or local law, that grants to individuals with disabilities protection greater than or equivalent to that provided by the ADA. This means that the existence of a lesser standard of protection to individuals with disabilities under the ADA will not provide a defense to failing to meet a higher standard under another law. Thus, for example, title I of the ADA would not be a defense to failing to collect information required to satisfy the affirmative action requirements of section 503 of the Rehabilitation Act. On the other hand, the existence of a lesser standard under another law will not provide a defense to failing to meet a higher standard under the ADA. See House Labor Report at 135; House Judiciary Report at 69–70.

This also means that an individual with a disability could choose to pursue claims under a state discrimination or tort law that does not confer greater substantive rights, or even confers fewer substantive rights, if the potential available remedies would be greater than those available under the ADA and this part. The ADA does not restrict an individual with a disability from pursuing such claims in addition to charges brought under this part. House Judiciary at 69–70.

The ADA does not automatically preempt medical standards or safety requirements established by Federal law or regulations. It does not preempt State, county, or local laws, ordinances or regulations that are consistent with this part, and are designed to protect the public health from individuals who pose a direct threat, that cannot be eliminated or reduced by reasonable accommodation, to the health or safety of others. However, the ADA does preempt inconsistent requirements established by state or local law for safety or security sensitive positions. See Senate Report at 27; House Labor Report at 57.

An employer allegedly in violation of this part cannot successfully defend its actions by relying on the obligation to comply with the requirements of any state or local law that imposes prohibitions or limitations on the eligibility of qualified individuals with disabilities to practice any occupation or profession. For example, suppose a municipality has an ordinance that prohibits individuals with tuberculosis from teaching school children. If an individual with dormant tuberculosis challenges a private school's refusal to hire him or her because of the tuberculosis, the private school would not be able to rely on the city ordinance as a defense under the ADA.

Sections 1630.2(a)–(f) Commission, Covered Entity, etc.

The definitions section of part 1630 includes several terms that are identical, or almost identical, to the terms found in title VII of the Civil Rights Act of 1964. Among these terms are "Commission," "Person," "State," and "Employer." These terms are to be given the same meaning under the ADA that they are given under title VII.

In general, the term "employee" has the same meaning that it is given under title VII. However, the ADA's definition of "employee" does not contain an exception, as does title VII, for elected officials and their personal staffs. It should be further noted that all state and local governments are covered by title II of the ADA whether or not they are also covered by this part. Title II, which is enforced by the Department of Justice, becomes effective on January 26, 1992. See 28 CFR part 35.

The term "covered entity" is not found in title VII. However, the title VII definitions of the entities included in the term "covered entity" (e.g., employer, employment agency, etc.) are applicable to the ADA.

Section 1630.2(g) Disability

In addition to the term "covered entity," there are several other terms that are unique to the ADA. The first of these is the term "disability." Congress adopted the definition of this term from the Rehabilitation Act definition of the term "individual with handicaps." By so doing, Congress intended that the relevant caselaw developed under the Rehabilitation Act be generally applicable to the term "disability" as used in the ADA. Senate Report at 21; House Labor Report at 50; House Judiciary Report at 27.

The definition of the term "disability" is divided into three parts. An individual must satisfy at least one of these parts in order to be considered an individual with a disability for purposes of this part. An individual is considered to have a "disability" if that individual either (1) has a physical or mental impairment which substantially limits one or more of that person's major life activities, (2) has a record of such an impairment, or, (3) is regarded by the covered entity as having such an impairment. To understand the meaning of the term "disability," it is necessary to understand, as a preliminary matter, what is meant by the terms "physical or mental impairment," "major life activity," and "substantially limits." Each of these terms is discussed below.

Section 1630.2(h) Physical or Mental Impairment

This term adopts the definition of the term "physical or mental impairment" found in the regulations implementing section 504 of the Rehabilitation Act at 34 CFR part 104. It defines physical or mental impairment as any physiological disorder or condition, cosmetic disfigurement, or anatomical loss affecting one or more of several body systems, or any mental or psychological disorder.

The existence of an impairment is to be determined without regard to mitigating measures such as medicines, or assistive or prosthetic devices. See Senate Report at 23,

House Labor Report at 52, House Judiciary Report at 28. For example, an individual with epilepsy would be considered to have an impairment even if the symptoms of the disorder were completely controlled by medicine. Similarly, an individual with hearing loss would be considered to have an impairment even if the condition were correctable through the use of a hearing aid.

It is important to distinguish between conditions that are impairments and physical, psychological, environmental, cultural and economic characteristics that are not impairments. The definition of the term "impairment" does not include physical characteristics such as eye color, hair color, left-handedness, or height, weight or muscle tone that are within "normal" range and are not the result of a physiological disorder. The definition, likewise, does not include characteristic predisposition to illness or disease. Other conditions, such as pregnancy, that are not the result of a physiological disorder are also not impairments. Similarly, the definition does not include common personality traits such as poor judgment or a quick temper where these are not symptoms of a mental or psychological disorder. Environmental, cultural, or economic disadvantages such as poverty, lack of education or a prison record are not impairments. Advanced age, in and of itself, is also not an impairment. However, various medical conditions commonly associated with age, such as hearing loss, osteoporosis, or arthritis would constitute impairments within the meaning of this part. See Senate Report at 22–23; House Labor Report at 51–52; House Judiciary Report at 28–29.

Section 1630.2(i)   Major Life Activities

This term adopts the definition of the term "major life activities" found in the regulations implementing section 504 of the Rehabilitation Act at 34 CFR part 104. "Major life activities" are those basic activities that the average person in the general population can perform with little or no difficulty. Major life activities include caring for oneself, performing manual tasks, walking, seeing, hearing, speaking, breathing, learning, and working. This list is not exhaustive. For example, other major life activities include, but are not limited to, sitting, standing, lifting, reaching. See Senate Report at 22; House Labor Report at 52; House Judiciary Report at 28.

Section 1630.2(j)   Substantially Limits

Determining whether a physical or mental impairment exists is only the first step in determining whether or not an individual is disabled. Many impairments do not impact an individual's life to the degree that they constitute disabling impairments. An impairment rises to the level of disability if the impairment substantially limits one or more of the individual's major life activities. Multiple impairments that combine to substantially limit one or more of an individual's major life activities also constitute a disability.

The ADA and this part, like the Rehabilitation Act of 1973, do not attempt a "laundry list" of impairments that are "disabilities." The determination of whether

an individual has a disability is not necessarily based on the name or diagnosis of the impairment the person has, but rather on the effect of that impairment on the life of the individual. Some impairments may be disabling for particular individuals but not for others, depending on the stage of the disease or disorder, the presence of other impairments that combine to make the impairment disabling or any number of other factors.

Other impairments, however, such as HIV infection, are inherently substantially limiting.

On the other hand, temporary, non-chronic impairments of short duration, with little or no long term or permanent impact, are usually not disabilities. Such impairments may include, but are not limited to, broken limbs, sprained joints, concussions, appendicitis, and influenza. Similarly, except in rare circumstances, obesity is not considered a disabling impairment.

An impairment that prevents an individual from performing a major life activity substantially limits that major life activity. For example, an individual whose legs are paralyzed is substantially limited in the major life activity of walking because he or she is unable, due to the impairment, to perform that major life activity.

Alternatively, an impairment is substantially limiting if it significantly restricts the duration, manner or condition under which an individual can perform a particular major life activity as compared to the average person in the general population's ability to perform that same major life activity. Thus, for example, an individual who, because of an impairment, can only walk for very brief periods of time would be substantially limited in the major life activity of walking. An individual who uses artificial legs would likewise be substantially limited in the major life activity of walking because the individual is unable to walk without the aid of prosthetic devices. Similarly, a diabetic who without insulin would lapse into a coma would be substantially limited because the individual cannot perform major life activities without the aid of medication. See Senate Report at 23; House Labor Report at 52. It should be noted that the term "average person" is not intended to imply a precise mathematical "average."

Part 1630 notes several factors that should be considered in making the determination of whether an impairment is substantially limiting. These factors are (1) the nature and severity of the impairment, (2) the duration or expected duration of the impairment, and (3) the permanent or long term impact, or the expected permanent or long term impact of, or resulting from, the impairment. The term "duration," as used in this context, refers to the length of time an impairment persists, while the term "impact" refers to the residual effects of an impairment. Thus, for example, a broken leg that takes eight weeks to heal is an impairment of fairly brief duration. However, if the broken leg heals improperly, the "impact" of the impairment would be the resulting permanent limp. Likewise, the effect on cognitive functions resulting from traumatic head injury would be the "impact" of that impairment.

The determination of whether an individual is substantially limited in a major life activity must be made on a case by case basis, without regard to mitigating measures such as medicines, or assistive or prosthetic devices. An individual is not substantially limited in a major life activity if the limitation, when viewed in light of the factors noted above, does not amount to a significant restriction when compared with the abilities of the average person. For example, an individual who had once been able to walk at an extraordinary speed would not be substantially limited in the major life activity of walking if, as a result of a physical impairment, he or she were only able to walk at an average speed, or even at moderately below average speed.

It is important to remember that the restriction on the performance of the major life activity must be the result of a condition that is an impairment. As noted earlier, advanced age, physical or personality characteristics, and environmental, cultural, and economic disadvantages are not impairments. Consequently, even if such factors substantially limit an individual's ability to perform a major life activity, this limitation will not constitute a disability. For example, an individual who is unable to read because he or she was never taught to read would not be an individual with a disability because lack of education is not an impairment. However, an individual who is unable to read because of dyslexia would be an individual with a disability because dyslexia, a learning disability, is an impairment.

If an individual is not substantially limited with respect to any other major life activity, the individual's ability to perform the major life activity of working should be considered. If an individual is substantially limited in any other major life activity, no determination should be made as to whether the individual is substantially limited in working. For example, if an individual is blind, *i.e.,* substantially limited in the major life activity of seeing, there is no need to determine whether the individual is also substantially limited in the major life activity of working. The determination of whether an individual is substantially limited in working must also be made on a case by case basis.

This part lists specific factors that may be used in making the determination of whether the limitation in working is "substantial." These factors are:

(1) The geographical area to which the individual has reasonable access;

(2) The job from which the individual has been disqualified because of an impairment, and the number and types of jobs utilizing similar training, knowledge, skills or abilities, within that geographical area, from which the individual is also disqualified because of the impairment (class of jobs); and/or

(3) The job from which the individual has been disqualified because of an impairment, and the number and types of other jobs not utilizing similar training, knowledge, skills or abilities, within that geographical area, from which the individual is also disqualified because of the impairment (broad range of jobs in various classes).

Thus, an individual is not substantially limited in working just because he or she is unable to perform a particular job for one employer, or because he or she is unable to perform a specialized job or profession requiring extraordinary skill, prowess or talent. For example, an individual who cannot be a commercial airline pilot because of a minor vision impairment, but who can be a commercial airline co-pilot or a pilot for a courier service, would not be substantially limited in the major life activity of working. Nor would a professional baseball pitcher who develops a bad elbow and can no longer throw a baseball be considered substantially limited in the major life activity of working. In both of these examples, the individuals are not substantially limited in the ability to perform any other major life activity and, with regard to the major life activity of working, are only unable to perform either a particular specialized job or a narrow range of jobs. See *Forrisi* v. *Bowen*, 794 F.2d 931 (4th Cir. 1986); *Jasany* v. *U.S. Postal Service*, 755 F.2d 1244 (6th Cir. 1985); *E.E Black, Ltd.* v. *Marshall*, 497 F. Supp. 1088 (D. Hawaii 1980).

On the other hand, an individual does not have to be totally unable to work in order to be considered substantially limited in the major life activity of working. An individual is substantially limited in working if the individual is significantly restricted in the ability to perform a class of jobs or a broad range of jobs in various classes, when compared with the ability of the average person with comparable qualifications to perform those same jobs. For example, an individual who has a back condition that prevents the individual from performing any heavy labor job would be substantially limited in the major life activity of working because the individual's impairment eliminates his or her ability to perform a class of jobs. This would be so even if the individual were able to perform jobs in another class, *e.g.*, the class of semi-skilled jobs. Similarly, suppose an individual has an allergy to a substance found in most high rise office buildings, but seldom found elsewhere, that makes breathing extremely difficult. Since this individual would be substantially limited in the ability to perform the broad range of jobs in various classes that are conducted in high rise office buildings within the geographical area to which he or she has reasonable access, he or she would be substantially limited in working.

The terms "number and types of jobs" and "number and types of other jobs," as used in the factors discussed above, are not intended to require an onerous evidentiary showing. Rather, the terms only require the presentation of evidence of general employment demographics and/or of recognized occupational classifications that indicate the approximate number of jobs (*e.g.*, "few," "many," "most") from which an individual would be excluded because of an impairment.

If an individual has a "mental or physical impairment" that "substantially limits" his or her ability to perform one or more "major life activities," that individual will satisfy the first part of the regulatory definition of "disability" and will be considered an individual with a disability. An individual

who satisfies this first part of the definition of the term "disability" is not required to demonstrate that he or she satisfies either of the other parts of the definition. However, if an individual is unable to satisfy this part of the definition, he or she may be able to satisfy one of the other parts of the definition.

Section 1630.2(k) Record of a Substantially Limiting Condition

The second part of the definition provides that an individual with a record of an impairment that substantially limits a major life activity is an individual with a disability. The intent of this provision, in part, is to ensure that people are not discriminated against because of a history of disability. For example, this provision protects former cancer patients from discrimination based on their prior medical history. This provision also ensures that individuals are not discriminated against because they have been misclassified as disabled. For example, individuals misclassified as learning disabled are protected from discrimination on the basis of that erroneous classification. Senate Report at 23; House Labor Report at 52–53; House Judiciary Report at 29.

This part of the definition is satisfied if a record relied on by an employer indicates that the individual has or has had a substantially limiting impairment. The impairment indicated in the record must be an impairment that would substantially limit one or more of the individual's major life activities. There are many types of records that could potentially contain this information, including but not limited to, education, medical, or employment records.

The fact that an individual has a record of being a disabled veteran, or of disability retirement, or is classified as disabled for other purposes does not guarantee that the individual will satisfy the definition of "disability" under part 1630. Other statutes, regulations and programs may have a definition of "disability" that is not the same as the definition set forth in the ADA and contained in part 1630. Accordingly, in order for an individual who has been classified in a record as "disabled" for some other purpose to be considered disabled for purposes of part 1630, the impairment indicated in the record must be a physical or mental impairment that substantially limits one or more of the individual's major life activities.

Section 1630.2(l) Regarded as Substantially Limited in a Major Life Activity

If an individual cannot satisfy either the first part of the definition of "disability" or the second "record of" part of the definition, he or she may be able to satisfy the third part of the definition. The third part of the definition provides that an individual who is regarded by an employer or other covered entity as having an impairment that substantially limits a major life activity is an individual with a disability.

There are three different ways in which an individual may satisfy the definition of "being regarded as having a disability":

(1) The individual may have an impairment which is not substantially limiting but is perceived by the employer or other covered entity as constituting a substantially limiting impairment;

(2) The individual may have an impairment which is only substantially limiting because of the attitudes of others toward the impairment; or

(3) The individual may have no impairment at all but is regarded by the employer or other covered entity as having a substantially limiting impairment.
Senate Report at 23; House Labor Report at 53; House Judiciary Report at 29.

An individual satisfies the first part of this definition if the individual has an impairment that is not substantially limiting, but the covered entity perceives the impairment as being substantially limiting. For example, suppose an employee has controlled high blood pressure that is not substantially limiting. If an employer reassigns the individual to less strenuous work because of unsubstantiated fears that the individual will suffer a heart attack if he or she continues to perform strenuous work, the employer would be regarding the individual as disabled.

An individual satisfies the second part of the "regarded as" definition if the individual has an impairment that is only substantially limiting because of the attitudes of others toward the condition. For example, an individual may have a prominent facial scar or disfigurement, or may have a condition that periodically causes an involuntary jerk of the head but does not limit the individual's major life activities. If an employer discriminates against such an individual because of the negative reactions of customers, the employer would be regarding the individual as disabled and acting on the basis of that perceived disability. See Senate Report at 24; House Labor Report at 53; House Judiciary Report at 30–31.

An individual satisfies the third part of the "regarded as" definition of "disability" if the employer or other covered entity erroneously believes the individual has a substantially limiting impairment that the individual actually does not have. This situation could occur, for example, if an employer discharged an employee in response to a rumor that the employee is infected with Human Immunodeficiency Virus (HIV). Even though the rumor is totally unfounded and the individual has no impairment at all, the individual is considered an individual with a disability because the employer perceived of this individual as being disabled. Thus, in this example, the employer, by discharging this employee, is discriminating on the basis of disability.

The rationale for the "regarded as" part of the definition of disability was articulated by the Supreme Court in the context of the Rehabilitation Act of 1973 in *School Board of Nassau County* v. *Arline*, 480 U.S. 273 (1987). The Court noted that, although an individual may have an impairment that does not in fact substantially limit a major life activity, the reaction of others may prove just as disabling. "Such an impairment might not diminish a person's physical or mental capabilities, but could nevertheless substantially limit that person's ability to work as a result of the negative reactions of others to the impairment." 480 U.S. at 283. The Court concluded that by including "regarded as" in the Rehabilitation Act's definition. "Congress acknowledged that society's accumulated myths and fears about disability and diseases are as handicapping as are the physical limitations that flow from actual impairment." 480 U.S. at 284.

An individual rejected from a job because of the "myths, fears and stereotypes" associated with disabilities would be covered under this part of the definition of disability, whether or not the employer's or other covered entity's perception were shared by others in the field and whether or not the individual's actual physical or mental condition would be considered a disability under the first or second part of this definition. As the legislative history notes, sociologists have identified common attitudinal barriers that frequently result in employers excluding individuals with disabilities. These include concerns regarding productivity, safety, insurance, liability, attendance, cost of accommodation and accessibility, workers' compensation costs, and acceptance by coworkers and customers.

Therefore, if an individual can show that an employer or other covered entity made an employment decision because of a perception of disability based on "myth, fear or stereotype," the individual will satisfy the "regarded as" part of the definition of disability. If the employer cannot articulate a non-discriminatory reason for the employment action, an inference that the employer is acting on the basis of "myth, fear or stereotype" can be drawn.

Section 1630.2(m)   Qualified Individual With a Disability

The ADA prohibits discrimination on the basis of disability against qualified individuals with disabilities. The determination of whether an individual with a disability is "qualified" should be made in two steps. The first step is to determine if the individual satisfies the prerequisites for the position, such as possessing the appropriate educational background, employment experience, skills, licenses, etc. For example, the first step in determining whether an accountant who is paraplegic is qualified for a certified public accountant (CPA) position is to examine the individual's credentials to determine whether the individual is a licensed CPA. This is sometimes referred to in the Rehabilitation Act caselaw as determining whether the individual is "otherwise qualified" for the position. See Senate Report at 33; House Labor Report at 64–65. (See § 1630.9 Not Making Reasonable Accommodation).

The second step is to determine whether or not the individual can perform the essential functions of the position held or desired, with or without reasonable accommodation. The purpose of this second step is to ensure that individuals with disabilities who can perform the essential functions of the position held or desired are not denied employment opportunities because they are not able to perform marginal functions of the position. House Labor Report at 55.

The determination of whether an individual with a disability is qualified is to be made at the time of the employment decision. This determination should be based on the capabilities of the individual with a disability at the time of the employment decision, and should not be based on speculation that the employee may become unable in the future or may cause increased health insurance premiums or workers compensation costs.

Section 1630.2(n)   Essential Functions

The determination of which functions are essential may be critical to the determination of whether or not the individual with a disability is qualified. The essential functions are those functions that the individual who holds the position must be able to perform unaided or with the assistance of a reasonable accommodation.

The inquiry into whether a particular function is essential initially focuses on whether the employer actually requires employees in the position to perform the functions that the employer asserts are essential. For example, an employer may state that typing is an essential function of a position. If, in fact, the employer has never required any employee in that particular position to type, this will be evidence that typing is not actually an essential function of the position.

If the individual who holds the position is actually required to perform the function the employer asserts is an essential function, the inquiry will then center around whether removing the function would fundamentally alter that position. This determination of whether or not a particular function is essential will generally include one or more of the following factors listed in part 1630.

The first factor is whether the position exists to perform a particular function. For example, an individual may be hired to proofread documents. The ability to proofread the documents would then be an essential function, since this is the only reason the position exists.

The second factor in determining whether a function is essential is the number of other employees available to perform that job function or among whom the performance of that job function can be distributed. This may be a factor either because the total number of available employees is low, or because of the fluctuating demands of the business operation. For example, if an employer has a relatively small number of available employees for the volume of work to be performed, it may be necessary that each employee perform a multitude of different functions. Therefore, the performance of those functions by each employee becomes more critical and the options for reorganizing the work become more limited. In such a situation, functions that might not be essential if there were a larger staff may become essential because the staff size is small compared to the volume of work that has to be done. See Treadwell v. Alexander, 707 F.2d 473 (11th Cir. 1983).

A similar situation might occur in a larger work force if the workflow follows a cycle of heavy demand for labor intensive work followed by low demand periods. This type of workflow might also make the performance of each function during the peak periods more critical and might limit the employer's flexibility in reorganizing operating procedures. See Dexler v. Tisch, 660 F. Supp. 1418 (D. Conn. 1987).

The third factor is the degree of expertise or skill required to perform the function. In certain professions and highly skilled positions the employee is hired for his or her expertise or ability to perform the particular function. In such a situation, the performance of that specialized task would be an essential function.

Whether a particular function is essential is a factual determination that must be made on a case by case basis. In determining whether or not a particular function is essential, all relevant evidence should be considered. Part 1630 lists various types of evidence, such as an established job description, that should be considered in determining whether a particular function is essential. Since the list is not exhaustive, other relevant evidence may also be presented. Greater weight will not be granted to the types of evidence included on the list than to the types of evidence not listed.

Although part 1630 does not require employers to develop or maintain job descriptions, written job descriptions prepared before advertising or interviewing applicants for the job, as well as the employer's judgment as to what functions are essential are among the relevant evidence to be considered in determining whether a particular function is essential. The terms of a collective bargaining agreement are also relevant to the determination of whether a particular function is essential. The work experience of past employees in the job or of current employees in similar jobs is likewise relevant to the determination of whether a particular function is essential. See H.R. Conf. Rep. No. 101–596, 101st Cong., 2d Sess. 58 (1990) [hereinafter Conference Report]; House Judiciary Report at 33–34. See also Hall v. U.S. Postal Service, 857 F.2d 1073 (6th Cir. 1988).

The time spent performing the particular function may also be an indicator of whether that function is essential. For example, if an employee spends the vast majority of his or her time working at a cash register, this would be evidence that operating the cash register is an essential function. The consequences of failing to require the employee to perform the function may be another indicator of whether a particular function is essential. For example, although a firefighter may not regularly have to carry an unconscious adult out of a burning building, the consequence of failing to require the firefighter to be able to perform this function would be serious.

It is important to note that the inquiry into essential functions is not intended to second guess an employer's business judgment with regard to production standards, whether qualitative or quantitative, nor to require employers to lower such standards. (See § 1630.10 Qualification Standards, Tests and Other Selection Criteria). If an employer requires its typists to be able to accurately type 75 words per minute, it will not be called upon to explain why an inaccurate work product, or a typing speed of 65 words per minute, would not be adequate. Similarly, if a hotel requires its service workers to thoroughly clean 16 rooms per day, it will not have to explain why it requires thorough cleaning, or why it chose a 16 room rather than a 10 room requirement. However, if an employer does require accurate 75 word per minute typing or the thorough cleaning of 16 rooms, it will have to show that it actually imposes such requirements on its employees in fact, and not simply on paper. It should also be noted that, if it is alleged that the employer intentionally selected the particular level of production to exclude individuals with disabilities, the employer may have to offer a legitimate, nondiscriminatory reason for its selection.

Section 1630.2(o) Reasonable Accommodation

An individual is considered a "qualified individual with a disability" if the individual can perform the essential functions of the position held or desired with or without reasonable accommodation. In general, an accommodation is any change in the work environment or in the way things are customarily done that enables an individual with a disability to enjoy equal employment opportunities. There are three categories of reasonable accommodation. These are (1) accommodations that are required to ensure equal opportunity in the application process; (2) accommodations that enable the employer's employees with disabilities to perform the essential functions of the position held or desired; and (3) accommodations that enable the employer's employees with disabilities to enjoy equal benefits and privileges of employment as are enjoyed by employees without disabilities. It should be noted that nothing in this part prohibits employers or other covered entities from providing accommodations beyond those required by this part.

Part 1630 lists the examples, specified in title I of the ADA, of the most common types of accommodation that an employer or other covered entity may be required to provide. There are any number of other specific accommodations that may be appropriate for particular situations but are not specifically mentioned in this listing. This listing is not intended to be exhaustive of accommodation possibilities. For example, other accommodations could include permitting the use of accrued paid leave or providing additional unpaid leave for necessary treatment, making employer provided transportation accessible, and providing reserved parking spaces. Providing personal assistants, such as a page turner for an employee with no hands or a travel attendant to act as a sighted guide to assist a blind employee on occasional business trips, may also be a reasonable accommodation. Senate Report at 31; House Labor Report at 62; House Judiciary Report at 39.

It may also be a reasonable accommodation to permit an individual with a disability the opportunity to provide and utilize equipment, aids or services that an employer is not required to provide as a reasonable accommodation. For example, it would be a reasonable accommodation for an employer to permit an individual who is blind to use a guide dog at work, even though the employer would not be required to provide a guide dog for the employee.

The accommodations included on the list of reasonable accommodations are generally self explanatory. However, there are a few that require further explanation. One of these is the accommodation of making existing facilities used by employees readily accessible to, and usable by, individuals with disabilities. This accommodation includes both those areas that must be accessible for the employee to perform essential job functions, as well as non-work areas used by the employer's employees for other purposes. For example, accessible break rooms, lunch rooms, training rooms, restrooms etc., may be required as reasonable accommodations.

Another of the potential accommodations listed is "job restructuring." An employer or other covered entity may restructure a job by reallocating or redistributing nonessential, marginal job functions. For example, an employer may have two jobs, each of which entails the performance of a number of marginal functions. The employer hires a qualified individual with a disability who is able to perform some of the marginal functions of each job but not all of the marginal functions of either job. As an accommodation, the employer may redistribute the marginal functions so that all of the marginal functions that the qualified individual with a disability can perform are made a part of the position to be filled by the qualified individual with a disability. The remaining marginal functions that the individual with a disability cannot perform would then be transferred to the other position. See Senate Report at 31; House Labor Report at 62.

An employer or other covered entity is not required to reallocate essential functions. The essential functions are by definition those that the individual who holds the job would have to perform, with or without reasonable accommodation, in order to be considered qualified for the position. For example, suppose a security guard position requires the individual who holds the job to inspect identification cards. An employer would not have to provide an individual who is legally blind with an assistant to look at the identification cards for the legally blind employee. In this situation the assistant would be performing the job for the individual with a disability rather than assisting the individual to perform the job. See *Coleman* v. *Darden*, 595 F.2d 533 (10th Cir. 1979).

An employer or other covered entity may also restructure a job by altering when and/or how an essential function is performed. For example, an essential function customarily performed in the early morning hours may be rescheduled until later in the day as a reasonable accommodation to a disability that precludes performance of the function at the customary hour. Likewise, as a reasonable accommodation, an employee with a disability that inhibits the ability to write, may be permitted to computerize records that were customarily maintained manually.

Reassignment to a vacant position is also listed as a potential reasonable accommodation. In general, reassignment should be considered only when accommodation within the individual's current position would pose an undue hardship. Reassignment is not available to applicants. An applicant for a position must be qualified for, and be able to perform the essential functions of, the position sought with or without reasonable accommodation.

Reassignment may not be used to limit, segregate, or otherwise discriminate against employees with disabilities by forcing reassignments to undesirable positions or to designated offices or facilities. Employers should reassign the individual to an equivalent position, in terms of pay, status, etc., if the individual is qualified, and if the position is vacant within a reasonable amount of time. A "reasonable amount of time" should be determined in light of the totality of the circumstances. As an example, suppose there is no vacant position available at the time that an individual with a disability requests reassignment as a reasonable accommodation. The employer, however, knows that an equivalent position for which the individual is qualified, will become vacant next week. Under these circumstances, the employer should reassign the individual to the position when it becomes available.

An employer may reassign an individual to a lower graded position if there are no accommodations that would enable the employee to remain in the current position and there are no vacant equivalent positions for which the individual is qualified with or without reasonable accommodation. An employer, however, is not required to maintain the reassigned individual with a disability at the salary of the higher graded position if it does not so maintain reassigned employees who are not disabled. It should also be noted that an employer is not required to promote an individual with a disability as an accommodation. See Senate Report at 31–32; House Labor Report at 63.

The determination of which accommodation is appropriate in a particular situation involves a process in which the employer and employee identify the precise limitations imposed by the disability and explore potential accommodations that would overcome those limitations. This process is discussed more fully in § 1630.9 Not Making Reasonable Accommodation.

Section 1630.2(p) Undue Hardship

An employer or other covered entity is not required to provide an accommodation that will impose an undue hardship on the operation of the employer's or other covered entity's business. The term "undue hardship" means significant difficulty or expense in, or resulting from, the provision of the accommodation. The "undue hardship" provision takes into account the financial realities of the particular employer or other covered entity. However, the concept of undue hardship is not limited to financial difficulty. "Undue hardship" refers to any accommodation that would be unduly costly, extensive, substantial, or disruptive, or that would fundamentally alter the nature or operation of the business. See Senate Report at 35; House Labor Report at 67.

For example, suppose an individual with a disabling visual impairment that makes it extremely difficult to see in dim lighting applies for a position as a waiter in a nightclub and requests that the club be brightly lit as a reasonable accommodation. Although the individual may be able to perform the job in bright lighting, the nightclub will probably be able to demonstrate that that particular accommodation, though inexpensive, would impose an undue hardship if the bright lighting would destroy the ambience of the nightclub and/or make it difficult for the customers to see the stage show. The fact that that particular accommodation poses an undue hardship, however, only means that the employer is not required to provide that accommodation. If there is another accommodation that will not create an undue hardship, the employer would be required to provide the alternative accommodation.

An employer's claim that the cost of a particular accommodation will impose an undue hardship will be analyzed in light of the factors outlined in part 1630. In part, this analysis requires a determination of whose financial resources should be considered in deciding whether the accommodation is unduly costly. In some cases the financial resources of the employer or other covered entity in its entirety should be considered in determining whether the cost of an accommodation poses an undue hardship. In other cases, consideration of the financial resources of the employer or other covered entity as a whole may be inappropriate because it may not give an accurate picture of the financial resources available to the particular facility that will actually be required to provide the accommodation. See House Labor Report at 68–69; House Judiciary Report at 40–41; see also Conference Report at 56–57.

If the employer or other covered entity asserts that only the financial resources of the facility where the individual will be employed should be considered, part 1630 requires a factual determination of the relationship between the employer or other covered entity and the facility that will provide the accommodation. As an example, suppose that an independently owned fast food franchise that receives no money from the franchisor refuses to hire an individual with a hearing impairment because it asserts that it would be an undue hardship to provide an interpreter to enable the individual to participate in monthly staff meetings. Since the financial relationship between the franchisor and the franchise is limited to payment of an annual franchise fee, only the financial resources of the franchise would be considered in determining whether or not providing the accommodation would be an undue hardship. See House Labor Report at 68; House Judiciary Report at 40.

If the employer or other covered entity can show that the cost of the accommodation would impose an undue hardship, it would still be required to provide the accommodation if the funding is available from another source, e.g., a State vocational rehabilitation agency, or if Federal, State or local tax deductions or tax credits are available to offset the cost of the accommodation. If the employer or other covered entity receives, or is eligible to receive, monies from an external source that would pay the entire cost of the

accommodation, it cannot claim cost as an undue hardship. In the absence of such funding, the individual with a disability requesting the accommodation should be given the option of providing the accommodation or of paying that portion of the cost which constitutes the undue hardship on the operation of the business. To the extent that such monies pay or would pay for only part of the cost of the accommodation, only that portion of the cost of the accommodation that could not be recovered—the final net cost to the entity—may be considered in determining undue hardship. (See § 1630.9 Not Making Reasonable Accommodation). See Senate Report at 36; House Labor Report at 69.

Section 1630.2(r)   Direct Threat

An employer may require, as a qualification standard, that an individual not pose a direct threat to the health or safety of himself/herself or others. Like any other qualification standard, such a standard must apply to all applicants or employees and not just to individuals with disabilities. If, however, an individual poses a direct threat as a result of a disability, the employer must determine whether a reasonable accommodation would either eliminate the risk or reduce it to an acceptable level. If no accommodation exists that would either eliminate or reduce the risk, the employer may refuse to hire an applicant or may discharge an employee who poses a direct threat.

An employer, however, is not permitted to deny an employment opportunity to an individual with a disability merely because of a slightly increased risk. The risk can only be considered when it poses a significant risk, i.e., high probability, of substantial harm; a speculative or remote risk is insufficient. See Senate Report at 27; House Report Labor Report at 56–57; House Judiciary Report at 45.

Determining whether an individual poses a significant risk of substantial harm to others must be made on a case by case basis. The employer should identify the specific risk posed by the individual. For individuals with mental or emotional disabilities, the employer must identify the specific behavior on the part of the individual that would pose the direct threat. For individuals with physical disabilities, the employer must identify the aspect of the disability that would pose the direct threat. The employer should then consider the four factors listed in part 1630:

(1) The duration of the risk;

(2) The nature and severity of the potential harm;

(3) The likelihood that the potential harm will occur; and

(4) The imminence of the potential harm.

Such consideration must rely on objective, factual evidence—not on subjective perceptions, irrational fears, patronizing attitudes, or stereotypes—about the nature or effect of a particular disability, or of disability generally. See Senate Report at 27; House Labor Report at 56–57; House Judiciary Report at 45–46. See also *Strathie* v. *Department of Transportation*, 716 F.2d 227 (3d Cir. 1983). Relevant evidence may include input from the individual with a disability,

the experience of the individual with a disability in previous similar positions, and opinions of medical doctors, rehabilitation counselors, or physical therapists who have expertise in the disability involved and/or direct knowledge of the individual with the disability.

An employer is also permitted to require that an individual not pose a direct threat of harm to his or her own safety or health. If performing the particular functions of a job would result in a high probability of substantial harm to the individual, the employer could reject or discharge the individual unless a reasonable accommodation that would not cause an undue hardship would avert the harm. For example, an employer would not be required to hire an individual, disabled by narcolepsy, who frequently and unexpectedly loses consciousness for a carpentry job the essential functions of which require the use of power saws and other dangerous equipment, where no accommodation exists that will reduce or eliminate the risk.

The assessment that there exists a high probability of substantial harm to the individual, like the assessment that there exists a high probability of substantial harm to others, must be strictly based on valid medical analyses and/or on other objective evidence. This determination must be based on individualized factual data, using the factors discussed above, rather than on stereotypic or patronizing assumptions and must consider potential reasonable accommodations. Generalized fears about risks from the employment environment, such as exacerbation of the disability caused by stress, cannot be used by an employer to disqualify an individual with a disability. For example, a law firm could not reject an applicant with a history of disabling mental illness based on a generalized fear that the stress of trying to make partner might trigger a relapse of the individual's mental illness. Nor can generalized fears about risks to individuals with disabilities in the event of an evacuation or other emergency be used by an employer to disqualify an individual with a disability. See Senate Report at 56; House Labor Report at 73–74; House Judiciary Report at 45. See also *Mantolete* v. *Bolger*, 767 F.2d 1416 (9th Cir. 1985); *Bentivegna* v. *U.S. Department of Labor*, 694 F.2d 619 (9th Cir.1982).

Section 1630.3   Exceptions to the Definitions of "Disability" and "Qualified Individual with a Disability"

Section 1630.3 (a) through (c)   Illegal Use of Drugs

Part 1630 provides that an individual currently engaging in the illegal use of drugs is not an individual with a disability for purposes of this part when the employer or other covered entity acts on the basis of such use. Illegal use of drugs refers both to the use of unlawful drugs, such as cocaine, and to the unlawful use of prescription drugs.

Employers, for example, may discharge or deny employment to persons who illegally use drugs, on the basis of such use, without fear of being held liable for discrimination. The term "currently engaging" is not intended to be limited to the use of drugs on the day of, or within a matter of days or weeks before, the employment action in question. Rather, the provision is intended to apply to the illegal use of drugs that has occurred recently enough to indicate that the individual is actively engaged in such conduct. See Conference Report at 64.

Individuals who are erroneously perceived as engaging in the illegal use of drugs, but are not in fact illegally using drugs are not excluded from the definitions of the terms "disability" and "qualified individual with a disability." Individuals who are no longer illegally using drugs and who have either been rehabilitated successfully or are in the process of completing a rehabilitation program are, likewise, not excluded from the definitions of those terms. The term "rehabilitation program" refers to both in-patient and out-patient programs, as well as to appropriate employee assistance programs, professionally recognized self-help programs, such as Narcotics Anonymous, or other programs that provide professional (not necessarily medical) assistance and counseling for individuals who illegally use drugs. See Conference Report at 64; see also House Labor Report at 77; House Judiciary Report at 47.

It should be noted that this provision simply provides that certain individuals are not excluded from the definitions of "disability" and "qualified individual with a disability." Consequently, such individuals are still required to establish that they satisfy the requirements of these definitions in order to be protected by the ADA and this part. An individual erroneously regarded as illegally using drugs, for example, would have to show that he or she was regarded as a drug addict in order to demonstrate that he or she meets the definition of "disability" as defined in this part.

Employers are entitled to seek reasonable assurances that no illegal use of drugs is occurring or has occurred recently enough so that continuing use is a real and ongoing problem. The reasonable assurances that employers may ask applicants or employees to provide include evidence that the individual is participating in a drug treatment program and/or evidence, such as drug test results, to show that the individual is not currently engaging in the illegal use of drugs. An employer, such as a law enforcement agency, may also be able to impose a qualification standard that excludes individuals with a history of illegal use of drugs if it can show that the standard is job-related and consistent with business necessity. (See § 1630.10 Qualification Standards, Tests and Other Selection Criteria) See Conference Report at 64.

Section 1630.4   Discrimination Prohibited

This provision prohibits discrimination against a qualified individual with a disability in all aspects of the employment relationship. The range of employment decisions covered by this nondiscrimination mandate is to be construed in a manner consistent with the regulations implementing section 504 of the Rehabilitation Act of 1973.

Part 1630 is not intended to limit the ability of covered entities to choose and maintain a qualified workforce. Employers can continue to use job-related criteria to select qualified employees, and can continue to hire employees who can perform the essential functions of the job.

Section 1630.5   Limiting, Segregating and Classifying

This provision and the several provisions that follow describe various specific forms of discrimination that are included within the general prohibition of § 1630.4. Covered entities are prohibited from restricting the employment opportunities of qualified individuals with disabilities on the basis of stereotypes and myths about the individual's disability. Rather, the capabilities of qualified individuals with disabilities must be determined on an individualized, case by case basis. Covered entities are also prohibited from segregating qualified employees with disabilities into separate work areas or into separate lines of advancement.

Thus, for example, it would be a violation of this part for an employer to limit the duties of an employee with a disability based on a presumption of what is best for an individual with such a disability, or on a presumption about the abilities of an individual with such a disability. It would be a violation of this part for an employer to adopt a separate track of job promotion or progression for employees with disabilities based on a presumption that employees with disabilities are uninterested in, or incapable of, performing particular jobs. Similarly, it would be a violation for an employer to assign or reassign (as a reasonable accommodation) employees with disabilities to one particular office or installation, or to require that employees with disabilities only use particular employer provided non-work facilities such as segregated break-rooms, lunch rooms, or lounges. It would also be a violation of this part to deny employment to an applicant or employee with a disability based on generalized fears about the safety of an individual with such a disability, or based on generalized assumptions about the absenteeism rate of an individual with such a disability.

In addition, it should also be noted that this part is intended to require that employees with disabilities be accorded equal access to whatever health insurance coverage the employer provides to other employees. This part does not, however, affect pre-existing condition clauses included in health insurance policies offered by employers. Consequently, employers may continue to offer policies that contain such clauses, even if they adversely affect individuals with disabilities, so long as the clauses are not used as a subterfuge to evade the purposes of this part.

So, for example, it would be permissible for an employer to offer an insurance policy that limits coverage for certain procedures or treatments to a specified number per year. Thus, if a health insurance plan provided coverage for five blood transfusions a year to all covered employees, it would not be discriminatory to offer this plan simply because a hemophiliac employee may require more than five blood transfusions annually.

However, it would not be permissible to limit or deny the hemophiliac employee coverage for other procedures, such as heart surgery or the setting of a broken leg, even though the plan would not have to provide coverage for the additional blood transfusions that may be involved in these procedures. Likewise, limits may be placed on reimbursements for certain procedures or on the types of drugs or procedures covered (e.g. limits on the number of permitted X-rays or non-coverage of experimental drugs or procedures), but that limitation must be applied equally to individuals with and without disabilities. See Senate Report at 28–29; House Labor Report at 58–59; House Judiciary Report at 36.

Leave policies or benefit plans that are uniformly applied do not violate this part simply because they do not address the special needs of every individual with a disability. Thus, for example, an employer that reduces the number of paid sick leave days that it will provide to all employees, or reduces the amount of medical insurance coverage that it will provide to all employees, is not in violation of this part, even if the benefits reduction has an impact on employees with disabilities in need of greater sick leave and medical coverage. Benefits reductions adopted for discriminatory reasons are in violation of this part. See *Alexander* v. *Choate*, 469 U.S. 287 (1985). See Senate Report at 85; House Labor Report at 137. (See also, the discussion at § 1630.16(f) Health Insurance, Life Insurance, and Other Benefit Plans).

Section 1630.6   Contractual or Other Arrangements

An employer or other covered entity may not do through a contractual or other relationship what it is prohibited from doing directly. This provision does not affect the determination of whether or not one is a "covered entity" or "employer" as defined in § 1630.2.

This provision only applies to situations where an employer or other covered entity has entered into a contractual relationship that has the effect of discriminating against its own employees or applicants with disabilities. Accordingly, it would be a violation for an employer to participate in a contractual relationship that results in discrimination against the employer's employees with disabilities in hiring, training, promotion, or in any other aspect of the employment relationship. This provision applies whether or not the employer or other covered entity intended for the contractual relationship to have the discriminatory effect.

Part 1630 notes that this provision applies to parties on either side of the contractual or other relationship. This is intended to highlight that an employer whose employees provide services to others, like an employer whose employees receive services, must ensure that those employees are not discriminated against on the basis of disability. For example, a copier company whose service representative is a dwarf could be required to provide a stepstool, as a reasonable accommodation, to enable him to perform the necessary repairs. However, the employer would not be required, as a reasonable accommodation, to make structural changes to its customer s inaccessible premises.

The existence of the contractual relationship adds no new obligations under part 1630. The employer, therefore, is not liable through the contractual arrangement for any discrimination by the contractor against the contractors own employees or applicants, although the contractor, as an employer, may be liable for such discrimination.

An employer or other covered entity, on the other hand, cannot evade the obligations imposed by this part by engaging in a contractual or other relationship. For example, an employer cannot avoid its responsibility to make reasonable accommodation subject to the undue hardship limitation through a contractual arrangement. See Conference Report at 59; House Labor Report at 59–61; House Judiciary Report at 36–37.

To illustrate, assume that an employer is seeking to contract with a company to provide training for its employees. Any responsibilities of reasonable accommodation applicable to the employer in providing the training remain with that employer even if it contracts with another company for this service. Thus, if the training company were planning to conduct the training at an inaccessible location, thereby making it impossible for an employee who uses a wheelchair to attend, the employer would have a duty to make reasonable accommodation unless to do so would impose an undue hardship. Under these circumstances, appropriate accommodations might include (1) having the training company identify accessible training sites and relocate the training program; (2) having the training company make the training site accessible; (3) directly making the training site accessible or providing the training company with the means by which to make the site accessible; (4) identifying and contracting with another training company that uses accessible sites; or (5) any other accommodation that would result in making the training available to the employee.

As another illustration, assume that instead of contracting with a training company, the employer contracts with a hotel to host a conference for its employees. The employer will have a duty to ascertain and ensure the accessibility of the hotel and its conference facilities. To fulfill this obligation the employer could, for example, inspect the hotel first-hand or ask a local disability group to inspect the hotel. Alternatively, the employer could ensure that the contract with the hotel specifies it will provide accessible guest rooms for those who need them and that all rooms to be used for the conference, including exhibit and meeting rooms, are accessible. If the hotel breaches this accessibility provision, the hotel may be liable to the employer, under a non-ADA breach of contract theory, for the cost of any accommodation needed to provide access to the hotel and conference, and for any other costs accrued by the employer. (In addition, the hotel may also be independently liable under title III of the ADA). However, this would not relieve the employer of its

responsibility under this part nor shield it from charges of discrimination by its own employees. See House Labor Report at 40; House Judiciary Report at 37.

Section 1630.8 Relationship or Association With an Individual With a Disability

This provision is intended to protect any qualified individual, whether or not that individual has a disability, from discrimination because that person is known to have an association or relationship with an individual who has a known disability. This protection is not limited to those who have a familial relationship with an individual with a disability.

To illustrate the scope of this provision, assume that a qualified applicant without a disability applies for a job and discloses to the employer that his or her spouse has a disability. The employer thereupon declines to hire the applicant because the employer believes that the applicant would have to miss work or frequently leave work early in order to care for the spouse. Such a refusal to hire would be prohibited by this provision. Similarly, this provision would prohibit an employer from discharging an employee because the employee does volunteer work with people who have AIDS, and the employer fears that the employee may contract the disease.

This provision also applies to other benefits and privileges of employment. For example, an employer that provides health insurance benefits to its employees for their dependents may not reduce the level of those benefits to an employee simply because that employee has a dependent with a disability. This is true even if the provision of such benefits would result in increased health insurance costs for the employer.

It should be noted, however, that an employer need not provide the applicant or employee without a disability with a reasonable accommodation because that duty only applies to qualified applicants or employees with disabilities. Thus, for example, an employee would not be entitled to a modified work schedule as an accommodation to enable the employee to care for a spouse with a disability. See Senate Report at 30; House Labor Report at 61–62; House Judiciary Report at 38–39.

Section 1630.9 Not Making Reasonable Accommodation

The obligation to make reasonable accommodation is a form of non-discrimination. It applies to all employment decisions and to the job application process. This obligation does not extend to the provision of adjustments or modifications that are primarily for the personal benefit of the individual with a disability. Thus, if an adjustment or modification is job-related, *e.g.,* specifically assists the individual in performing the duties of a particular job, it will be considered a type of reasonable accommodation. On the other hand, if an adjustment or modification assists the individual throughout his or her daily activities, on and off the job, it will be considered a personal item that the employer is not required to provide. Accordingly, an employer would generally not be required to

provide an employee with a disability with a prosthetic limb, wheelchair, or eyeglasses. Nor would an employer have to provide as an accommodation any amenity or convenience that is not job-related, such as a private hot plate, hot pot or refrigerator that is not provided to employees without disabilities. See Senate Report at 31; House Labor Report at 62.

It should be noted, however, that the provision of such items may be required as a reasonable accommodation where such items are specifically designed or required to meet job-related rather than personal needs. An employer, for example, may have to provide an individual with a disabling visual impairment with eyeglasses specifically designed to enable the individual to use the office computer monitors, but that are not otherwise needed by the individual outside of the office.

The term "supported employment," which has been applied to a wide variety of programs to assist individuals with severe disabilities in both competitive and non-competitive employment, is not synonymous with reasonable accommodation. Examples of supported employment include modified training materials, restructuring essential functions to enable an individual to perform a job, or hiring an outside professional ("job coach") to assist in job training. Whether a particular form of assistance would be required as a reasonable accommodation must be determined on an individualized, case by case basis without regard to whether that assistance is referred to as "supported employment." For example, an employer, under certain circumstances, may be required to provide modified training materials or a temporary "job coach" to assist in the training of a qualified individual with a disability as a reasonable accommodation. However, an employer would not be required to restructure the essential functions of a position to fit the skills of an individual with a disability who is not otherwise qualified to perform the position, as is done in certain supported employment programs. See 34 CFR part 363. It should be noted that it would not be a violation of this part for an employer to provide any of these personal modifications or adjustments, or to engage in supported employment or similar rehabilitative programs.

The obligation to make reasonable accommodation applies to all services and programs provided in connection with employment, and to all non-work facilities provided or maintained by an employer for use by its employees. Accordingly, the obligation to accommodate is applicable to employer sponsored placement or counseling services, and to employer provided cafeterias, lounges, gymnasiums, auditoriums, transportation and the like.

The reasonable accommodation requirement is best understood as a means by which barriers to the equal employment opportunity of an individual with a disability are removed or alleviated. These barriers may, for example, be physical or structural obstacles that inhibit or prevent the access of an individual with a disability to job sites, facilities or equipment. Or they may be rigid work schedules that permit no flexibility as to when work is performed or when breaks may be taken, or inflexible job procedures that unduly limit the modes of communication that are used on the job, or the way in which particular tasks are accomplished.

The term "otherwise qualified" is intended to make clear that the obligation to make reasonable accommodation is owed only to an individual with a disability who is qualified within the meaning of § 1630.2(m) in that he or she satisfies all the skill, experience, education and other job-related selection criteria. An individual with a disability is "otherwise qualified," in other words, if he or she is qualified for a job, except that, because of the disability, he or she needs a reasonable accommodation to be able to perform the job's essential functions.

For example, if a law firm requires that all incoming lawyers have graduated from an accredited law school and have passed the bar examination, the law firm need not provide an accommodation to an individual with a visual impairment who has not met these selection criteria. That individual is not entitled to a reasonable accommodation because the individual is not "otherwise qualified" for the position.

On the other hand, if the individual has graduated from an accredited law school and passed the bar examination, the individual would be "otherwise qualified." The law firm would thus be required to provide a reasonable accommodation, such as a machine that magnifies print, to enable the individual to perform the essential functions of the attorney position, unless the necessary accommodation would impose an undue hardship on the law firm. See Senate Report at 33–34; House Labor Report at 64–65.

The reasonable accommodation that is required by this part should provide the qualified individual with a disability with an equal employment opportunity. Equal employment opportunity means an opportunity to attain the same level of performance, or to enjoy the same level of benefits and privileges of employment as are available to the average similarly situated employee without a disability. Thus, for example, an accommodation made to assist an employee with a disability in the performance of his or her job must be adequate to enable the individual to perform the essential functions of the relevant position. The accommodation, however, does not have to be the "best" accommodation possible, so long as it is sufficient to meet the job-related needs of the individual being accommodated. Accordingly, an employer would not have to provide an employee disabled by a back impairment with a state-of-the art mechanical lifting device if it provided the employee with a less expensive or more readily available device that enabled the employee to perform the essential functions of the job. See Senate Report at 35; House Labor Report at 66; see also *Carter v. Bennett*, 840 F.2d 63 (DC Cir. 1988).

Employers are obligated to make reasonable accommodation only to the physical or mental limitations resulting from the disability of a qualified individual with a disability that is known to the employer.

Thus, an employer would not be expected to accommodate disabilities of which it is unaware. If an employee with a known disability is having difficulty performing his or her job, an employer may inquire whether the employee is in need of a reasonable accommodation. In general, however, it is the responsibility of the individual with a disability to inform the employer that an accommodation is needed. When the need for an accommodation is not obvious, an employer, before providing a reasonable accommodation, may require that the individual with a disability provide documentation of the need for accommodation.

See Senate Report at 34; House Labor Report at 65.

Process of Determining the Appropriate Reasonable Accommodation

Once a qualified individual with a disability has requested provision of a reasonable accommodation, the employer must make a reasonable effort to determine the appropriate accommodation. The appropriate reasonable accommodation is best determined through a flexible, interactive process that involves both the employer and the qualified individual with a disability. Although this process is described below in terms of accommodations that enable the individual with a disability to perform the essential functions of the position held or desired, it is equally applicable to accommodations involving the job application process, and to accommodations that enable the individual with a disability to enjoy equal benefits and privileges of employment. See Senate Report at 34–35; House Labor Report at 65–67.

When a qualified individual with a disability has requested a reasonable accommodation to assist in the performance of a job, the employer, using a problem solving approach, should:

(1) Analyze the particular job involved and determine its purpose and essential functions;

(2) Consult with the individual with a disability to ascertain the precise job-related limitations imposed by the individual's disability and how those limitations could be overcome with a reasonable accommodation;

(3) In consultation with the individual to be accommodated, identify potential accommodations and assess the effectiveness each would have in enabling the individual to perform the essential functions of the position; and

(4) Consider the preference of the individual to be accommodated and select and implement the accommodation that is most appropriate for both the employee and the employer.

In many instances, the appropriate reasonable accommodation may be so obvious to either or both the employer and the qualified individual with a disability that it may not be necessary to proceed in this step-by-step fashion. For example, if an employee who uses a wheelchair requests that his or her desk be placed on blocks to elevate the desktop above the arms of the wheelchair and the employer complies, an appropriate accommodation has been requested, identified, and provided without either the employee or employer being aware

of having engaged in any sort of "reasonable accommodation process."

However, in some instances neither the individual requesting the accommodation nor the employer can readily identify the appropriate accommodation. For example, the individual needing the accommodation may not know enough about the equipment used by the employer or the exact nature of the work site to suggest an appropriate accommodation. Likewise, the employer may not know enough about the individual's disability or the limitations that disability would impose on the performance of the job to suggest an appropriate accommodation. Under such circumstances, it may be necessary for the employer to initiate a more defined problem solving process, such as the step-by-step process described above, as part of its reasonable effort to identify the appropriate reasonable accommodation.

This process requires the individual assessment of both the particular job at issue, and the specific physical or mental limitations of the particular individual in need of reasonable accommodation. With regard to assessment of the job, "individual assessment" means analyzing the actual job duties and determining the true purpose or object of the job. Such an assessment is necessary to ascertain which job functions are the essential functions that an accommodation must enable an individual with a disability to perform.

After assessing the relevant job, the employer, in consultation with the individual requesting the accommodation, should make an assessment of the specific limitations imposed by the disability on the individual's performance of the job's essential functions. This assessment will make it possible to ascertain the precise barrier to the employment opportunity which, in turn, will make it possible to determine the accommodation(s) that could alleviate or remove that barrier.

If consultation with the individual in need of the accommodation still does not reveal potential appropriate accommodations, then the employer, as part of this process, may find that technical assistance is helpful in determining how to accommodate the particular individual in the specific situation. Such assistance could be sought from the Commission, from state or local rehabilitation agencies, or from disability constituent organizations. It should be noted, however, that, as provided in § 1630.9(c) of this part, the failure to obtain or receive technical assistance from the federal agencies that administer the ADA will not excuse the employer from its reasonable accommodation obligation.

Once potential accommodations have been identified, the employer should assess the effectiveness of each potential accommodation in assisting the individual in need of the accommodation in the performance of the essential functions of the position. If more than one of these accommodations will enable the individual to perform the essential functions or if the individual would prefer to provide his or her own accommodation, the preference of the individual with a disability should be given primary consideration. However, the employer providing the accommodation has the ultimate discretion to choose between effective accommodations, and may choose the less expensive accommodation or the accommodation that is easier for it to provide. It should also be noted that the individual's willingness to provide his or her own accommodation does not relieve the employer of the duty to provide the accommodation should the individual for any reason be unable or unwilling to continue to provide the accommodation.

Reasonable Accommodation Process Illustrated

The following example illustrates the informal reasonable accommodation process. Suppose a Sack Handler position requires that the employee pick up fifty pound sacks and carry them from the company loading dock to the storage room, and that a sack handler who is disabled by a back impairment requests a reasonable accommodation. Upon receiving the request, the employer analyzes the Sack Handler job and determines that the essential function and purpose of the job is not the requirement that the job holder physically lift and carry the sacks, but the requirement that the job holder cause the sack to move from the loading dock to the storage room.

The employer then meets with the sack handler to ascertain precisely the barrier posed by the individual's specific disability to the performance of the job's essential function of relocating the sacks. At this meeting the employer learns that the individual can, in fact, lift the sacks to waist‐level, but is prevented by his or her disability from carrying the sacks from the loading dock to the storage room. The employer and the individual agree that any of a number of potential accommodations, such as the provision of a dolly, hand truck, or cart, could enable the individual to transport the sacks that he or she has lifted.

Upon further consideration, however, it is determined that the provision of a cart is not a feasible effective option. No carts are currently available at the company, and those that can be purchased by the company are the wrong shape to hold many of the bulky and irregularly shaped sacks that must be moved. Both the dolly and the hand truck, on the other hand, appear to be effective options. Both are readily available to the company, and either will enable the individual to relocate the sacks that he or she has lifted. The sack handler indicates his or her preference for the dolly. In consideration of this expressed preference, and because the employer feels that the dolly will allow the individual to move more sacks at a time and so be more efficient than would a hand truck, the employer ultimately provides the sack handler with a dolly in fulfillment of the obligation to make reasonable accommodation.

Section 1630.9(b)

This provision states that an employer or other covered entity cannot prefer or select a qualified individual without a disability over an equally qualified individual with a disability merely because the individual with a disability will require a reasonable

accommodation. In other words, an individual's need for an accommodation cannot enter into the employer's or other covered entity's decision regarding hiring, discharge, promotion, or other similar employment decisions, unless the accommodation would impose an undue hardship on the employer. See House Labor Report at 70.

Section 1630.9(d)

The purpose of this provision is to clarify that an employer or other covered entity may not compel a qualified individual with a disability to accept an accommodation, where that accommodation is neither requested nor needed by the individual. However, if a necessary reasonable accommodation is refused, the individual may not be considered qualified. For example, an individual with a visual impairment that restricts his or her field of vision but who is able to read unaided would not be required to accept a reader as an accommodation. However, if the individual were not able to read unaided and reading was an essential function of the job, the individual would not be qualified for the job if he or she refused a reasonable accommodation that would enable him or her to read. See Senate Report at 34; House Labor Report at 65; House Judiciary Report at 71–72.

Section 1630.10   Qualification Standards, Tests, and Other Selection Criteria

The purpose of this provision is to ensure that individuals with disabilities are not excluded from job opportunities unless they are actually unable to do the job. It is to ensure that there is a fit between job criteria and an applicant's (or employee's) actual ability to do the job. Accordingly, job criteria that even unintentionally screen out, or tend to screen out, an individual with a disability or a class of individuals with disabilities because of their disability may not be used unless the employer demonstrates that that criteria, as used by the employer, are job‐related to the position to which they are being applied and are consistent with business necessity. The concept of "business necessity" has the same meaning as the concept of "business necessity" under section 504 of the Rehabilitation Act of 1973.

Selection criteria that exclude, or tend to exclude, an individual with a disability or a class of individuals with disabilities because of their disability but do not concern an essential function of the job would not be consistent with business necessity.

The use of selection criteria that are related to an essential function of the job may be consistent with business necessity. However, selection criteria that are related to an essential function of the job may not be used to exclude an individual with a disability if that individual could satisfy the criteria with the provision of a reasonable accommodation. Experience under a similar provision of the regulations implementing section 504 of the Rehabilitation Act indicates that challenges to selection criteria are, in fact, most often resolved by reasonable accommodation. It is therefore anticipated that challenges to selection criteria brought under this part will generally be resolved in a like manner.

This provision is applicable to all types of selection criteria, including safety requirements, vision or hearing requirements, walking requirements, lifting requirements, and employment tests. See Senate Report at 37–39; House Labor Report at 70–72; House Judiciary Report at 42. As previously noted, however, it is not the intent of this part to second guess an employer's business judgment with regard to production standards. (See section 1630.2(n) Essential Functions). Consequently, production standards will generally not be subject to a challenge under this provision.

The Uniform Guidelines on Employee Selection Procedures (UGESP) 29 CFR part 1607 do not apply to the Rehabilitation Act and are similarly inapplicable to this part.

Section 1630.11   Administration of Tests

The intent of this provision is to further emphasize that individuals with disabilities are not to be excluded from jobs that they can actually perform merely because a disability prevents them from taking a test, or negatively influences the results of a test, that is a prerequisite to the job. Read together with the reasonable accommodation requirement of section 1630.9, this provision requires that employment tests be administered to eligible applicants or employees with disabilities that impair sensory, manual, or speaking skills in formats that do not require the use of the impaired skill.

The employer or other covered entity is, generally, only required to provide such reasonable accommodation if it knows, prior to the administration of the test, that the individual is disabled and that the disability impairs sensory, manual or speaking skills. Thus, for example, it would be unlawful to administer a written employment test to an individual who has informed the employer, prior to the administration of the test, that he is disabled with dyslexia and unable to read. In such a case, as a reasonable accommodation and in accordance with this provision, an alternative oral test should be administered to that individual. By the same token, a written test may need to be substituted for an oral test if the applicant taking the test is an individual with a disability that impairs speaking skills or impairs the processing of auditory information.

Occasionally, an individual with a disability may not realize, prior to the administration of a test, that he or she will need an accommodation to take that particular test. In such a situation, the individual with a disability, upon becoming aware of the need for an accommodation, must so inform the employer or other covered entity. For example, suppose an individual with a disabling visual impairment does not request an accommodation for a written examination because he or she is usually able to take written tests with the aid of his or her own specially designed lens. When the test is distributed, the individual with a disability discovers that the lens is insufficient to distinguish the words of the test because of the unusually low color contrast between the paper and the ink, the individual would be entitled, at that point, to request an accommodation. The employer or other covered entity would, thereupon, have to provide a test with higher contrast, schedule a retest, or provide any other effective accommodation unless to do so would impose an undue hardship.

Other alternative or accessible test modes or formats include the administration of tests in large print or braille, or via a reader or sign interpreter. Where it is not possible to test in an alternative format, the employer may be required, as a reasonable accommodation, to evaluate the skill to be tested in another manner (e.g., through an interview, or through education license, or work experience requirements). An employer may also be required, as a reasonable accommodation, to allow more time to complete the test. In addition, the employer's obligation to make reasonable accommodation extends to ensuring that the test site is accessible. (See § 1630.9 Not Making Reasonable Accommodation) See Senate Report at 37–38; House Labor Report at 70–72; House Judiciary Report at 42; see also *Stutts* v. *Freeman*, 694 F.2d 666 (11th Cir. 1983); *Crane* v. *Dole*, 617 F. Supp. 156 (D.D.C. 1985).

This provision does not require that an employer offer every applicant his or her choice of test format. Rather, this provision only requires that an employer provide, upon advance request, alternative, accessible tests to individuals with disabilities that impair sensory, manual, or speaking skills needed to take the test.

This provision does not apply to employment tests that require the use of sensory, manual, or speaking skills where the tests are intended to measure those skills. Thus, an employer could require that an applicant with dyslexia take a written test for a particular position if the ability to read is the skill the test is designed to measure. Similarly, an employer could require that an applicant complete a test within established time frames if speed were one of the skills for which the applicant was being tested. However, the results of such a test could not be used to exclude an individual with a disability unless the skill was necessary to perform an essential function of the position and no reasonable accommodation was available to enable the individual to perform that function, or the necessary accommodation would impose an undue hardship.

Section 1630.13 Prohibited Medical Examinations and Inquiries

Section 1630.13(a) Pre-employment Examination or Inquiry

This provision makes clear that an employer cannot inquire as to whether an individual has a disability at the pre-offer stage of the selection process. Nor can an employer inquire at the pre-offer stage about an applicant's workers' compensation history.

Employers may ask questions that relate to the applicant's ability to perform job-related functions. However, these questions should not be phrased in terms of disability. An employer, for example, may ask whether the applicant has a driver's license, if driving is a job function, but may not ask whether the

applicant has a visual disability. Employers may ask about an applicant's ability to perform both essential and marginal job functions. Employers, though, may not refuse to hire an applicant with a disability because the applicant's disability prevents him or her from performing marginal functions. See Senate Report at 39; House Labor Report at 72–73; House Judiciary Report at 42–43.

Section 1630.13(b) Examination or Inquiry of Employees

The purpose of this provision is to prevent the administration to employees of medical tests or inquiries that do not serve a legitimate business purpose. For example, if an employee suddenly starts to use increased amounts of sick leave or starts to appear sickly, an employer could not require that employee to be tested for AIDS, HIV infection, or cancer unless the employer can demonstrate that such testing is job-related and consistent with business necessity. See Senate Report at 39; House Labor Report at 75; House Judiciary Report at 44.

Section 1630.14 Medical Examinations and Inquiries Specifically Permitted

Section 1630.14(a) Pre-employment Inquiry

Employers are permitted to make pre-employment inquiries into the ability of an applicant to perform job-related functions. This inquiry must be narrowly tailored. The employer may describe or demonstrate the job function and inquire whether or not the applicant can perform that function with or without reasonable accommodation. For example, an employer may explain that the job requires assembling small parts and ask if the individual will be able to perform that function, with or without reasonable accommodation. See Senate Report at 39; House Labor Report at 73; House Judiciary Report at 43.

An employer may also ask an applicant to describe or to demonstrate how, with or without reasonable accommodation, the applicant will be able to perform job-related functions. Such a request may be made of all applicants in the same job category regardless of disability. Such a request may also be made of an applicant whose known disability may interfere with or prevent the performance of a job-related function, whether or not the employer routinely makes such a request of all applicants in the job category. For example, an employer may ask an individual with one leg who applies for a position as a home washing machine repairman to demonstrate or to explain how, with or without reasonable accommodation, he would be able to transport himself and his tools down basement stairs. However, the employer may not inquire as to the nature or severity of the disability. Therefore, for example, the employer cannot ask how the individual lost the leg or whether the loss of the leg is indicative of an underlying impairment.

On the other hand, if the known disability of an applicant will not interfere with or prevent the performance of a job-related function, the employer may only request a description or demonstration by the applicant if it routinely makes such a request of all applicants in the same job category. So, for

example, it would not be permitted for an employer to request that an applicant with one leg demonstrate his ability to assemble small parts while seated at a table, if the employer does not routinely request that all applicants provide such a demonstration.

An employer that requires an applicant with a disability to demonstrate how he or she will perform a job-related function must either provide the reasonable accommodation the applicant needs to perform the function or permit the applicant to explain how, with the accommodation, he or she will perform the function. If the job-related function is not an essential function, the employer may not exclude the applicant with a disability because of the applicant's inability to perform that function. Rather, the employer must, as a reasonable accommodation, either provide an accommodation that will enable the individual to perform the function, transfer the function to another position, or exchange the function for one the applicant is able to perform.

An employer may not use an application form that lists a number of potentially disabling impairments and ask the applicant to check any of the impairments he or she may have. In addition, as noted above, an employer may not ask how a particular individual became disabled or the prognosis of the individual's disability. The employer is also prohibited from asking how often the individual will require leave for treatment or use leave as a result of incapacitation because of the disability. However, the employer may state the attendance requirements of the job and inquire whether the applicant can meet them.

An employer is permitted to ask, on a test announcement or application form, that individuals with disabilities who will require a reasonable accommodation in order to take the test so inform the employer within a reasonable established time period prior to the administration of the test. The employer may also request that documentation of the need for the accommodation accompany the request. Requested accommodations may include accessible testing sites, modified testing conditions and accessible test formats. (See § 1630.11 Administration of Tests).

Physical agility tests are not medical examinations and so may be given at any point in the application or employment process. Such tests must be given to all similarly situated applicants or employees regardless of disability. If such tests screen out or tend to screen out an individual with a disability or a class of individuals with disabilities, the employer would have to demonstrate that the test is job-related and consistent with business necessity and that performance cannot be achieved with reasonable accommodation. (See § 1630.9 Not Making Reasonable Accommodation: Process of Determining the Appropriate Reasonable Accommodation).

As previously noted, collecting information and inviting individuals to identify themselves as individuals with disabilities as required to satisfy the affirmative action requirements of Section 503 of the Rehabilitation Act is not restricted by this part. (See § 1630.1 (b) and (c) Applicability and Construction).

Section 1630.14(b)   Employment Entrance Examination

An employer is permitted to require post-offer medical examinations before the employee actually starts working. The employer may condition the offer of employment on the results of the examination, provided that all entering employees in the same job category are subjected to such an examination, regardless of disability, and that the confidentiality requirements specified in this part are met.

This provision recognizes that in many industries, such as air transportation or construction, applicants for certain positions are chosen on the basis of many factors including physical and psychological criteria, some of which may be identified as a result of post-offer medical examinations given prior to entry on duty. Only those employees who meet the employer's physical and psychological criteria for the job, with or without reasonable accommodation, will be qualified to receive confirmed offers of employment and begin working.

Medical examinations permitted by this section are not required to be job-related and consistent with business necessity. However, if an employer withdraws an offer of employment because the medical examination reveals that the employee does not satisfy certain employment criteria, either the exclusionary criteria must not screen out or tend to screen out an individual with a disability or a class of individuals with disabilities, or they must be job-related and consistent with business necessity. As part of the showing that an exclusionary criteria is job-related and consistent with business necessity, the employer must also demonstrate that there is no reasonable accommodation that will enable the individual with a disability to perform the essential functions of the job. See Conference Report at 59–60; Senate Report at 39; House Labor Report at 73–74; House Judiciary Report at 43.

As an example, suppose an employer makes a conditional offer of employment to an applicant, and it is an essential function of the job that the incumbent be available to work every day for the next three months. An employment entrance examination then reveals that the applicant has a disabling impairment that, according to reasonable medical judgment that relies on the most current medical knowledge, will require treatment that will render the applicant unable to work for a portion of the three month period. Under these circumstances, the employer would be able to withdraw the employment offer without violating this part.

The information obtained in the course of a permitted entrance examination or inquiry is to be treated as a confidential medical record and may only be used in a manner not inconsistent with this part. State workers' compensation laws are not preempted by the ADA or this part. These laws require the collection of information from individuals for state administrative purposes that do not conflict with the ADA or this part. Consequently, employers or other covered entities may submit information to state workers' compensation offices or second injury funds in accordance with state workers' compensation laws without violating this part.

Consistent with this section and with § 1630.16(f) of this part, information obtained in the course of a permitted entrance examination or inquiry may be used for insurance purposes described in § 1630.16(f).

Section 1630.14(c)   Examination of Employees

This provision permits employers to make inquiries or require medical examinations (fitness for duty exams) when there is a need to determine whether an employee is still able to perform the essential functions of his or her job. The provision permits employers or other covered entities to make inquiries or require medical examinations necessary to the reasonable accommodation process described in this part. This provision also permits periodic physicals to determine fitness for duty or other medical monitoring if such physicals or monitoring are required by medical standards or requirements established by Federal, state, or local law that are consistent with the ADA and this part (or in the case of a federal standard, with section 504 of the Rehabilitation Act) in that they are job-related and consistent with business necessity.

Such standards may include federal safety regulations that regulate bus and truck driver qualifications, as well as laws establishing medical requirements for pilots or other air transportation personnel. These standards also include health standards promulgated pursuant to the Occupational Safety and Health Act of 1970, the Federal Coal Mine Health and Safety Act of 1969, or other similar statutes that require that employees exposed to certain toxic and hazardous substances be medically monitored at specific intervals. See House Labor Report at 74–75.

The information obtained in the course of such examination or inquiries is to be treated as a confidential medical record and may only be used in a manner not inconsistent with this part.

Section 1630.14(d)   Other Acceptable Examinations and Inquiries

Part 1630 permits voluntary medical examinations, including voluntary medical histories, as part of employee health programs. These programs often include, for example, medical screening for high blood pressure, weight control counseling, and cancer detection. Voluntary activities, such as blood pressure monitoring and the administering of prescription drugs, such as insulin, are also permitted. It should be noted, however, that the medical records developed in the course of such activities must be maintained in the confidential manner required by this part and must not be used for any purpose in violation of this part, such as limiting health insurance eligibility. House Labor Report at 75; House Judiciary Report at 43–44.

Section 1630.15   Defenses

The section on defenses in part 1630 is not intended to be exhaustive. However, it is intended to inform employers of some of the potential defenses available to a charge of discrimination under the ADA and this part.

Section 1630.15(a)   Disparate Treatment Defenses

The "traditional" defense to a charge of disparate treatment under title VII, as expressed in *McDonnell Douglas Corp.* v. *Green*, 411 U.S. 792 (1973), *Texas Department of Community Affairs* v. *Burdine*, 450 U.S. 248 (1981), and their progeny, may be applicable to charges of disparate treatment brought under the ADA. See *Prewitt* v. *U.S. Postal Service*, 662 F.2d 292 (5th Cir. 1981). Disparate treatment means, with respect to title I of the ADA, that an individual was treated differently on the basis of his or her disability. For example, disparate treatment has occurred where an employer excludes an employee with a severe facial disfigurement from staff meetings because the employer does not like to look at the employee. The individual is being treated differently because of the employer's attitude towards his or her perceived disability. Disparate treatment has also occurred where an employer has a policy of not hiring individuals with AIDS regardless of the individuals' qualifications.

The crux of the defense to this type of charge is that the individual was treated differently not because of his or her disability but for a legitimate nondiscriminatory reason such as poor performance unrelated to the individual's disability. The fact that the individual's disability is not covered by the employer's current insurance plan or would cause the employer's insurance premiums or workers' compensation costs to increase, would not be a legitimate nondiscriminatory reason justifying disparate treatment of an individual with a disability. Senate Report at 85; House Labor Report at 136 and House Judiciary Report at 70. The defense of a legitimate nondiscriminatory reason is rebutted if the alleged nondiscriminatory reason is shown to be pretextual.

Section 1630.15 (b) and (c)   Disparate Impact Defenses

Disparate impact means, with respect to title I of the ADA and this part, that uniformly applied criteria have an adverse impact on an individual with a disability or a disproportionately negative impact on a class of individuals with disabilities. Section 1630.15(b) clarifies that an employer may use selection criteria that have such a disparate impact, i.e., that screen out or tend to screen out an individual with a disability or a class of individuals with disabilities only when they are job-related and consistent with business necessity.

For example, an employer interviews two candidates for a position, one of whom is blind. Both are equally qualified. The employer decides that while it is not essential to the job it would be convenient to have an employee who has a driver's license and so could occasionally be asked to run errands by car. The employer hires the individual who is sighted because this individual has a driver's license. This is an example of a uniformly applied criterion, having a driver's permit, that screens out an individual who has a disability that makes it impossible to obtain a driver's permit. The employer would, thus, have to show that this criterion is job-related and consistent with business necessity. See House Labor Report at 55.

However, even if the criterion is job-related and consistent with business necessity, an employer could not exclude an individual with a disability if the criterion could be met or job performance accomplished with a reasonable accommodation. For example, suppose an employer requires, as part of its application process, an interview that is job-related and consistent with business necessity. The employer would not be able to refuse to hire a hearing impaired applicant because he or she could not be interviewed. This is so because an interpreter could be provided as a reasonable accommodation that would allow the individual to be interviewed, and thus satisfy the selection criterion.

With regard to safety requirements that screen out or tend to screen out an individual with a disability or a class of individuals with disabilities, an employer must demonstrate that the requirement, as applied to the individual, satisfies the "direct threat" standard in § 1630.2(r) in order to show that the requirement is job-related and consistent with business necessity.

Section 1630.15(c) clarifies that there may be uniformly applied standards, criteria and policies not relating to selection that may also screen out or tend to screen out an individual with a disability or a class of individuals with disabilities. Like selection criteria that have a disparate impact, non-selection criteria having such an impact may also have to be job-related and consistent with business necessity, subject to consideration of reasonable accommodation.

It should be noted, however, that some uniformly applied employment policies or practices, such as leave policies, are not subject to challenge under the adverse impact theory. "No-leave" policies (e.g., no leave during the first six months of employment) are likewise not subject to challenge under the adverse impact theory. However, an employer, in spite of its "no-leave" policy, may, in appropriate circumstances, have to consider the provision of leave to an employee with a disability as a reasonable accommodation, unless the provision of leave would impose an undue hardship. See discussion at § 1630.5 Limiting, Segregating and Classifying, and § 1630.10 Qualification Standards, Tests, and Other Selection Criteria.

Section 1630.15(d)   Defense to Not Making Reasonable Accommodation

An employer or other covered entity alleged to have discriminated because it did not make a reasonable accommodation, as required by this part, may offer as a defense that it would have been an undue hardship to make the accommodation.

It should be noted, however, that an employer cannot simply assert that a needed accommodation will cause it undue hardship, as defined in § 1630.2(p), and thereupon be relieved of the duty to provide accommodation. Rather, an employer will have to present evidence and demonstrate

that the accommodation will, in fact, cause it undue hardship. Whether a particular accommodation will impose an undue hardship for a particular employer is determined on a case by case basis. Consequently, an accommodation that poses an undue hardship for one employer at a particular time may not pose an undue hardship for another employer, or even for the same employer at another time. Likewise, an accommodation that poses an undue hardship for one employer in a particular job setting, such as a temporary construction worksite, may not pose an undue hardship for another employer, or even for the same employer at a permanent worksite. See House Judiciary Report at 42.

The concept of undue hardship that has evolved under Section 504 of the Rehabilitation Act and is embodied in this part is unlike the "undue hardship" defense associated with the provision of religious accommodation under title VII of the Civil Rights Act of 1964. To demonstrate undue hardship pursuant to the ADA and this part, an employer must show substantially more difficulty or expense than would be needed to satisfy the "de minimis" title VII standard of undue hardship. For example, to demonstrate that the cost of an accommodation poses an undue hardship, an employer would have to show that the cost is undue as compared to the employer's budget. Simply comparing the cost of the accommodation to the salary of the individual with a disability in need of the accommodation will not suffice. Moreover, even if it is determined that the cost of an accommodation would unduly burden an employer, the employer cannot avoid making the accommodation if the individual with a disability can arrange to cover that portion of the cost that rises to the undue hardship level, or can otherwise arrange to provide the accommodation. Under such circumstances, the necessary accommodation would no longer pose an undue hardship. See Senate Report at 36; House Labor Report at 68–69; House Judiciary Report at 40–41.

Excessive cost is only one of several possible bases upon which an employer might be able to demonstrate undue hardship. Alternatively, for example, an employer could demonstrate that the provision of a particular accommodation would be unduly disruptive to its other employees or to the functioning of its business. The terms of a collective bargaining agreement may be relevant to this determination. By way of illustration, an employer would likely be able to show undue hardship if the employer could show that the requested accommodation of the upward adjustment of the business' thermostat would result in it becoming unduly hot for its other employees, or for its patrons or customers. The employer would thus not have to provide this accommodation. However, if there were an alternate accommodation that would not result in undue hardship, the employer would have to provide that accommodation.

It should be noted, moreover, that the employer would not be able to show undue hardship if the disruption to its employees were the result of those employees fears or prejudices toward the individual's disability and not the result of the provision of the

accommodation. Nor would the employer be able to demonstrate undue hardship by showing that the provision of the accommodation has a negative impact on the morale of its other employees but not on the ability of these employees to perform their jobs.

Section 1630.15(e)   Defense—Conflicting Federal Laws and Regulations

There are several Federal laws and regulations that address medical standards and safety requirements. If the alleged discriminatory action was taken in compliance with another Federal law or regulation, the employer may offer its obligation to comply with the conflicting standard as a defense. The employer's defense of a conflicting Federal requirement or regulation may be rebutted by a showing of pretext, or by showing that the Federal standard did not require the discriminatory action, or that there was a nonexclusionary means to comply with the standard that would not conflict with this part. See House Labor Report at 74.

Section 1630.16   Specific Activities Permitted

Section 1630.16(a)   Religious Entities

Religious organizations are not exempt from title I of the ADA or this part. A religious corporation, association, educational institution, or society may give a preference in employment to individuals of the particular religion, and may require that applicants and employees conform to the religious tenets of the organization. However, a religious organization may not discriminate against an individual who satisfies the permitted religious criteria because that individual is disabled. The religious entity, in other words, is required to consider qualified individuals with disabilities who satisfy the permitted religious criteria on an equal basis with qualified individuals without disabilities who similarly satisfy the religious criteria. See Senate Report at 42; House Labor Report at 76–77; House Judiciary Report at 46.

Section 1630.16(b)   Regulation of Alcohol and Drugs

This provision permits employers to establish or comply with certain standards regulating the use of drugs and alcohol in the workplace. It also allows employers to hold alcoholics and persons who engage in the illegal use of drugs to the same performance and conduct standards to which it holds all of its other employees. Individuals disabled by alcoholism are entitled to the same protections accorded other individuals with disabilities under this part. As noted above, individuals currently engaging in the illegal use of drugs are not individuals with disabilities for purposes of part 1630 when the employer acts on the basis of such use.

Section 1630.16(c)   Drug Testing

This provision reflects title I's neutrality toward testing for the illegal use of drugs. Such drug tests are neither encouraged, authorized nor prohibited. The results of such drug tests may be used as a basis for disciplinary action. Tests for the illegal use of drugs are not considered medical examinations for purposes of this part. If the results reveal information about an individual's medical condition beyond whether the individual is currently engaging in the illegal use of drugs, this additional information is to be treated as a confidential medical record. For example, if a test for the illegal use of drugs reveals the presence of a controlled substance that has been lawfully prescribed for a particular medical condition, this information is to be treated as a confidential medical record. See House Labor Report at 79; House Judiciary Report at 47.

Section 1630.16(e)   Infectious and Communicable Diseases; Food Handling Jobs

This provision addressing food handling jobs applies the "direct threat" analysis to the particular situation of accommodating individuals with infectious or communicable diseases that are transmitted through the handling of food. The Department of Health and Human Services is to prepare a list of infectious and communicable diseases that are transmitted through the handling of food. If an individual with a disability has one of the listed diseases and works in or applies for a position in food handling, the employer must determine whether there is a reasonable accommodation that will eliminate the risk of transmitting the disease through the handling of food. If there is an accommodation that will not pose an undue hardship, and that will prevent the transmission of the disease through the handling of food, the employer must provide the accommodation to the individual. The employer, under these circumstances, would not be permitted to discriminate against the individual because of the need to provide the reasonable accommodation and would be required to maintain the individual in the food handling job.

If no such reasonable accommodation is possible, the employer may refuse to assign, or to continue to assign the individual to a position involving food handling. This means that if such an individual is an applicant for a food handling position the employer is not required to hire the individual. However, if the individual is a current employee, the employer would be required to consider the accommodation of reassignment to a vacant position not involving food handling for which the individual is qualified. Conference Report at 61–63. (See § 1630.2(r) Direct Threat).

Section 1630.16(f)   Health Insurance, Life Insurance, and Other Benefit Plans

This provision is a limited exemption that is only applicable to those who establish, sponsor, observe or administer benefit plans, such as health and life insurance plans. It does not apply to those who establish, sponsor, observe or administer plans not involving benefits, such as liability insurance plans.

The purpose of this provision is to permit the development and administration of benefit plans in accordance with accepted principles of risk assessment. This provision is not intended to disrupt the current regulatory structure for self-insured employers. These employers may establish,

sponsor, observe, or administer the terms of a bona fide benefit plan not subject to state laws that regulate insurance. This provision is also not intended to disrupt the current nature of insurance underwriting, or current insurance industry practices in sales, underwriting, pricing, administrative and other services, claims and similar insurance related activities based on classification of risks as regulated by the States.

The activities permitted by this provision do not violate part 1630 even if they result in limitations on individuals with disabilities, provided that these activities are not used as a subterfuge to evade the purposes of this part. Whether or not these activities are being used as a subterfuge is to be determined without regard to the date the insurance plan or employee benefit plan was adopted.

However, an employer or other covered entity cannot deny a qualified individual with a disability equal access to insurance or subject a qualified individual with a disability to different terms or conditions of insurance based on disability alone, if the disability does not pose increased risks. Part 1630 requires that decisions not based on risk classification be made in conformity with non-discrimination requirements. See Senate Report at 84–86; House Labor Report at 136–138; House Judiciary Report at 70–71. See the discussion of § 1630.5 Limiting, Segregating and Classifying.

[FR Doc. 91–17512 Filed 7–25–91; 8:45 am]
BILLING CODE 6750-06-M

EQUAL EMPLOYMENT OPPORTUNITY COMMISSION

29 CFR Parts 1602 and 1627

Recordkeeping and Reporting Under Title VII and the ADA

AGENCY: Equal Employment Opportunity Commission (EEOC).

ACTION: Final rule.

SUMMARY: This final rule is based on two separate Notices of Proposed Rulemaking (NPRM) published on February 13, 1989 (54 FR 6551), and March 5, 1991 (56 FR 9185). This final rule amends 29 CFR part 1602, EEOC's regulations on Recordkeeping and Reporting under title VII of the Civil Rights Act of 1964 (title VII), to add recordkeeping requirements under the Americans with Disabilities Act of 1990 (ADA). It increases the records retention period required in part 1602 for title VII and the ADA from 6 months to one year. The Commission also is adding a new subpart R to part 1602, 29 CFR 1602.56, that will clarify that the Commission has the authority to investigate persons to determine whether they comply with the reporting or recordkeeping requirements of part 1602. In addition, the Commission is making several minor changes to §§ 1602.7 and 1602.10.

The Commission also is deleting § 1602.14(b) of its title VII recordkeeping regulations, which provides that the § 1602 recordkeeping requirements do not apply to temporary or seasonal positions. Information regarding such employees now must be reported on Standard Form 100 on September 30 of each year, in the same fashion as information regarding permanent employees is reported. Similarly, the Commission is deleting §§ 1627.3(b) and 1627.4(a)(2) of the Age Discrimination in Employment Act recordkeeping regulations, which provide for a 90-day retention period for temporary positions, and is clarifying the mandatory nature of such recordkeeping. The Commission is not issuing a final rule on proposed § 1602.57 at this time.

EFFECTIVE DATE: August 26, 1991.

FOR FURTHER INFORMATION CONTACT: Thomas J. Schlageter, Acting Assistant Legal Counsel, Grace C. Karmiol, General Attorney, or Wendy Adams, General Attorney, at (202) 663–4669 (voice) or (202) 663–4399 (TDD).

SUPPLEMENTARY INFORMATION: The Commission received nine comments in response to the NPRM published in the March 5, 1991 Federal Register on Recordkeeping and Reporting under title VII and the ADA. The comments responded to the invitation in the preamble of the NPRM for comment on whether there should be a reporting requirement under the ADA, how the reported information should be used, and how it should be collected. Four comments recommended that there be a reporting requirement although one of them suggested that it be collected by sampling rather than universal reporting. Five comments opposed any new reporting requirements on the grounds of administrative burden. One of these suggested that no reporting requirement be imposed at this time, but that the need for reporting be reassessed at a later date. Another of these argued that if a reporting requirement is necessary, it should be accomplished by using the existing EEO-1 rather than a separate report, should be collected by both employer visual identification and employee self-identification, and should be used to monitor the impact of the ADA and to document utilization of persons with disabilities, not for affirmative action purposes. The Commission is continuing its consideration of possible reporting requirements under the ADA and will confer with the Department of Labor, and any other affected federal agency, to discuss whether a reporting requirement would be appropriate under the ADA. If it concludes that a reporting requirement may be appropriate, it will issue an NPRM.

The Commission received over 20 comments in response to the February 13, 1989 NPRM. While this preamble does not address each individual comment, it addresses the most significant issues raised in the comments. Current § 1602.7 concerns the filing of Standard Form 100, and has been interpreted in conjunction with the instructions accompanying the form. In order to clarify which of the employers that are subject to title VII must file the report, the Commission has incorporated some of the information that is contained in the instructions into § 1602.7.

Current § 1602.14 provides that personnel or employment records made or kept by an employer shall be preserved by the employer for a period of six months from the date of the making of the record or of the personnel action involved, whichever is later. This requirement was promulgated before title VII was amended in 1972 to change the time limit for filing a charge from 90 days to 180 days (or, in some instances, to 300 days). Requiring an employer or labor organization to maintain records for six months when the charge filing limit was 90 days ensured that all applicable records were kept. Due to the lengthening of the filing period, however, it no longer is true that employers or labor organizations necessarily will have retained records until the title VII filing period expires. Under the current regulation, an employer or labor organization may have already lawfully destroyed its employment records before it is notified that a charge has been filed. Moreover, a one year retention period for employers and labor organizations subject to title VII and the ADA will make the records retention period the same as that required by the Commission's regulations under the Age Discrimination in Employment Act, 29 U.S.C. 621 *et seq.* (ADEA), 29 CFR 1627.3(b)(1) and 1627.4(a)(1). This uniform retention period will simplify and clarify recordkeeping for employers who are also subject to the ADEA.

In order to promote efficiency and to eliminate confusion as to recordkeeping requirements regarding temporary and seasonal employees, the Commission is deleting § 1602.14(b) which provides that the part 1602 recordkeeping requirements do not apply to temporary or seasonal positions. Similarly, the Commission is deleting §§ 1627.3(b)(3) and 1627.4(a)(2) of the ADEA recordkeeping regulations, which

provide for a 90 day records retention period for temporary positions, and is clarifying the mandatory nature of such recordkeeping. These changes will require employers to retain records on all employees, permanent and temporary, for a one year period. They will, however, impose a new recordkeeping requirement only on the relatively few employers who are not subject to the recordkeeping provisions of the ADEA.

Section 709(c) of title VII, 42 U.S.C. 2000e–8(c), provides, *inter alia,* that any person who fails to maintain information as required by that subsection and by Commission regulations may, upon application of the Commission or the Attorney General in a case involving a government, governmental agency or political subdivision, be ordered to comply by the appropriate United States district court. At present, Commission regulations do not explicitly provide that the Commission may conduct an investigation when it has reason to believe an employer or other entity subject to title VII has failed to comply with the recordkeeping requirements of part 1602, as when, for example, an employer does not provide the required recordkeeping information to the Commission. The Commission is adding § 1602.56 to give clear notice of its authority to enforce section 709(c) of title VII. The addition of this section is consistent with the Commission's authority to issue suitable procedural regulations to carry out the provisions of title VII, 42 U.S.C. 2000e–12(a), and is an appropriate procedural mechanism for investigating apparent violations of those provisions.

The revisions to § 1602.7 change the annual Standard Form 100 reporting date from March 31 to September 30. By changing the reporting date the Commission also is changing the dates for which the information should be reported, i.e., from the three months preceding March 31, to the three months preceding September 30. Any employer that has received permission to use a different period for reporting may continue to use that approved period. The Commission has determined that this change will result in a reporting date that is less affected by the variation in seasonal employment, such as employment in the construction industry, than the present date and will provide employment figures which reflect annual average employment more closely than the present date does. This change will not affect the date by which employers must report VETS information to the United States

Department of Labor, as the VETS data and the Standard Form 100 data are processed separately. The revisions also change the address for obtaining necessary reporting supplies from "Jeffersonville, Indiana" to "the Commission or its delegate."

The revision to § 1602.10 deletes the reference to "section 4(c) of the instructions" and substitutes "section 5 of the instructions." The reference to the 100 employee jurisdictional test of section 701(b) of title VII is deleted since the number of employees required for an employer to be subject to title VII now is 15 or more. This change in no way affects the present Standard Form 100 reporting requirement of 100 or more employees that is set out in the instructions accompanying the form and now is made explicit in the regulation.

In order to provide a mechanism for those subject to the reporting requirements to seek a change in the reporting date or the date by which data should be reported, the Commission has revised § 1602.10 to permit employers to seek changes in those requirements. The Commission notes that retention of the records for the period of one year will increase only minimally, if at all, the employer's cost of maintaining the records. Employers already are required to maintain the records for a period of six months. The cost of retaining the records for an additional six months will be minimal. Moreover, most employers subject to Title VII also are subject to the ADEA, which presently requires that these records be retained for a period of one year.

The Commission estimates that the changes to §§ 1602.14 and 1602.28(a) increasing the title VII records retention period from six months to one year will result in an increased recordkeeping burden on employers of approximately 9,000 burden hours annually. The Commission estimates that the changes in the title VII and ADEA recordkeeping requirements for employers with temporary employees will result in an increased recordkeeping burden of approximately 20,800 burden hours annually. The Commission believes that this increase in burden hours is *de minimis* and that the modifications will not have a significant impact on a substantial number of small employers. Further, the Commission believes that the above cited benefits of the modifications, by establishing a uniform period of recordkeeping for full time and part time employees under title VII, ADA and the ADEA, outweigh the minimal increase in recordkeeping burden hours on employers. For the above reasons, the regulatory change will simplify the recordkeeping requirements. The Commission also certifies under 5 U.S.C. 605(b), enacted by the Regulatory Flexibility Act (Pub. L. No. 96–354), that these modifications will not result in a significant economic impact on a substantial number of small employers and that a regulatory flexibility analysis therefore is not required.

List of Subjects in 29 CFR Parts 1602 and 1627

Equal employment opportunity, Reporting and recordkeeping requirements.

For the Commission.

Evan J. Kemp, Jr.,

Chairman.

Accordingly, 29 CFR parts 1602 and 1627 are amended as follows:

PART 1602—[AMENDED]

1. The heading for part 1602 is revised to read as follows:

PART 1602—RECORDKEEPING AND REPORTING REQUIREMENTS UNDER TITLE VII AND THE ADA

2. The authority citation for part 1602 is revised to read as follows:

Authority: 42 U.S.C. 2000e–8, 2000e–12; 44 U.S.C. 3501 et seq.; 42 U.S.C. 12117.

3. Section 1602.1 is revised to read as follows:

§ 1602.1 Purpose and scope.

Section 709 of title VII (42 U.S.C. 2000e) and section 107 of the Americans with Disabilities Act (ADA) (42 U.S.C. 12117) require the Commission to establish regulations pursuant to which employers, labor organizations, joint labor-management committees, and employment agencies subject to those Acts shall make and preserve certain records and shall furnish specified information to aid in the administration and enforcement of the Acts.

4. The heading for Subpart A is revised to read as follows:

Subpart A—General

§ 1602.1 [Amended]

5. Section 1602.1 is moved under subpart A.

§§ 1602.2–1602.6 [Removed]

6. Sections 1602.2–1602.6 are removed and reserved.

§ 1602.7 [Amended]

7. Section 1602.7 is amended by revising the first and last sentences to read as follows:

§ 1602.7 Requirement for filing of report.

On or before September 30 of each year, every employer that is subject to title VII of the Civil Rights Act of 1964, as amended, and that has 100 or more employees, shall file with the Commission or its delegate executed copies of Standard Form 100, as revised (otherwise known as "Employer Information Report EEO–1") in conformity with the directions set forth in the form and accompanying instructions. * * * Appropriate copies of Standard Form 100 in blank will be supplied to every employer known to the Commission to be subject to the reporting requirements, but it is the responsibility of all such employers to obtain necessary supplies of the form from the Commission or its delegate prior to the filing date.

8. Section 1602.10 is revised to read as follows:

§ 1602.10 Employer's exemption from reporting requirements.

If an employer claims that the preparation or filing of the report would create undue hardship, the employer may apply to the Commission for an exemption from the requirements set forth in this part, according to instruction 5. If an employer is engaged in activities for which the reporting unit criteria described in section 5 of the instructions are not readily adaptable, special reporting procedures may be required. If an employer seeks to change the date for filing its Standard Form 100 or seeks to change the period for which data are reported, an alternative reporting date or period may be permitted. In such instances, the employer should so advise the Commission by submitting to the Commission or its delegate a specific written proposal for an alternative reporting system prior to the date on which the report is due.

§ 1602.11 [Amended]

9. Section 1602.11 is amended as follows:

a. In the first sentence, after "purposes of title VII" insert "or the ADA".

b. In the second sentence, after "section 709(c) of title VII" insert "or section 107 of the ADA".

§ 1602.12 [Amended]

10. Section 1602.12 is amended as follows:

a. In the first sentence, after "purposes of Title VII" insert "or the ADA".

b. In the second sentence, after "section 709(c)" insert "of Title VII, or section 107 of the ADA".

c. By revising the parenthetical at the end of the section to read as follows:

(Approved by the Office of Management and Budget under control number 3046–0040)

§ 1602.14 [Amended]

11. Section 1602.14(a) is amended as follows:

a. By removing the words "6 months" wherever they appear and replacing them with the words "one year".

b. In the first sentence, after "not necessarily limited to" insert "requests for reasonable accommodation,".

c. In the third sentence, after "under title VII" insert "or the ADA".

d. By revising the parenthetical at the end of the section to read as follows:

(Approved by the Office of Management and Budget under control number 3046–0040)

§ 1602.14 [Amended]

12. Section 1602.14 is amended by removing paragraph (b), by removing the designation from paragraph (a), and by revising the parenthetical at the end of the section to read as follows:

(Approved by the Office of Management and Budget under control number 3046–0040)

§ 1602.19 [Amended]

13. Section 1602.19 is amended as follows:

a. In the first sentence, after "purpose of Title VII" insert "or the ADA".

b. In the second sentence, after "section 709(c) of title VII" insert "or section 107 of the ADA".

§ 1602.21 [Amended]

14. Section 1602.21(b) is amended as follows:

a. In the first sentence, after "not necessarily limited to" insert "requests for reasonable accommodation,".

b. In the second sentence, after "under Title VII" insert "or the ADA".

§ 1602.26 [Amended]

15. Section 1602.26 is amended as follows:

a. In the first sentence, after "purposes of Title VII" insert "or the ADA".

b. In the second sentence, after "section 709(c)" insert "of Title VII or section 107 of the ADA".

§ 1602.28 [Amended]

16. Section 1602.28(a) is amended as follows:

a. By removing the words "6 months" wherever they appear and replacing them with the words "one year".

b. In the third sentence, after "under title VII" insert "or the ADA".

c. By revising the parenthetical at the end of the section to read as follows:

(Approved by the Office of Management and Budget under control number 3046–0040)

§ 1602.31 [Amended]

17. Section 1602.31 is amended as follows:

a. By removing paragraph (b) and the designation from paragraph (a).

b. In the first sentence, after "not necessarily limited to" insert "requests for reasonable accommodation,".

c. In the third sentence, after "under title VII" insert "or the ADA".

d. By revising the parenthetical at the end of the section to read as follows:

(Approved by the Office of Management and Budget under control number 3046–0040)

§ 1602.37 [Amended]

18. Section 1602.37 is amended as follows:

a. In the first sentence, after "purposes of title VII" insert "or the ADA".

b. In the second sentence, after "section 709(c) of title VII" insert "or section 107 of the ADA".

§ 1602.40 [Amended]

19. Section 1602.40 is amended as follows:

a. By removing paragraph (b) and the designation from paragraph (a).

b. In the first sentence, after "not necessarily limited to" insert "requests for reasonable accommodation,".

c. By revising the parenthetical at the end of the section to read as follows:

(Approved by the Office of Management and Budget under control number 3046–0040)

§ 1602.45 [Amended]

20. Section 1602.45 is amended as follows:

a. In the first sentence, after "purposes of title VII" insert "or the ADA".

b. In the second sentence, after "section 709(c) of title VII" insert "or section 107 of the ADA".

§ 1602.49 [Amended]

21. Section 1602.49 is amended as follows:

a. By removing paragraph (b) and redesignating paragraph (c) as new paragraph (b).

b. In the first sentence of paragraph (a), after "not necessarily limited to" insert "requests for reasonable accommodation,".

c. By revising the parenthetical at the end of the section to read as follows:

(Approved by the Office of Management and Budget under control number 3046–0040)

§ 1602.54 [Amended]

22. Section 1602.54 is amended as follows:

a. In the first sentence, after "purposes of title VII" insert "or the ADA".

b. In the second sentence, after "section 709(c) of title VII" insert "or section 107 of the ADA".

23. A new subpart R consisting of § 1602.56 is added, to read as follows:

Subpart R—Investigation of Reporting or Recordkeeping Violations

§ 1602.56 Investigation of reporting or recordkeeping violations.

When it has received an allegation, or has reason to believe, that a person has not complied with the reporting or recordkeeping requirements of this Part or of Part 1607 of this chapter, the Commission may conduct an investigation of the alleged failure to comply.

Part 1627—[Amended]

24. The authority citation for 29 CFR part 1627 continues to read as follows:

Authority: Sec. 7, 81 Stat. 604; 29 U.S.C. 626; sec. 11, 52 Stat. 1066; 29 U.S.C. 211; sec. 12, 29 U.S.C. 631, Pub. L. No. 99–592, 100 Stat. 3342; sec. 2, Reorg. Plan No. 1 of 1978, 43 FR 19807

§ 1627.3 [Amended]

25. In § 1627.3, paragraph (b)(3) is removed and paragraph (b)(4) is redesignated as new paragraph (b)(3).

26. Newly designated § 1627.3(b)(3) is amended by removing the word "may" and replacing it with the word "shall" and by revising the words "paragraph (b) (1), (2), or (3)" to read "paragraph (b) (1) or (2)".

§ 1627.4 [Amended]

27. In § 1627.4, paragraph (a)(2) is removed and paragraph (a)(3) is redesignated as new paragraph (a)(2).

28. Newly designated § 1627.4(a)(2) is amended by removing the word "may" and replacing it with the word "shall" and by revising the words "paragraph (a) (1) or (2)" to read "paragraph (a)(1)".

§ 1627.5 [Amended]

29. Section 1627.5(c) is amended by removing the word "may" and replacing it with the word "shall".

[FR Doc. 91–17513 Filed 7–25–91; 8:45 am]

BILLING CODE 8750–06–M

O
U.S. DOJ REGULATIONS IMPLEMENTING TITLE II OF THE ADA

This appendix presents the full text of the Justice Department regulations implementing Title II of the Americans with Disabilities Act.

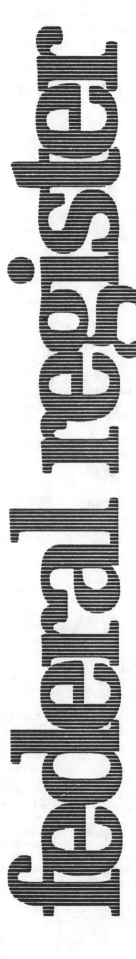

Friday
July 26, 1991

Part IV

Department of Justice

Office of the Attorney General

28 CFR Part 35
Nondiscrimination on the Basis of
Disability in State and Local Government
Services; Final Rule

DEPARTMENT OF JUSTICE

28 CFR Part 35

[Order No. 1512–91]

Nondiscrimination on the Basis of Disability in State and Local Government Services

AGENCY: Department of Justice.

ACTION: Final rule.

SUMMARY: This rule implements subtitle A of title II of the Americans with Disabilities Act, Public Law 101–336, which prohibits discrimination on the basis of disability by public entities. Subtitle A protects qualified individuals with disabilities from discrimination on the basis of disability in the services, programs, or activities of all State and local governments. It extends the prohibition of discrimination in federally assisted programs established by section 504 of the Rehabilitation Act of 1973 to all activities of State and local governments, including those that do not receive Federal financial assistance, and incorporates specific prohibitions of discrimination on the basis of disability from titles I, III, and V of the Americans with Disabilities Act. This rule, therefore, adopts the general prohibitions of discrimination established under section 504, as well as the requirements for making programs accessible to individuals with disabilities and for providing equally effective communications. It also sets forth standards for what constitutes discrimination on the basis of mental or physical disability, provides a definition of disability and qualified individual with a disability, and establishes a complaint mechanism for resolving allegations of discrimination.

EFFECIVE DATE: January 26, 1992.

FOR FURTHER INFORMATION CONTACT: Barbara S. Drake, Deputy Assistant Attorney General, Civil Rights Division; Stewart B. Oneglia, Chief, Coordination and Review Section, Civil Rights Division; John L. Wodatch, Director, Office on the Americans with Disabilities Act, Civil Rights Division; all of the U.S. Department of Justice, Washington, DC 20530. These individuals may be contacted through the Division's ADA Information Line at (202) 514–0301 (Voice), (202) 514–0381 (TDD), or (202) 514–0383 (TDD). These telephone numbers are not toll-free numbers.

SUPPLEMENTARY INFORMATION:

Background

The landmark Americans with Disabilities Act ("ADA" or "the Act"),

enacted on July 26, 1990, provides comprehensive civil rights protections to individuals with disabilities in the areas of employment, public accommodations, State and local government services, and telecommunications.

This regulation implements subtitle A of title II of the ADA, which applies to State and local governments. Most programs and activities of State and local governments are recipients of Federal financial assistance from one or more Federal funding agencies and, therefore, are already covered by section 504 of the Rehabilitation Act of 1973, as amended (29 U.S.C. 794) ("section 504"), which prohibits discrimination on the basis of handicap in federally assisted programs and activities. Because title II of the ADA essentially extends the nondiscrimination mandate of section 504 to those State and local governments that do not receive Federal financial assistance, this rule hews closely to the provisions of existing section 504 regulations. This approach is also based on section 204 of the ADA, which provides that the regulations issued by the Attorney General to implement title II shall be consistent with the ADA and with the Department of Health, Education, and Welfare's coordination regulation, now codified at 28 CFR part 41, and, with respect to "program accessibility, existing facilities," and "communications," with the Department of Justice's regulation for its federally conducted programs and activities, codified at 28 CFR part 39.

The first regulation implementing section 504 was issued in 1977 by the Department of Health, Education, and Welfare (HEW) for the programs and activities to which it provided Federal financial assistance. The following year, pursuant to Executive Order 11914, HEW issued its coordination regulation for federally assisted programs, which served as the model for regulations issued by the other Federal agencies that administer grant programs. HEW's coordination authority, and the coordination regulation issued under that authority, were transferred to the Department of Justice by Executive Order 12250 in 1980.

In 1978, Congress extended application of section 504 to programs and activities conducted by Federal Executive agencies and the United States Postal Service. Pursuant to Executive Order 12250, the Department of Justice developed a prototype regulation to implement the 1978 amendment for federally conducted programs and activities. More than 80 Federal agencies have now issued final regulations based on that prototype,

prohibiting discrimination based on handicap in the programs and activities they conduct.

Despite the large number of regulations implementing section 504 for federally assisted and federally conducted programs and activities, there is very little variation in their substantive requirements, or even in their language. Major portions of this regulation, therefore, are taken directly from the existing regulations.

In addition, section 204(b) of the ADA requires that the Department's regulation implementing subtitle A of title II be consistent with the ADA. Thus, the Department's final regulation includes provisions and concepts from titles I and III of the ADA.

Rulemaking History

On February 22, 1991, the Department of Justice published a notice of proposed rulemaking (NPRM) implementing title III of the ADA in the **Federal Register**. 56 FR 7452. On February 28, 1991, the Department published a notice of proposed rulemaking implementing subtitle A of title II of the ADA in the **Federal Register**. 56 FR 8538. Each NPRM solicited comments on the definitions, standards, and procedures of the proposed rules. By the April 29, 1991, close of the comment period of the NPRM for title II, the Department had received 2,718 comments. Following the close of the comment period, the Department received an additional 222 comments.

In order to encourage public participation in the development of the Department's rules under the ADA, the Department held four public hearings. Hearings were held in Dallas, Texas on March 4–5, 1991, in Washington, DC on March 13–15, 1991, in San Francisco, California on March 18–19, 1991, and in Chicago, Illinois on March 27–28, 1991. At these hearings, 329 persons testified and 1,567 pages of testimony were compiled. Transcripts of the hearings were included in the Department's rulemaking docket.

The comments that the Department received occupy almost six feet of shelf space and contain over 10,000 pages. The Department received comments from individuals from all fifty States and the District of Columbia. Nearly 75% of the comments that the Department received came from individuals and from organizations representing the interests of persons with disabilities. The Department received 292 comments from entities covered by the ADA and trade associations representing businesses in the private sector, and 67 from government units, such as mayors' offices, public school districts, and various State agencies working with individuals with disabilities.

The Department received one comment from a consortium of 540 organizations representing a broad spectrum of persons with disabilities. In addition, at least another 25 commenters endorsed the position expressed by this consortium, or submitted identical comments on one or both proposed regulations.

An organization representing persons with hearing impairments submitted a large number of comments. This organization presented the Department with 479 individual comments, each providing in chart form a detailed representation of what type of auxiliary aid or service would be useful in the various categories of places of public accommodation.

The Department received a number of comments based on almost ten different form letters. For example, individuals who have a heightened sensitivity to a variety of chemical substances submitted 266 post cards detailing how exposure to various environmental conditions restricts their access to public and commercial buildings. Another large group of form letters came from groups affiliated with independent living centers.

The vast majority of the comments addressed the Department's proposal implementing title III. Slightly more than 100 comments addressed only issues presented in the proposed title II regulation.

The Department read and analyzed each comment that was submitted in a timely fashion. Transcripts of the four hearings were analyzed along with the written comments. The decisions that the Department has made in response to these comments, however, were not made on the basis of the number of commenters addressing any one point but on a thorough consideration of the merits of the points of view expressed in the comments. Copies of the written comments, including transcripts of the four hearings, will remain available for public inspection in room 854 of the HOLC Building, 320 First Street, NW., Washington, DC from 10 a.m. to 5 p.m., Monday through Friday, except for legal holidays, until August 30, 1991.

Overview of the Rule

The rule is organized into seven subparts. Subpart A, "General," includes the purpose and application sections, describes the relationship of the Act to other laws, and defines key terms used in the regulation. It also includes administrative requirements adapted from section 504 regulations for

self-evaluations, notices, designation of responsible employees, and adoption of grievance procedures by public entities.

Subpart B, "General Requirements," contains the general prohibitions of discrimination based on the Act and the section 504 regulations. It also contains certain "miscellaneous" provisions derived from title V of the Act that involve issues such as retaliation and coercion against those asserting ADA rights, illegal use of drugs, and restrictions on smoking. These provisions are also included in the Department's proposed title III regulation, as is the general provision on maintenance of accessible features.

Subpart C addresses employment by public entities, which is also covered by title I of the Act. Subpart D, which is also based on the section 504 regulations, sets out the requirements for program accessibility in existing facilities and for new construction and alterations. Subpart E contains specific requirements relating to communications.

Subpart F establishes administrative procedures for enforcement of title II. As provided by section 203 of the Act, these are based on the procedures for enforcement of section 504, which, in turn, are based on the enforcement procedures for title VI of the Civil Rights Act of 1964 (42 U.S.C. 2000d to 2000d–4a). Subpart F also restates the provisions of title V of the ADA on attorneys fees, alternative means of dispute resolution, the effect of unavailability of technical assistance, and State immunity.

Subpart G designates the Federal agencies responsible for investigation of complaints under this part. It assigns enforcement responsibility for particular public entities, on the basis of their major functions, to eight Federal agencies that currently have substantial responsibilities for enforcing section 504. It provides that the Department of Justice would have enforcement responsibility for all State and local government entities not specifically assigned to other designated agencies, but that the Department may further assign specific functions to other agencies. The part would not, however, displace the existing enforcement authorities of the Federal funding agencies under section 504.

Regulatory Process Matters

This final rule has been reviewed by the Office of Management and Budget under Executive Order 12291. The Department is preparing a final regulatory impact analysis (RIA) of this rule and the Architectural and Transportation Barriers Compliance

Board is preparing an RIA for its Americans with Disabilities Act Accessibility Guidelines for Buildings and Facilities (ADAAG) that are incorporated in appendix A of the Department's final rule implementing title III of the ADA. Draft copies of both preliminary RIAs are available for comment; the Department will provide copies of these documents to the public upon request. Commenters are urged to provide additional information as to the costs and benefits associated with this rule. This will facilitate the development of a final RIA by January 1, 1992.

The Department's RIA will evaluate the economic impact of the final rule. Included among those title II provisions that are likely to result in significant economic impact are the requirements for auxiliary aids, barrier removal in existing facilities, and readily accessible new construction and alterations. An analysis of these costs will be included in the RIA.

The Preliminary RIA prepared for the notice of proposed rulemaking contained all of the available information that would have been included in a preliminary regulatory flexibility analysis, had one been prepared under the Regulatory Flexibility Act, concerning the rule's impact on small entities. The final RIA will contain all of the information that is required in a final regulatory flexibility analysis and will serve as such an analysis. Moreover, the extensive notice and comment procedure followed by the Department in the promulgation of this rule, which included public hearings, dissemination of materials, and provision of speakers to affected groups, clearly provided any interested small entities with the notice and opportunity for comment provided for under the Regulatory Flexibility Act procedures.

The Department is preparing a statement of the federalism impact of the rule under Executive Order 12612 and will provide copies of this statement on request.

The reporting and recordkeeping requirements described in the rule are considered to be information collection requirements as that term is defined by the Office of Management and Budget in 5 CFR part 1320. Accordingly, those information collection requirements have been submitted to OMB for review pursuant to the Paperwork Reduction Act.

Section-by-Section Analysis

Subpart A—General

Section 35.101 Purpose

Section 35.101 states the purpose of the rule, which is to effectuate subtitle A of title II of the Americans with Disabilities Act of 1990 (the Act), which prohibits discrimination on the basis of disability by public entities. This part does not, however, apply to matters within the scope of the authority of the Secretary of Transportation under subtitle B of title II of the Act.

Section 35.102 Application

This provision specifies that, except as provided in paragraph (b), the regulation applies to all services, programs, and activities provided or made available by public entities, as that term is defined in § 35.104. Section 504 of the Rehabilitation Act of 1973 (29 U.S.C. 794), which prohibits discrimination on the basis of handicap in federally assisted programs and activities, already covers those programs and activities of public entities that receive Federal financial assistance. Title II of the ADA extends this prohibition of discrimination to include all services, programs, and activities provided or made available by State and local governments or any of their instrumentalities or agencies, regardless of the receipt of Federal financial assistance. Except as provided in § 35.134, this part does not apply to private entities.

The scope of title II's coverage of public entities is comparable to the coverage of Federal Executive agencies under the 1978 amendment to section 504, which extended section 504's application to all programs and activities "conducted by" Federal Executive agencies, in that title II applies to anything a public entity does. Title II coverage, however, is not limited to "Executive" agencies, but includes activities of the legislative and judicial branches of State and local governments. All governmental activities of public entities are covered, even if they are carried out by contractors. For example, a State is obligated by title II to ensure that the services, programs, and activities of a State park inn operated under contract by a private entity are in compliance with title II's requirements. The private entity operating the inn would also be subject to the obligations of public accommodations under title III of the Act and the Department's title III regulations at 28 CFR part 36.

Aside from employment, which is also covered by title I of the Act, there are two major categories of programs or activities covered by this regulation: those involving general public contact as part of ongoing operations of the entity and those directly administered by the entities for program beneficiaries and participants. Activities in the first category include communication with the public (telephone contacts, office walk-ins, or interviews) and the public's use of the entity's facilities. Activities in the second category include programs that provide State or local government services or benefits.

Paragraph (b) of § 35.102 explains that to the extent that the public transportation services, programs, and activities of public entities are covered by subtitle B of title II of the Act, they are subject to the regulation of the Department of Transportation (DOT) at 49 CFR part 37, and are not covered by ·this part. The Department of Transportation's ADA regulation establishes specific requirements for construction of transportation facilities and acquisition of vehicles. Matters not covered by subtitle B, such as the provision of auxiliary aids, are covered by this rule. For example, activities that are covered by the Department of Transportation's regulation implementing subtitle B are not required to be included in the self-evaluation required by § 35.105. In addition, activities not specifically addressed by DOT's ADA regulation may be covered by DOT's regulation implementing section 504 for its federally assisted programs and activities at 49 CFR part 27. Like other programs of public entities that are also recipients of Federal financial assistance, those programs would be covered by both the section 504 regulation and this part. Although airports operated by public entities are not subject to DOT's ADA regulation, they are subject to subpart A of title II and to this rule.

Some commenters asked for clarification about the responsibilities of public school systems under section 504 and the ADA with respect to programs, services, and activities that are not covered by the Individuals with Disabilities Education Act (IDEA), including, for example, programs open to parents or to the public, graduation ceremonies, parent-teacher organization meetings, plays and other events open to the public, and adult education classes. Public school systems must comply with the ADA in all of their services, programs, or activities, including those that are open to parents or to the public. For instance, public school systems must provide program accessibility to parents and guardians with disabilities to these programs, activities, or services, and appropriate auxiliary aids and services whenever necessary to ensure effective communication, as long as the provision of the auxiliary aids results neither in an undue burden or in a fundamental alteration of the program.

Section 35.103 Relationship to Other Laws

Section 35.103 is derived from sections 501 (a) and (b) of the ADA. Paragraph (a) of this section provides that, except as otherwise specifically provided by this part, title II of the ADA is not intended to apply lesser standards than are required under title V of the Rehabilitation Act of 1973, as amended (29 U.S.C. 790–94), or the regulations implementing that title. The standards of title V of the Rehabilitation Act apply for purposes of the ADA to the extent that the ADA has not explicitly adopted a different standard than title V. Because title II of the ADA essentially extends the antidiscrimination prohibition embodied in section 504 to all actions of State and local governments, the standards adopted in this part are generally the same as those required under section 504 for federally assisted programs. Title II, however, also incorporates those provisions of titles I and III of the ADA that are not inconsistent with the regulations implementing section 504. Judiciary Committee report, H.R. Rep. No. 485, 101st Cong., 2d Sess., pt. 3, at 51 (1990) (hereinafter "Judiciary report") ; Education and Labor Committee report. H.R. Rep. No. 485, 101st Cong., 2d Sess., pt. 2, at 84 (1990) (hereinafter "Education and Labor report"). Therefore, this part also includes appropriate provisions derived from the regulations implementing those titles. The inclusion of specific language in this part, however, should not be interpreted as an indication that a requirement is not included under a regulation implementing section 504.

Paragraph (b) makes clear that Congress did not intend to displace any of the rights or remedies provided by other Federal laws (including section 504) or other State laws (including State common law) that provide greater or equal protection to individuals with disabilities. As discussed above, the standards adopted by title II of the ADA for State and local government services are generally the same as those required under section 504 for federally assisted programs and activities. Subpart F of the regulation establishes compliance procedures for processing complaints covered by both this part and section 504.

With respect to State law, a plaintiff may choose to pursue claims under a State law that does not confer greater substantive rights, or even confers fewer substantive rights, if the alleged violation is protected under the alternative law and the remedies are greater. For example, a person with a physical disability could seek damages under a State law that allows compensatory and punitive damages for discrimination on the basis of physical disability, but not on the basis of mental disability. In that situation, the State law would provide narrower coverage, by excluding mental disabilities, but broader remedies, and an individual covered by both laws could choose to bring an action under both laws. Moreover, State tort claims confer greater remedies and are not preempted by the ADA. A plaintiff may join a State tort claim to a case brought under the ADA. In such a case, the plaintiff must, of course, prove all the elements of the State tort claim in order to prevail under that cause of action.

Section 35.104 Definitions

"Act." The word "Act" is used in this part to refer to the Americans with Disabilities Act of 1990, Public Law 101–336, which is also referred to as the "ADA."

"Assistant Attorney General." The term "Assistant Attorney General" refers to the Assistant Attorney General of the Civil Rights Division of the Department of Justice.

"Auxiliary aids and services." Auxiliary aids and services include a wide range of services and devices for ensuring effective communication. The proposed definition in § 35.104 provided a list of examples of auxiliary aids and services that were taken from the definition of auxiliary aids and services in section 3(1) of the ADA and were supplemented by examples from regulations implementing section 504 in federally conducted programs (see 28 CFR 39.103).

A substantial number of commenters suggested that additional examples be added to this list. The Department has added several items to this list but wishes to clarify that the list is not an all-inclusive or exhaustive catalogue of possible or available auxiliary aids or services. It is not possible to provide an exhaustive list, and an attempt to do so would omit the new devices that will become available with emerging technology.

Subparagraph (1) lists several examples, which would be considered auxiliary aids and services to make aurally delivered materials available to individuals with hearing impairments.

The Department has changed the phrase used in the proposed rules, "orally delivered materials," to the statutory phrase, "aurally delivered materials," to track section 3 of the ADA and to include non-verbal sounds and alarms, and computer generated speech.

The Department has added videotext displays, transcription services, and closed and open captioning to the list of examples. Videotext displays have become an important means of accessing auditory communications through a public address system. Transcription services are used to relay aurally delivered material almost simultaneously in written form to persons who are deaf or hearing-impaired. This technology is often used at conferences, conventions, and hearings. While the proposed rule expressly included television decoder equipment as an auxiliary aid or service, it did not mention captioning itself. The final rule rectifies this omission by mentioning both closed and open captioning.

Several persons and organizations requested that the Department replace the term "telecommunications devices for deaf persons" or "TDD's" with the term "text telephone." The Department has declined to do so. The Department is aware that the Architectural and Transportation Barriers Compliance Board (ATBCB) has used the phrase "text telephone" in lieu of the statutory term "TDD" in its final accessibility guidelines. Title IV of the ADA, however, uses the term "Telecommunications Device for the Deaf" and the Department believes it would be inappropriate to abandon this statutory term at this time.

Several commenters urged the Department to include in the definition of "auxiliary aids and services" devices that are now available or that may become available with emerging technology. The Department declines to do so in the rule. The Department, however, emphasizes that, although the definition would include "state of the art" devices, public entities are not required to use the newest or most advanced technologies as long as the auxiliary aid or service that is selected affords effective communication.

Subparagraph (2) lists examples of aids and services for making visually delivered materials accessible to persons with visual impairments. Many commenters proposed additional examples, such as signage or mapping, audio description services, secondary auditory programs, telebraillers, and reading machines. While the Department declines to add these items to the list, they are auxiliary aids and

services and may be appropriate depending on the circumstances.

Subparagraph (3) refers to acquisition or modification of equipment or devices. Several commenters suggested the addition of current technological innovations in microelectronics and computerized control systems (e.g., voice recognition systems, automatic dialing telephones, and infrared elevator and light control systems) to the list of auxiliary aids. The Department interprets auxiliary aids and services as those aids and services designed to provide effective communications, i.e., making aurally and visually delivered information available to persons with hearing, speech, and vision impairments. Methods of making services, programs, or activities accessible to, or usable by, individuals with mobility or manual dexterity impairments are addressed by other sections of this part, including the provision for modifications in policies, practices, or procedures (§ 35.130 (b)(7)).

Paragraph (b)(4) deals with other similar services and actions. Several commenters asked for clarification that "similar services and actions" include retrieving items from shelves, assistance in reaching a marginally accessible seat, pushing a barrier aside in order to provide an accessible route, or assistance in removing a sweater or coat. While retrieving an item from a shelf might be an "auxiliary aid or service" for a blind person who could not locate the item without assistance, it might be a method of providing program access for a person using a wheelchair who could not reach the shelf, or a reasonable modification to a self-service policy for an individual who lacked the ability to grasp the item. As explained above, auxiliary aids and services are those aids and services required to provide effective communications. Other forms of assistance are more appropriately addressed by other provisions of the final rule.

"Complete complaint." "Complete complaint" is defined to include all the information necessary to enable the Federal agency designated under subpart G as responsible for investigation of a complaint to initiate its investigation.

"Current illegal use of drugs." The phrase "current illegal use of drugs" is used in § 35.131. Its meaning is discussed in the preamble for that section.

"Designated agency." The term "designated agency" is used to refer to the Federal agency designated under subpart G of this rule as responsible for carrying out the administrative enforcement responsibilities established by subpart F of the rule.

"Disability." The definition of the term "disability" is the same as the definition in the title III regulation codified at 28 CFR part 36. It is comparable to the definition of the term "individual with handicaps" in section 7(8) of the Rehabilitation Act and section 802(h) of the Fair Housing Act. The Education and Labor Committee report makes clear that the analysis of the term "individual with handicaps" by the Department of Health, Education, and Welfare (HEW) in its regulations implementing section 504 (42 FR 22685 (May 4, 1977)) and the analysis by the Department of Housing and Urban Development in its regulation implementing the Fair Housing Amendments Act of 1988 (54 FR 3232 (Jan. 23, 1989)) should also apply fully to the term "disability" (Education and Labor report at 50).

The use of the term "disability" instead of "handicap" and the term "individual with a disability" instead of "individual with handicaps" represents an effort by Congress to make use of up-to-date, currently accepted terminology. As with racial and ethnic epithets, the choice of terms to apply to a person with a disability is overlaid with stereotypes, patronizing attitudes, and other emotional connotations. Many individuals with disabilities, and organizations representing such individuals, object to the use of such terms as "handicapped person" or "the handicapped." In other recent legislation, Congress also recognized this shift in terminology, e.g., by changing the name of the National Council on the Handicapped to the National Council on Disability (Pub. L. 100-630).

In enacting the Americans with Disabilities Act, Congress concluded that it was important for the current legislation to use terminology most in line with the sensibilities of most Americans with disabilities. No change in definition or substance is intended nor should one be attributed to this change in phraseology.

The term "disability" means, with respect to an individual—

(A) A physical or mental impairment that substantially limits one or more of the major life activities of such individual;

(B) A record of such an impairment; or

(C) Being regarded as having such an impairment. If an individual meets any one of these three tests, he or she is considered to be an individual with a disability for purposes of coverage under the Americans with Disabilities Act.

Congress adopted this same basic definition of "disability," first used in the Rehabilitation Act of 1973 and in the Fair Housing Amendments Act of 1988, for a number of reasons. First, it has worked well since it was adopted in 1974. Second, it would not be possible to guarantee comprehensiveness by providing a list of specific disabilities, especially because new disorders may be recognized in the future, as they have since the definition was first established in 1974.

Test A—A physical or mental impairment that substantially limits one or more of the major life activities of such individual

Physical or mental impairment. Under the first test, an individual must have a physical or mental impairment. As explained in paragraph (1)(i) of the definition, "impairment" means any physiological disorder or condition, cosmetic disfigurement, or anatomical loss affecting one or more of the following body systems: neurological; musculoskeletal; special sense organs (which would include speech organs that are not respiratory such as vocal cords, soft palate, tongue, etc.); respiratory, including speech organs; cardiovascular; reproductive; digestive; genitourinary; hemic and lymphatic; skin; and endocrine. It also means any mental or psychological disorder, such as mental retardation, organic brain syndrome, emotional or mental illness, and specific learning disabilities. This list closely tracks the one used in the regulations for section 504 of the Rehabilitation Act of 1973 (see, *e.g.*, 45 CFR 84.3(j)(2)(i)).

Many commenters asked that "traumatic brain injury" be added to the list in paragraph (1)(i). Traumatic brain injury is already included because it is a physiological condition affecting one of the listed body systems, i.e., "neurological." Therefore, it was unnecessary to add the term to the regulation, which only provides representative examples of physiological disorders.

It is not possible to include a list of all the specific conditions, contagious and noncontagious diseases, or infections that would constitute physical or mental impairments because of the difficulty of ensuring the comprehensiveness of such a list, particularly in light of the fact that other conditions or disorders may be identified in the future. However, the list of examples in paragraph (1)(ii) of the definition includes: orthopedic, visual, speech and hearing impairments, cerebral palsy, epilepsy, muscular dystrophy, multiple sclerosis, cancer, heart disease, diabetes, mental

retardation, emotional illness, specific learning disabilities, HIV disease (symptomatic or asymptomatic), tuberculosis, drug addiction, and alcoholism. The phrase "symptomatic or asymptomatic" was inserted in the final rule after "HIV disease" in response to commenters who suggested the clarification was necessary.

The examples of "physical or mental impairments" in paragraph (1)(ii) are the same as those contained in many section 504 regulations, except for the addition of the phrase "contagious and noncontagious" to describe the types of diseases and conditions included, and the addition of "HIV disease (symptomatic or asymptomatic)" and "tuberculosis" to the list of examples. These additions are based on the committee reports, caselaw, and official legal opinions interpreting section 504. In *School Board of Nassau County* v. *Arline*, 480 U.S. 273 (1987), a case involving an individual with tuberculosis, the Supreme Court held that people with contagious diseases are entitled to the protections afforded by section 504. Following the *Arline* decision, this Department's Office of Legal Counsel issued a legal opinion that concluded that symptomatic HIV disease is an impairment that substantially limits a major life activity; therefore it has been included in the definition of disability under this part. The opinion also concluded that asymptomatic HIV disease is an impairment that substantially limits a major life activity, either because of its actual effect on the individual with HIV disease or because the reactions of other people to individuals with HIV disease cause such individuals to be treated as though they are disabled. See Memorandum from Douglas W. Kmiec, Acting Assistant Attorney General, Office of Legal Counsel, Department of Justice, to Arthur B. Culvahouse, Jr., Counsel to the President (Sept. 27, 1988), reprinted in Hearings on S. 933, the Americans with Disabilities Act, Before the Subcomm. on the Handicapped of the Senate Comm. on Labor and Human Resources, 101st. Cong., 1st Sess. 346 (1989).

Paragraph (1)(iii) states that the phrase "physical or mental impairment" does not include homosexuality or bisexuality. These conditions were never considered impairments under other Federal disability laws. Section 511(a) of the statute makes clear that they are likewise not to be considered impairments under the Americans with Disabilities Act.

Physical or mental impairment does not include simple physical characteristics, such as blue eyes or black hair. Nor does it include environmental, cultural, economic, or other disadvantages, such as having a prison record, or being poor. Nor is age a disability. Similarly, the definition does not include common personality traits such as poor judgment or a quick temper where these are not symptoms of a mental or psychological disorder. However, a person who has these characteristics and also has a physical or mental impairment may be considered as having a disability for purposes of the Americans with Disabilities Act based on the impairment.

Substantial Limitation of a Major Life Activity. Under Test A, the impairment must be one that "substantially limits a major life activity." Major life activities include such things as caring for one's self, performing manual tasks, walking, seeing, hearing, speaking, breathing, learning, and working.

For example, a person who is paraplegic is substantially limited in the major life activity of walking, a person who is blind is substantially limited in the major life activity of seeing, and a person who is mentally retarded is substantially limited in the major life activity of learning. A person with traumatic brain injury is substantially limited in the major life activities of caring for one's self, learning, and working because of memory deficit, confusion, contextual difficulties, and inability to reason appropriately.

A person is considered an individual with a disability for purposes of Test A, the first prong of the definition, when the individual's important life activities are restricted as to the conditions, manner, or duration under which they can be performed in comparison to most people. A person with a minor, trivial impairment, such as a simple infected finger, is not impaired in a major life activity. A person who can walk for 10 miles continuously is not substantially limited in walking merely because, on the eleventh mile, he or she begins to experience pain, because most people would not be able to walk eleven miles without experiencing some discomfort.

The Department received many comments on the proposed rule's inclusion of the word "temporary" in the definition of "disability." The preamble indicated that impairments are not necessarily excluded from the definition of "disability" simply because they are temporary, but that the duration, or expected duration, of an impairment is one factor that may properly be considered in determining whether the impairment substantially limits a major life activity. The preamble recognized,

however, that temporary impairments, such as a broken leg, are not commonly regarded as disabilities, and only in rare circumstances would the degree of the limitation and its expected duration be substantial. Nevertheless, many commenters objected to inclusion of the word "temporary" both because it is not in the statute and because it is not contained in the definition of "disability" set forth in the title I regulations of the Equal Employment Opportunity Commission (EEOC). The word "temporary" has been deleted from the final rule to conform with the statutory language.

The question of whether a temporary impairment is a disability must be resolved on a case-by-case basis, taking into consideration both the duration (or expected duration) of the impairment and the extent to which it actually limits a major life activity of the affected individual.

The question of whether a person has a disability should be assessed without regard to the availability of mitigating measures, such as reasonable modification or auxiliary aids and services. For example, a person with hearing loss is substantially limited in the major life activity of hearing, even though the loss may be improved through the use of a hearing aid. Likewise, persons with impairments, such as epilepsy or diabetes, that substantially limit a major life activity, are covered under the first prong of the definition of disability, even if the effects of the impairment are controlled by medication.

Many commenters asked that environmental illness (also known as multiple chemical sensitivity) as well as allergy to cigarette smoke be recognized as disabilities. The Department, however, declines to state categorically that these types of allergies or sensitivities are disabilities, because the determination as to whether an impairment is a disability depends on whether, given the particular circumstances at issue, the impairment substantially limits one or more major life activities (or has a history of, or is regarded as having such an effect).

Sometimes respiratory or neurological functioning is so severely affected that an individual will satisfy the requirements to be considered disabled under the regulation. Such an individual would be entitled to all of the protections afforded by the Act and this part. In other cases, individuals may be sensitive to environmental elements or to smoke but their sensitivity will not rise to the level needed to constitute a disability. For example, their major life activity of breathing may be somewhat,

but not substantially, impaired. In such circumstances, the individuals are not disabled and are not entitled to the protections of the statute despite their sensitivity to environmental agents.

In sum, the determination as to whether allergies to cigarette smoke, or allergies or sensitivities characterized by the commenters as environmental illness are disabilities covered by the regulation must be made using the same case-by-case analysis that is applied to all other physical or mental impairments. Moreover, the addition of specific regulatory provisions relating to environmental illness in the final rule would be inappropriate at this time pending future consideration of the issue by the Architectural and Transportation Barriers Compliance Board, the Environmental Protection Agency, and the Occupational Safety and Health Administration of the Department of Labor.

Test B—A record of such an impairment

This test is intended to cover those who have a record of an impairment. As explained in paragraph (3) of the rule's definition of disability, this includes a person who has a history of an impairment that substantially limited a major life activity, such as someone who has recovered from an impairment. It also includes persons who have been misclassified as having an impairment.

This provision is included in the definition in part to protect individuals who have recovered from a physical or mental impairment that previously substantially limited them in a major life activity. Discrimination on the basis of such a past impairment is prohibited. Frequently occurring examples of the first group (those who have a history of an impairment) are persons with histories of mental or emotional illness, heart disease, or cancer; examples of the second group (those who have been misclassified as having an impairment) are persons who have been misclassified as having mental retardation or mental illness.

Test C—Being regarded as having such an impairment

This test, as contained in paragraph (4) of the definition, is intended to cover persons who are treated by a public entity as having a physical or mental impairment that substantially limits a major life activity. It applies when a person is treated as if he or she has an impairment that substantially limits a major life activity, regardless of whether that person has an impairment.

The Americans with Disabilities Act uses the same "regarded as" test set forth in the regulations implementing section 504 of the Rehabilitation Act. See, e.g., 28 CFR 42.540(k)(2)(iv), which provides:

(iv) "Is regarded as having an impairment" means (A) Has a physical or mental impairment that does not substantially limit major life activities but that is treated by a recipient as constituting such a limitation; (B) Has a physical or mental impairment that substantially limits major life activities only as a result of the attitudes of others toward such impairment; or (C) Has none of the impairments defined in paragraph (k)(2)(i) of this section but is treated by a recipient as having such an impairment.

The perception of the covered entity is a key element of this test. A person who perceives himself or herself to have an impairment, but does not have an impairment, and is not treated as if he or she has an impairment, is not protected under this test.

A person would be covered under this test if a public entity refused to serve the person because it perceived that the person had an impairment that limited his or her enjoyment of the goods or services being offered.

For example, persons with severe burns often encounter discrimination in community activities, resulting in substantial limitation of major life activities. These persons would be covered under this test based on the attitudes of others towards the impairment, even if they did not view themselves as "impaired."

The rationale for this third test, as used in the Rehabilitation Act of 1973, was articulated by the Supreme Court in *Arline*, 480 U.S. 273 (1987). The Court noted that although an individual may have an impairment that does not in fact substantially limit a major life activity, the reaction of others may prove just as disabling. "Such an impairment might not diminish a person's physical or mental capabilities, but could nevertheless substantially limit that person's ability to work as a result of the negative reactions of others to the impairment." *Id.* at 283. The Court concluded that, by including this test in the Rehabilitation Act's definition, "Congress acknowledged that society's accumulated myths and fears about disability and diseases are as handicapping as are the physical limitations that flow from actual impairment." *Id.* at 284.

Thus, a person who is denied services or benefits by a public entity because of myths, fears, and stereotypes associated with disabilities would be covered under this third test whether or not the person's physical or mental condition would be considered a disability under the first or second test in the definition.

If a person is refused admittance on the basis of an actual or perceived physical or mental condition, and the public entity can articulate no legitimate reason for the refusal (such as failure to meet eligibility criteria), a perceived concern about admitting persons with disabilities could be inferred and the individual would qualify for coverage under the "regarded as" test. A person who is covered because of being regarded as having an impairment is not required to show that the public entity's perception is inaccurate (e.g., that he will be accepted by others) in order to receive benefits from the public entity.

Paragraph (5) of the definition lists certain conditions that are not included within the definition of "disability." The excluded conditions are: Transvestism, transsexualism, pedophilia, exhibitionism, voyeurism, gender identity disorders not resulting from physical impairments, other sexual behavior disorders, compulsive gambling, kleptomania, pyromania, and psychoactive substance use disorders resulting from current illegal use of drugs. Unlike homosexuality and bisexuality, which are not considered impairments under either section 504 or the Americans with Disabilities Act (see the definition of "disability," paragraph (1)(iv)), the conditions listed in paragraph (5), except for transvestism, are not necessarily excluded as impairments under section 504. (Transvestism was excluded from the definition of disability for section 504 by the Fair Housing Amendments Act of 1988, Pub. L. 100–430, section 6(b)).

"Drug." The definition of the term "drug" is taken from section 510(d)(2) of the ADA.

"Facility." "Facility" means all or any portion of buildings, structures, sites, complexes, equipment, rolling stock or other conveyances, roads, walks, passageways, parking lots, or other real or personal property, including the site where the building, property, structure, or equipment is located. It includes both indoor and outdoor areas where human-constructed improvements, structures, equipment, or property have been added to the natural environment.

Commenters raised questions about the applicability of this part to activities operated in mobile facilities, such as bookmobiles or mobile health screening units. Such activities would be covered by the requirement for program accessibility in § 35.150, and would be included in the definition of "facility" as "other real or personal property," although standards for new construction and alterations of such facilities are not yet included in the accessibility standards adopted by § 35.151. Sections

35.150 and 35.151 specifically address the obligations of public entities to ensure accessibility by providing curb ramps at pedestrian walkways.

"Historic preservation programs" and "Historic properties" are defined in order to aid in the interpretation of §§ 35.150 (a)(2) and (b)(2), which relate to accessibility of historic preservation programs, and § 35.151(d), which relates to the alteration of historic properties.

"Illegal use of drugs." The definition of "illegal use of drugs" is taken from section 510(d)(1) of the Act and clarifies that the term includes the illegal use of one or more drugs.

"Individual with a disability" means a person who has a disability but does not include an individual who is currently illegally using drugs, when the public entity acts on the basis of such use. The phrase "current illegal use of drugs" is explained in § 35.131.

"Public entity." The term "public entity" is defined in accordance with section 201(1) of the ADA as any State or local government; any department, agency, special purpose district, or other instrumentality of a State or States or local government; or the National Railroad Passenger Corporation, and any commuter authority (as defined in section 103(8) of the Rail Passenger Service Act).

"Qualified individual with a disability." The definition of "qualified individual with a disability" is taken from section 201(2) of the Act, which is derived from the definition of "qualified handicapped person" in the Department of Health and Human Services' regulation implementing section 504 (45 CFR § 84.3(k)). It combines the definition at 45 CFR 84.3(k)(1) for employment ("a handicapped person who, with reasonable accommodation, can perform the essential functions of the job in question") with the definition for other services at 45 CFR 84.3(k)(4) ("a handicapped person who meets the essential eligibility requirements for the receipt of such services").

Some commenters requested clarification of the term "essential eligibility requirements." Because of the variety of situations in which an individual's qualifications will be at issue, it is not possible to include more specific criteria in the definition. The "essential eligibility requirements" for participation in some activities covered under this part may be minimal. For example, most public entities provide information about their operations as a public service to anyone who requests it. In such situations, the only "eligibility requirement" for receipt of such information would be the request for it.

Where such information is provided by telephone, even the ability to use a voice telephone is not an "essential eligibility requirement," because § 35.161 requires a public entity to provide equally effective telecommunication systems for individuals with impaired hearing or speech.

For other activities, identification of the "essential eligibility requirements" may be more complex. Where questions of safety are involved, the principles established in § 36.208 of the Department's regulation implementing title III of the ADA, to be codified at 28 CFR, part 36, will be applicable. That section implements section 302(b)(3) of the Act, which provides that a public accommodation is not required to permit an individual to participate in or benefit from the goods, services, facilities, privileges, advantages and accommodations of the public accommodation, if that individual poses a direct threat to the health or safety of others.

A "direct threat" is a significant risk to the health or safety of others that cannot be eliminated by a modification of policies, practices, or procedures, or by the provision of auxiliary aids or services. In *School Board of Nassau County* v. *Arline*, 480 U.S. 273 (1987), the Supreme Court recognized that there is a need to balance the interests of people with disabilities against legitimate concerns for public safety. Although persons with disabilities are generally entitled to the protection of this part, a person who poses a significant risk to others will not be "qualified," if reasonable modifications to the public entity's policies, practices, or procedures will not eliminate that risk.

The determination that a person poses a direct threat to the health or safety of others may not be based on generalizations or stereotypes about the effects of a particular disability. It must be based on an individualized assessment, based on reasonable judgment that relies on current medical evidence or on the best available objective evidence, to determine: the nature, duration, and severity of the risk; the probability that the potential injury will actually occur; and whether reasonable modifications of policies, practices, or procedures will mitigate the risk. This is the test established by the Supreme Court in *Arline*. Such an inquiry is essential if the law is to achieve its goal of protecting disabled individuals from discrimination based on prejudice, stereotypes, or unfounded fear, while giving appropriate weight to legitimate concerns, such as the need to avoid exposing others to significant

health and safety risks. Making this assessment will not usually require the services of a physician. Sources for medical knowledge include guidance from public health authorities, such as the U.S. Public Health Service, the Centers for Disease Control, and the National Institutes of Health, including the National Institute of Mental Health.

"Qualified interpreter." The _ Department received substantial comment regarding the lack of a definition of "qualified interpreter." The proposed rule defined auxiliary aids and services to include the statutory term, "qualified interpreters" (§ 35.104), but did not define it. Section 35.160 requires the use of auxiliary aids including qualified interpreters and commenters stated that a lack of guidance on what the term means would create confusion among those trying to secure interpreting services and often result in less than effective communication.

Many commenters were concerned that, without clear guidance on the issue of "qualified" interpreter, the rule would be interpreted to mean "available, rather than qualified" interpreters. Some claimed that few public entities would understand the difference between a qualified interpreter and a person who simply knows a few signs or how to fingerspell.

In order to clarify what is meant by "qualified interpreter" the Department has added a definition of the term to the final rule. A qualified interpreter means an interpreter who is able to interpret effectively, accurately, and impartially both receptively and expressively, using any necessary specialized vocabulary. This definition focuses on the actual ability of the interpreter in a particular interpreting context to facilitate effective communication between the public entity and the individual with disabilities.

Public comment also revealed that public entities have at times asked persons who are deaf to provide family members or friends to interpret. In certain circumstances, notwithstanding that the family member of friend is able to interpret or is a certified interpreter, the family member or friend may not be qualified to render the necessary interpretation because of factors such as emotional or personal involvement or considerations of confidentiality that may adversely affect the ability to interpret "effectively, accurately, and impartially."

The definition of "qualified interpreter" in this rule does not invalidate or limit standards for interpreting services of any State or local law that are equal to or more

stringent than those imposed by this definition. For instance, the definition would not supersede any requirement of State law for use of a certified interpreter in court proceedings.

"Section 504." The Department added a definition of "section 504" because the term is used extensively in subpart F of this part.

"State." The definition of "State" is identical to the statutory definition in section 3(3) of the ADA.

Section 35.105   Self-evaluation

Section 35.105 establishes a requirement, based on the section 504 regulations for federally assisted and federally conducted programs, that a public entity evaluate its current policies and practices to identify and correct any that are not consistent with the requirements of this part. As noted in the discussion of § 35.102, activities covered by the Department of Transportation's regulation implementing subtitle B of title II are not required to be included in the self-evaluation required by this section.

Experience has demonstrated the self-evaluation process to be a valuable means of establishing a working relationship with individuals with disabilities, which has promoted both effective and efficient implementation of section 504. The Department expects that it will likewise be useful to public entities newly covered by the ADA.

All public entities are required to do a self-evaluation. However, only those that employ 50 or more persons are required to maintain the self-evaluation on file and make it available for public inspection for three years. The number 50 was derived from the Department of Justice's section 504 regulations for federally assisted programs, 28 CFR 42.505(c). The Department received comments critical of this limitation, some suggesting the requirement apply to all public entities and others suggesting that the number be changed from 50 to 15. The final rule has not been changed. Although many regulations implementing section 504 for federally assisted programs do use 15 employees as the cut-off for this record-keeping requirement, the Department believes that it would be inappropriate to extend it to those smaller public entities covered by this regulation that do not receive Federal financial assistance. This approach has the benefit of minimizing paperwork burdens on small entities.

Paragraph (d) provides that the self-evaluation required by this section shall apply only to programs not subject to section 504 or those policies and practices, such as those involving communications access, that have not already been included in a self-evaluation required under an existing regulation implementing section 504. Because most self-evaluations were done from five to twelve years ago, however, the Department expects that a great many public entities will be reexamining all of their policies and programs. Programs and functions may have changed, and actions that were supposed to have been taken to comply with section 504 may not have been fully implemented or may no longer be effective. In addition, there have been statutory amendments to section 504 which have changed the coverage of section 504, particularly the Civil Rights Restoration Act of 1987, Public Law No. 100–259, 102 Stat. 28 (1988), which broadened the definition of a covered "program or activity."

Several commenters suggested that the Department clarify public entities' liability during the one-year period for compliance with the self-evaluation requirement. The self-evaluation requirement does not stay the effective date of the statute nor of this part. Public entities are, therefore, not shielded from discrimination claims during that time.

Other commenters suggested that the rule require that every self-evaluation include an examination of training efforts to assure that individuals with disabilities are not subjected to discrimination because of insensitivity, particularly in the law enforcement area. Although the Department has not added such a specific requirement to the rule, it would be appropriate for public entities to evaluate training efforts because, in many cases, lack of training leads to discriminatory practices, even when the policies in place are nondiscriminatory.

Section 35.106 Notice

Section 35.106 requires a public entity to disseminate sufficient information to applicants, participants, beneficiaries, and other interested persons to inform them of the rights and protections afforded by the ADA and this regulation. Methods of providing this information include, for example, the publication of information in handbooks, manuals, and pamphlets that are distributed to the public to describe a public entity's programs and activities; the display of informative posters in service centers and other public places; or the broadcast of information by television or radio. In providing the notice, a public entity must comply with the requirements for effective communication in § 35.160. The

preamble to that section gives guidance on how to effectively communicate with individuals with disabilities.

Section 35.107 Designation of Responsible Employee and Adoption of Grievance Procedures

Consistent with § 35.105, self-evaluation, the final rule requires that public entities with 50 or more employees designate a responsible employee and adopt grievance procedures. Most of the commenters who suggested that the requirement that self-evaluation be maintained on file for three years not be limited to those employing 50 or more persons made a similar suggestion concerning § 35.107. Commenters recommended either that all public entities be subject to § 35.107, or that "50 or more persons" be changed to "15 or more persons." As explained in the discussion of § 35.105, the Department has not adopted this suggestion.

The requirement for designation of an employee responsible for coordination of efforts to carry out responsibilities under this part is derived from the HEW regulation implementing section 504 in federally assisted programs. The requirement for designation of a particular employee and dissemination of information about how to locate that employee helps to ensure that individuals dealing with large agencies are able to easily find a responsible person who is familiar with the requirements of the Act and this part and can communicate those requirements to other individuals in the agency who may be unaware of their responsibilities. This paragraph in no way limits a public entity's obligation to ensure that all of its employees comply with the requirements of this part, but it ensures that any failure by individual employees can be promptly corrected by the designated employee.

Section 35.107(b) requires public entities with 50 or more employees to establish grievance procedures for resolving complaints of violations of this part. Similar requirements are found in the section 504 regulations for federally assisted programs (see, e.g., 45 CFR 84.7(b)). The rule, like the regulations for federally assisted programs, provides for investigation and resolution of complaints by a Federal enforcement agency. It is the view of the Department that public entities subject to this part should be required to establish a mechanism for resolution of complaints at the local level without requiring the complainant to resort to the Federal complaint procedures established under subpart F. Complainants would not, however, be required to exhaust the

public entity's grievance procedures before filing a complaint under subpart F. Delay in filing the complaint at the Federal level caused by pursuit of the remedies available under the grievance procedure would generally be considered good cause for extending the time allowed for filing under § 35.170(b).

Subpart B—General Requirements

Section 35.130 General Prohibitions Against Discrimination

The general prohibitions against discrimination in the rule are generally based on the prohibitions in existing regulations implementing section 504 and, therefore, are already familiar to State and local entities covered by section 504. In addition, § 35.130 includes a number of provisions derived from title III of the Act that are implicit to a certain degree in the requirements of regulations implementing section 504.

Several commenters suggested that this part should include the section of the proposed title III regulation that implemented section 309 of the Act, which requires that courses and examinations related to applications, licensing, certification, or credentialing be provided in an accessible place and manner or that alternative accessible arrangements be made. The Department has not adopted this suggestion. The requirements of this part, including the general prohibitions of discrimination in this section, the program access requirements of subpart D, and the communications requirements of subpart E, apply to courses and examinations provided by public entities. The Department considers these requirements to be sufficient to ensure that courses and examinations administered by public entities meet the requirements of section 309. For example, a public entity offering an examination must ensure that modifications of policies, practices, or procedures or the provision of auxiliary aids and services furnish the individual with a disability an equal opportunity to demonstrate his or her knowledge or ability. Also, any examination specially designed for individuals with disabilities must be offered as often and in as timely a manner as are other examinations. Further, under this part, courses and examinations must be offered in the most integrated setting appropriate. The analysis of § 35.130(d) is relevant to this determination.

A number of commenters asked that the regulation be amended to require training of law enforcement personnel to recognize the difference between criminal activity and the effects of seizures or other disabilities such as mental retardation, cerebral palsy, traumatic brain injury, mental illness, or deafness. Several disabled commenters gave personal statements about the abuse they had received at the hands of law enforcement personnel. Two organizations that commented cited the Judiciary report at 50 as authority to require law enforcement training.

The Department has not added such a training requirement to the regulation. Discriminatory arrests and brutal treatment are already unlawful police activities. The general regulatory obligation to modify policies, practices, or procedures requires law enforcement to make changes in policies that result in discriminatory arrests or abuse of individuals with disabilities. Under this section law enforcement personnel would be required to make appropriate efforts to determine whether perceived strange or disruptive behavior or unconsciousness is the result of a disability. The Department notes that a number of States have attempted to address the problem of arresting disabled persons for noncriminal conduct resulting from their disability through adoption of the Uniform Duties to Disabled Persons Act, and encourages other jurisdictions to consider that approach.

Paragraph (a) restates the nondiscrimination mandate of section 202 of the ADA. The remaining paragraphs in § 35.130 establish the general principles for analyzing whether any particular action of the public entity violates this mandate.

Paragraph (b) prohibits overt denials of equal treatment of individuals with disabilities. A public entity may not refuse to provide an individual with a disability with an equal opportunity to participate in or benefit from its program simply because the person has a disability.

Paragraph (b)(1)(i) provides that it is discriminatory to deny a person with a disability the right to participate in or benefit from the aid, benefit, or service provided by a public entity. Paragraph (b)(1)(ii) provides that the aids, benefits, and services provided to persons with disabilities must be equal to those provided to others, and paragraph (b)(1)(iii) requires that the aids, benefits, or services provided to individuals with disabilities must be as effective in affording equal opportunity to obtain the same result, to gain the same benefit, or to reach the same level of achievement as those provided to others. These paragraphs are taken from the regulations implementing section 504 and simply restate principles long established under section 504.

Paragraph (b)(1)(iv) permits the public entity to develop separate or different aids, benefits, or services when necessary to provide individuals with disabilities with an equal opportunity to participate in or benefit from the public entity's programs or activities, but only when necessary to ensure that the aids, benefits, or services are as effective as those provided to others. Paragraph (b)(1)(iv) must be read in conjunction with paragraphs (b)(2), (d), and (e). Even when separate or different aids, benefits, or services would be more effective, paragraph (b)(2) provides that a qualified individual with a disability still has the right to choose to participate in the program that is not designed to accommodate individuals with disabilities. Paragraph (d) requires that a public entity administer services, programs, and activities in the most integrated setting appropriate to the needs of qualified individuals with disabilities.

Paragraph (b)(2) specifies that, notwithstanding the existence of separate or different programs or activities provided in accordance with this section, an individual with a disability shall not be denied the opportunity to participate in such programs or activities that are not separate or different. Paragraph (e), which is derived from section 501(d) of the Americans with Disabilities Act, states that nothing in this part shall be construed to require an individual with a disability to accept an accommodation, aid, service, opportunity, or benefit that he or she chooses not to accept.

Taken together, these provisions are intended to prohibit exclusion and segregation of individuals with disabilities and the denial of equal opportunities enjoyed by others, based on, among other things, presumptions, patronizing attitudes, fears, and stereotypes about individuals with disabilities. Consistent with these standards, public entities are required to ensure that their actions are based on facts applicable to individuals and not on presumptions as to what a class of individuals with disabilities can or cannot do.

Integration is fundamental to the purposes of the Americans with Disabilities Act. Provision of segregated accommodations and services relegates persons with disabilities to second-class status. For example, it would be a violation of this provision to require persons with disabilities to eat in the back room of a government cafeteria or to refuse to allow a person with a disability the full use of recreation or exercise facilities because of

stereotypes about the person's ability to participate.

Many commenters objected to proposed paragraphs (b)(1)(iv) and (d) as allowing continued segregation of individuals with disabilities. The Department recognizes that promoting integration of individuals with disabilities into the mainstream of society is an important objective of the ADA and agrees that, in most instances, separate programs for individuals with disabilities will not be permitted. Nevertheless, section 504 does permit separate programs in limited circumstances, and Congress clearly intended the regulations issued under title II to adopt the standards of section 504. Furthermore, Congress included authority for separate programs in the specific requirements of title III of the Act. Section 302(b)(1)(A)(iii) of the Act provides for separate benefits in language similar to that in § 35.130(b)(1)(iv), and section 302(b)(1)(B) includes the same requirement for "the most integrated setting appropriate" as in § 35.130(d).

Even when separate programs are permitted, individuals with disabilities cannot be denied the opportunity to participate in programs that are not separate or different. This is an important and overarching principle of the Americans with Disabilities Act. Separate, special, or different programs that are designed to provide a benefit to persons with disabilities cannot be used to restrict the participation of persons with disabilities in general, integrated activities.

For example, a person who is blind may wish to decline participating in a special museum tour that allows persons to touch sculptures in an exhibit and instead tour the exhibit at his or her own pace with the museum's recorded tour. It is not the intent of this section to require the person who is blind to avail himself or herself of the special tour. Modified participation for persons with disabilities must be a choice, not a requirement.

In addition, it would not be a violation of this section for a public entity to offer recreational programs specially designed for children with mobility impairments. However, it would be a violation of this section if the entity then excluded these children from other recreational services for which they are qualified to participate when these services are made available to nondisabled children, or if the entity required children with disabilities to attend only designated programs.

Many commenters asked that the Department clarify a public entity's obligations within the integrated program when it offers a separate program but an individual with a disability chooses not to participate in the separate program. It is impossible to make a blanket statement as to what level of auxiliary aids or modifications would be required in the integrated program. Rather, each situation must be assessed individually. The starting point is to question whether the separate program is in fact necessary or appropriate for the individual. Assuming the separate program would be appropriate for a particular individual, the extent to which that individual must be provided with modifications in the integrated program will depend not only on what the individual needs but also on the limitations and defenses of this part. For example, it may constitute an undue burden for a public accommodation, which provides a full-time interpreter in its special guided tour for individuals with hearing impairments, to hire an additional interpreter for those individuals who choose to attend the integrated program. The Department cannot identify categorically the level of assistance or aid required in the integrated program.

Paragraph (b)(1)(v) provides that a public entity may not aid or perpetuate discrimination against a qualified individual with a disability by providing significant assistance to an agency, organization, or person that discriminates on the basis of disability in providing any aid, benefit, or service to beneficiaries of the public entity's program. This paragraph is taken from the regulations implementing section 504 for federally assisted programs.

Paragraph (b)(1)(vi) prohibits the public entity from denying a qualified individual with a disability the opportunity to participate as a member of a planning or advisory board.

Paragraph (b)(1)(vii) prohibits the public entity from limiting a qualified individual with a disability in the enjoyment of any right, privilege, advantage, or opportunity enjoyed by others receiving any aid, benefit, or service.

Paragraph (b)(3) prohibits the public entity from utilizing criteria or methods of administration that deny individuals with disabilities access to the public entity's services, programs, and activities or that perpetuate the discrimination of another public entity, if both public entities are subject to common administrative control or are agencies of the same State. The phrase "criteria or methods of administration" refers to official written policies of the public entity and to the actual practices of the public entity. This paragraph

prohibits both blatantly exclusionary policies or practices and nonessential policies and practices that are neutral on their face, but deny individuals with disabilities an effective opportunity to participate. This standard is consistent with the interpretation of section 504 by the U.S. Supreme Court in *Alexander* v. *Choate*, 469 U.S. 287 (1985). The Court in *Choate* explained that members of Congress made numerous statements during passage of section 504 regarding eliminating architectural barriers, providing access to transportation, and eliminating discriminatory effects of job qualification procedures. The Court then noted: "These statements would ring hollow if the resulting legislation could not rectify the harms resulting from action that discriminated by effect as well as by design." *Id.* at 297 (footnote omitted).

Paragraph (b)(4) specifically applies the prohibition enunciated in § 35.130(b)(3) to the process of selecting sites for construction of new facilities or selecting existing facilities to be used by the public entity. Paragraph (b)(4) does not apply to construction of additional buildings at an existing site.

Paragraph (b)(5) prohibits the public entity, in the selection of procurement contractors, from using criteria that subject qualified individuals with disabilities to discrimination on the basis of disability.

Paragraph (b)(6) prohibits the public entity from discriminating against qualified individuals with disabilities on the basis of disability in the granting of licenses or certification. A person is a "qualified individual with a disability" with respect to licensing or certification if he or she can meet the essential eligibility requirements for receiving the license or certification (see § 35.104).

A number of commenters were troubled by the phrase "essential eligibility requirements" as applied to State licensing requirements, especially those for health care professions. Because of the variety of types of programs to which the definition of "qualified individual with a disability" applies, it is not possible to use more specific language in the definition. The phrase "essential eligibility requirements," however, is taken from the definitions in the regulations implementing section 504, so caselaw under section 504 will be applicable to its interpretation. In *Southeastern Community College* v. *Davis*, 442 U.S. 397, for example, the Supreme Court held that section 504 does not require an institution to "lower or effect substantial modifications of standards to accommodate a handicapped person," 442 U.S. at 413, and that the school had

established that the plaintiff was not "qualified" because she was not able to "serve the nursing profession in all customary ways," *id.* Whether a particular requirement is "essential" will, of course, depend on the facts of the particular case.

In addition, the public entity may not establish requirements for the programs or activities of licensees or certified entities that subject qualified individuals with disabilities to discrimination on the basis of disability. For example, the public entity must comply with this requirement when establishing safety standards for the operations of licensees. In that case the public entity must ensure that standards that it promulgates do not discriminate against the employment of qualified individuals with disabilities in an impermissible manner.

Paragraph (b)(6) does not extend the requirements of the Act or this part directly to the programs or activities of licensees or certified entities themselves. The programs or activities of licensees or certified entities are not themselves programs or activities of the public entity merely by virtue of the license or certificate.

Paragraph (b)(7) is a specific application of the requirement under the general prohibitions of discrimination that public entities make reasonable modifications in policies, practices, or procedures where necessary to avoid discrimination on the basis of disability. Section 302(b)(2)(A)(ii) of the ADA sets out this requirement specifically for public accommodations covered by title III of the Act, and the House Judiciary Committee Report directs the Attorney General to include those specific requirements in the title II regulation to the extent that they do not conflict with the regulations implementing section 504. Judiciary report at 52.

Paragraph (b)(8), a new paragraph not contained in the proposed rule, prohibits the imposition or application of eligibility criteria that screen out or tend to screen out an individual with a disability or any class of individuals with disabilities from fully and equally enjoying any service, program, or activity, unless such criteria can be shown to be necessary for the provision of the service, program, or activity being offered. This prohibition is also a specific application of the general prohibitions of discrimination and is based on section 302(b)(2)(A)(i) of the ADA. It prohibits overt denials of equal treatment of individuals with disabilities, or establishment of exclusive or segregative criteria that would bar individuals with disabilities from participation in services, benefits, or activities.

Paragraph (b)(8) also prohibits policies that unnecessarily impose requirements or burdens on individuals with disabilities that are not placed on others. For example, public entities may not require that a qualified individual with a disability be accompanied by an attendant. A public entity is not, however, required to provide attendant care, or assistance in toileting, eating, or dressing to individuals with disabilities, except in special circumstances, such as where the individual is an inmate of a custodial or correctional institution.

In addition, paragraph (b)(8) prohibits the imposition of criteria that "tend to" screen out an individual with a disability. This concept, which is derived from current regulations under section 504 (see, e.g., 45 CFR 84.13), makes it discriminatory to impose policies or criteria that, while not creating a direct bar to individuals with disabilities, indirectly prevent or limit their ability to participate. For example, requiring presentation of a driver's license as the sole means of identification for purposes of paying by check would violate this section in situations where, for example, individuals with severe vision impairments or developmental disabilities or epilepsy are ineligible to receive a driver's license and the use of an alternative means of identification, such as another photo I.D. or credit card, is feasible.

A public entity may, however, impose neutral rules and criteria that screen out, or tend to screen out, individuals with disabilities if the criteria are necessary for the safe operation of the program in question. Examples of safety qualifications that would be justifiable in appropriate circumstances would include eligibility requirements for drivers' licenses, or a requirement that all participants in a recreational rafting expedition be able to meet a necessary level of swimming proficiency. Safety requirements must be based on actual risks and not on speculation, stereotypes, or generalizations about individuals with disabilities.

Paragraph (c) provides that nothing in this part prohibits a public entity from providing benefits, services, or advantages to individuals with disabilities, or to a particular class of individuals with disabilities, beyond those required by this part. It is derived from a provision in the section 504 regulations that permits programs conducted pursuant to Federal statute or Executive order that are designed to benefit only individuals with disabilities or a given class of individuals with

disabilities to be limited to those individuals with disabilities. Section 504 ensures that federally assisted programs are made available to all individuals, without regard to disabilities, unless the Federal program under which the assistance is provided is specifically limited to individuals with disabilities or a particular class of individuals with disabilities. Because coverage under this part is not limited to federally assisted programs, paragraph (c) has been revised to clarify that State and local governments may provide special benefits, beyond those required by the nondiscrimination requirements of this part, that are limited to individuals with disabilities or a particular class of individuals with disabilities, without thereby incurring additional obligations to persons without disabilities or to other classes of individuals with disabilities.

Paragraphs (d) and (e), previously referred to in the discussion of paragraph (b)(1)(iv), provide that the public entity must administer services, programs, and activities in the most integrated setting appropriate to the needs of qualified individuals with disabilities, i.e., in a setting that enables individuals with disabilities to interact with nondisabled persons to the fullest extent possible, and that persons with disabilities must be provided the option of declining to accept a particular accommodation.

Some commenters expressed concern that § 35.130(e), which states that nothing in the rule requires an individual with a disability to accept special accommodations and services provided under the ADA, could be interpreted to allow guardians of infants or older people with disabilities to refuse medical treatment for their wards. Section 35.130(e) has been revised to make it clear that paragraph (e) is inapplicable to the concern of the commenters. A new paragraph (e)(2) has been added stating that nothing in the regulation authorizes the representative or guardian of an individual with a disability to decline food, water, medical treatment, or medical services for that individual. New paragraph (e) clarifies that neither the ADA nor the regulation alters current Federal law ensuring the rights of incompetent individuals with disabilities to receive food, water, and medical treatment. See, e.g., Child Abuse Amendments of 1984 (42 U.S.C. 5106a(b)(10), 5106g(10)); Rehabilitation Act of 1973, as amended (29 U.S.C. 794); the Developmentally Disabled Assistance and Bill of Rights Act (42 U.S.C. 6042).

Sections 35.130(e) (1) and (2) are based on section 501(d) of the ADA.

Section 501(d) was designed to clarify that nothing in the ADA requires individuals with disabilities to accept special accommodations and services for individuals with disabilities that may segregate them:

The Committee added this section [501(d)] to clarify that nothing in the ADA is intended to permit discriminatory treatment on the basis of disability, even when such treatment is rendered under the guise of providing an accommodation, service, aid or benefit to the individual with disability. For example, a blind individual may choose not to avail himself or herself of the right to go to the front of a line, even if a particular public accommodation has chosen to offer such a modification of a policy for blind individuals. Or, a blind individual may choose to decline to participate in a special museum tour that allows persons to touch sculptures in an exhibit and instead tour the exhibits at his or her own pace with the museum's recorded tour.

Judiciary report at 71–72. The Act is not to be construed to mean that an individual with disabilities must accept special accommodations and services for individuals with disabilities when that individual can participate in the regular services already offered. Because medical treatment, including treatment for particular conditions, is not a special accommodation or service for individuals with disabilities under section 501(d), neither the Act nor this part provides affirmative authority to suspend such treatment. Section 501(d) is intended to clarify that the Act is not designed to foster discrimination through mandatory acceptance of special services when other alternatives are provided; this concern does not reach to the provision of medical treatment for the disabling condition itself.

Paragraph (f) provides that a public entity may not place a surcharge on a particular individual with a disability, or any group of individuals with disabilities, to cover any costs of measures required to provide that individual or group with the nondiscriminatory treatment required by the Act or this part. Such measures may include the provision of auxiliary aids or of modifications required to provide program accessibility.

Several commenters asked for clarification that the costs of interpreter services may not be assessed as an element of "court costs." The Department has already recognized that imposition of the cost of courtroom interpreter services is impermissible under section 504. The preamble to the Department's section 504 regulation for its federally assisted programs states that where a court system has an obligation to provide qualified interpreters, "it has the corresponding responsibility to pay for the services of the interpreters." (45 FR 37630 (June 3, 1980)). Accordingly, recouping the costs of interpreter services by assessing them as part of court costs would also be prohibited.

Paragraph (g), which prohibits discrimination on the basis of an individual's or entity's known relationship or association with an individual with a disability, is based on sections 102(b)(4) and 302(b)(1)(E) of the ADA. This paragraph was not contained in the proposed rule. The individuals covered under this paragraph are any individuals who are discriminated against because of their known association with an individual with a disability. For example, it would be a violation of this paragraph for a local government to refuse to allow a theater company to use a school auditorium on the grounds that the company had recently performed for an audience of individuals with HIV disease.

This protection is not limited to those who have a familial relationship with the individual who has a disability. Congress considered, and rejected, amendments that would have limited the scope of this provision to specific associations and relationships. Therefore, if a public entity refuses admission to a person with cerebral palsy and his or her companions, the companions have an independent right of action under the ADA and this section.

During the legislative process, the term "entity" was added to section 302(b)(1)(E) to clarify that the scope of the provision is intended to encompass not only persons who have a known association with a person with a disability, but also entities that provide services to or are otherwise associated with such individuals. This provision was intended to ensure that entities such as health care providers, employees of social service agencies, and others who provide professional services to persons with disabilities are not subjected to discrimination because of their professional association with persons with disabilities.

Section 35.131   Illegal Use of Drugs

Section 35.131 effectuates section 510 of the ADA, which clarifies the Act's application to people who use drugs illegally. Paragraph (a) provides that this part does not prohibit discrimination based on an individual's current illegal use of drugs.

The Act and the regulation distinguish between illegal use of drugs and the legal use of substances, whether or not

those substances are "controlled substances," as defined in the Controlled Substances Act (21 U.S.C. 812). Some controlled substances are prescription drugs that have legitimate medical uses. Section 35.131 does not affect use of controlled substances pursuant to a valid prescription under supervision by a licensed health care professional, or other use that is authorized by the Controlled Substances Act or any other provision of Federal law. It does apply to illegal use of those substances, as well as to illegal use of controlled substances that are not prescription drugs. The key question is whether the individual's use of the substance is illegal, not whether the substance has recognized legal uses. Alcohol is not a controlled substance, so use of alcohol is not addressed by § 35.131 (although alcoholics are individuals with disabilities, subject to the protections of the statute).

A distinction is also made between the use of a substance and the status of being addicted to that substance. Addiction is a disability, and addicts are individuals with disabilities protected by the Act. The protection, however, does not extend to actions based on the illegal use of the substance. In other words, an addict cannot use the fact of his or her addiction as a defense to an action based on illegal use of drugs. This distinction is not artificial. Congress intended to deny protection to people who engage in the illegal use of drugs, whether or not they are addicted, but to provide protection to addicts so long as they are not currently using drugs.

A third distinction is the difficult one between current use and former use. The definition of "current illegal use of drugs" in § 35.104, which is based on the report of the Conference Committee, H.R. Conf. Rep. No. 596, 101st Cong., 2d Sess. 64 (1990) (hereinafter "Conference report"), is "illegal use of drugs that occurred recently enough to justify a reasonable belief that a person's drug use is current or that continuing use is a real and ongoing problem."

Paragraph (a)(2)(i) specifies that an individual who has successfully completed a supervised drug rehabilitation program or has otherwise been rehabilitated successfully and who is not engaging in current illegal use of drugs is protected. Paragraph (a)(2)(ii) clarifies that an individual who is currently participating in a supervised rehabilitation program and is not engaging in current illegal use of drugs is protected. Paragraph (a)(2)(iii) provides that a person who is erroneously regarded as engaging in current illegal use of drugs, but who is not engaging in such use, is protected.

Paragraph (b) provides a limited exception to the exclusion of current illegal users of drugs from the protections of the Act. It prohibits denial of health services, or services provided in connection with drug rehabilitation to an individual on the basis of current illegal use of drugs, if the individual is otherwise entitled to such services. A health care facility, such as a hospital or clinic, may not refuse treatment to an individual in need of the services it provides on the grounds that the individual is illegally using drugs, but it is not required by this section to provide services that it does not ordinarily provide. For example, a health care facility that specializes in a particular type of treatment, such as care of burn victims, is not required to provide drug rehabilitation services, but it cannot refuse to treat a individual's burns on the grounds that the individual is illegally using drugs.

Some commenters pointed out that abstention from the use of drugs is an essential condition of participation in some drug rehabilitation programs, and may be a necessary requirement in inpatient or residential settings. The Department believes that this comment is well-founded. Congress clearly intended to prohibit exclusion from drug treatment programs of the very individuals who need such programs because of their use of drugs, but, once an individual has been admitted to a program, abstention may be a necessary and appropriate condition to continued participation. The final rule therefore provides that a drug rehabilitation or treatment program may prohibit illegal use of drugs by individuals while they are participating in the program.

Paragraph (c) expresses Congress' intention that the Act be neutral with respect to testing for illegal use of drugs. This paragraph implements the provision in section 510(b) of the Act that allows entities "to adopt or administer reasonable policies or procedures, including but not limited to drug testing," that ensure that an individual who is participating in a supervised rehabilitation program, or who has completed such a program or otherwise been rehabilitated successfully is no longer engaging in the illegal use of drugs. The section is not to be "construed to encourage, prohibit, restrict, or authorize the conducting of testing for the illegal use of drugs."

Paragraph 35.131(c) clarifies that it is not a violation of this part to adopt or administer reasonable policies or procedures to ensure that an individual who formerly engaged in the illegal use of drugs is not currently engaging in illegal use of drugs. Any such policies or procedures must, of course, be reasonable, and must be designed to identify accurately the illegal use of drugs. This paragraph does not authorize inquiries, tests, or other procedures that would disclose use of substances that are not controlled substances or are taken under supervision by a licensed health care professional, or other uses authorized by the Controlled Substances Act or other provisions of Federal law, because such uses are not included in the definition of "illegal use of drugs." A commenter argued that the rule should permit testing for lawful use of prescription drugs, but most commenters preferred that tests must be limited to unlawful use in order to avoid revealing the lawful use of prescription medicine used to treat disabilities.

Section 35.132 Smoking

Section 35.132 restates the clarification in section 501(b) of the Act that the Act does not preclude the prohibition of, or imposition of restrictions on, smoking in transportation covered by title II. Some commenters argued that this section is too limited in scope, and that the regulation should prohibit smoking in all facilities used by public entities. The reference to smoking in section 501, however, merely clarifies that the Act does not require public entities to accommodate smokers by permitting them to smoke in transportation facilities.

Section 35.133 Maintenance of Accessible Features

Section 35.133 provides that a public entity shall maintain in operable working condition those features of facilities and equipment that are required to be readily accessible to and usable by persons with disabilities by the Act or this part. The Act requires that, to the maximum extent feasible, facilities must be accessible to, and usable by, individuals with disabilities. This section recognizes that it is not sufficient to provide features such as accessible routes, elevators, or ramps, if those features are not maintained in a manner that enables individuals with disabilities to use them. Inoperable elevators, locked accessible doors, or "accessible" routes that are obstructed by furniture, filing cabinets, or potted plants are neither "accessible to" nor "usable by" individuals with disabilities.

Some commenters objected that this section appeared to establish an absolute requirement and suggested that language from the preamble be included

in the text of the regulation. It is, of course, impossible to guarantee that mechanical devices will never fail to operate. Paragraph (b) of the final regulation provides that this section does not prohibit isolated or temporary interruptions in service or access due to maintenance or repairs. This paragraph is intended to clarify that temporary obstructions or isolated instances of mechanical failure would not be considered violations of the Act or this part. However, allowing obstructions or "out of service" equipment to persist beyond a reasonable period of time would violate this part, as would repeated mechanical failures due to improper or inadequate maintenance. Failure of the public entity to ensure that accessible routes are properly maintained and free of obstructions, or failure to arrange prompt repair of inoperable elevators or other equipment intended to provide access would also violate this part.

Other commenters requested that this section be expanded to include specific requirements for inspection and maintenance of equipment, for training staff in the proper operation of equipment, and for maintenance of specific items. The Department believes that this section properly establishes the general requirement for maintaining access and that further details are not necessary.

Section 35.134 Retaliation or Coercion

Section 35.134 implements section 503 of the ADA, which prohibits retaliation against any individual who exercises his or her rights under the Act. This section is unchanged from the proposed rule. Paragraph (a) of § 35.134 provides that no private or public entity shall discriminate against any individual because that individual has exercised his or her right to oppose any act or practice made unlawful by this part, or because that individual made a charge, testified, assisted, or participated in any manner in an investigation, proceeding, or hearing under the Act or this part.

Paragraph (b) provides that no private or public entity shall coerce, intimidate, threaten, or interfere with any individual in the exercise of his or her rights under this part or because that individual aided or encouraged any other individual in the exercise or enjoyment of any right granted or protected by the Act or this part.

This section protects not only individuals who allege a violation of the Act or this part, but also any individuals who support or assist them. This section applies to all investigations or proceedings initiated under the Act or this part without regard to the ultimate

resolution of the underlying allegations. Because this section prohibits any act of retaliation or coercion in response to an individual's effort to exercise rights established by the Act and this part (or to support the efforts of another individual), the section applies not only to public entities subject to this part, but also to persons acting in an individual capacity or to private entities. For example, it would be a violation of the Act and this part for a private individual to harass or intimidate an individual with a disability in an effort to prevent that individual from attending a concert in a State-owned park. It would, likewise, be a violation of the Act and this part for a private entity to take adverse action against an employee who appeared as a witness on behalf of an individual who sought to enforce the Act.

Section 35.135 Personal Devices and Services

The final rule includes a new § 35.135, entitled "Personal devices and services," which states that the provision of personal devices and services is not required by title II. This new section, which serves as a limitation on all of the requirements of the regulation, replaces § 35.160(b)(2) of the proposed rule, which addressed the issue of personal devices and services explicitly only in the context of communications. The personal devices and services limitation was intended to have general application in the proposed rule in all contexts where it was relevant. The final rule, therefore, clarifies this point by including a general provision that will explicitly apply not only to auxiliary aids and services but across-the-board to include other relevant areas such as, for example, modifications in policies, practices, and procedures (§ 35.130(b)(7)). The language of § 35.135 parallels an analogous provision in the Department's title III regulations (28 CFR 36.306) but preserves the explicit reference to "readers for personal use or study" in § 35.160(b)(2) of the proposed rule. This section does not preclude the short-term loan of personal receivers that are part of an assistive listening system.

Subpart C—Employment

Section 35.140 Employment Discrimination Prohibited

Title II of the ADA applies to all activities of public entities, including their employment practices. The proposed rule cross-referenced the definitions, requirements, and procedures of title I of the ADA, as established by the Equal Employment

Opportunity Commission in 29 CFR part 1630. This proposal would have resulted in use, under § 35.140, of the title I definition of "employer," so that a public entity with 25 or more employees would have become subject to the requirements of § 35.140 on July 26, 1992, one with 15 to 24 employees on July 26, 1994, and one with fewer than 15 employees would have been excluded completely.

The Department received comments objecting to this approach. The commenters asserted that Congress intended to establish nondiscrimination requirements for employment by all public entities, including those that employ fewer than 15 employees; and that Congress intended the employment requirements of title II to become effective at the same time that the other requirements of this regulation become effective, January 26, 1992. The Department has reexamined the statutory language and legislative history of the ADA on this issue and has concluded that Congress intended to cover the employment practices of all public entities and that the applicable effective date is that of title II.

The statutory language of section 204(b) of the ADA requires the Department to issue a regulation that is consistent with the ADA and the Department's coordination regulation under section 504, 28 CFR part 41. The coordination regulation specifically requires nondiscrimination in employment, 28 CFR 41.52–41.55, and does not limit coverage based on size of employer. Moreover, under all section 504 implementing regulations issued in accordance with the Department's coordination regulation, employment coverage under section 504 extends to all employers with federally assisted programs or activities, regardless of size, and the effective date for those employment requirements has always been the same as the effective date for nonemployment requirements established in the same regulations. The Department therefore concludes that § 35.140 must apply to all public entities upon the effective date of this regulation.

In the proposed regulation the Department cross-referenced the regulations implementing title I of the ADA, issued by the Equal Employment Opportunity Commission at 29 CFR part 1630, as a compliance standard for § 35.140 because, as proposed, the scope of coverage and effective date of coverage under title II would have been coextensive with title I. In the final regulation this language is modified slightly. Subparagraph (1) of new

paragraph (b) makes it clear that the standards established by the Equal Employment Opportunity Commission in 29 CFR part 1630 will be the applicable compliance standards if the public entity is subject to title I. If the public entity is not covered by title I, or until it is covered by title I, subparagraph (b)(2) cross-references section 504 standards for what constitutes employment discrimination, as established by the Department of Justice in 28 CFR part 41. Standards for title I of the ADA and section 504 of the Rehabilitation Act are for the most part identical because title I of the ADA was based on requirements set forth in regulations implementing section 504.

The Department, together with the other Federal agencies responsible for the enforcement of Federal laws prohibiting employment discrimination on the basis of disability, recognizes the potential for jurisdictional overlap that exists with respect to coverage of public entities and the need to avoid problems related to overlapping coverage. The other Federal agencies include the Equal Employment Opportunity Commission, which is the agency primarily responsible for enforcement of title I of the ADA, the Department of Labor, which is the agency responsible for enforcement of section 503 of the Rehabilitation Act of 1973, and 26 Federal agencies with programs of Federal financial assistance, which are responsible for enforcing section 504 in those programs. Section 107 of the ADA requires that coordination mechanisms be developed in connection with the administrative enforcement of complaints alleging discrimination under title I and complaints alleging discrimination in employment in violation of the Rehabilitation Act. Although the ADA does not specifically require inclusion of employment complaints under title II in the coordinating mechanisms required by title I, Federal investigations of title II employment complaints will be coordinated on a government-wide basis also. The Department is currently working with the EEOC and other affected Federal agencies to develop effective coordinating mechanisms, and final regulations on this issue will be issued on or before January 26, 1992.

Subpart D—Program Accessibility

Section 35.149 Discrimination Prohibited

Section 35.149 states the general nondiscrimination principle underlying the program accessibility requirements of §§ 35.150 and 35.151.

Section 35.150 Existing Facilities

Consistent with section 204(b) of the Act, this regulation adopts the program accessibility concept found in the section 504 regulations for federally conducted programs or activities (e.g., 28 CFR part 39). The concept of "program accessibility" was first used in the section 504 regulation adopted by the Department of Health, Education, and Welfare for its federally assisted programs and activities in 1977. It allowed recipients to make their federally assisted programs and activities available to individuals with disabilities without extensive retrofitting of their existing buildings and facilities, by offering those programs through alternative methods. Program accessibility has proven to be a useful approach and was adopted in the regulations issued for programs and activities conducted by Federal Executive agencies. The Act provides that the concept of program access will continue to apply with respect to facilities now in existence, because the cost of retrofitting existing facilities is often prohibitive.

Section 35.150 requires that each service, program, or activity conducted by a public entity, when viewed in its entirety, be readily accessible to and usable by individuals with disabilities. The regulation makes clear, however, that a public entity is not required to make each of its existing facilities accessible (§ 35.150(a)(1)). Unlike title III of the Act, which requires public accommodations to remove architectural barriers where such removal is "readily achievable," or to provide goods and services through alternative methods, where those methods are "readily achievable," title II requires a public entity to make its programs accessible in all cases, except where to do so would result in a fundamental alteration in the nature of the program or in undue financial and administrative burdens. Congress intended the "undue burden" standard in title II to be significantly higher than the "readily achievable" standard in title III. Thus, although title II may not require removal of barriers in some cases where removal would be required under title III, the program access requirement of title II should enable individuals with disabilities to participate in and benefit from the services, programs, or activities of public entities in all but the most unusual cases.

Paragraph (a)(2), which establishes a special limitation on the obligation to ensure program accessibility in historic preservation programs, is discussed below in connection with paragraph (b).

Paragraph (a)(3), which is taken from the section 504 regulations for federally conducted programs, generally codifies case law that defines the scope of the public entity's obligation to ensure program accessibility. This paragraph provides that, in meeting the program accessibility requirement, a public entity is not required to take any action that would result in a fundamental alteration in the nature of its service, program, or activity or in undue financial and administrative burdens. A similar limitation is provided in § 35.164.

This paragraph does not establish an absolute defense; it does not relieve a public entity of all obligations to individuals with disabilities. Although a public entity is not required to take actions that would result in a fundamental alteration in the nature of a service, program, or activity or in undue financial and administrative burdens, it nevertheless must take any other steps necessary to ensure that individuals with disabilities receive the benefits or services provided by the public entity.

It is the Department's view that compliance with § 35.150(a), like compliance with the corresponding provisions of the section 504 regulations for federally conducted programs, would in most cases not result in undue financial and administrative burdens on a public entity. In determining whether financial and administrative burdens are undue, all public entity resources available for use in the funding and operation of the service, program, or activity should be considered. The burden of proving that compliance with paragraph (a) of § 35.150 would fundamentally alter the nature of a service, program, or activity or would result in undue financial and administrative burdens rests with the public entity.

The decision that compliance would result in such alteration or burdens must be made by the head of the public entity or his or her designee and must be accompanied by a written statement of the reasons for reaching that conclusion. The Department recognizes the difficulty of identifying the official responsible for this determination, given the variety of organizational forms that may be taken by public entities and their components. The intention of this paragraph is that the determination must be made by a high level official, no lower than a Department head, having budgetary authority and responsibility for making spending decisions.

Any person who believes that he or she or any specific class of persons has been injured by the public entity head's decision or failure to make a decision may file a complaint under the compliance procedures established in subpart F.

Paragraph (b)(1) sets forth a number of means by which program accessibility may be achieved, including redesign of equipment, reassignment of services to accessible buildings, and provision of aides.

The Department wishes to clarify that, consistent with longstanding interpretation of section 504, carrying an individual with a disability is considered an ineffective and therefore an unacceptable method for achieving program accessibility. Department of Health, Education, and Welfare, Office of Civil Rights, Policy Interpretation No. 4, 43 FR 36035 (August 14, 1978). Carrying will be permitted only in manifestly exceptional cases, and only if all personnel who are permitted to participate in carrying an individual with a disability are formally instructed on the safest and least humiliating means of carrying. "Manifestly exceptional" cases in which carrying would be permitted might include, for example, programs conducted in unique facilities, such as an oceanographic vessel, for which structural changes and devices necessary to adapt the facility for use by individuals with mobility impairments are unavailable or prohibitively expensive. Carrying is not permitted as an alternative to structural modifications such as installation of a ramp or a chairlift.

In choosing among methods, the public entity shall give priority consideration to those that will be consistent with provision of services in the most integrated setting appropriate to the needs of individuals with disabilities. Structural changes in existing facilities are required only when there is no other feasible way to make the public entity's program accessible. (It should be noted that "structural changes" include all physical changes to a facility; the term does not refer only to changes to structural features, such as removal of or alteration to a load-bearing structural member.) The requirements of § 35.151 for alterations apply to structural changes undertaken to comply with this section. The public entity may comply with the program accessibility requirement by delivering services at alternate accessible sites or making home visits as appropriate.

Historic Preservation Programs

In order to avoid possible conflict between the congressional mandates to preserve historic properties, on the one hand, and to eliminate discrimination against individuals with disabilities on the other, paragraph (a)(2) provides that a public entity is not required to take any action that would threaten or destroy the historic significance of an historic property. The special limitation on program accessibility set forth in paragraph (a)(2) is applicable only to historic preservation programs, as defined in § 35.104, that is, programs that have preservation of historic properties as a primary purpose. Narrow application of the special limitation is justified because of the inherent flexibility of the program accessibility requirement. Where historic preservation is not a primary purpose of the program, the public entity is not required to use a particular facility. It can relocate all or part of its program to an accessible facility, make home visits, or use other standard methods of achieving program accessibility without making structural alterations that might threaten or destroy significant historic features of the historic property. Thus, government programs located in historic properties, such as an historic State capitol, are not excused from the requirement for program access.

Paragraph (a)(2), therefore, will apply only to those programs that uniquely concern the preservation and experience of the historic property itself. Because the primary benefit of an historic preservation program is the experience of the historic property, paragraph (b)(2) requires the public entity to give priority to methods of providing program accessibility that permit individuals with disabilities to have physical access to the historic property. This priority on physical access may also be viewed as a specific application of the general requirement that the public entity administer programs in the most integrated setting appropriate to the needs of qualified individuals with disabilities (§ 35.130(d)). Only when providing physical access would threaten or destroy the historic significance of an historic property, or would result in a fundamental alteration in the nature of the program or in undue financial and administrative burdens, may the public entity adopt alternative methods for providing program accessibility that do not ensure physical access. Examples of some alternative methods are provided in paragraph (b)(2).

Time Periods

Paragraphs (c) and (d) establish time periods for complying with the program accessibility requirement. Like the regulations for federally assisted programs (e.g., 28 CFR 41.57(b)), paragraph (c) requires the public entity to make any necessary structural changes in facilities as soon as practicable, but in no event later than three years after the effective date of this regulation.

The proposed rule provided that, aside from structural changes, all other necessary steps to achieve compliance with this part must be taken within sixty days. The sixty day period was taken from regulations implementing section 504, which generally were effective no more than thirty days after publication. Because this regulation will not be effective until January 26, 1992, the Department has concluded that no additional transition period for non-structural changes is necessary, so the sixty day period has been omitted in the final rule. Of course, this section does not reduce or eliminate any obligations that are already applicable to a public entity under section 504.

Where structural modifications are required, paragraph (d) requires that a transition plan be developed by an entity that employs 50 or more persons, within six months of the effective date of this regulation. The legislative history of title II of the ADA makes it clear that, under title II, "local and state governments are required to provide curb cuts on public streets." Education and Labor report at 84. As the rationale for the provision of curb cuts, the House report explains, "The employment, transportation, and public accommodation sections of * * * (the ADA) would be meaningless if people who use wheelchairs were not afforded the opportunity to travel on and between the streets." Id. Section 35.151(e), which establishes accessibility requirements for new construction and alterations, requires that all newly constructed or altered streets, roads, or highways must contain curb ramps or other sloped areas at any intersection having curbs or other barriers to entry from a street level pedestrian walkway, and all newly constructed or altered street level pedestrian walkways must have curb ramps or other sloped areas at intersections to streets, roads, or highways. A new paragraph (d)(2) has been added to the final rule to clarify the application of the general requirement for program accessibility to the provision of curb cuts at existing crosswalks. This paragraph requires that the transition plan include a schedule for providing curb ramps or other sloped areas at existing pedestrian walkways, giving priority to walkways serving entities covered by the Act, including State and local government offices and

facilities, transportation, public accommodations, and employers, followed by walkways serving other areas. Pedestrian "walkways" include locations where access is required for use of public transportation, such as bus stops that are not located at intersections or crosswalks.

Similarly, a public entity should provide an adequate number of accessible parking spaces in existing parking lots or garages over which it has jurisdiction.

Paragraph (d)(3) provides that, if a public entity has already completed a transition plan required by a regulation implementing section 504, the transition plan required by this part will apply only to those policies and practices that were not covered by the previous transition plan. Some commenters suggested that the transition plan should include all aspects of the public entity's operations, including those that may have been covered by a previous transition plan under section 504. The Department believes that such a duplicative requirement would be inappropriate. Many public entities may find, however, that it will be simpler to include all of their operations in the transition plan than to attempt to identify and exclude specifically those that were addressed in a previous plan. Of course, entities covered under section 504 are not shielded from their obligations under that statute merely because they are included under the transition plan developed under this section.

Section 35.151 New Construction and Alterations

Section 35.151 provides that those buildings that are constructed or altered by, on behalf of, or for the use of a public entity shall be designed, constructed, or altered to be readily accessible to and usable by individuals with disabilities if the construction was commenced after the effective date of this part. Facilities under design on that date will be governed by this section if the date that bids were invited falls after the effective date. This interpretation is consistent with Federal practice under section 504.

Section 35.151(c) establishes two standards for accessible new construction and alteration. Under paragraph (c), design, construction, or alteration of facilities in conformance with the Uniform Federal Accessibility Standards (UFAS) or with the Americans with Disabilities Act Accessibility Guidelines for Buildings and Facilities (hereinafter ADAAG) shall be deemed to comply with the requirements of this section with respect

to those facilities except that, if ADAAG is chosen, the elevator exemption contained at §§ 36.401(d) and 36.404 does not apply. ADAAG is the standard for private buildings and was issued as guidelines by the Architectural and Transportation Barriers Compliance Board (ATBCB) under title III of the ADA. It has been adopted by the Department of Justice and is published as appendix A to the Department's title III rule in today's Federal Register. Departures from particular requirements of these standards by the use of other methods shall be permitted when it is clearly evident that equivalent access to the facility or part of the facility is thereby provided. Use of two standards is a departure from the proposed rule.

The proposed rule adopted UFAS as the only interim accessibility standard because that standard was referenced by the regulations implementing section 504 of the Rehabilitation Act promulgated by most Federal funding agencies. It is, therefore, familiar to many State and local government entities subject to this rule. The Department, however, received many comments objecting to the adoption of UFAS. Commenters pointed out that, except for the elevator exemption, UFAS is not as stringent as ADAAG. Others suggested that the standard should be the same to lessen confusion.

Section 204(b) of the Act states that title II regulations must be consistent not only with section 504 regulations but also with "this Act." Based on this provision, the Department has determined that a public entity should be entitled to choose to comply either with ADAAG or UFAS.

Public entities who choose to follow ADAAG, however, are not entitled to the elevator exemption contained in title III of the Act and implemented in the title III regulation at § 36.401(d) for new construction and § 36.404 for alterations. Section 303(b) of title III states that, with some exceptions, elevators are not required in facilities that are less than three stories or have less than 3000 square feet per story. The section 504 standard, UFAS, contains no such exemption. Section 501 of the ADA makes clear that nothing in the Act may be construed to apply a lesser standard to public entities than the standards applied under section 504. Because permitting the elevator exemption would clearly result in application of a lesser standard than that applied under section 504, paragraph (c) states that the elevator exemption does not apply when public entities choose to follow ADAAG. Thus, a two-story courthouse, whether built according to UFAS or

ADAAG, must be constructed with an elevator. It should be noted that Congress did not include an elevator exemption for public transit facilities covered by subtitle B of title II, which covers public transportation provided by public entities, providing further evidence that Congress intended that public buildings have elevators.

Section 504 of the ADA requires the ATBCB to issue supplemental Minimum Guidelines and Requirements for Accessible Design of buildings and facilities subject to the Act, including title II. Section 204(c) of the ADA provides that the Attorney General shall promulgate regulations implementing title II that are consistent with the ATBCB's ADA guidelines. The ATBCB has announced its intention to issue title II guidelines in the future. The Department anticipates that, after the ATBCB's title II guidelines have been published, this rule will be amended to adopt new accessibility standards consistent with the ATBCB's rulemaking. Until that time, however, public entities will have a choice of following UFAS or ADAAG, without the elevator exemption.

Existing buildings leased by the public entity after the effective date of this part are not required by the regulation to meet accessibility standards simply by virtue of being leased. They are subject, however, to the program accessibility standard for existing facilities in § 35.150. To the extent the buildings are newly constructed or altered, they must also meet the new construction and alteration requirements of § 35.151.

The Department received many comments urging that the Department require that public entities lease only accessible buildings. Federal practice under section 504 has always treated newly leased buildings as subject to the existing facility program accessibility standard. Section 204(b) of the Act states that, in the area of "program accessibility, existing facilities," the title II regulations must be consistent with section 504 regulations. Thus, the Department has adopted the section 504 principles for these types of leased buildings. Unlike the construction of new buildings where architectural barriers can be avoided at little or no cost, the application of new construction standards to an existing building being leased raises the same prospect of retrofitting buildings as the use of an existing Federal facility, and the same program accessibility standard should apply to both owned and leased existing buildings. Similarly, requiring that public entities only lease accessible space would significantly restrict the

options of State and local governments in seeking leased space, which would be particularly burdensome in rural or sparsely populated areas.

On the other hand, the more accessible the leased space is, the fewer structural modifications will be required in the future for particular employees whose disabilities may necessitate barrier removal as a reasonable accommodation. Pursuant to the requirements for leased buildings contained in the Minimum Guidelines and Requirements for Accessible Design published under the Architectural Barriers Act by the ATBCB, 36 CFR 1190.34, the Federal Government may not lease a building unless it contains (1) One accessible route from an accessible entrance to those areas in which the principal activities for which the building is leased are conducted, (2) accessible toilet facilities, and (3) accessible parking facilities, if a parking area is included within the lease (36 CFR 1190.34). Although these requirements are not applicable to buildings leased by public entities covered by this regulation, such entities are encouraged to look for the most accessible space available to lease and to attempt to find space complying at least with these minimum Federal requirements.

Section 35.151(d) gives effect to the intent of Congress, expressed in section 504(c) of the Act, that this part recognize the national interest in preserving significant historic structures. Commenters criticized the Department's use of descriptive terms in the proposed rule that are different from those used in the ADA to describe eligible historic properties. In addition, some commenters criticized the Department's decision to use the concept of "substantially impairing" the historic features of a property, which is a concept employed in regulations implementing section 504 of the Rehabilitation Act of 1973. Those commenters recommended that the Department adopt the criteria of "adverse effect" published by the Advisory Council on Historic Preservation under the National Historic Preservation Act, 36 CFR 800.9, as the standard for determining whether an historic property may be altered.

The Department agrees with these comments to the extent that they suggest that the language of the rule should conform to the language employed by Congress in the ADA. A definition of "historic property," drawn from section 504 of the ADA, has been added to § 35.104 to clarify that the term applies to those properties listed or eligible for

listing in the National Register of Historic Places, or properties designated as historic under State or local law.

The Department intends that the exception created by this section be applied only in those very rare situations in which it is not possible to provide access to an historic property using the special access provisions established by UFAS and ADAAG. Therefore, paragraph (d)(1) of § 35.151 has been revised to clearly state that alterations to historic properties shall comply, to the maximum extent feasible, with section 4.1.7 of UFAS or section 4.1.7 of ADAAG. Paragraph (d)(2) has been revised to provide that, if it has been determined under the procedures established in UFAS and ADAAG that it is not feasible to provide physical access to an historic property in a manner that will not threaten or destroy the historic significance of the property, alternative methods of access shall be provided pursuant to the requirements of § 35.150.

In response to comments, the Department has added to the final rule a new paragraph (e) setting out the requirements of § 36.151 as applied to curb ramps. Paragraph (e) is taken from the statement contained in the preamble to the proposed rule that all newly constructed or altered streets, roads, and highways must contain curb ramps at any intersection having curbs or other barriers to entry from a street level pedestrian walkway, and that all newly constructed or altered street level pedestrian walkways must have curb ramps at intersections to streets, roads, or highways.

Subpart E—Communications

Section 35.160   General

Section 35.160 requires the public entity to take such steps as may be necessary to ensure that communications with applicants, participants, and members of the public with disabilities are as effective as communications with others.

Paragraph (b)(1) requires the public entity to furnish appropriate auxiliary aids and services when necessary to afford an individual with a disability an equal opportunity to participate in, and enjoy the benefits of, the public entity's service, program, or activity. The public entity must provide an opportunity for individuals with disabilities to request the auxiliary aids and services of their choice. This expressed choice shall be given primary consideration by the public entity (§ 35.160(b)(2)). The public entity shall honor the choice unless it can demonstrate that another effective means of communication exists or that use of the means chosen would not be required under § 35.164.

Deference to the request of the individual with a disability is desirable because of the range of disabilities, the variety of auxiliary aids and services, and different circumstances requiring effective communication. For instance, some courtrooms are now equipped for "computer-assisted transcripts," which allow virtually instantaneous transcripts of courtroom argument and testimony to appear on displays. Such a system might be an effective auxiliary aid or service for a person who is deaf or has a hearing loss who uses speech to communicate, but may be useless for someone who uses sign language.

Although in some circumstances a notepad and written materials may be sufficient to permit effective communication, in other circumstances they may not be sufficient. For example, a qualified interpreter may be necessary when the information being communicated is complex, or is exchanged for a lengthy period of time. Generally, factors to be considered in determining whether an interpreter is required include the context in which the communication is taking place, the number of people involved, and the importance of the communication.

Several commenters asked that the rule clarify that the provision of readers is sometimes necessary to ensure access to a public entity's services, programs or activities. Reading devices or readers should be provided when necessary for equal participation and opportunity to benefit from any governmental service, program, or activity, such as reviewing public documents, examining demonstrative evidence, and filling out voter registration forms or forms needed to receive public benefits. The importance of providing qualified readers for examinations administered by public entities is discussed under § 35.130. Reading devices and readers are appropriate auxiliary aids and services where necessary to permit an individual with a disability to participate in or benefit from a service, program, or activity.

Section 35.160(b)(2) of the proposed rule, which provided that a public entity need not furnish individually prescribed devices, readers for personal use or study, or other devices of a personal nature, has been deleted in favor of a new section in the final rule on personal devices and services (see § 35.135).

In response to comments, the term "auxiliary aids and services" is used in place of "auxiliary aids" in the final rule. This phrase better reflects the

range of aids and services that may be required under this section.

A number of comments raised questions about the extent of a public entity's obligation to provide access to television programming for persons with hearing impairments. Television and videotape programming produced by public entities are covered by this section. Access to audio portions of such programming may be provided by closed captioning.

Section 35.161   Telecommunication Devices for the Deaf (TDD's)

Section 35.161 requires that, where a public entity communicates with applicants and beneficiaries by telephone, TDD's or equally effective telecommunication systems be used to communicate with individuals with impaired speech or hearing.

Problems arise when a public entity which does not have a TDD needs to communicate with an individual who uses a TDD or vice versa. Title IV of the ADA addresses this problem by requiring establishment of telephone relay services to permit communications between individuals who communicate by TDD and individuals who communicate by the telephone alone. The relay services required by title IV would involve a relay operator using both a standard telephone and a TDD to type the voice messages to the TDD user and read the TDD messages to the standard telephone user.

Section 204(b) of the ADA requires that the regulation implementing title II with respect to communications be consistent with the Department's regulation implementing section 504 for its federally conducted programs and activities at 28 CFR part 39. Section 35.161, which is taken from § 39.160(a)(2) of that regulation, requires the use of TDD's or equally effective telecommunication systems for communication with people who use TDD's. Of course, where relay services, such as those required by title IV of the ADA are available, a public entity may use those services to meet the requirements of this section.

Many commenters were concerned that public entities should not rely heavily on the establishment of relay services. The commenters explained that while relay services would be of vast benefit to both public entities and individuals who use TDD's, the services are not sufficient to provide access to all telephone services. First, relay systems do not provide effective access to the increasingly popular automated systems that require the caller to respond by pushing a button on a touch tone phone. Second, relay systems cannot operate

fast enough to convey messages on answering machines, or to permit a TDD user to leave a recorded message. Third, communication through relay systems may not be appropriate in cases of crisis lines pertaining to rape, domestic violence, child abuse, and drugs. The Department believes that it is more appropriate for the Federal Communications Commission to address these issues in its rulemaking under title IV.

Some commenters requested that those entities with frequent contacts with clients who use TDD's have on-site TDD's to provide for direct communication between the entity and the individual. The Department encourages those entities that have extensive telephone contact with the public such as city halls, public libraries, and public aid offices, to have TDD's to insure more immediate access. Where the provision of telephone service is a major function of the entity, TDD's should be available.

Section 35.162   Telephone Emergency Services

Many public entities provide telephone emergency services by which individuals can seek immediate assistance from police, fire, ambulance, and other emergency services. These telephone emergency services—including "911" services—are clearly an important public service whose reliability can be a matter of life or death. The legislative history of title II specifically reflects congressional intent that public entities must ensure that telephone emergency services, including 911 services, be accessible to persons with impaired hearing and speech through telecommunication technology (Conference report at 67; Education and Labor report at 84–85).

Proposed § 35.162 mandated that public entities provide emergency telephone services to persons with disabilities that are "functionally equivalent" to voice services provided to others. Many commenters urged the Department to revise the section to make clear that direct access to telephone emergency services is required by title II of the ADA as indicated by the legislative history (Conference report at 67–68; Education and Labor report at 85). In response, the final rule mandates "direct access," instead of "access that is functionally equivalent" to that provided to all other telephone users. Telephone emergency access through a third party or through a relay service would not satisfy the requirement for direct access.

Several commenters asked about a separate seven-digit emergency call number for the 911 services. The requirement for direct access disallows the use of a separate seven-digit number where 911 service is available. Separate seven-digit emergency call numbers would be unfamiliar to many individuals and also more burdensome to use. A standard emergency 911 number is easier to remember and would save valuable time spent in searching in telephone books for a local seven-digit emergency number.

Many commenters requested the establishment of minimum standards of service (e.g., the quantity and location of TDD's and computer modems needed in a given emergency center). Instead of establishing these scoping requirements, the Department has established a performance standard through the mandate for direct access.

Section 35.162 requires public entities to take appropriate steps, including equipping their emergency systems with modern technology, as may be necessary to promptly receive and respond to a call from users of TDD's and computer modems. Entities are allowed the flexibility to determine what is the appropriate technology for their particular needs. In order to avoid mandating use of particular technologies that may become outdated, the Department has eliminated the references to the Baudot and ASCII formats in the proposed rule.

Some commenters requested that the section require the installation of a voice amplification device on the handset of the dispatcher's telephone to amplify the dispatcher's voice. In an emergency, a person who has a hearing loss may be using a telephone that does not have an amplification device. Installation of speech amplification devices on the handsets of the dispatchers' telephones would respond to that situation. The Department encourages their use.

Several commenters emphasized the need for proper maintenance of TDD's used in telephone emergency services. Section 35.133, which mandates maintenance of accessible features, requires public entities to maintain in operable working condition TDD's and other devices that provide direct access to the emergency system.

Section 35.163   Information and Signage

Section 35.163(a) requires the public entity to provide information to individuals with disabilities concerning accessible services, activities, and facilities. Paragraph (b) requires the public entity to provide signage at all inaccessible entrances to each of its facilities that directs users to an accessible entrance or to a location with information about accessible facilities.

Several commenters requested that, where TDD-equipped pay phones or portable TDD's exist, clear signage should be posted indicating the location of the TDD. The Department believes that this is required by paragraph (a). In addition, the Department recommends that, in large buildings that house TDD's, directional signage indicating the location of available TDD's should be placed adjacent to banks of telephones that do not contain a TDD.

Section 35.164   Duties

Section 35.164, like paragraph (a)(3) of § 35.150, is taken from the section 504 regulations for federally conducted programs. Like paragraph (a)(3), it limits the obligation of the public entity to ensure effective communication in accordance with *Davis* and the circuit court opinions interpreting it. It also includes specific requirements for determining the existence of undue financial and administrative burdens. The preamble discussion of § 35.150(a) regarding that determination is applicable to this section and further explains the public entity's obligation to comply with §§ 35.160–35.164. Because of the essential nature of the services provided by telephone emergency systems, the Department assumes that § 35.164 will rarely be applied to § 35.162.

Subpart F—Compliance Procedures

Subpart F sets out the procedures for administrative enforcement of this part. Section 203 of the Act provides that the remedies, procedures, and rights set forth in section 505 of the Rehabilitation Act of 1973 (29 U.S.C. 794a) for enforcement of section 504 of the Rehabilitation Act, which prohibits discrimination on the basis of handicap in programs and activities that receive Federal financial assistance, shall be the remedies, procedures, and rights for enforcement of title II. Section 505, in turn, incorporates by reference the remedies, procedures, and rights set forth in title VI of the Civil Rights Act of 1964 (42 U.S.C. 2000d to 2000d–4a). Title VI, which prohibits discrimination on the basis of race, color, or national origin in federally assisted programs, is enforced by the Federal agencies that provide the Federal financial assistance to the covered programs and activities in question. If voluntary compliance cannot be achieved, Federal agencies enforce title VI either by the termination of Federal funds to a program that is found to discriminate, following an administrative hearing, or by a referral to this Department for judicial enforcement.

Title II of the ADA extended the requirements of section 504 to all services, programs, and activities of State and local governments, not only those that receive Federal financial assistance. The House Committee on Education and Labor explained the enforcement provisions as follows:

It is the Committee's intent that administrative enforcement of section 202 of the legislation should closely parallel the Federal government's experience with section 504 of the Rehabilitation Act of 1973. The Attorney General should use section 504 enforcement procedures and the Department's coordination role under Executive Order 12250 as models for regulation in this area.

The Committee envisions that the Department of Justice will identify appropriate Federal agencies to oversee compliance activities for State and local governments. As with section 504, these Federal agencies, including the Department of Justice, will receive, investigate, and where possible, resolve complaints of discrimination. If a Federal agency is unable to resolve a complaint by voluntary means, * * * the major enforcement sanction for the Federal government will be referral of cases by these Federal agencies to the Department of Justice.

The Department of Justice may then proceed to file suits in Federal district court. As with section 504, there is also a private right of action for persons with disabilities, which includes the full panoply of remedies. Again, consistent with section 504, it is not the Committee's intent that persons with disabilities need to exhaust Federal administrative remedies before exercising their private right of action.

Education & Labor report at 98. See also S. Rep. No. 116, 101st Cong., 1st Sess., at 57–58 (1989).

Subpart F effectuates the congressional intent by deferring to section 504 procedures where those procedures are applicable, that is, where a Federal agency has jurisdiction under section 504 by virtue of its provision of Federal financial assistance to the program or activity in which the discrimination is alleged to have occurred. Deferral to the 504 procedures also makes the sanction of fund termination available where necessary to achieve compliance. Because the Civil Rights Restoration Act (Pub. L. 100–259) extended the application of section 504 to all of the operations of the public entity receiving the Federal financial assistance, many activities of State and local governments are already covered by section 504. The procedures in subpart F apply to complaints concerning services, programs, and activities of public entities that are covered by the ADA.

Subpart G designates the Federal agencies responsible for enforcing the ADA with respect to specific components of State and local government. It does not, however, displace existing jurisdiction under section 504 of the various funding agencies. Individuals may still file discrimination complaints against recipients of Federal financial assistance with the agencies that provide that assistance, and the funding agencies will continue to process those complaints under their existing procedures for enforcing section 504. The substantive standards adopted in this part for title II of the ADA are generally the same as those required under section 504 for federally assisted programs, and public entities covered by the ADA are also covered by the requirements of section 504 to the extent that they receive Federal financial assistance. To the extent that title II provides greater protection to the rights of individuals with disabilities, however, the funding agencies will also apply the substantive requirements established under title II and this part in processing complaints covered by both this part and section 504, except that fund termination procedures may be used only for violations of section 504.

Subpart F establishes the procedures to be followed by the agencies designated in subpart G for processing complaints against State and local government entities when the designated agency does not have jurisdiction under section 504.

Section 35.170 Complaints

Section 35.170 provides that any individual who believes that he or she or a specific class of individuals has been subjected to discrimination on the basis of disability by a public entity may, by himself or herself or by an authorized representative, file a complaint under this part within 180 days of the date of the alleged discrimination, unless the time for filing is extended by the agency for good cause. Although § 35.107 requires public entities that employ 50 or more persons to establish grievance procedures for resolution of complaints, exhaustion of those procedures is not a prerequisite to filing a complaint under this section. If a complainant chooses to follow the public entity's grievance procedures, however, any resulting delay may be considered good cause for extending the time allowed for filing a complaint under this part.

Filing the complaint with any Federal agency will satisfy the requirement for timely filing. As explained below, a complaint filed with an agency that has jurisdiction under section 504 will be processed under the agency's procedures for enforcing section 504.

Some commenters objected to the complexity of allowing complaints to be filed with different agencies. The multiplicity of enforcement jurisdiction is the result of following the statutorily mandated enforcement scheme. The Department has, however, attempted to simplify procedures for complainants by making the Federal agency that receives the complaint responsible for referring it to an appropriate agency.

The Department has also added a new paragraph (c) to this section providing that a complaint may be filed with any agency designated under subpart G of this part, or with any agency that provides funding to the public entity that is the subject of the complaint, or with the Department of Justice. Under § 35.171(a)(2), the Department of Justice will refer complaints for which it does not have jurisdiction under section 504 to an agency that does have jurisdiction under section 504, or to the agency designated under subpart G as responsible for complaints filed against the public entity that is the subject of the complaint or in the case of an employment complaint that is also subject to title I of the Act, to the Equal Employment Opportunity Commission. Complaints filed with the Department of Justice may be sent to the Coordination and Review Section, P.O. Box 66118, Civil Rights Division, U.S. Department of Justice, Washington, DC 20035–6118.

Section 35.171 Acceptance of Complaints

Section 35.171 establishes procedures for determining jurisdiction and responsibility for processing complaints against public entities. The final rule provides complainants an opportunity to file with the Federal funding agency of their choice. If that agency does not have jurisdiction under section 504, however, and is not the agency designated under subpart G as responsible for that public entity, the agency must refer the complaint to the Department of Justice, which will be responsible for referring it either to an agency that does have jurisdiction under section 504 or to the appropriate designated agency, or in the case of an employment complaint that is also subject to title I of the Act, to the Equal Employment Opportunity Commission.

Whenever an agency receives a complaint over which it has jurisdiction under section 504, it will process the complaint under its section 504 procedures. When the agency designated under subpart G receives a complaint for which it does not have jurisdiction under section 504, it will treat the complaint as an ADA complaint under the procedures established in this subpart.

Section 35.171 also describes agency responsibilities for the processing of employment complaints. As described in connection with § 35.140, additional procedures regarding the coordination of employment complaints will be established in a coordination regulation issued by DOJ and EEOC. Agencies with jurisdiction under section 504 for complaints alleging employment discrimination also covered by title I will follow the procedures established by the coordination regulation for those complaints. Complaints covered by title I but not section 504 will be referred to the EEOC, and complaints covered by this part but not title I will be processed under the procedures in this part.

Section 35.172 Resolution of Complaints

Section 35.172 requires the designated agency to either resolve the complaint or issue to the complainant and the public entity a Letter of Findings containing findings of fact and conclusions of law and a description of a remedy for each violation found.

The Act requires the Department of Justice to establish administrative procedures for resolution of complaints, but does not require complainants to exhaust these administrative remedies. The Committee Reports make clear that Congress intended to provide a private right of action with the full panoply of remedies for individual victims of discrimination. Because the Act does not require exhaustion of administrative remedies, the complainant may elect to proceed with a private suit at any time.

Section 35.173 Voluntary Compliance Agreements

Section 35.173 requires the agency to attempt to resolve all complaints in which it finds noncompliance through voluntary compliance agreements enforceable by the Attorney General.

Section 35.174 Referral

Section 35.174 provides for referral of the matter to the Department of Justice if the agency is unable to obtain voluntary compliance.

Section 35.175 Attorney's Fees

Section 35.175 states that courts are authorized to award attorneys fees, including litigation expenses and costs, as provided in section 505 of the Act. Litigation expenses include items such as expert witness fees, travel expenses, etc. The Judiciary Committee Report specifies that such items are included under the rubric of "attorneys fees" and not "costs" so that such expenses will be assessed against a plaintiff only under the standard set forth in *Christiansburg Garment Co.* v. *Equal Employment Opportunity Commission,* 434 U.S. 412 (1978). (Judiciary report at 73.)

Section 35.176   Alternative Means of Dispute Resolution

Section 35.176 restates section 513 of the Act, which encourages use of alternative means of dispute resolution.

Section 35.177   Effect of Unavailability of Technical Assistance

Section 35.177 explains that, as provided in section 506(e) of the Act, a public entity is not excused from compliance with the requirements of this part because of any failure to receive technical assistance.

Section 35.178   State Immunity

Section 35.178 restates the provision of section 502 of the Act that a State is not immune under the eleventh amendment to the Constitution of the United States from an action in Federal or State court for violations of the Act, and that the same remedies are available for any such violations as are available in an action against an entity other than a State.

Subpart G—Designated Agencies

Section 35.190   Designated Agencies

Subpart G designates the Federal agencies responsible for investigating complaints under this part. At least 26 agencies currently administer programs of Federal financial assistance that are subject to the nondiscrimination requirements of section 504 as well as other civil rights statutes. A majority of these agencies administer modest programs of Federal financial assistance and/or devote minimal resources exclusively to "external" civil rights enforcement activities. Under Executive Order 12250, the Department of Justice has encouraged the use of delegation agreements under which certain civil rights compliance responsibilities for a class of recipients funded by more than one agency are delegated by an agency or agencies to a "lead" agency. For example, many agencies that fund institutions of higher education have signed agreements that designate the Department of Education as the "lead" agency for this class of recipients.

The use of delegation agreements reduces overlap and duplication of effort, and thereby strengthens overall civil rights enforcement. However, the

use of these agreements to date generally has been limited to education and health care recipients. These classes of recipients are funded by numerous agencies and the logical connection to a lead agency is clear (e.g., the Department of Education for colleges and universities, and the Department of Health and Human Services for hospitals).

The ADA's expanded coverage of State and local government operations further complicates the process of establishing Federal agency jurisdiction for the purpose of investigating complaints of discrimination on the basis of disability. Because all operations of public entities now are covered irrespective of the presence or absence of Federal financial assistance, many additional State and local government functions and organizations now are subject to Federal jurisdiction. In some cases, there is no historical or single clear-cut subject matter relationship with a Federal agency as was the case in the education example described above. Further, the 33,000 governmental jurisdictions subject to the ADA differ greatly in their organization, making a detailed and workable division of Federal agency jurisdiction by individual State, county, or municipal entity unrealistic.

This regulation applies the delegation concept to the investigation of complaints of discrimination on the basis of disability by public entities under the ADA. It designates eight agencies, rather than all agencies currently administering programs of Federal financial assistance, as responsible for investigating complaints under this part. These "designated agencies" generally have the largest civil rights compliance staffs, the most experience in complaint investigations and disability issues, and broad yet clear subject area responsibilities. This division of responsibilities is made functionally rather than by public entity type or name designation. For example, all entities (regardless of their title) that exercise responsibilities, regulate, or administer services or programs relating to lands and natural resources fall within the jurisdiction of the Department of Interior.

Complaints under this part will be investigated by the designated agency most closely related to the functions exercised by the governmental component against which the complaint is lodged. For example, a complaint against a State medical board, where such a board is a recognizable entity, will be investigated by the Department of Health and Human Services (the designated agency for regulatory

activities relating to the provision of health care), even if the board is part of a general umbrella department of planning and regulation (for which the Department of Justice is the designated agency). If two or more agencies have apparent responsibility over a complaint, § 35.190(c) provides that the Assistant Attorney General shall determine which one of the agencies shall be the designated agency for purposes of that complaint.

Thirteen commenters, including four proposed designated agencies, addressed the Department of Justice's identification in the proposed regulation of nine "designated agencies" to investigate complaints under this part. Most comments addressed the proposed specific delegations to the various individual agencies. The Department of Justice agrees with several commenters who pointed out that responsibility for "historic and cultural preservation" functions appropriately belongs with the Department of Interior rather than the Department of Education. The Department of Justice also agrees with the Department of Education that "museums" more appropriately should be delegated to the Department of Interior, and that "preschool and daycare programs" more appropriately should be assigned to the Department of Health and Human Services, rather than to the Department of Education. The final rule reflects these decisions.

The Department of Commerce opposed its listing as the designated agency for "commerce and industry, including general economic development, banking and finance, consumer protection, insurance, and small business". The Department of Commerce cited its lack of a substantial existing section 504 enforcement program and experience with many of the specific functions to be delegated. The Department of Justice accedes to the Department of Commerce's position, and has assigned itself as the designated agency for these functions.

In response to a comment from the Department of Health and Human Services, the regulation's category of "medical and nursing schools" has been clarified to read "schools of medicine, dentistry, nursing, and other health-related fields". Also in response to a comment from the Department of Health and Human Services, "correctional institutions" have been specifically added to the public safety and administration of justice functions assigned to the Department of Justice.

The regulation also assigns the Department of Justice as the designated agency responsible for all State and local government functions not assigned to other designated agencies. The Department of Justice, under an agreement with the Department of the Treasury, continues to receive and coordinate the investigation of complaints filed under the Revenue Sharing Act. This entitlement program, which was terminated in 1986, provided civil rights compliance jurisdiction for a wide variety of complaints regarding the use of Federal funds to support various general activities of local governments. In the absence of any similar program of Federal financial assistance administered by another Federal agency, placement of designated agency responsibilities for miscellaneous and otherwise undesignated functions with the Department of Justice is an appropriate continuation of current practice.

The Department of Education objected to the proposed rule's inclusion of the functional area of "arts and humanities" within its responsibilities, and the Department of Housing and Urban Development objected to its proposed designation as responsible for activities relating to rent control, the real estate industry, and housing code enforcement. The Department has deleted these areas from the lists assigned to the Departments of Education and Housing and Urban Development, respectively, and has added a new paragraph (c) to § 35.190, which provides that the Department of Justice may assign responsibility for components of State or local governments that exercise responsibilities, regulate, or administer services, programs, or activities relating to functions not assigned to specific designated agencies by paragraph (b) of this section to other appropriate agencies. The Department believes that this approach will provide more flexibility in determining the appropriate agency for investigation of complaints involving those components of State and local governments not specifically addressed by the listings in paragraph (b). As provided in §§ 35.170 and 35.171, complaints filed with the Department of Justice will be referred to the appropriate agency.

Several commenters proposed a stronger role for the Department of Justice, especially with respect to the receipt and assignment of complaints, and the overall monitoring of the effectiveness of the enforcement activities of Federal agencies. As discussed above, §§ 35.170 and 35.171 have been revised to provide for referral of complaints by the Department of Justice to appropriate enforcement

agencies. Also, language has been added to § 35.190(a) of the final regulation stating that the Assistant Attorney General shall provide policy guidance and interpretations to designated agencies to ensure the consistent and effective implementation of this part.

List of Subjects in 28 CFR Part 35

Administrative practice and procedure, Alcoholism, Americans with disabilities, Buildings, Civil rights, Drug abuse, Handicapped, Historic preservation, Intergovernmental relations, Reporting and recordkeeping requirements.

By the authority vested in me as Attorney General by 28 U.S.C. 509, 510, 5 U.S.C. 301, and section 204 of the Americans with Disabilities Act, and for the reasons set forth in the preamble, chapter I of title 28 of the Code of Federal Regulations is amended by adding a new part 35 to read as follows:

PART 35—NONDISCRIMINATION ON THE BASIS OF DISABILITY IN STATE AND LOCAL GOVERNMENT SERVICES

Subpart A—General

Sec.
35.101   Purpose.
35.102   Application.
35.103   Relationship to other laws.
35.104   Definitions.
35.105   Self-evaluation.
35.106   Notice.
35.107   Designation of responsible employee and adoption of grievance procedures.
35.108–35.129   [Reserved]

Subpart B—General Requirements

35.130   General prohibitions against discrimination.
35.131   Illegal use of drugs.
35.132   Smoking.
35.133   Maintenance of accessible features.
35.134   Retaliation or coercion.
35.135   Personal devices and services.
35.136–35.139   [Reserved]

Subpart C—Employment

35.140   Employment discrimination prohibited.
35.141–35.148   [Reserved]

Subpart D—Program Accessibility

35.149   Discrimination prohibited.
35.150   Existing facilities.
35.151   New construction and alterations.
35.152–35.159   [Reserved]

Subpart E—Communications

35.160   General.
35.161   Telecommunication devices for the deaf (TDD's).
35.162   Telephone emergency services.
35.163   Information and signage.
35.164   Duties.
35.165–35.169   [Reserved]

Subpart F—Compliance Procedures

35.170   Complaints.
35.171   Acceptance of complaints.
35.172   Resolution of complaints.
35.173   Voluntary compliance agreements.
35.174   Referral.
35.175   Attorney's fees.
35.176   Alternative means of dispute resolution.
35.177   Effect of unavailability of technical assistance.
35.178   State immunity.
35.179–35.189   [Reserved]

Subpart G—Designated Agencies

35.190   Designated agencies.
35.191–35.999   [Reserved]

Appendix A to Part 35—Preamble to Regulation on Nondiscrimination on the Basis of Disability in State and Local Government Services (Published July 26, 1991)

Authority: 5 U.S.C. 301; 28 U.S.C. 509, 510; Title II, Pub. L. 101–336 (42 U.S.C. 12134).

Subpart A—General

§ 35.101   Purpose.

The purpose of this part is to effectuate subtitle A of title II of the Americans with Disabilities Act of 1990. (42 U.S.C. 12131), which prohibits discrimination on the basis of disability by public entities.

§ 35.102   Application.

(a) Except as provided in paragraph (b) of this section, this part applies to all services, programs, and activities provided or made available by public entities.

(b) To the extent that public transportation services, programs, and activities of public entities are covered by subtitle B of title II of the ADA (42 U.S.C. 12141), they are not subject to the requirements of this part.

§ 35.103   Relationship to other laws.

(a) *Rule of interpretation.* Except as otherwise provided in this part, this part shall not be construed to apply a lesser standard than the standards applied under title V of the Rehabilitation Act of 1973 (29 U.S.C. 791) or the regulations issued by Federal agencies pursuant to that title.

(b) *Other laws.* This part does not invalidate or limit the remedies, rights, and procedures of any other Federal laws, or State or local laws (including State common law) that provide greater or equal protection for the rights of individuals with disabilities or individuals associated with them.

§ 35.104   Definitions.

For purposes of this part, the term—
Act means the Americans with Disabilities Act (Pub. L. 101–336, 104

Stat. 327, 42 U.S.C. 12101–12213 and 47 U.S.C. 225 and 611).

Assistant Attorney General means the Assistant Attorney General, Civil Rights Division, United States Department of Justice.

Auxiliary aids and services includes—

(1) Qualified interpreters, notetakers, transcription services, written materials, telephone handset amplifiers, assistive listening devices, assistive listening systems, telephones compatible with hearing aids, closed caption decoders, open and closed captioning, telecommunications devices for deaf persons (TDD's), videotext displays, or other effective methods of making aurally delivered materials available to individuals with hearing impairments;

(2) Qualified readers, taped texts, audio recordings, Brailled materials, large print materials, or other effective methods of making visually delivered materials available to individuals with visual impairments;

(3) Acquisition or modification of equipment or devices; and

(4) Other similar services and actions.

Complete complaint means a written statement that contains the complainant's name and address and describes the public entity's alleged discriminatory action in sufficient detail to inform the agency of the nature and date of the alleged violation of this part. It shall be signed by the complainant or by someone authorized to do so on his or her behalf. Complaints filed on behalf of classes or third parties shall describe or identify (by name, if possible) the alleged victims of discrimination.

Current illegal use of drugs means illegal use of drugs that occurred recently enough to justify a reasonable belief that a person's drug use is current or that continuing use is a real and ongoing problem.

Designated agency means the Federal agency designated under subpart G of this part to oversee compliance activities under this part for particular components of State and local governments.

Disability means, with respect to an individual, a physical or mental impairment that substantially limits one or more of the major life activities of such individual; a record of such an impairment; or being regarded as having such an impairment.

(1)(i) The phrase *physical or mental impairment* means—

(A) Any physiological disorder or condition, cosmetic disfigurement, or anatomical loss affecting one or more of the following body systems: Neurological, musculoskeletal, special sense organs, respiratory (including speech organs), cardiovascular, reproductive, digestive, genitourinary, hemic and lymphatic, skin, and endocrine;

(B) Any mental or psychological disorder such as mental retardation, organic brain syndrome, emotional or mental illness, and specific learning disabilities.

(ii) The phrase *physical or mental impairment* includes, but is not limited to, such contagious and noncontagious diseases and conditions as orthopedic, visual, speech and hearing impairments, cerebral palsy, epilepsy, muscular dystrophy, multiple sclerosis, cancer, heart disease, diabetes, mental retardation, emotional illness, specific learning disabilities, HIV disease (whether symptomatic or asymptomatic), tuberculosis, drug addiction, and alcoholism.

(iii) The phrase *physical or mental impairment* does not include homosexuality or bisexuality.

(2) The phrase *major life activities* means functions such as caring for one's self, performing manual tasks, walking, seeing, hearing, speaking, breathing, learning, and working.

(3) The phrase *has a record of such an impairment* means has a history of, or has been misclassified as having, a mental or physical impairment that substantially limits one or more major life activities.

(4) The phrase *is regarded as having an impairment means*—

(i) Has a physical or mental impairment that does not substantially limit major life activities but that is treated by a public entity as constituting such a limitation;

(ii) Has a physical or mental impairment that substantially limits major life activities only as a result of the attitudes of others toward such impairment; or

(iii) Has none of the impairments defined in paragraph (1) of this definition but is treated by a public entity as having such an impairment.

(5) The term *disability* does not include—

(i) Transvestism, transsexualism, pedophilia, exhibitionism, voyeurism, gender identity disorders not resulting from physical impairments, or other sexual behavior disorders;

(ii) Compulsive gambling, kleptomania, or pyromania; or

(iii) Psychoactive substance use disorders resulting from current illegal use of drugs.

Drug means a controlled substance, as defined in schedules I through V of section 202 of the Controlled Substances Act (21 U.S.C. 812).

Facility means all or any portion of buildings, structures, sites, complexes, equipment, rolling stock or other conveyances, roads, walks, passageways, parking lots, or other real or personal property, including the site where the building, property, structure, or equipment is located.

Historic preservation programs means programs conducted by a public entity that have preservation of historic properties as a primary purpose.

Historic Properties means those properties that are listed or eligible for listing in the National Register of Historic Places or properties designated as historic under State or local law.

Illegal use of drugs means the use of one or more drugs, the possession or distribution of which is unlawful under the Controlled Substances Act (21 U.S.C. 812). The term *illegal use of drugs* does not include the use of a drug taken under supervision by a licensed health care professional, or other uses authorized by the Controlled Substances Act or other provisions of Federal law.

Individual with a disability means a person who has a disability. The term *individual with a disability* does not include an individual who is currently engaging in the illegal use of drugs, when the public entity acts on the basis of such use.

Public entity means—

(1) Any State or local government;

(2) Any department, agency, special purpose district, or other instrumentality of a State or States or local government; and

(3) The National Railroad Passenger Corporation, and any commuter authority (as defined in section 103(8) of the Rail Passenger Service Act).

Qualified individual with a disability means an individual with a disability who, with or without reasonable modifications to rules, policies, or practices, the removal of architectural, communication, or transportation barriers, or the provision of auxiliary aids and services, meets the essential eligibility requirements for the receipt of services or the participation in programs or activities provided by a public entity.

Qualified interpreter means an interpreter who is able to interpret effectively, accurately, and impartially both receptively and expressively, using any necessary specialized vocabulary.

Section 504 means section 504 of the Rehabilitation Act of 1973 (Pub. L. 93–112, 87 Stat. 394 (29 U.S.C. 794)), as amended.

State means each of the several States, the District of Columbia, the Commonwealth of Puerto Rico, Guam, American Samoa, the Virgin Islands, the

Trust Territory of the Pacific Islands, and the Commonwealth of the Northern Mariana Islands.

§ 35.105 Self-evaluation.

(a) A public entity shall, within one year of the effective date of this part, evaluate its current services, policies, and practices, and the effects thereof, that do not or may not meet the requirements of this part and, to the extent modification of any such services, policies, and practices is required, the public entity shall proceed to make the necessary modifications.

(b) A public entity shall provide an opportunity to interested persons, including individuals with disabilities or organizations representing individuals with disabilities, to participate in the self-evaluation process by submitting comments.

(c) A public entity that employs 50 or more persons shall, for at least three years following completion of the self-evaluation, maintain on file and make available for public inspection:

(1) A list of the interested persons consulted;

(2) A description of areas examined and any problems identified; and

(3) A description of any modifications made.

(d) If a public entity has already complied with the self-evaluation requirement of a regulation implementing section 504 of the Rehabilitation Act of 1973, then the requirements of this section shall apply only to those policies and practices that were not included in the previous self-evaluation.

§ 35.106 Notice.

A public entity shall make available to applicants, participants, beneficiaries, and other interested persons information regarding the provisions of this part and its applicability to the services, programs, or activities of the public entity, and make such information available to them in such manner as the head of the entity finds necessary to apprise such persons of the protections against discrimination assured them by the Act and this part.

§ 35.107 Designation of responsible employee and adoption of grievance procedures.

(a) *Designation of responsible employee.* A public entity that employs 50 or more persons shall designate at least one employee to coordinate its efforts to comply with and carry out its responsibilities under this part, including any investigation of any complaint communicated to it alleging its noncompliance with this part or

alleging any actions that would be prohibited by this part. The public entity shall make available to all interested individuals the name, office address, and telephone number of the employee or employees designated pursuant to this paragraph.

(b) *Complaint procedure.* A public entity that employs 50 or more persons shall adopt and publish grievance procedures providing for prompt and equitable resolution of complaints alleging any action that would be prohibited by this part.

§§ 35.108–35.129 [Reserved]

Subpart B—General Requirements

§ 35.130 General prohibitions against discrimination.

(a) No qualified individual with a disability shall, on the basis of disability, be excluded from participation in or be denied the benefits of the services, programs, or activities of a public entity, or be subjected to discrimination by any public entity.

(b) (1) A public entity, in providing any aid, benefit, or service, may not, directly or through contractual, licensing, or other arrangements, on the basis of disability—

(i) Deny a qualified individual with a disability the opportunity to participate in or benefit from the aid, benefit, or service;

(ii) Afford a qualified individual with a disability an opportunity to participate in or benefit from the aid, benefit, or service that is not equal to that afforded others;

(iii) Provide a qualified individual with a disability with an aid, benefit, or service that is not as effective in affording equal opportunity to obtain the same result, to gain the same benefit, or to reach the same level of achievement as that provided to others;

(iv) Provide different or separate aids, benefits, or services to individuals with disabilities or to any class of individuals with disabilities than is provided to others unless such action is necessary to provide qualified individuals with disabilities with aids, benefits, or services that are as effective as those provided to others;

(v) Aid or perpetuate discrimination against a qualified individual with a disability by providing significant assistance to an agency, organization, or person that discriminates on the basis of disability in providing any aid, benefit, or service to beneficiaries of the public entity's program;

(vi) Deny a qualified individual with a disability the opportunity to participate as a member of planning or advisory boards;

(vii) Otherwise limit a qualified individual with a disability in the enjoyment of any right, privilege, advantage, or opportunity enjoyed by others receiving the aid, benefit, or service.

(2) A public entity may not deny a qualified individual with a disability the opportunity to participate in services, programs, or activities that are not separate or different, despite the existence of permissibly separate or different programs or activities.

(3) A public entity may not, directly or through contractual or other arrangements, utilize criteria or methods of administration:

(i) That have the effect of subjecting qualified individuals with disabilities to discrimination on the basis of disability;

(ii) That have the purpose or effect of defeating or substantially impairing accomplishment of the objectives of the public entity's program with respect to individuals with disabilities; or

(iii) That perpetuate the discrimination of another public entity if both public entities are subject to common administrative control or are agencies of the same State.

(4) A public entity may not, in determining the site or location of a facility, make selections—

(i) That have the effect of excluding individuals with disabilities from, denying them the benefits of, or otherwise subjecting them to discrimination; or

(ii) That have the purpose or effect of defeating or substantially impairing the accomplishment of the objectives of the service, program, or activity with respect to individuals with disabilities.

(5) A public entity, in the selection of procurement contractors, may not use criteria that subject qualified individuals with disabilities to discrimination on the basis of disability.

(6) A public entity may not administer a licensing or certification program in a manner that subjects qualified individuals with disabilities to discrimination on the basis of disability, nor may a public entity establish requirements for the programs or activities of licensees or certified entities that subject qualified individuals with disabilities to discrimination on the basis of disability. The programs or activities of entities that are licensed or certified by a public entity are not, themselves, covered by this part.

(7) A public entity shall make reasonable modifications in policies, practices, or procedures when the modifications are necessary to avoid discrimination on the basis of disability,

unless the public entity can demonstrate that making the modifications would fundamentally alter the nature of the service, program, or activity.

(8) A public entity shall not impose or apply eligibility criteria that screen out or tend to screen out an individual with a disability or any class of individuals with disabilities from fully and equally enjoying any service, program, or activity, unless such criteria can be shown to be necessary for the provision of the service, program, or activity being offered.

(c) Nothing in this part prohibits a public entity from providing benefits, services, or advantages to individuals with disabilities, or to a particular class of individuals with disabilities beyond those required by this part.

(d) A public entity shall administer services, programs, and activities in the most integrated setting appropriate to the needs of qualified individuals with disabilities.

(e)(1) Nothing in this part shall be construed to require an individual with a disability to accept an accommodation, aid, service, opportunity, or benefit provided under the ADA or this part which such individual chooses not to accept.

(2) Nothing in the Act or this part authorizes the representative or guardian of an individual with a disability to decline food, water, medical treatment, or medical services for that individual.

(f) A public entity may not place a surcharge on a particular individual with a disability or any group of individuals with disabilities to cover the costs of measures, such as the provision of auxiliary aids or program accessibility, that are required to provide that individual or group with the nondiscriminatory treatment required by the Act or this part.

(g) A public entity shall not exclude or otherwise deny equal services, programs, or activities to an individual or entity because of the known disability of an individual with whom the individual or entity is known to have a relationship or association.

§ 35.131 Illegal use of drugs.

(a) *General.* (1) Except as provided in paragraph (b) of this section, this part does not prohibit discrimination against an individual based on that individual's current illegal use of drugs.

(2) A public entity shall not discriminate on the basis of illegal use of drugs against an individual who is not engaging in current illegal use of drugs and who—

(i) Has successfully completed a supervised drug rehabilitation program

or has otherwise been rehabilitated successfully;

(ii) Is participating in a supervised rehabilitation program; or

(iii) Is erroneously regarded as engaging in such use.

(b) *Health and drug rehabilitation services.* (1) A public entity shall not deny health services, or services provided in connection with drug rehabilitation, to an individual on the basis of that individual's current illegal use of drugs, if the individual is otherwise entitled to such services.

(2) A drug rehabilitation or treatment program may deny participation to individuals who engage in illegal use of drugs while they are in the program.

(c) *Drug testing.* (1) This part does not prohibit a public entity from adopting or administering reasonable policies or procedures, including but not limited to drug testing, designed to ensure that an individual who formerly engaged in the illegal use of drugs is not now engaging in current illegal use of drugs.

(2) Nothing in paragraph (c) of this section shall be construed to encourage, prohibit, restrict, or authorize the conduct of testing for the illegal use of drugs.

§ 35.132 Smoking.

This part does not preclude the prohibition of, or the imposition of restrictions on, smoking in transportation covered by this part.

§ 35.133 Maintenance of accessible features.

(a) A public accommodation shall maintain in operable working condition those features of facilities and equipment that are required to be readily accessible to and usable by persons with disabilities by the Act or this part.

(b) This section does not prohibit isolated or temporary interruptions in service or access due to maintenance or repairs.

§ 35.134 Retaliation or coercion.

(a) No private or public entity shall discriminate against any individual because that individual has opposed any act or practice made unlawful by this part, or because that individual made a charge, testified, assisted, or participated in any manner in an investigation, proceeding, or hearing under the Act or this part.

(b) No private or public entity shall coerce, intimidate, threaten, or interfere with any individual in the exercise or enjoyment of, or on account of his or her having exercised or enjoyed, or on account of his or her having aided or encouraged any other individual in the

exercise or enjoyment of, any right granted or protected by the Act or this part.

§ 35.135 Personal devices and services.

This part does not require a public entity to provide to individuals with disabilities personal devices, such as wheelchairs; individually prescribed devices, such as prescription eyeglasses or hearing aids; readers for personal use or study; or services of a personal nature including assistance in eating, toileting, or dressing.

§§ 35.136–35.139 [Reserved]

Subpart C—Employment

§ 35.140 Employment discrimination prohibited.

(a) No qualified individual with a disability shall, on the basis of disability, be subjected to discrimination in employment under any service, program, or activity conducted by a public entity.

(b)(1) For purposes of this part, the requirements of title I of the Act, as established by the regulations of the Equal Employment Opportunity Commission in 29 CFR part 1630, apply to employment in any service, program, or activity conducted by a public entity if that public entity is also subject to the jurisdiction of title I.

(2) For the purposes of this part, the requirements of section 504 of the Rehabilitation Act of 1973, as established by the regulations of the Department of Justice in 28 CFR part 41, as those requirements pertain to employment, apply to employment in any service, program, or activity conducted by a public entity if that public entity is not also subject to the jurisdiction of title I.

§§ 35.141–35.148 [Reserved]

Subpart D—Program Accessibility

§ 35.149 Discrimination prohibited.

Except as otherwise provided in § 35.150, no qualified individual with a disability shall, because a public entity's facilities are inaccessible to or unusable by individuals with disabilities, be excluded from participation in, or be denied the benefits of the services, programs, or activities of a public entity, or be subjected to discrimination by any public entity.

§ 35.150 Existing facilities.

(a) *General.* A public entity shall operate each service, program, or activity so that the service, program, or activity, when viewed in its entirety, is readily accessible to and usable by individuals with disabilities. This paragraph does not—

(1) Necessarily require a public entity to make each of its existing facilities accessible to and usable by individuals with disabilities;

(2) Require a public entity to take any action that would threaten or destroy the historic significance of an historic property; or

(3) Require a public entity to take any action that it can demonstrate would result in a fundamental alteration in the nature of a service, program, or activity or in undue financial and administrative burdens. In those circumstances where personnel of the public entity believe that the proposed action would fundamentally alter the service, program, or activity or would result in undue financial and administrative burdens, a public entity has the burden of proving that compliance with § 35.150(a) of this part would result in such alteration or burdens. The decision that compliance would result in such alteration or burdens must be made by the head of a public entity or his or her designee after considering all resources available for use in the funding and operation of the service, program, or activity, and must be accompanied by a written statement of the reasons for reaching that conclusion. If an action would result in such an alteration or such burdens, a public entity shall take any other action that would not result in such an alteration or such burdens but would nevertheless ensure that individuals with disabilities receive the benefits or services provided by the public entity.

(b) *Methods*—(1) *General.* A public entity may comply with the requirements of this section through such means as redesign of equipment, reassignment of services to accessible buildings, assignment of aides to beneficiaries, home visits, delivery of services at alternate accessible sites, alteration of existing facilities and construction of new facilities, use of accessible rolling stock or other conveyances, or any other methods that result in making its services, programs, or activities readily accessible to and usable by individuals with disabilities. A public entity is not required to make structural changes in existing facilities where other methods are effective in achieving compliance with this section. A public entity, in making alterations to existing buildings, shall meet the accessibility requirements of § 35.151. In choosing among available methods for meeting the requirements of this section, a public entity shall give priority to those methods that offer services, programs, and activities to qualified

individuals with disabilities in the most integrated setting appropriate.

(2) *Historic preservation programs.* In meeting the requirements of § 35.150(a) in historic preservation programs, a public entity shall give priority to methods that provide physical access to individuals with disabilities. In cases where a physical alteration to an historic property is not required because of paragraph (a)(2) or (a)(3) of this section, alternative methods of achieving program accessibility include—

(i) Using audio-visual materials and devices to depict those portions of an historic property that cannot otherwise be made accessible;

(ii) Assigning persons to guide individuals with handicaps into or through portions of historic properties that cannot otherwise be made accessible; or

(iii) Adopting other innovative methods.

(c) *Time period for compliance.* Where structural changes in facilities are undertaken to comply with the obligations established under this section, such changes shall be made within three years of January 26, 1992, but in any event as expeditiously as possible.

(d) *Transition plan.* (1) In the event that structural changes to facilities will be undertaken to achieve program accessibility, a public entity that employs 50 or more persons shall develop, within six months of January 26, 1992, a transition plan setting forth the steps necessary to complete such changes. A public entity shall provide an opportunity to interested persons, including individuals with disabilities or organizations representing individuals with disabilities, to participate in the development of the transition plan by submitting comments. A copy of the transition plan shall be made available for public inspection.

(2) If a public entity has responsibility or authority over streets, roads, or walkways, its transition plan shall include a schedule for providing curb ramps or other sloped areas where pedestrian walks cross curbs, giving priority to walkways serving entities covered by the Act, including State and local government offices and facilities, transportation, places of public accommodation, and employers, followed by walkways serving other areas.

(3) The plan shall, at a minimum—

(i) Identify physical obstacles in the public entity's facilities that limit the accessibility of its programs or activities to individuals with disabilities;

(ii) Describe in detail the methods that will be used to make the facilities accessible;

(iii) Specify the schedule for taking the steps necessary to achieve compliance with this section and, if the time period of the transition plan is longer than one year, identify steps that will be taken during each year of the transition period; and

(iv) Indicate the official responsible for implementation of the plan.

(4) If a public entity has already complied with the transition plan requirement of a Federal agency regulation implementing section 504 of the Rehabilitation Act of 1973, then the requirements of this paragraph (d) shall apply only to those policies and practices that were not included in the previous transition plan.

§ 35.151 New construction and alterations.

(a) *Design and construction.* Each facility or part of a facility constructed by, on behalf of, or for the use of a public entity shall be designed and constructed in such manner that the facility or part of the facility is readily accessible to and usable by individuals with disabilities, if the construction was commenced after January 26, 1992.

(b) *Alteration.* Each facility or part of a facility altered by, on behalf of, or for the use of a public entity in a manner that affects or could affect the usability of the facility or part of the facility shall, to the maximum extent feasible, be altered in such manner that the altered portion of the facility is readily accessible to and usable by individuals with disabilities, if the alteration was commenced after January 26, 1992.

(c) *Accessibility standards.* Design, construction, or alteration of facilities in conformance with the Uniform Federal Accessibility Standards (UFAS) (Appendix A to 41 CFR part 101–19.6) or with the Americans with Disabilities Act Accessibility Guidelines for Buildings and Facilities (ADAAG) (Appendix A to 28 CFR part 36) shall be deemed to comply with the requirements of this section with respect to those facilities, except that the elevator exemption contained at section 4.1.3(5) and section 4.1.6(1)(j) of ADAAG shall not apply. Departures from particular requirements of either standard by the use of other methods shall be permitted when it is clearly evident that equivalent access to the facility or part of the facility is thereby provided.

(d) *Alterations: Historic properties.* (1) Alterations to historic properties shall comply, to the maximum extent feasible, with section 4.1.7 of UFAS or section 4.1.7 of ADAAG.

(2) If it is not feasible to provide physical access to an historic property in a manner that will not threaten or destroy the historic significance of the building or facility, alternative methods of access shall be provided pursuant to the requirements of § 35.150.

(e) *Curb ramps.* (1) Newly constructed or altered streets, roads, and highways must contain curb ramps or other sloped areas at any intersection having curbs or other barriers to entry from a street level pedestrian walkway.

(2) Newly constructed or altered street level pedestrian walkways must contain curb ramps or other sloped areas at intersections to streets, roads, or highways.

§§ 35.152–35.159 [Reserved]

Subpart E—Communications

§ 35.160 General.

(a) A public entity shall take appropriate steps to ensure that communications with applicants, participants, and members of the public with disabilities are as effective as communications with others.

(b)(1) A public entity shall furnish appropriate auxiliary aids and services where necessary to afford an individual with a disability an equal opportunity to participate in, and enjoy the benefits of, a service, program, or activity conducted by a public entity.

(2) In determining what type of auxiliary aid and service is necessary, a public entity shall give primary consideration to the requests of the individual with disabilities.

§ 35.161 Telecommunication devices for the deaf (TDD's).

Where a public entity communicates by telephone with applicants and beneficiaries, TDD's or equally effective telecommunication systems shall be used to communicate with individuals with impaired hearing or speech.

§ 35.162 Telephone emergency services.

Telephone emergency services, including 911 services, shall provide direct access to individuals who use TDD's and computer modems.

§ 35.163 Information and signage.

(a) A public entity shall ensure that interested persons, including persons with impaired vision or hearing, can obtain information as to the existence and location of accessible services, activities, and facilities.

(b) A public entity shall provide signage at all inaccessible entrances to each of its facilities, directing users to an accessible entrance or to a location at which they can obtain information

about accessible facilities. The international symbol for accessibility shall be used at each accessible entrance of a facility.

§ 35.164 Duties.

This subpart does not require a public entity to take any action that it can demonstrate would result in a fundamental alteration in the nature of a service, program, or activity or in undue financial and administrative burdens. In those circumstances where personnel of the public entity believe that the proposed action would fundamentally alter the service, program, or activity or would result in undue financial and administrative burdens, a public entity has the burden of proving that compliance with this subpart would result in such alteration or burdens. The decision that compliance would result in such alteration or burdens must be made by the head of the public entity or his or her designee after considering all resources available for use in the funding and operation of the service, program, or activity and must be accompanied by a written statement of the reasons for reaching that conclusion. If an action required to comply with this subpart would result in such an alteration or such burdens, a public entity shall take any other action that would not result in such an alteration or such burdens but would nevertheless ensure that, to the maximum extent possible, individuals with disabilities receive the benefits or services provided by the public entity.

§§ 35.165–35.169 [Reserved]

Subpart F—Compliance Procedures

§ 35.170 Complaints.

(a) *Who may file.* An individual who believes that he or she or a specific class of individuals has been subjected to discrimination on the basis of disability by a public entity may, by himself or herself or by an authorized representative, file a complaint under this part.

(b) *Time for filing.* A complaint must be filed not later than 180 days from the date of the alleged discrimination, unless the time for filing is extended by the designated agency for good cause shown. A complaint is deemed to be filed under this section on the date it is first filed with any Federal agency.

(c) *Where to file.* An individual may file a complaint with any agency that he or she believes to be the appropriate agency designated under subpart G of this part, or with any agency that provides funding to the public entity that is the subject of the complaint, or with

the Department of Justice for referral as provided in § 35.171(a)(2).

§ 35.171 Acceptance of complaints.

(a) *Receipt of complaints.* (1)(i) Any Federal agency that receives a complaint of discrimination on the basis of disability by a public entity shall promptly review the complaint to determine whether it has jurisdiction over the complaint under section 504.

(ii) If the agency does not have section 504 jurisdiction, it shall promptly determine whether it is the designated agency under subpart G of this part responsible for complaints filed against that public entity.

(2)(i) If an agency other than the Department of Justice determines that it does not have section 504 jurisdiction and is not the designated agency, it shall promptly refer the complaint, and notify the complainant that it is referring the complaint to the Department of Justice.

(ii) When the Department of Justice receives a complaint for which it does not have jurisdiction under section 504 and is not the designated agency, it shall refer the complaint to an agency that does have jurisdiction under section 504 or to the appropriate agency designated in subpart G of this part or, in the case of an employment complaint that is also subject to title I of the Act, to the Equal Employment Opportunity Commission.

(3)(i) If the agency that receives a complaint has section 504 jurisdiction, it shall process the complaint according to its procedures for enforcing section 504.

(ii) If the agency that receives a complaint does not have section 504 jurisdiction, but is the designated agency, it shall process the complaint according to the procedures established by this subpart.

(b) *Employment complaints.* (1) If a complaint alleges employment discrimination subject to title I of the Act, and the agency has section 504 jurisdiction, the agency shall follow the procedures issued by the Department of Justice and the Equal Employment Opportunity Commission under section 107(b) of the Act.

(2) If a complaint alleges employment discrimination subject to title I of the Act, and the designated agency does not have section 504 jurisdiction, the agency shall refer the complaint to the Equal Employment Opportunity Commission for processing under title I of the Act.

(3) Complaints alleging employment discrimination subject to this part, but not to title I of the Act shall be processed in accordance with the procedures established by this subpart.

(c) *Complete complaints.* (1) A designated agency shall accept all complete complaints under this section and shall promptly notify the complainant and the public entity of the receipt and acceptance of the complaint.

(2) If the designated agency receives a complaint that is not complete, it shall notify the complainant and specify the additional information that is needed to make the complaint a complete complaint. If the complainant fails to complete the complaint, the designated agency shall close the complaint without prejudice.

§ 35.172 Resolution of complaints.

(a) The designated agency shall investigate each complete complaint. attempt informal resolution, and, if resolution is not achieved, issue to the complainant and the public entity a Letter of Findings that shall include—

(1) Findings of fact and conclusions of law;

(2) A description of a remedy for each violation found; and

(3) Notice of the rights available under paragraph (b) of this section.

(b) If the designated agency finds noncompliance, the procedures in §§ 35.173 and 35.174 shall be followed. At any time, the complainant may file a private suit pursuant to section 203 of the Act, whether or not the designated agency finds a violation.

§ 35.173 Voluntary compliance agreements.

(a) When the designated agency issues a noncompliance Letter of Findings, the designated agency shall—

(1) Notify the Assistant Attorney General by forwarding a copy of the Letter of Findings to the Assistant Attorney General; and

(2) Initiate negotiations with the public entity to secure compliance by voluntary means.

(b) Where the designated agency is able to secure voluntary compliance, the voluntary compliance agreement shall—

(1) Be in writing and signed by the parties;

(2) Address each cited violation;

(3) Specify the corrective or remedial action to be taken, within a stated period of time, to come into compliance;

(4) Provide assurance that discrimination will not recur; and

(5) Provide for enforcement by the Attorney General.

§ 35.174 Referral.

If the public entity declines to enter into voluntary compliance negotiations or if negotiations are unsuccessful, the designated agency shall refer the matter to the Attorney General with a recommendation for appropriate action.

§ 35.175 Attorney's fees.

In any action or administrative proceeding commenced pursuant to the Act or this part, the court or agency, in its discretion, may allow the prevailing party, other than the United States, a reasonable attorney's fee, including litigation expenses, and costs, and the United States shall be liable for the foregoing the same as a private individual.

§ 35.176 Alternative means of dispute resolution.

Where appropriate and to the extent authorized by law, the use of alternative means of dispute resolution, including settlement negotiations, conciliation, facilitation, mediation, factfinding, minitrials, and arbitration, is encouraged to resolve disputes arising under the Act and this part.

§ 35.177 Effect of unavailability of technical assistance.

A public entity shall not be excused from compliance with the requirements of this part because of any failure to receive technical assistance, including any failure in the development or dissemination of any technical assistance manual authorized by the Act.

§ 35.178 State immunity.

A State shall not be immune under the eleventh amendment to the Constitution of the United States from an action in Federal or State court of competent jurisdiction for a violation of this Act. In any action against a State for a violation of the requirements of this Act, remedies (including remedies both at law and in equity) are available for such a violation to the same extent as such remedies are available for such a violation in an action against any public or private entity other than a State.

§§ 35.179–35.189 [Reserved]

Subpart G—Designated Agencies

§ 35.190 Designated agencies.

(a) The Assistant Attorney General shall coordinate the compliance activities of Federal agencies with respect to State and local government components, and shall provide policy guidance and interpretations to designated agencies to ensure the consistent and effective implementation of the requirements of this part.

(b) The Federal agencies listed in paragraph (b) (1) through (8) of this section shall have responsibility for the implementation of subpart F of this part for components of State and local governments that exercise responsibilities, regulate, or administer services, programs, or activities in the following functional areas.

(1) *Department of Agriculture:* All programs, services, and regulatory activities relating to farming and the raising of livestock, including extension services.

(2) *Department of Education:* All programs, services, and regulatory activities relating to the operation of elementary and secondary education systems and institutions, institutions of higher education and vocational education (other than schools of medicine, dentistry, nursing, and other health-related schools), and libraries.

(3) *Department of Health and Human Services:* All programs, services, and regulatory activities relating to the provision of health care and social services, including schools of medicine, dentistry, nursing, and other health-related schools, the operation of health care and social service providers and institutions, including "grass-roots" and community services organizations and programs, and preschool and daycare programs.

(4) *Department of Housing and Urban Development:* All programs, services, and regulatory activities relating to state and local public housing, and housing assistance and referral.

(5) *Department of Interior:* All programs, services, and regulatory activities relating to lands and natural resources, including parks and recreation, water and waste management, environmental protection, energy, historic and cultural preservation, and museums.

(6) *Department of Justice:* All programs, services, and regulatory activities relating to law enforcement, public safety, and the administration of justice, including courts and correctional institutions; commerce and industry, including general economic development, banking and finance, consumer protection, insurance, and small business; planning, development, and regulation (unless assigned to other designated agencies); state and local government support services (e.g., audit, personnel, comptroller, administrative services); all other government functions not assigned to other designated agencies.

(7) *Department of Labor:* All programs, services, and regulatory activities relating to labor and the work force.

(8) *Department of Transportation:* All programs, services, and regulatory activities relating to transportation, including highways, public transportation, traffic management (non-

law enforcement), automobile licensing and inspection, and driver licensing.

(c) Responsibility for the implementation of subpart F of this part for components of State or local governments that exercise responsibilities, regulate, or administer services, programs, or activities relating to functions not assigned to specific designated agencies by paragraph (b) of this section may be assigned to other specific agencies by the Department of Justice.

(d) If two or more agencies have apparent responsibility over a

complaint, the Assistant Attorney General shall determine which one of the agencies shall be the designated agency for purposes of that complaint.

§§ 35.191–35.999   [Reserved]

Appendix A to Part 35—Preamble to Regulation on Nondiscrimination on the Basis of Disability in State and Local Government Services (Published July 26, 1991)

Note: For the convenience of the reader, this appendix contains the text of the preamble to the final regulation on nondiscrimination on the basis of disability in State and local government services

beginning at the heading "Section-by-Section Analysis" and ending before "List of Subjects in 28 CFR Part 35" (56 FR (INSERT FR PAGE CITATIONS); July 26, 1991).

Dated: July 17, 1991.

Dick Thornburgh,

Attorney General.

[FR Doc. 91–17368 Filed 7–25–91; 8:45 am]

BILLING CODE 4410-01-M